LECTURES ON THE PHILOSOPHY OF KANT

AND OTHER

PHILOSOPHICAL LECTURES & ESSAYS

LECTURES
ON THE PHILOSOPHY OF KANT

AND OTHER

PHILOSOPHICAL LECTURES & ESSAYS

BY THE LATE

HENRY SIDGWICK

KNIGHTBRIDGE PROFESSOR OF MORAL PHILOSOPHY IN THE UNIVERSITY OF CAMBRIDGE

WIPF & STOCK · Eugene, Oregon

Wipf and Stock Publishers
199 W 8th Ave, Suite 3
Eugene, OR 97401

Lectures on the Philosophy of Kant
and other Philosophical Lectures and Essays
By Sidgwick, Henry
ISBN 13: 978-1-62564-032-1
Publication date 4/15/2013
Previously published by Macmillan, 1905

EDITORIAL NOTE

THE first portion of this volume consists of lectures given by Professor Sidgwick as part of a long course on Metaphysics, which he delivered for the last time in the academic year 1899-1900. It was his intention eventually to work up these lectures into a book on Kant and Kantism in England. The gap between the lectures on Kant and those on Green and Spencer was to have been filled up with a sketch of the influence of post-Kantian philosophy on English thought. But the two fragments, placed one as appendix to the last lecture on Kant, and the other as 'introductory' to the lectures on Spencer, are all that seemed now available of the material prepared for this sketch. The lectures on Kant, the author felt, were left "tolerably complete," but "the study of Green" he knew was "not in the form required for a book." Appended to it is the chief part of a lecture—the last he ever gave—on Green's philosophy, which the author thought "might be somehow combined with the lectures" as here printed. And no doubt it may be, but the editor is of opinion that most readers will prefer to do the combining themselves. This decision to meddle as little as possible with what the author has left us has also entailed the retention of sundry repetitions which he would doubtless have removed (cf. *e.g.* pp. 235, 244).

The second portion of the volume consists of articles, all but the first of which have—with the editor's permission—been reprinted from *Mind*. The first, on the Sophists, from the *Journal of Philology*,[1] has been inserted, though incomplete, on the advice of Dr. Henry Jackson, who has kindly undertaken its revision for the press. A small portion of the last article, that on "Criteria of Truth and Error," occurs also in the lectures on Spencer (cf. pp. 318, 456); and as already stated in the editorial note to the author's *Philosophy, its Scope and Relations*, a few passages from the same article are reproduced there. This article too was left unfinished, but there is now appended to it portions of two lectures which show the lines on which the author intended to complete it. These lectures were themselves an amplification of a paper read to the Metaphysical Society and afterwards published in the *Contemporary Review* (July 1871).

Passages and references in square brackets, other than those occurring in quotations, are editorial additions.

---

[1] Published by Messrs. Macmillan and Co.

The Index has been kindly prepared by Miss E. E. C. Jones, the Mistress of Girton College, and the proof sheets have been carefully revised by Mrs. Sidgwick.

JAMES WARD.

Trinity College, Cambridge,
April 23, 1905.

ERRATA

Page 4, line 3 from foot, *delete* (1).
,, 64, ,, 6, *for* principle *read* principles.
,, 67, ,, 15, *for* context *read* content.
,, 121, ,, 15, *for* scheme *read* schema.
,, 188, ,, 3, *add a comma after* derivative.
,, 202, ,, 4, *delete comma after* as God.
,, 231, ,, 9, *for* relation *read* relations.
,, 286, lines 9 and 10 from foot, *for* "obvious to me" *read* 'obvious' to me.
,, 331, line 5, *add* to *at end of line.*
,, 372, ,, 3 of title, *for* vol. iii. *read* vol. vii.

CONTENTS

LECTURES

THE METAPHYSICS OF KANT—

		PAGE
1.	The Critical Standpoint	1
2.	The Transcendental Æsthetic	21
3.	Kant's 'Expositions' of Space and Time	38
4.	The Transcendental Analytic	58
5.	The Mathematical Categories and Principles	75
6.	Substance	98
7.	Causality, Community, Modality	106
8.	The Transcendental Dialectic	128
9.	Rational Psychology	143
10.	The Mathematical Antinomies	152
11.	The Dynamical Antinomies	162
12.	Rational Theology	179
	Appendix to Lecture 12 : The Unconditioned	196

THE METAPHYSICS OF T. H. GREEN—

	PAGE
1. Summary Account	209
2. The Spiritual Principle in Knowledge and in Nature	222
3. The Relation of Man to the Spiritual Principle in Nature	238
Appendix to these Lectures	257

THE PHILOSOPHY OF MR. HERBERT SPENCER—

Introductory: Agnosticism and Relativism . . 267

1. Metaphysical Doctrines 275

2. Metaphysical and Epistemological Doctrines . . 302

ESSAYS

1. The Sophists. (Two papers from *The Journal of Philology*, 1872 and 1873) . . . 323

2. Incoherence of Empirical Philosophy (from *Mind*, vol. vii. O.S., October 1882) . . . 372

3. A Dialogue on Time and Common Sense (from *Mind*, vol. iii. N.S., October 1894) . . . 392

4. The Philosophy of Common Sense (from *Mind*, vol. iv. N.S., April 1895) . . . 406

5. Criteria of Truth and Error (from *Mind*, vol. ix. N.S., January 1900) . . . 430

Appendix to the preceding Essay . . 461

INDEX 469

THE METAPHYSICS OF KANT

LECTURE I

THE CRITICAL STANDPOINT

KANT is selected by me as a philosopher to study, not merely on account of his historical importance—that is a consideration for another department of study, undertaken by another teacher [1]—but because it is partly at least to Kant that we trace the origin of the systems of metaphysical thought which have most vogue at the present day—the Agnosticism of Spencer (though here the influence is indirect, through Hamilton and Mansel), and more directly the Idealism or Spiritualism of which I take Green as a representative.[2]

---

[1] And, I may add, if that were the sole reason, it would be an instance of the irony of fate that Kant should be studied on that ground. Cf. *Prolegomena*, Mahaffy's Trans. pp. 1 f. [References throughout to this edition.]

[2] However, I may support my selection by a reference to the space given to Kant in current histories. You will observe that Falckenberg gives Kant much the largest space that he gives to any one thinker in the whole history of modern thought; and, if you suggest that this is due to German patriotism, I point out that Falckenberg allots to Kant *nearly three* times the space that he allots to any other *German* philosopher. And I point out that in other cases Falckenberg's preference for Germans is kept within bounds: since he gives Locke a *somewhat* larger space than either Leibniz, Fichte, Schelling, or Hegel.

But what treatise of Kant's shall we study? His great treatise, the one to which his influence is mainly due, the *Critique of Pure Reason* (1781), or the *Prolegomena to any Future Metaphysic*, written two years later?

The aim of the latter book (as he explains, p. 10) is to remove a "certain obscurity arising partly from the extent of the plan" of the earlier work, which rendered it difficult "to gather into one view the principal points of the investigation." This difficulty is no doubt diminished by Professor Watson's abridgment.[1] But if we want to learn what a philosopher is driving at, no one can tell us quite as well as the philosopher himself; and I often think that if every eminent thinker who has written an epoch-making work had also written a supplementary one to explain what he aimed at doing, and what he believes himself to have done, in the first,—there would be fewer unsettled questions in the history of philosophy than is actually the case. I cannot, however, take the *Prolegomena* (intelligently translated—though not with *perfect* accuracy—by the versatile Professor Mahaffy) as the primary textbook of this course, because it presupposes the earlier work too much; but I shall endeavour, so far as I can, to make the lectures suitable both to those who have read the *Critique of Pure Reason* (either as Kant wrote it or as abridged by Watson) and to those who have read the *Prolegomena*. I shall have

---

[1] *The Philosophy of Kant, as contained in Extracts from his own Writings* (1888).

to refer to this for certain important parts of the argument, and shall point out the passages that should be especially read along with the *Critique*.

What, then, is briefly Kant's aim? It is clearly stated in the *Prolegomena* (but not quite rightly translated by Professor Mahaffy): "My aim is to convince all who find it worth while to busy themselves with metaphysics, that it is indispensably necessary for them to suspend their business for the present, and start with the question 'Whether such a thing as Metaphysic is at all possible?'"[1]

What, then, is the answer to the question, and are the metaphysicians allowed to resume their business? Well, this answer properly and logically comes at the end of the book. But as there are some who seem to me slightly to misunderstand Kant's attitude to Metaphysics, I will presently give you my view of his verdict before we examine the arguments in detail.

But, first, there is a prior question on which we may profitably spend a few minutes. *Why suspend metaphysicians in particular from their business*, among all the groups of persons engaged in the pursuit of truth? The human mind has a moral preference for equality of treatment. Why not suspend Mathematicians and Scientists also, and have a general closing of intellectual workshops, until this prior question as to the possibility of producing the commodity offered has been tried with regard to all branches of what is currently taught as

[1] Cf. p. 37, where—the question having become more definite—"all metaphysicians are solemnly and legitimately suspended from their occupations" till they have answered it.

knowledge? To this question Kant's answer is simple, and I think clear. (1) Metaphysics has not the characteristics by which a Science is known. It has not been able to obtain "universal and permanent approval." (2) "Every other science is continually advancing, while in this, notwithstanding its high pretensions, we perpetually revolve round the same point without gaining a step."[1] On the other hand, as regards 'pure mathematic and pure physical science'[2] "we can say with certainty" that these parts of professed knowledge "are actual and given." What then is meant as 'given'? Kant answers that both contain propositions which obtain thoroughgoing recognition as apodictically certain: (*a*) partly by mere reason, (*b*) partly "by general consent arising from experience and yet as independent of experience."[3]

Mathematics and Physics, then, stand in no need of criticism; and the only reason for this, as it seems to me, is that they have the *consensus* and steady progress which Metaphysics lacks. This is not, indeed, the only reason that Kant gives. In fact, in another passage (§ 40, p. 114) he seems to give only other reasons: viz. (1) that Mathematics "rests on its own evidence" and (2) Physical Science on the confirmation of experience. But neither of these reasons is really available. For (1) Metaphysics, in the view of the dogmatic metaphysicians whom Kant criticises, rested on its own evidence; and it is

---

[1] *Prolegomena*, pp. 2 f. Observe that 'Science' is used for *any* Systematic Knowledge, not as I used it in *Philosophy: its Scope and Relations*, pp. 2 f.
[2] By 'pure' Kant means what is *a priori* in these sciences.
[3] *Prolegomena*, § 4, p. 32.

only to a mathematician that Mathematics rests on this. We cannot therefore make this characteristic a difference between the two that necessitates a critical inquiry in the latter case which does not exist in the former. The real difference is the *consensus* in the former case, the *uncontested* condition of the evidence in contrast with the absence of "universal and permanent recognition" in the latter.

The case is different with Physics. Here the basis is said to be "experience and its thoroughgoing confirmation," and certainly the Metaphysics that Kant has in view cannot claim any such basis. But then can this basis be adequate even for Physics? Certainly not for Pure Physics as conceived by Kant. For the distinctive characteristic of this—what is meant by its 'purity'—is that it "propounds *a priori*, and as necessary, laws to which nature is subject" (§ 15, p. 64); and there is no point on which Kant is more emphatic than he is on the impossibility of establishing such laws by induction from particular experiences. But if the universals of Pure Physics cannot be thus established, it would seem clear that they cannot receive from such experiences *adequate* confirmation.

We are left, therefore, with the lack of consensus and steady progress as the only valid reasons for suspending metaphysicians from their work, until a preliminary critical inquiry into the possibility of accomplishing that work has been completed.[1]

---

[1] But now observe the 'presuppositions':—Consensus implies plurality of minds; Progress implies Time. Cf. below, p. 35 *fin*.

It may be said that these provisional criteria are not essential, but that in every case it is important, before attempting to gain knowledge on any subject, that we should satisfy ourselves of the possibility of gaining it. I answer that this must also apply to the knowledge of the possibility, etc. Indeed the reasons Kant gives for suspending Metaphysicians from their business must be admitted to apply now to Criticists or Critical Epistemologists.[1] However, we will grant the need of inquiry, and only demand *consistency* in the assumptions and conclusions of Criticism.

One point we may note in the view of knowledge from which Kant starts, because it throws important light on the movement of the modern mind in respect to the relation of Metaphysics to Physical Science. According to Kant, as we have seen, Physical Science has no occasion for a critical inquiry to remove doubts as to the validity of its fundamental principles: it does not require this "for its own safety and certainty." It is, indeed, important in the systematic study of human knowledge to show—as Kant holds that he has shown—that Physics has an *a priori* element, contains certain universal and necessary principles, "sprung from pure sources of the understanding." But though this is important for the study of human knowledge as a whole—what we now call philosophy—it is not required for the secure establishment and steady progress of Physical Science

---

[1] Cf. my article, "A Criticism of the Critical Philosophy," *Mind*, 1883, vol. viii. pp. 73 f.

itself. This Kant emphatically declares; and, so declaring, he was no doubt in harmony with the instructed common sense of his time. But turn back something less than a century and a half, to the system which begins distinctively modern thought, and you find a very different view. Descartes, in his treatise on Method, when describing his state of mind at the outset of his independent study, speaks of the Philosophy offered to his youthful mind very much as Kant speaks of the prevalent dogmatic metaphysics: "Of Philosophy[1] I will say nothing, except that when I saw that it had been cultivated for many ages by the most distinguished men, and that yet there is not a single matter within its sphere which is not still in dispute, and nothing therefore which is above doubt," etc. (*Discourse on Method*, Veitch's edn. p. 9). But unlike Kant, Descartes holds that this defect of Philosophy extends to the Sciences. "Inasmuch as these borrow their principles from Philosophy," he continues, "I judged that no solid superstructures could be reared on foundations so infirm." Between 1637 and 1783 the Sciences and Natural Philosophy seemed to have managed to struggle out of the mire of controversy in which Metaphysics is still up to the neck. They have got their feet on firm ground and are making steady progress, to which the critic points as a contrast that

[1] Philosophy as here used included more than Metaphysics, *i.e.* it included Natural Philosophy, which became effectively independent in Newton, and has since—like other subjects who have achieved independence—shown a disposition to turn and trample on its former lord. But Philosophy was throughout conceived by Descartes as a system of which Metaphysics formed the fundamental part (cf. Preface to the *Principles*, Veitch's edn. p. 185).

puts to shame the unfortunate study, of greater pretensions, which they have left behind. An examination of the source of their principles will, Kant holds, be useful, even indispensable, to any one who proposes to embark on the bewildering, unstable element where Metaphysics has been turning round; but he does not pretend that it will be useful to the Sciences themselves, or be in any way needed for their security. I draw attention to this, because this humbler attitude of Philosophy towards the Sciences, casting longing looks at the consensus of experts and continuity of progress which the latter have attained, is in the main the attitude of our own time. And it is this aspect of Kant's philosophy which makes him seem in some ways still so near to us; when more pretentious systems, that have intervened in the century and a quarter which separates him from us, have been swept irrevocably to the limbo of the past.

Let us take this, then, as Kant's point of departure. We have knowledge, mathematical and physical—uncontested, progressive knowledge, of which it would be idle to doubt. But what is offered us as knowledge, under the name of Metaphysics—what has been offered to human minds under this name for many centuries—is not uncontested, not progressive: system succeeds system, and we seem to be always revolving on the same spot and never getting on. Does it not look as if the human mind had been trying all this time to get knowledge beyond its powers? Is it not time to suspend these ineffectual toils and to ask *whether metaphysical knowledge* is at all possible? The *Critique* gives the systematic answer to this question: the *Prolegomena* is intended to drive the answer home. It is this answer that we have to examine. But before we examine it, it seems desirable to get a closer view of the professed knowledge whose possibility is being inquired into.

What Metaphysics has Kant in view? Now first it is evident that Kant's criticism is not, in his own view of it, limited to any particular metaphysical system. For the characteristics to which he appeals as justifying the critical procedure are not found in any one system: it is the whole results of the effort of the human mind to obtain metaphysical knowledge which taken together exhibit the perpetual unsettled disputes, the dreary round of unprogressive change, on which Kant lays stress. Still, in considering the detail of the metaphysical thought that Kant had chiefly before his mind, we may limit our view very much.

In the first place, we may limit it mainly to modern philosophy. Kant's interest in, and acquaintance with, Greek metaphysical thought seems to have been of a slight and general kind.[1] As to mediæval

---

[1] It is true that he makes references to Plato in more than one passage in the *Critique*, and a specially important reference in one passage* (to which I shall refer again) where he is contrasting Dogmatism with Empiricism. The Dogmatist is a thinker who proves to his own satisfaction that the world is limited in time and space, is ultimately composed of simple indivisible beings (atoms), and that—in order to explain the chain of contingent, causally connected, conditionally necessary, facts in the world's process—we require to assume an absolutely necessary Being and an unconditioned or free causality. The Empiricist, on his part, proves neither more nor less cogently the negative of these four dogmas, maintaining the unlimited extension of the world in time and space, the unlimited divisibility of matter, and

* *Transcendental Dialectic*, Book ii. chap. ii. § 3 [M. Müller's trans. p. 411].

thought again, he seems to have been almost entirely incurious. Practically, then, the Metaphysics into the possibility of which he is inquiring may be taken to be modern Metaphysics, not going back further than the seventeenth century. But we may limit the inquiry still further to Continental Metaphysics from Descartes onward. For with the English line of metaphysical thought, developed side by side with the Continental, Kant has again only imperfect acquaintance.[1] He does not seriously argue with either Locke or Berkeley. He treats the former as the author of a celebrated but unsuccessful attempt to derive the pure concepts of the understanding from experience, and an obviously inconsistent attempt to use the notions so derived for obtaining knowledge beyond the limits of experience. He finds, indeed, in Locke's fourth book, a hint of the distinction between analytical and synthetical judgments; but Locke's undeniable want of definite, systematic coherence seems to have prevented Kant from finding in him the instruction which—I

denying unconditioned or free causality and an unconditioned or absolutely necessary Being. Having compared the advantages and drawbacks of the two lines of thought in an impartial manner, Kant says that "this opposition all along the line of Empiricism to Dogmatism constitutes the opposition of Epicureanism to Platonism." But this remark strikingly shows the imperfection of his historical knowledge; for two cardinal points in Epicureanism—which by the way was primarily opposed to Stoicism rather than Platonism—are its assumption of material atoms and its maintenance of the freedom of the Will in antithesis to Stoic Determinism. "One might as well swallow the fables about the gods as bow to the yoke of Destiny" is an Epicurean dictum.[*] Similarly, his references to Plato show only a general popular knowledge of Platonic Idealism.

[1] The mentalistic Empiricism which leads in its three stages to the very diverse conclusions of Locke, Berkeley, and Hume is not to be confounded with the cosmological Empiricism to which I just referred.

[*] Cf. Diogenes Laertius [x. 134. R.D.H.].

venture to think—he might have found on this topic. Again, he shows no sign of having understood Berkeley, whom he treats as a mere visionary idealist not requiring serious refutation. Of Hume he speaks with emphatic admiration, and acknowledges that Hume's discussion of causality first "woke him from his dogmatic slumber"; but he only knows Hume's doctrine in the later and more guarded form in which it appears in the *Inquiry concerning Human Understanding*—of the frank, comprehensive, and uncompromising scepticism of Hume's *Treatise on Human Nature* he seems to have known nothing.

It is, then, on the metaphysical doctrines of the line of Continental thinkers which begins with Descartes and ends with Wolff, that Kant's attention is almost entirely concentrated when he thinks and speaks of Metaphysics and metaphysical dogmatism. And here again we may make a yet further reduction: we may omit Spinoza. There is, I think, no direct reference to Spinoza in either of the books we are to study, certainly no evidence that Kant had ever seriously considered his position and arguments. Apart from Hume—whose metaphysical view, as I said, Kant only knows in respect of the concept of Cause—the only leading thinkers whose metaphysical doctrines Kant knows sufficiently well to criticise with real grasp and penetration are Descartes, Leibniz, and Wolff.

Speaking broadly, Wolff's philosophy is that of Leibniz, with the paradoxical element pared down so far as to make the doctrine acceptable to Common Sense. Kant refers to both together as 'Leibniz-

Wolffian.' Perhaps, on the whole, it is Wolff's system that he has most before his mind: partly, I think, because Leibniz, though a more original and penetrating thinker than Wolff, was less of a system-maker, and Kant himself had a decided turn for system-making. But it is more important to note that the philosophy of Wolff, with minor modifications introduced by disciples, was the prevalent philosophy—the system that held the field, though by no means unassailed—not only when Kant was a learner, but for some time after he began to teach: though we gather from the Preface to the first edition of the *Critique* that in 1770-80 its influence had rather given way before the stream of general culture and enlightenment flowing from France; and that "Indifferentism, mother of chaos and night," was tending to take its place.

I propose therefore, when we come to study Kant's criticism of Metaphysics, to state briefly under each head the chief doctrines of Metaphysics as conceived by Wolff, with such references to Descartes and Leibniz as seem to be required. And it is all the more important for us to try to get an idea of the scope and method of pre-Kantian Metaphysics, because it is not easy to get it from Kant himself. For the new view of the problems of philosophy which Kant is introducing requires new lines of distinction which he does not always draw, or does not draw clearly and consistently.

To show this, it will be convenient to give by anticipation Kant's answer to the question 'Whether Metaphysics is possible?' The answer is 'Yes' and

'No' according as the term is used; and Kant seems to me to say 'no' or 'yes' according as he has the old method or doctrine of Metaphysics—what he sometimes calls 'dogmatical' Metaphysics, sometimes "the common Metaphysic of the schools"—in view, or the new method to which the *Critique* has shown the way. He means the former when he says that "all vain wisdom lasts its time but finally destroys itself," and that "this time has come for Metaphysics." He means the latter when he says that one who has grasped the principles of the *Critique* will "look forward to Metaphysics, which is now indeed within his power, with a certain delight." He means the former vain wisdom when he explains the *genesis* of Metaphysic, how "before men began to question nature methodically, they questioned isolated reason, which is ever present . . . ," and "so Metaphysic floated to the surface like foam—like it also in this, that when what had been gathered was dissolved there immediately appeared a new supply on the surface."[1] On the other hand, it is not this 'vain wisdom' but true knowledge that he means when he say in the concluding section of the *Prolegomena* that "Metaphysics alone of all possible sciences can be brought"—at once seemingly—"to such completion and fixity as to be incapable of further change or any augmentation by new discoveries."

It is largely this doubleness of view which gave Kantism its vogue both in the age of its appearance and in times nearer our own. It appealed both to

---

[1] [*Prolegomena*, § 4, p. 27.]

the foes and the friends of Metaphysics. Were you inclined to despise Metaphysics as antiquated rubbish, eternal sterile word-debates, speculative spinning of unsubstantial thought-cobwebs—here was a professor of philosophy who used the same language, and justified your vague contempt by laborious demonstrations, conducted according to all the rules of the scholastic game. Were you, on the other hand, disposed to think that these many centuries of efforts of great minds must have some deep meaning, some true end and goal, must spring from an intellectual need for which satisfaction was to be found somewhere in the nature of things—the same professor undertook to explain to you the meaning, show you the goal close at hand, satisfy the philosophic need by a symmetrical, well-articulated, coherent system of far-reaching truths. Whether you ran with the hare or with the hounds, Kant ran with you: you might not quite understand him, but you knew that he was on your side.

Let us look closer at the two kinds of Metaphysics: the good and the bad, the sham wisdom and the true. In the first place, it is true of both kinds of metaphysical propositions, the good and the bad alike, that they are synthetic *a priori* propositions, and that neither they nor the concepts used in them can be derived from experience. That they must be *a priori* is implied in the very conception of them 'metaphysical' knowledge has always been understood to mean knowledge lying 'on the other side' (*jenseits*) of the physical knowledge of which external experience is the source. Again, they must be 'synthetical': that is, the truths which it is the end and aim of metaphysical inquiry to ascertain must be expressible in judgments or propositions in which the predicate is not implicitly thought in thinking the subject. Analytical judgments no doubt belong to Metaphysics, and are of course independent of experience. But as such judgments merely state in the predicate what is implicitly thought in the subject-notion, we can get no extension of knowledge by making them: *e.g.* we can reflect on the metaphysical notion of substance, and make it more distinct by the purely analytical judgment "substance is that which only exists as the subject of predicates"; but this merely tells us what is meant by substance, and does not extend our knowledge of substances. And such analytical judgments are in no way distinctive of Metaphysics, as we can equally well analyse merely empirical concepts as 'body' and get from them equally certain judgments with regard to it—as that 'body is extended'—which equally add nothing to our knowledge of bodies.

To make the definition of metaphysical propositions complete, we require both characteristics, they must be at once 'synthetical' and '*a priori*': neither alone will do. Such propositions extend our knowledge, and at the same time are not empirical: the latter point is otherwise clear from the fact that they are universal and necessary. For merely empirical judgments cannot have true and strict universality, and therefore not necessity; "experience can only tell us that, so far as our observation has gone, there is no exception to this or that rule." But, as I have said, these characteristics belong equally to the sham knowledge and the true, the Metaphysics that we are to adopt and the Metaphysics we are to eschew. The question then is: What is the distinction between the two?

Perhaps the best way of expressing this distinction is to take Kant's phrase that "metaphysical knowledge," as its very term implies, must be knowledge " on the other or further side (*jenseits*) of experience"; and to show that the term 'on the further side' may have two different meanings, which we might express briefly as 'beyond' and 'behind' experience. Metaphysical study before Kant had tried to go *beyond* experience: that is to say, it had tried to get, and professed to have succeeded in getting, real knowledge—synthetical judgments—with regard to realities that never were nor could be objects of experience. Whereas the Metaphysics that Kant offers aims mainly at going *behind* experience: by analysing the object and conditions of experience it seeks to separate and exhibit systematically that element in our thought about experience and its objects which is not obtained from without, but from the nature and constitution of the knowing mind—regarded first as *per*ceiving through its senses, outer and inner, secondly as *con*ceiving and judging, thirdly as reasoning, passing from step to step of inference, and tending to unify its knowledge into a systematic whole. It is this latter kind of knowledge that Kant sometimes calls Critical Philosophy: what he gives under this name is not, he tells us, a complete metaphysical system of the right kind—Transcendental Philosophy, as he sometimes prefers to call it; for it does not profess to contain a complete detailed analysis of all the pure non-empirical concepts that the human mind possesses, the derivative as well as the primary. But—as *Prolegomena*, p. 177, shows—Kant does not think it a difficult matter to work out such a system, final and complete; and the fundamental principles and plan of such a system he thought he had completely given.

Is this, then, all? it may be said. Is this the end of all the high aspirations and pretensions of the Metaphysics—

> that seemed so fair,
> Such splendid purpose in her eyes?

Is she to confine herself to the task of making clear and systematic the *a priori* elements in our knowledge of the empirical world—which seems quite able to get on without her—and to tell us nothing of the great realities that she once sought to know: of God, and the human soul, and the relation between the two? Are we doomed to know nothing of God by the exercise of our reason, and nothing of the soul except what empirical psychology can tell us? No: that is not exactly Kant's meaning. The ultimate aim of the whole of his philosophy is to establish the beliefs in 'Immortality, Freedom, and God.' It is true that he establishes them primarily as postulates of the practical reason, resting ultimately on our certain, irrefragable conviction of duty, together with our equally strong conviction that, in order that morality may be more than an idle dream, reason must assume a supersensible world in which happiness depends on the performance of duty. But though this is the basis of the certitude of our faith in God, Freedom, and Immortality, speculative reason has nevertheless a function with regard to these postulates: although, as I understand Kant, it is of very different importance in the three cases.

In the case of Immortality, speculative reason—the non-empirical study of the soul, when duly critical—appears to do nothing but guard against materialistic explanations of mental phenomena. Rational psychology, with its idea of an absolute subject, "is merely a discipline which prevents us . . . from throwing ourselves into the arms of a soulless materialism,"[1] and serves as a regulative principle totally to destroy all materialistic explanations of the internal phenomena of the soul—for these can never account for self-consciousness,—but it gives no ground for inferring the permanence of the soul beyond the period of mundane life. I may observe that as regards the practical postulate of Immortality, Kant's ideas appear to have undergone a development between the *Critique of Pure Reason* (1781) and the *Critique of Practical Reason* (1788). In the former, he does not distinguish between the belief in

[1] Watson's *Selections*, p. 153.

immortality and the belief in 'a future life,' or 'future world' in which the connexion which reason demands between morality and happiness may be realised. But by the time he came to compose the *Critique of Practical Reason*, it seems to have occurred to him that the postulate of a future life, adequate to the rewarding of desert with happiness, does not necessarily involve endlessness of life. Here, accordingly, he rests the argument for immortality on the necessity for the realisation of the highest good by man, of 'perfect harmony' between this disposition and the moral law. "Such a harmony," he says, "must be possible, as it is implied in the command to promote the highest good"—a form in which the command to do duty may be conceived; on the other hand, 'a finite rational being' cannot *attain* moral perfection, it is only "capable of infinite progress towards it." Hence, as we must postulate that our "existence should continue long enough to permit of the complete realisation of the moral law," we must postulate that it will continue for ever. I shall have occasion to refer to this argument later. It always seems to me to illustrate well both the ingenuity of Kant and what I may perhaps be allowed to call his *naïveté*.

I turn to the second practical postulate, Freedom of Will. Here, again, our positive certain conviction of Free Will is based entirely on the conviction of duty. Still, speculative reason has a not unimportant function with regard to this belief, though only in the way of showing that it is not excluded by the no less necessary assumption of physical science. We may say that a discussion of the possibility of explaining natural effects by natural causality only, shows us a gap in our system of empirical knowledge which *may* be filled by the 'free causality' of the human individual as a transcendental reality, though we cannot positively say that it is so filled.

But in the case of Theology somewhat more is done.[1]

---

[1] Cf. [in the *Critique of Pure Reason* the section entitled "Criticism of all Speculative Theology"] Watson's *Selections*, p. 222. [In the *Critique of Practical Reason* that entitled "Possibility of an extension of Pure Practical Reason without a corresponding extension of Pure Speculative Reason," Watson's *Selections*, pp. 300-302. See also the Appendix at the end of these Lectures.]

LECTURE II

THE TRANSCENDENTAL ÆSTHETIC

HAVING given this bird's-eye view of its conclusions, I pass now to examine in detail the principles and method of the True Metaphysics.

It must be remembered that, according to Kant, we are not to expect from him a complete metaphysical system, according to his definition of Metaphysics, *i.e.* mainly a complete systematic statement of the *a priori* concepts and synthetic judgments—of the knowledge attainable by the human mind, apart from particular experiences. Such a system may be worked out hereafter: the *Critique* only gives the principles and method of constructing such a system.

The exposition of the Critical or Transcendental Philosophy is divided into three parts, in accordance with the traditional threefold division of the cognitive faculties of the human mind into Sense, Understanding, and Reason. It is to be observed, however, that Reason seems to be also used in the title in a wider sense, to denote the source of the *a priori* elements in cognition as a whole. This is due to another antithesis, which Kant finds in the thought handed down to him, between 'rational' and 'empirical' knowledge. For elements of *a priori* knowledge real or supposed are found not only in the ideas and conclusions of Reason in the narrower sense: they are found also in the forms of Sense-perception, Space, and Time, and in the forms of synthesis by which the understanding constitutes empirical objects, and connects them into coherent elements of an empirical world, conceived as extended through space and perduring through time. But the treatment of the three sources has to be fundamentally different. For the *a priori* element derived from the forms of Sense, and the forms of Understanding, has been in the main rightly conceived by the thinkers who have employed it in the systematic sciences of Mathematics and Physics.

The recognised appeal to intuition in the case of Mathematics, and the control of experience in the case of Physics, have kept the human mind—on the whole—from serious vagaries in these departments. In fact, as we have seen, these sciences are now enjoying uncontested acceptance and steady progress, and Transcendentalism assumes them as given. The case is otherwise with the *a priori* ideas peculiar to Reason—which are, in fact, various forms of the idea of unconditioned being or existence—the temptation to use these in answers to questions that carry us beyond the limits of possible experience has been too strong, and has produced the long stream of bad dogmatic Metaphysics, which Kant hopes effectually to dam up. Here, therefore, in this third part of

Transcendental Philosophy, we have first to expose the vain semblance of knowledge by which the human mind has so strong a natural tendency to be deluded: and then, after destroying the vain semblance of knowledge, a sound criticism of these *a priori* ideas will show their use—(1) in systematising as far as possible the additions to real knowledge which we are continually obtaining through experience; (2) in so making clear, when we stand at the limits of empirical knowledge, what may be reasonably thought of its relation to the unknown realities that lie beyond these limits; and thus (3) clearing the ground for the erection not of a structure of speculative knowledge, but still of well-grounded, rational, positive conviction on the great questions of the Existence of God, the Freedom of the Will, the Immortality of the Soul, and generally the Moral Order of the World.

As we said, for these great convictions—always fundamentally important to Kant—the Practical Reason, in his view, affords the only adequate rational basis.

In this last part of Kant's work—as will appear from what I have said—the true use of the ideas of Reason, the right direction of man's natural, ineradicable impulse to penetrate beyond the conditioned to the unconditioned, can only be understood when we have fully seen with his eyes through the illusions of the old Metaphysics.

We have therefore to begin by examining Sensibility and Understanding, as sources of *a priori* knowledge. The *a priori* cognitions of which Sensibility is the primary source have been elaborated into a great, coherent, progressive system of knowledge, which, from the outset of modern philosophy, has presented itself to the philosophic mind as a model of certainty in its premises, method, and conclusions, and as at the same time entirely independent of empirical basis. This we call Pure Mathematics. Here Transcendental Philosophy, Kant holds, has no work to do in distinguishing and separating the pure or non-empirical element of the object of knowledge from the empirical element: it finds the separation completely made and universally recognised. It has only to make clear the source of this non-empirical knowledge, in the universal forms—Space and Time—in which the human mind receives and arranges the particular data of Sensibility.

The case is different with Physical Science—including the application of Mathematics to that world of empirical objects with undetermined limits of extension in Space and duration in Time, concerning which Physical Science seeks systematic general knowledge. These objects and all their parts and their relations and changes in Time and Space are all measurable and numerable, and so far objects of the *a priori* mathematical knowledge just mentioned.

But there is another non-empirical element, besides the mathematical, in the knowledge we commonly conceive ourselves to possess of the general laws of our common world of empirical objects; and this element is much more difficult to exhibit in clear separation from the empirical element that is blended with it in the view of ordinary physical science. Here, in fact, lies the most difficult task for Transcendental Philosophy, so far as its work is constructive rather than destructive. This will occupy us in detail hereafter: the fundamental question is, How, from the subjective data of sense— the various impressions on each individual's sensibility which we distinguish as sights, sounds, touches, pressures, muscular feelings, etc.—is it possible to pass to universally valid knowledge of the laws of an objective world, common to all human minds? The uncontested establishment and progress of Physical Science shows that we commonly conceive this transition to be legitimate, and that experience confirms the assumption of its legitimacy; but how is it legitimate? There is a great gap between the data of sense-perception, as reflective analysis shows them, and the general truths of science which we all accept—*e.g.* the laws of motion. How is the gap filled up? The presence of a non-empirical element is manifest, according to Kant, in the conclusions of science if there are—as physical science holds—any ascertained universal laws of the physical world. For a universal conclusion cannot be validly attained by any number of mere particular experiences. But to show what this non-empirical element is, and how it is related to the empirical element, requires elaborate analysis. In the *Critique* this is given in the Transcendental Analytic, and again in the 'second part of the General Transcendental Problem' in the *Prolegomena*.

The arguments in the first part of the Transcendental Philosophy, the Transcendental Æsthetic, are comparatively easy of apprehension; and they seem to have been found convincing by thinkers who have been able only very partially to assimilate the elaborate and difficult system of the forms of understanding expounded in the second part (the *Analytic*) or the anti-spiritualistic conclusions—negativing speculative knowledge of Self and God—of the third part (the *Dialectic*).

The arguments of the *Æsthetic* may be read in Watson's *Selections*, pp. 22-39. What is called the 'metaphysical exposition' gives the context and characteristics of the notions of Space and Time: in the 'transcendental exposition' they are regarded as *sources* of synthetic *a priori* judgments. The conclusion is simple and striking.

Space and Time are unalterable forms of sensibility, and therefore necessary conditions of the apprehension of phenomena by the human mind, but not attributes, elements, or conditions of the existence of things apart from their relation to the percipient human mind, nor even of human minds themselves, regarded simply as existing. Even Time is only a form of the appearance of a human mind to itself, not an attribute of its real existence. "If," says Kant, "I could be perceived by myself or by any other being without the condition of sensibility, the very same determinations, which now appear as changes, would not be known as in Time, and therefore would not be known as changes."[1]

Distinguishing the two forms, Space is the necessary form of external perception—perception of things outside me—Time the necessary form primarily of the perception of ourselves and our mental state; but, as external perceptions are states —or elements of states—of the perceiving mind, Time is a formal *a priori* condition of all phenomena without exception. This brought on Kant the charge of Idealism, vehemently repudiated by him in the *Prolegomena* and also in the second edition of the *Critique*.[2]

It is, then, undeniable that Kant's metaphysical view as here given is not to be classed as Idealism or Mentalism, on account of its strong assertion of the existence of things other than percipient human minds, "unknown to us as to what they are in themselves," but yet 'known'—in a sense—as operating on us and causing impressions on our senses. It is rather to be called Phenomenalism—so far as the existence of a material world is concerned —since it holds that all the attributes of what we commonly call body, Locke's primary qualities as well as his secondary, are mere phenomena.

But it is remarkable how little *proof* Kant ever

[1] [Watson's *Selections*, p. 35.]
[2] *Prolegomena*. § 13, Remark ii. pp. 54 f.   *Critique*, second edition, "Refutation of Idealism."

offers of the anti-mentalistic element in his doctrine. In the passage in the *Prolegomena* we have simple 'assertion and not proof. In the 'Refutation of Idealism' in the second edition of the *Critique*, Kant is apparently demonstrating the existence not of things independent of human perception but of phenomenal things in space, which are ultimately only impressions on our minds, received in the forms of sensibility and combined into connected objects of experience by the judgments of the understanding. As regards, indeed, the reality underlying the phenomenal subject which Common Sense conceives as a soul or spirit, Kant (in the *Critique of the Practical Reason*) finds evidence of its existence in the freedom which our moral consciousness leads us to attribute to the 'noumenal' self. But as regards 'body,' no such evidence is of course available, and yet Kant does not anywhere offer any other.

The explanation may be partly found in the fact that Kant's thought is not consistent on this fundamental point, though of course this fundamental inconsistency, in a thinker so acute and so laboriously systematic, itself needs explanation. He never, indeed, *denies* the existence of an unknown thing-in-itself which, acting on our minds, produces the manifold sensations that, when bound together by the understanding, we call a 'body'; but in the concluding chapter of the Transcendental Analytic he certainly treats its existence as *problematical*. The most definite passage is the following: "The understanding limits the sensibility without enlarging its own scope; and, warning the latter not to presume to deal with things-in-themselves, but only with phenomena, it forms the thought of an object in itself; but only as a transcendental object that is the cause of the phenomenon (and hence not itself phenomenon), and that cannot be thought of either as magnitude or as reality or as substance, because these concepts always require sensuous forms in order to be applicable to an object. We cannot say, therefore, of this transcendental object, *whether it is in us or also outside us*; or *whether, if sensibility were taken away, it would disappear along with it or would still remain.*"[1]

It is impossible to reconcile this passage—especially the last sentence—with that in the *Prolegomena*, where Kant says:—" I grant by all means that there are bodies without us, that is things which though quite unknown to us as to what they are in themselves . . . are not therefore less real."[2] In both cases, indeed, not only the 'secondary' qualities of Locke, which Common Sense, but not physical science, attributes to bodies as they exist unperceived — colour, odour, flavour, heat, — but also Locke's 'primary' qualities—extension, place, figure, impenetrability,—are regarded as merely phenomenal, merely mental, results of the understanding combining the data of sense. But in the *Prolegomena*,

---

[1] *Critique*, Max Müller's trans., p. 250. [Italics Prof. Sidgwick's.] This passage is not given by Watson, but the whole chapter is in this sense. See Watson, pp. 129-134.
[2] *Prolegomena*, p. 54.

empirical body is the appearance of a thing 'influencing sensibility,' a thing none the less real because it is unknown: which must therefore be conceived to remain, if the sensibility influenced by it were to vanish. In the passage just quoted, it is expressly said that we do not know whether the thing in itself would remain or not, if sensibility were to vanish. Now if, as Kant says, Idealism—which *I* prefer to call Mentalism—"consists in the assertion that all the things other than thinking beings, which we believe ourselves to cognise in external perception, are nothing but representations (*Vorstellungen*) in thinking beings,"[1] there can be no doubt that the view taken in the passage in the *Critique* is—to use the phrase that Kant applies to Descartes—'problematical Idealism': since we cannot say whether the 'transcendental object' is only in us or also without us. On the other hand, there can be equally no doubt that in the *Prolegomena* Kant vehemently repudiates all Idealism, problematical or dogmatic.

No reconciliation is possible; and I have tried to make this quite clear, because it is important that students of Kant should fully apprehend his weak points as well as his strong points. He is one of the most original, penetrating, ingenious, and laboriously systematic of modern thinkers; so that the close study of his system—for those who can and will go through it—is a most valuable metaphysical education. But I am convinced that he is a profoundly

[1] *Prolegomena*, § 13, p. 54.

inconsistent thinker, profoundly unaware of his own inconsistency. On the most important questions of theoretical and practical philosophy, and the relation between the two—the deepest and most difficult of philosophical problems—I continually find him saying different things in different treatises, and I never find him showing the least consciousness of the difference.[1] What remains to be said of Kant's relation to Idealism or Mentalism must be deferred till we have examined the second part of his Transcendental Philosophy— which deals with the fundamental conceptions and assumptions of physical science.

I return, then, to the doctrine of the Transcendental Æsthetic, as to which Kant never wavers or qualifies. There are two main points: First, that Space and Time are mental forms, existing in the mind *prior* to experience; and, secondly, that they are forms of perception or sense and not of understanding. The first two paragraphs in the 'Metaphysical Exposition' deal with the first point; the third and fourth paragraphs with the second point. I may say at once that with these latter arguments I substantially agree; and what Kant here says can be accepted whether or not we follow him in regarding (*e.g.*) Space as an *a priori* mental form. That is, to me as to Kant, Space, as an element of the empirical world, presents itself as essentially single and in a logical sense individual. It is not merely a notion of a class of relations; for the essential characteristic of all spatial relations of real things, as Common Sense

---

[1] Cf. what I have said on Freedom in *Methods of Ethics*.

conceives them—things that have empirical reality—is that they are relations of things occupying different parts of one and the same space. I do not, indeed, think it strictly correct to say with Kant's translator that Space is presented as an infinite given magnitude; but the *Prolegomena* (§ 12, p. 47) seems to make clear that Kant's '*unendlich*' here means only "extended without assignable limit *in indefinitum*." The same may be said, with similar qualification, of Time.

To show the gain in precision obtained from this part of the discussion, we may compare Mr. Spencer's view in his essay on the *Classification of the Sciences*. The point is that, after referring to the Kantian view—which he obviously only knows inaccurately and at second-hand—as the view that "Space and Time are forms of thought," Mr. Spencer says: "Space is the abstract of all relations of coexistence," "Time is the abstract of all relations of sequence."[1] Now this statement seems to me hasty and inaccurate for more than one reason. For coexistence is certainly a time-relation, and, in its widest sense, is only a *time*-relation. No doubt material things coexist spatially; but mental facts do not. As Hume says, "A moral reflection cannot be placed on the right or the left hand of a passion."[2] Or if it be said that mental and material facts are "two sides or aspects of the same fact,"—so that a moral reflection is an 'aspect' of a material fact that

---

[1] [*Essays, Scientific, Political, and Speculative*, vol. iii., 1874, p. 11.]

[2] *Treatise of Human Nature*, Bk. iv. § 5, Green and Grose's edition, p. 520.

is spatially related to another material fact of which a passion is an aspect,—at any rate the two aspects (mental and material) are not spatially related like the two sides of a merely material thing. You may call them sides, but you only call them so metaphorically. Suppose that a certain movement in the grey matter of my brain is inseparably connected with my moral reflection; and suppose an intelligent observer able to see this movement, and able to see it from any position. He might look all round it, but however he might vary his position, we cannot conceive that he would see a moral reflection anywhere. Here, therefore, we have a case of coexistence which is merely temporal and not spatial at all. But the point that now mainly concerns us turns on the word 'abstract.' The statement that " Space is the *abstract* of all relations of coexistence" ignores or blurs the characteristics of Space brought out in the paragraphs of Kant that we have been discussing. I am not indeed quite clear how Mr. Spencer uses the phrase, 'abstract of relations,' for this substantival use of 'abstract' is unfamiliar. But suppose we take another kind of relation, Likeness, and try to think what would be meant—what could be meant—by the 'abstract of all relations of likeness.' It seems clear that the phrase must mean the general conception of likeness or resemblance abstracted from the particularities of all particular resemblances: and I certainly think that Kant has shown that Space is not merely or primarily the general or abstract conception of the various relations of spatial coexistence.

In accordance with Kant's paragraphs, then, it seems to me clear that Time and Space, as objects of ordinary and of scientific thought—apart from any question of their a-priority or mentality—are not relations or 'abstracts' of relations, but entities of relational quality. We no doubt conceive the manifold things of the material world as arranged in Space, and connected through their spatial relations in a kind of order different from the order which they occupy in a scientific classification that systematises their relations of resemblance; the essential characteristics of the spatial relations of real things, as Common Sense thinks, is that they are relations of position in *one* space.[1] And as there is one apparently real Space for all things, so there is one Time in which all events are temporally related. This remains true of Space and Time as ordinarily conceived, whether we regard them as belonging only to percipient and conscious human minds as such, or also to a real world existing independently of such perceptions.

But are we to regard them as belonging only to the percipient mind? To Kant's arguments in support of this momentous conclusion I now turn. First, however, let us consider for a moment how momentous it is. I ask you to realise this, because I am not sure that Kant always realises it. For he seems to suppose that, even after being convinced by the arguments of the Transcendental Æsthetic, when we come

---

[1] I say 'real things' because, as Sigwart points out, we may and do construct scenes and geometrical figures in imaginary Space, having no definite relation to real Space.

to the third part of the treatise, we shall still take a serious interest in the great questions of Rational Cosmology:—whether the physical world has bounds in Space, and had a beginning in Time, whether its parts are ultimately simple or infinitely divisible, etc. etc. But surely, for a mind of the least intelligence, all these questions are altogether cut off and precluded by the acceptance of the conclusions of the Æsthetic: we can no more ask them than we can ask how many angels can stand on the point of a pin (a question which is said to have interested the mediæval mind). For the *real* physical world, as we must then hold, not being in Space, can have no bounds; and not being extended, the question of ultimate divisibility cannot be raised with regard to it. Again, not being in Time, neither beginning, nor duration, nor succession of events can be predicated of it; and, neither changing nor enduring, it can have no causality, in the sense of necessary connexion of antecedents and consequents. These conclusions, indeed, are what Kant himself draws; but there are others, that concern us more intimately, which he has not expressly drawn, and which indeed I hardly see how he could have drawn without something like inconsistency. For these latter negations are true of the spiritual no less than the material world: since all temporal determinations must be held to belong to appearance, not to real existence, in the case of spirits no less than in the case of bodies. As Kant says in a passage before quoted: "If I could be perceived by myself or by any other being without the condition of sensibility, the very same determinations which now appear as changes would not be known as in time, and therefore would not be known as changes."[1]

The notion of spiritual progress is therefore merely phenomenal and unreal: and hence it would seem that the objection to Metaphysics, put forward as the starting-point of the transcendental inquiry, that it does not progress like other sciences, but goes on turning round and round without advancing, is deprived of its force—since the progress is in any case merely apparent. And this, of course, applies to moral as well as to intellectual progress. Hence the conception of moral progress, on which the practical postulate of immortality—as we saw—is based, is a conception that represents no real fact of any soul's existence, but merely an appearance due to the imperfection of its faculty of cognition. But if moral progress is thus reduced to mere appearance, what becomes of the belief in the immortality of the soul which Kant (in the *Critique of the Practical Reason*) bases on it? Indeed, in any case, if Time is merely a form of human sensibility,—due to an imperfection of man's nature which prevents him from knowing things as they are,—the postulate of immortality seems to become a postulate for the endless continuance of an imperfection. It does not seem that this can afford an inspiring hope for a truth-loving mind. I do not find that Kant has fully contemplated these consequences of his doctrine of Time: though I ought to say that in his practical Philosophy he

[1] Cf. above, p. 27.

certainly throws over Time—if I may so express myself—when he finds it convenient. Since, indeed, his defence of the notion of Freedom is expressly based on the assumption that the momentous choice between good and evil which every human soul makes is in reality not subject to the condition of time, so that any change that may appear in a man's character is illusory: his character as manifested in his conduct is made by himself though a timeless act of will in which there is no before and after.[1]

Well, the consequences, we see, are tremendous: in the next lecture we shall have therefore to consider carefully the proof of the doctrine from which they flow.

[1] [Cf. *Methods of Ethics*, 6th edn. Appendix.]

LECTURE III

KANT'S 'EXPOSITION' OF SPACE AND TIME

LET us, for simplicity and definiteness, concentrate attention on the notion of Space: and take first the 'Metaphysical Exposition.' Here Kant's points are two: (1) The notion of Space cannot be derived from external experience; because, in order that I may apprehend things as out of me and out of each other, I must have the notion of Space already in my mind; and (2) that the notion of Space is a necessary, *a priori* one; for I cannot imagine Space annihilated, though I can very well think it emptied of objects.[1]

Now it appears to me that in discussing these arguments—and all that Kant says on the subject—we are liable to two confusions of thought: one relating to the notion of 'externality,' and the other to the notion of 'a-priority' (if I may be allowed the word): and that when these confusions are cleared away, Kant's arguments are clearly inadequate to prove their conclusion.

First as regards *externality*. What is meant

[1] Cf. Watson's *Selections*, p. 24.

here by 'external,' 'outside of'? There are two distinct meanings possible: (1) 'Spatial externality.' This seems clearly meant in speaking of the apparent perception of things 'outside of and beside' one another: the word 'beside' definitely determines 'outside' to this meaning. But 'outside' (*ausser*) is sometimes used by Kant, definitely in the sense of (2) 'otherness of existence'—'distinct and independent existence.'[1] Now if we get these two meanings quite distinct, and then turn to the argument that I have just summarised, we shall find, I think, that any force it may seem to have is derived from a more or less unconscious fusion of the two: and that if we apply either separately, it loses all force or contains a manifestly unwarranted assumption.

First, take externality in the sense of spatial externality. Then 'outside of me' must mean 'outside my body,' as Kant does not conceive my *mind* as occupying space. This being so, the statement that I cannot apprehend things as being outside my body and outside each other, without apprehending them as occupying different parts of Space, is undeniable but insignificant; since material outsideness is a spatial notion, involved in and involving the notion of 'location in different parts of Space.' But the statement has no tendency to prove that the whole notion of Space and spatial externality is not empirical. I might as well argue that the notion of colour is not derived from visual perception, but

---

[1] Cf. *Prolegomena*, p. 54, where 'without us' must mean 'having an existence distinct from and independent of our existence, an existence made known by some action on our senses.'

'presupposed in it,' because I cannot visually perceive things to be there at all without perceiving them to be coloured.

It is of course true—and I think this partly accounts for Kant's view—that so far as, in any fresh apprehension of things around me, I definitely apply spatial notions,—perceiving and judging that they are in front or to the right, of such and such size, at such and such distance from me or each other—I seem to bring these notions with me to the fresh experience and not to derive them from it. But this applies equally to my perceptions and judgments of colour, or any other admittedly empirical conception. I can only definitely apprehend any fresh experience by applying to it the system of notions that my mind has derived from past experience: though so far as the fresh experience contains novel elements, it will tend to modify and enlarge my previously formed system of notions—sometimes perceptibly, but more often imperceptibly. Observable progress in our experience of objects almost always takes place, not by sudden definite acquisitions of entirely new notions, but partly by new combinations of old notions, partly by the gradual consolidation into definiteness of vague apprehensions of new differences and resemblances. I see no reason why we should not suppose a similar gradual emergence into definiteness of our spatial notions, along with other notions admittedly empirical.

Here perhaps it may be suggested that when

Kant says that the notion of Space is already presupposed in external perception, he only means '*logically* presupposed': and similarly that 'a-priority' in the second argument[1] only refers to logical not chronological priority. Now the distinction between these two meanings of priority has often been drawn—in the form of a distinction between what is '*naturally* prior' in knowledge and what is 'prior for us' it is as old as Aristotle—and it may be said to be now current and familiar. But it is not easy to get it quite clear: that is, to get the conception of logical priority purged of all chronological suggestion: but when this purgation is effected, it seems to me that a merely *logical* presupposition of the notion of Space in external perception is quite irrelevant to Kant's argument. For what is meant by priority in a purely logical sense? Merely that the concept (or judgment) said to be logically prior to another requires to be made explicit before and in order that the concept to which it is prior may be perfectly clear and distinct (or that the judgment may be arrived at by a perfectly cogent process of inference). In this sense the notion of a straight line is logically prior to the notion of a triangle as a figure bounded by straight lines: and Euclid's axiom relating to parallels is logically prior to his 29th proposition—it is a more elementary proposition, without which the other cannot be cogently established. In this sense the notion of pure Space may no doubt be said to be logically prior to the

---

[1] Watson's *Selections*, p. 24 *fin.*

notion of a material thing. But when this meaning is made clear, it is, I think, evident that 'logical priority' is quite irrelevant to the question whether Space really belongs to the object perceived, independently; or is only a form under which the human mind is by its constitution compelled to perceive it.

Secondly, Kant argues that the notion of Space is necessary, as is shown by the psychological experiment of trying to get rid of it. "By no effort can we think Space away, though we can quite easily think Space empty of objects." This argument has been regarded as weighty by writers deserving of respect: but I confess that it seems to me to have all the worst defects that an argument can have: (1) it is not strictly true; (2) the distinction drawn in it between Space and Matter is inconsistent with another fundamental principle elsewhere laid down by Kant; and (3) so far as it has any force it really tends in my opinion to prove the contrary of the conclusion which Kant draws from it. When I say that it is not strictly true, I mean that there are cases in which, so far as I can perform the psychological experiment suggested, it does seem to me that Space is eliminated from my consciousness nearly or altogether for brief moments:—*e.g.* when I am absorbed in listening to music. But I quite admit what I rather understand Kant to mean, that when I turn my attention to Space, I am unable to conceive it annihilated. Only I do not find that this characteristic—inconceivability of annihilation—

distinguishes Space from Matter, as Kant affirms: I do not find that I can readily think of Space as empty of material things:—*i.e.* not all Space of all Matter. Such a complete emptying of Space is no less impossible to me than the complete elimination of Space from my thought. And further, I should have supposed that Kant would have found the same impossibility, since he elsewhere[1] gives as a synthetical *a priori* cognition "that the quantum of substance in Nature can neither be increased or diminished." He holds this to have been admitted in all ages by men of common understanding no less than by philosophers, and expressed in the ancient *Gigni de nihilo nihil, in nihilum nil posse reverti*— nothing can be produced from nothing or return into nothing. But how can we readily think Space emptied of all Matter, if the permanence of material substance is a necessary condition of experience? Whither is the Matter of which Space is emptied conceived to go; and when it has gone where does the permanent substance hide?

But, lastly, granting it true that I can conceive Matter annihilated, but cannot conceive Space annihilated, the Space that I am unable to conceive annihilated is not conceived by me as a form of my cognition, or of human cognition, but as something that exists independently of my cognition of it. Now, I concede to the Empiricists that we cannot infer with absolute certitude the existence

---

[1] Watson's *Selections*, "First Analogy of Experience," p. 106. Cf. *Prolegomena*, § 15, p. 65.

of anything from the impossibility of conceiving it non-existent. At the same time, I think the 'inconceivability of the opposite' is of some value as a test of truth. But surely, if it is legitimate to infer anything from the inconceivability of annihilating Space, it is the necessary existence of Space apart from my sensibility; for it is that Space that I cannot conceive annihilated and not Space regarded as a form of my sensibility. For this—being a notion I never found till I came across Kant—is one of which I can get rid with the utmost ease.

It would take too long to go through in the same way the metaphysical exposition of Time. I think it will be found that the reasoning I have employed in criticising the metaphysical exposition of Space applies, *mutatis mutandis*, to that of Time. I now pass to the 'Transcendental Exposition.'

I have tried to show that the arguments Kant uses in his 'Metaphysical Exposition,' viz. that the notion of Space is presupposed in external perception, and that it is a necessary notion which we cannot by any effort think away, are ineffective to prove that Space is a form of human sensibility and not a determination that belongs to objects when abstraction is made from our subjective conditions of perception. I ought, however, to say that I do not think Kant would have regarded them as effective, apart from an assumption which lies at the basis of the Transcendental Exposition. This is the assumption that I could not have universal knowledge, universal synthetic—not merely analytical—judgments with regard to Space and its properties, if Space existed independently of my (or any human) perception; but only if it be regarded as a form and subjective condition of such perception. Now doubtless geometry as commonly accepted does give us such synthetical universals: I know that all triangles inscribed in a semicircle must be right-angled triangles, and I could not obtain this knowledge by mere analysis of the notions of 'semicircle' and 'right-angled triangle.' But why am I to infer from this that the proposition is not true of a real extended world existing as such, independently of human cognition'?

Kant's answer to this question is perhaps most clearly given in the *Prolegomena*, § 9, p. 43. He there says: (1) "I can only know what is contained in the object itself when it is present and given to me"; and (2) "Even then it is incomprehensible how the intuition of a present thing should make me know the thing as it is in itself, since its properties cannot migrate into my faculty of cognition (*Vorstellungskraft*)." The second of these arguments, if valid at all, would render it unnecessary to consider the first or talk any further about things as existing apart from my perception. For if I cannot have immediate knowledge of any entity, because it cannot migrate into my faculty of cognition, it must surely for the same reason be impossible to have mediate knowledge of it or any rational conviction with regard to its existence: so that Rational Cosmology and Theology would vanish in a twinkling, leaving nothing for the Critical Philosophy to confute. But with them also would vanish the conception of the reality of things in themselves, and Kant must inevitably fall into the Idealism that he repudiates. But this is not all: not only would material things in themselves be thus eliminated, but all knowledge of other minds would equally be cut off: for another mind cannot migrate into my faculty of cognition any more than anything else. If the mind can only know what can get into the mind, then, as I certainly cannot *be* anything except myself, I cannot know anything except myself. We are thus reduced from Idealism to Solipsism: and the Critical Philosophy is thereby rendered absurd; for what is the meaning of suspending all metaphysicians from their business and appealing to the 'uncontested' position of Mathematics, if I do not know whether there are any metaphysicians or mathematicians except myself? This short-cut to agnosticism which has tempted others besides Kant —the strange dogma that in order to *know* a thing I have to *be* it—has thus led us into a quagmire of absurdities and inconsistencies. Let us abandon it once for all, and pass to the other contention, that I cannot know a thing unless it is 'present and given' to me.

This at first sight seems more plausible: but on looking closer, I think it will be found to involve a confusion between physical and psychical fact. It surreptitiously transforms a merely empirically known condition of bodies acting on bodies, into a condition, dogmatically assumed, of a purely mental function. In our ordinary experience of material changes, the bodies that appear to act on other bodies appear generally to be locally contiguous with them. It is true that gravitation constitutes a vast *prima facie* exception to this generalisation: but efforts have been made to explain away this exception, and it is possible that they may some day succeed. But what then? How can this physical generalisation as to the causation of motion justify us in dogmatically limiting the possibilities of the purely psychical fact that we call knowledge of Matter or Space? Kant certainly does not mean to materialise mind so far as to localise it: and if not, the object of knowledge can never be properly said to be in local contiguity to the knowing mind. What meaning, then, can be attached to the statement that the mind can only know what is 'present and given to it,' except that it can only know—in fact what there is to be known? It may be said that our apparent particular knowledge of the relations in space of particular things is scientifically known to be obtained only through a chain of movements between the things and our brains, throughout which contiguity of moving particles is always a condition of the transmission of motion. But granting this, how can we legitimately infer from this empirical generalisation the impossibility of obtaining by reflection *universal* knowledge of the spatial relations of real things? To the ordinary geometer it undoubtedly appears that certain universal spatial relations, applicable to a real external world, are presented to his mind as necessary: surely the assumption that this is impossible is a mere dogma, which cannot be justified by any empirical generalisation based on our empirical knowledge of the particular spatial relations of particular things.

But, further, if I could have no universal knowledge of anything except the forms of my own sensibility, why should I suppose that I can have universally valid synthetic judgments with regard to these? This is a question which Kant never seems to have asked himself: but it is of fundamental importance to examine it, when we are considering the *pros* and *cons* of the question as to the subjectivity or objectivity of Space and Time. If I can only know—or let us say "only know with the certainty that Mathematics claims"—what is 'present and given,' surely I can only thus know the form of my sensibility as it is here and now: I cannot know what it has been in the past, nor what it will be in the future: I cannot know that it has not changed, or that it will not change: still less can I know that it is precisely similar to the forms of sensibility of other human minds. But if this is so, what can possibly be gained for the explanation of the universal validity of our geometrical cognitions by transferring Space from the *non-ego* to the *ego*?

I have gone into this at some length because the view to which I am replying is a part of Kant's doctrine which has been more widely accepted than many other parts. In pursuing this argument so far, I have followed Kant in assuming that the synthetic universals of Pure Mathematics depend on intuition; and therefore that the objects of mathematical cognition cannot be merely thought but require to be *constructed in concreto*. This is the distinction which Kant draws between mathematical cognition and philosophical (under which term he includes both Physics and Metaphysics). "Philosophical cognition," he says, "is the rational cognition obtained from concepts, mathematical that obtained from the construction of concepts. . . . By *constructing* a concept I mean representing *a priori* the intuition belonging to it. For the construction of a concept, therefore, a *non-empirical* intuition is required which as an intuition is a *single* object, though as the construction of a concept or general notion it must express relations generally valid for all possible intuitions that come under the same concept." He takes the instance of a triangle: in order to reason about triangles generally I 'construct' the concept either by representing a particular triangle "by mere imagination in pure intuition, or after this upon paper also in empirical intuition, in both cases however *a priori*, without borrowing the pattern for it from any experience."[1]

Now no doubt what Kant says here is broadly true of ordinary geometry: when we reason about triangles, or squares, or circles we do draw in imagination or on paper particular triangles, etc.

[1] *Kritik der reinen Vernunft*, Hartenstein's edition, p. 478 [M. Müller's translation (emended), p. 611.]

It seems to me, however, bold to affirm that these simple figures are not borrowed from experience. We had got empirical ideas of these before our earliest studies in geometry: we called a plate circular, and the sides of dice and boxes square, and the flaps of envelopes triangular: and when we came to get more precise ideas of these from Euclid, and to be introduced to unfamiliar figures—such as the rhombus—they were always drawn for us on paper before we represented them in imagination. Doubtless, as we came to understand geometrical reasoning we realised that the square we reasoned about was not the square we drew: for first, the latter was a particular square of a particular size on a particular piece of paper, whereas our reasoning was about any square of any size anywhere; and secondly, the lines of the drawn square were slightly wabbly and unequal, while the square of our thought was a perfect square. This distinction between the real general object of geometrical thought and the imperfect particular copy that we use to aid that thought has been a starting-point for philosophical Idealism since Plato: but this imperfection and this particularity belong no less to any square I may imagine, if I try to solve a geometrical problem in my head. Indeed, in my poor experience, the circle of my imagination is much inferior to that which I draw as a representation of the general or abstract circle about which I think: the circle I draw is not quite round, but it is clear and stable, whereas the circle I imagine is dim and fluctuating. It seems to me indubitable that the latter is a copy of the drawn circle, and that there is nothing of pure intuition about it. No doubt, as my geometrical faculty develops, I can imagine more or less definitely new figures, even surfaces of complicated convolution which I could not draw on paper. But I see no difference in this respect between geometrical and mechanical reasoning. The inventor of a machine imagines new combinations of wheels, levers, screws, cranks, etc., varying the data of his mechanical experience to produce a novel result; in the same way proceeds the geometer, whose imagination, guided by and aiding his thought, constructs (*e.g.*) a pseudo-spherical surface. I do not see why a construction in 'pure intuition' should be interpolated between the thought and the empirically developed imagination in the case of the geometer any more than in that of the mechanician.

So far I have been considering, as Kant is, elementary geometry. But it seems to me important to note that, when we have learnt to apply analytical methods to algebraic figures and quantities, our thought is to an important extent able to dispense with the aid to reasoning furnished by the particular concrete specimens—drawn or imagined—of its general notions. It is able to grasp the law of construction of a regular curve, never presented or represented before, to know it to be possible and to deduce important properties of it without constructing any specimen of it at all, either in imagination or on paper. And, speaking from my own experience, when in my studies of analytical geometry I came to construct these unfamiliar curves:—the catenary, the cycloid and epicycloid, cissoid, conchoid, etc.—I could never trust imagination in the least to construct the curve as a whole. This had always to be done on paper: the imagination was reduced to the humble *rôle* of interpreting various simple cases of the general equation to the curve in the terms of very familiar relations of position and quantity.

But reflection on advanced geometrical reasoning introduces us to another notion, which establishes a still more striking exception to Kant's universal statement as to the dependence of mathematics on intuition: I mean the notion of a limit, to which certain varying quantitative relations approximate, as the quantities related are conceived to become very large or very small; though the limit is never attained, so long as the quantities in question have a finite value. Well, in geometrical reasoning beyond the most elementary, this conception of a limit is continually introduced. For example, in measuring the area of a circle, we suppose a regular polygon inscribed in it and a similar polygon circumscribed: it is easy to see that the area of the inscribed polygon is smaller than the area of the circle, and the area of the circumscribed polygon larger. So far intuition carries us: and also the judgment that the larger we make the number of sides of the two polygons, the smaller becomes the difference between the two areas, and therefore the difference between either and the area of the circle, is also intuitive up to a certain point : but in the final conclusion that by increasing sufficiently the number of sides of the two polygons, the difference between their two areas, and between either area and that of the circle may be made less than any assignable quantity, so that the area of the circle may be measured to any degree of exactness—this final step in the reasoning cannot be realised intuitively or imaginatively, any more than it can be drawn on paper: the notion of a difference less than any assignable quantity is one in which geometrical reason goes clearly beyond geometrical intuition. And this case is all the more important, because of the resemblance between this mathematical reasoning—as uncontested in validity as any other—and the philosophical reasoning in the department of Rational Cosmology which Kant criticises in the third part of his transcendental philosophy.[1]

So far I have been considering the case of geometry, and I have tried to show that the 'pure intuition' which Kant considers as indispensable to geometrical reasoning is not really to be found at any point of the development of the reasoning in question. For (1) in the more elementary stages, while we certainly rely on the aid of individual concrete specimens—or rather approximate though imperfect copies—of the ideal objects of thought whose relations we are examining, yet the imagination

---

[1] Further, mobility is commonly assumed in geometrical demonstrations, though 'motion' is not a 'pure' conception according to Kant.

or perception that aids the reasoning seems to be as empirical in the case of geometrical as it is in the closely analogous case of physical reasoning. While (2) in the more advanced stages of geometry our reason emancipates itself from this dependence on intuition, to an important extent; ascertains (*e.g.*) the properties of curves by purely algebraic and symbolical methods; and in dealing with limitary notions, presses forward to conclusions as to the limitary relations of varying quantities, in which it leaves intuition and imagination behind.

But it will be observed that I have been speaking only of Geometry, and Kant's distinction is drawn not between geometrical reasoning only and philosophical, but between Pure Mathematics and Philosophy. And here his case appears to me to lose the *prima facie* plausibility which it has in the case of elementary geometry. As I have indeed already assumed, algebraic reasoning—so long as it is pure and not applied—appears to be conducted without any semblance of reference to individual concrete objects of intuition. And this seems to me commonly the case even with Arithmetic, when we get beyond small numbers; though no doubt we learn Arithmetic with the aid of concrete examples. In Algebra, at any rate, and in all arithmetical reasoning except the most elementary, we reason about numbers and their relations, without any specimen of numbered objects to aid our general reasoning—as the particular figure aids it in the case of Geometry. How then can Kant say of Pure Mathematics generally that it cannot take a single step without exhibiting or constructing its concepts *in concreto*? The answer Kant gives to this question is rather surprising. He admits that in the case of Algebra "we abstract completely from the properties" of numerable objects. But he says that here "we adopt a certain notation for all constructions of quantities (numbers) in general—such as addition, subtraction, extraction of roots, etc., and . . . thus represent in intuition every operation by which quantity is produced and modified according to certain general rules. Thus when one quantity is to be divided by another we place the signs of both together according to the form denoting division, etc.: and thus Algebra arrives by means of a symbolical construction, no less than Geometry by means of an ostensive or geometrical construction, at results which discursive knowledge aided by mere conceptions could never have attained."[1]

But by this extension of the meaning of 'construction' to include the 'symbolic construction' that consists in the use of algebraic signs $+ - \times$ etc., the originally affirmed connexion between Mathematics and the pure forms of sensibility is entirely given up. The 'construction of a concept' was originally defined as the representation *a priori* of a single concrete object corresponding to the concept—as in Geometry the particular drawn square corresponds to the general notion of a square. But in the symbol construction of Algebra the objects of thought—$a, b, x, y,$

---

[1] [*Kritik der reinen Vernunft*, Hartenstein, p. 480, M. Müller's trans, p. 614.]

etc., representing numbers generally—are all general, highly general, in their character, and the operations of adding, subtracting, etc., must be as general as the numbers. In short, there is no single concrete object before the mind except the symbols written down on paper, and these are neither more nor less individual and concrete than the words used in philosophic reasoning. It seems to me evident that the universals of Algebra are as much contemplated *in abstracto* as the universals of Philosophy; the superiority of Algebra lying in the greater definiteness and clearness of the concepts, not in any intuitive presentation of single objects of intuition. And, finally, it is evident that the general concepts of quantity (or number) used in Algebra, including the concepts of the algebraic operations, have no more relation to the intuitions of Space and Time than the concepts of mass, force, motion, velocity which the student of mechanics employs: or rather the relation of the algebraic concepts to Space and Time is decidedly more remote.

So far, however, I have not considered the special relation between number and *Time* which Kant in some passages seeks to establish. I regard this attempt as a complete failure: 'counting' no doubt occupies time, but it certainly is not Time that we count except when we are thinking about dates. From the fact that it takes time to count six it cannot surely be inferred that the numerical notion six has any special reference to Time. For similarly any process of geometrical reasoning takes time: but we do not therefore argue that Time as well as Space is the subject of Geometry. A complete consideration, however, of this part of Kant's view requires us to have before us the scheme of the second part of the Transcendental Philosophy —the Transcendental Analytic, which deals with the fundamental concepts and principles of ordinary empirical, physical reasoning: and endeavours to exhibit the *a priori* element in such experience supplied by the understanding, as the Transcendental Æsthetic exhibits the elements supplied by the pure forms of Sensibility.

To this we shall pass next, bringing with us, I hope, at any rate a neutral mind as to the Transcendental Ideality of Space and Time.[1]

[1] Something might be said of the continually progressive characters of Mathematics, compared with Kant's assumption (*Prolegomena*, p. 177) that Metaphysics can be brought to completeness and fixity.

LECTURE IV

THE TRANSCENDENTAL ANALYTIC

THE aim of the second part of Kant's Transcendental Philosophy I shall take as defined in the heading of this part of the *Prolegomena* (§ 14). It is to answer the question, "How is the Pure Science of Nature possible?"

But there is a prior question on which we must spend a few minutes: viz. Is there a Pure Science of Nature? Let me first make clear the meaning of this prior question. 'Nature,' as Kant explains, is a term used in two significations, which he distinguishes—according to his favourite antithesis—as 'formal' and 'material' respectively. "Nature considered materially is the complex of all objects of experience."[1] And this, no doubt, expresses the common conception of the subject-matter of physical science. Possible experience is included as well as actual,—possible being taken in a wide sense, to cover objects whose existence cannot with our present faculties be perceived directly, but only conceived as analogous to that of objects of actual

[1] *Prolegomena*, § 16, p. 65.

experience, and is assumed in order to explain these—atoms and molecules, *e.g.*, are such objects of possible experience. But this does not, in Kant's view, exhaust the common meaning of the term. It is implied, he thinks, in the conception of Nature—it is certainly implied in the conception of a Science of Nature—that this complex of objects and changes, in spite of the manifold diversity it exhibits, is subject to general laws : and the aim of Science—as distinguished from mere natural history—is to ascertain these laws. Hence Kant regards this (uncontested) subjection to law of all objects of experience as the *formal* aspect or meaning of the term Nature : and includes it in his original definition of 'Nature'[1] as "the existence of things so far as it is determined according to universal laws"—'things' being afterwards limited to 'objects of experience.' A science of Nature, then, is understood to mean systematic knowledge of the laws by which the complex of empirical things and events is governed.

We know from our previous discussion that 'the *pure* Science of Nature' denotes the non-empirical element of this knowledge, the universal laws that may be known independently of particular experiences.

But are there such laws ? We cannot find them —at any rate without further analysis—even in such principles of wide application as the laws of motion. For the concept of 'motion' is not a pure concept ; it could not be formed apart from experience. Also,

[1] *Prolegomena*, § 14, p. 63.

Kant holds that strictly *a priori* and universal laws of nature must relate to all objects of experience, 'inner' no less than 'outer.' Still there are principles that have the required universality; *e.g.* the principle that "substance is permanent" and the principle that "everything that happens is predetermined by causes according to fixed laws."[1]

Observe that Kant thus gives the proposition that "substance is permanent" a wider scope than current science commonly assigns to it. We now regard it as a proposition belonging to physics as distinct from psychology. Thus the 'conservation of mass' in all transformations of *matter* is empirically proved or confirmed by weighing the products of any such transformation, and comparing them with the weights of the matter previous to transformation. But for us the proposition has no direct application to psychical experience. The wider scope that Kant gives it he found in the system of Wolff: in this system not only was everything in the material world conceived to consist ultimately of simple indestructible substances (atoms), but human souls were also such simple substances naturally indestructible and therefore immortal. This conception, with the momentous inference from simplicity to immortality, Kant afterwards assails with great force: he holds that mind, as an object of experience, cannot be speculatively known as having a permanent substance distinct from the substance that has to be conceived as

---

[1] *Prolegomena*, § 15, p. 65. Compare "Analogies of Experience," Watson's *Selections*, pp. 106, 110.

underlying all transformations of matter.[1] He thus reduces the proposition "substance is permanent" to its present purely physical scope: while still maintaining it as a universal law of Nature in general, *i.e.* of the whole complex of objects of experience.

The main problem, then, of the second part of Transcendental Philosophy is to show how this *a priori* element in our scientific knowledge of Nature is possible: which, in Kant's view, is equivalent to showing how it follows necessarily from the constitution of the mind—the laws of thought acting on the data of sensibility. But as this *a priori* element is not, in the pursuit of physical science, clearly distinguished from the empirical element, it is also a part of the task of Transcendental Philosophy to give it in the requisite systematic form.

But another problem, which may be partly distinguished from this—though the answer to the one, as we shall see, involves the answer to the other—is presented for Kant's solution, when he approaches this second part of his philosophy from the Transcendental Æsthetic, which formed the first, the problem, namely, How there comes to be a world of objects of experience for human minds at all? The Common Sense answer to this question is that this physical world has gradually come to be known through an innumerable mass of particular cognitions of material things, cognised as they exist apart from human minds;—such cognitions being remembered, recorded,

---

[1] The immortality of the soul he maintained only as a postulate of the Practical Reason.

communicated, combined, and finally rectified and generalised by Science. But from any such answer Kant is altogether precluded by the conclusions of the first part of his Transcendental Philosophy. For this world of empirical objects is certainly ordinarily conceived to exist in Space and Time: all our definite knowledge of it involves and is inseparable from spatial and temporal determinations. But Kant has already arrived at the conclusion that Space and Time do not belong to the world of reality, as it exists apart from human cognition, to 'transcendental reality' as we may call it. All that we know of this transcendental reality rests on impressions produced by it in human minds: and these, so far as yet analysed, consist of a manifold of sensations received in the two fundamental forms of human sensibility, Space and Time. But this result is obviously very unlike our common world of material things in complex motion. How then did we ever get from the one to the other? What is the transition from a mass of formed sensations to a world of matter in motion? This is a question which Kant must answer—and indeed every one must answer.who rejects the Common Sense assumption that we can know things as they exist apart from our cognition.

As I have said, Kant's answer to the two questions that I have just distinguished is the same: and indeed, it is in this identity that its interest and persuasiveness lies. It is, according to Kant, the synthetic or unifying action of the Understanding that converts the data of sense-perception into objects of experience: and it is because this is so, that we are able to lay down *a priori* certain fundamental laws to which experience and all objects of experience must conform. When I say that 'the synthetic action of the Understanding' converts our sensations or sense-perceptions into experience of objects, I ought to explain that the understanding alone—according to Kant's view of the faculties of the human mind—could not produce the result. The forms of intellectual synthesis which Kant calls categories are too heterogeneous from the data of sense-perception to be applied to them directly. "There must be some third element which is homogeneous on the one hand with the category, and on the other hand with the data of sense, so as to render possible the application of the one to the other."[1] This mediating element is furnished by Imagination, the faculty whose ordinary empirical use is to reproduce the data of sense. But Imagination is also capable of a pure or non-empirical exercise, in which its only matter is drawn from the pure form of all sensation and of all the empirical facts of consciousness—viz. Time. It is Pure Imagination influenced by Understanding which supplies what Kant calls the transcendental 'schemata.' These are the time-determinations which fit the categories of the Understanding to be applied in connecting the data of sense, and so enable the Mind to lay down principles to which all objects of sensible experience must conform.

[1] [Cf. Watson's *Selections*, "The Schematism of the Categories," p. 85.]

This complicated operation of faculties—though I have not as yet given its full complexity—is somewhat difficult to grasp in this general presentation of it. I will therefore illustrate by applying it to the two categories used in the *a priori* principles that I before quoted: the principles that 'Substance' in Nature is permanent and that every event is determined by antecedent 'Causes' of which it is the necessary consequent. Here the notions of Substance and Cause correspond respectively to the forms of the understanding which logicians distinguish as the Relations exhibited in the Categorical and Hypothetical judgment respectively. The relation in the categorical judgment is that of subject to predicate: this, applied to connect the data of sense into objects, becomes the relation of substance and attribute. 'Substance' so conceived as a pure category of thought, and applied to sensible data, is that in the object of experience which can only be thought as 'subject' and not as 'predicate'—the data connected with it would all be possible predicates. But there is nothing in the data of sense, so long as we consider them apart from the pure form of time, to which this conception of 'necessary subject' could be applied. Every empirical datum of sense that forms an element of the notion of a material thing can be and commonly is regarded as an attribute of the thing: and yet if our understanding is to *think* the thing at all, we must apply the notion of substance somehow, otherwise the requisite connexion or combination of data will not be effected. Here, then, the pure imagination comes in, and gives the rule for the application of this connecting form of subject and predicate, by the time-determination of 'permanence' or 'duration.' Substance is now recognised as that in objects of experience which remains permanent while their sensible qualities change: and this, and this alone, being the significance of 'substance' as applied to data of sense—so far as it is more than logical 'subject'—we can, Kant holds, lay down *a priori* that the substance in Nature is permanent amid all changes of phenomena, and that its *quantum* neither increases nor decreases.

Let us turn now to the notion of Cause. This has a special historical interest, because it was Hume's criticism of the supposed necessary connexion of causes and effects—as a truth evident to reason—that woke up Kant from his 'dogmatic slumber.' Here again we have the pure category distinct in the logical form of the Hypothetical judgment "If A is, B is," which expresses a rational dependence of B on A: but in this form, it is a purely rational dependence with no reference to time. And here again Imagination and the pure form of time render this form of thought-synthesis applicable to the data of sense, by the time-determinations of antecedence and consequence; and so enable us to define Cause as that in the phenomena of sensible experience which must come *before* the effect, and after which the effect must ensue.[1]

[1] I have had two reasons for the selection of these illustrations of the

We have traced the functions of Understanding and Imagination in supplying connexion to the data of sense : but we must now go deeper, and penetrate to the root of this complex operation. Synthesis or combination, as we have seen, is the essential function of the understanding : it is a function which reflective analysis of any ordinary conception shows us to have been exercised in the framing of such conception. It is not only that every general notion combines the similar elements of an indefinite number of particulars. Take the notion of any individual material thing, obtained through sense-perception : we find in it elements derived from different senses which must have been somehow put together. But that is not all : take the sensible quality belonging to one sense, *e.g.* vision, it is commonly a manifold : different parts of a coloured surface may be differently coloured, in conceiving it as 'a surface' we have unified the manifold. Even if it be perfectly uniform in colour, still as an extended surface it is analysable into parts which must—Kant says—have been put together. Nor is this true only of empirical notions.

syntheses of Understanding and Imagination, operating on the pure form of Time, thereby generating the fundamental connective elements in our common thought of objects of experience, and furnishing the *a priori* constituents, the necessary universal truths, that are the basis of our scientific knowledge of the empirical world. First, in these notions of Substance and Cause— especially the latter—and in the principles in which they are employed (Substance necessarily unchangeable and Causation necessarily universal) we have the historical starting-point of the Transcendental Philosophy ; as is shown by what Kant tells us of his relation to Hume. Again, this always seems to me the most impressive and plausible part of Kant's elaborated system—'forms of pure thought' applied through 'time-determinations' to sensory data, whereby an empirical world, a nature of things, is built up, the fundamental laws of which we may lay down *a priori.*

Take the simplest conception used in a geometrical proposition, take a straight line: in 'drawing' it, even in imagination, we put together its parts into a whole. And observe, the unity that results from this synthesis is not the category of unity as opposed to plurality (with which I shall deal later on); for it is found just as clearly in the notion of a 'number of things' as in the notion of 'one thing'—though in the case of 'a number' the synthesis is of a kind that keeps the parts put together distinctly before the mind.

Now this combination, which we find everywhere, which all our analysis presupposes, cannot be referred to mere sensibility. So far as the mind is merely passive, merely recipient, the context of perception is mere diversity. Sensation gives us a manifold of qualities: we have no sensation of oneness. The combination and the resulting unity must be referred to the mind *qua* active: it is not something that comes from without and is merely passively apprehended. Yet again this connexion that we find everywhere is not arbitrarily introduced by thought: it cannot but find it everywhere. We cannot conceive a datum of sense, a feeling of any quality, absolutely isolated, unconnected, unrelated: while at the same time we cannot, Kant holds, conceive this relation and connexion as merely given, merely passively apprehended.

How are we to explain this universality of connectedness in the data of sense, which yet mere sense cannot give? Kant finds the explanation in what he calls 'the original synthetic unity or the transcendental unity of self-consciousness or apperception'—the necessary reference of all the data of experience to one identical experiencing subject. He calls it 'transcendental' because it is not merely an empirical fact that I do refer all my sensations to one identical self, but I know that they *must* be so referred in order to be elements of experience at all. In fact, I am not always actually conscious of self-identity, at least not clearly conscious in every moment of sensible experience: still every datum of sense that can form an element of an object of experience for me, must be capable of being thought of as mine, must belong to one identical percipient self, though I may not actually be conscious of this reference in having the perception. This fundamental unity of self-consciousness, 'transcendental' because knowable *a priori* as necessary, is the root or basis of all the complex synthesis of Understanding and Imagination combined, of which the Transcendental Analytic gives the detail. It is because this self is an intelligent, not merely a percipient self, because the activity exercised in its synthesis of the data of sense is the activity of Thought or Understanding, that we find necessary thought-elements, forms of thought applied *a priori* through time-determinations, in our notions of empirical objects, and are able to lay down *a priori* laws to which such objects and their relations and changes must conform.

The detail of the system I shall examine in the

next lecture: but before we enter upon it, it seems necessary to understand more clearly and exactly Kant's use of the terms 'Object,' 'objective.' What precisely does Kant mean by the 'object' or complex of objects, of which he proposes to determine the necessary conditions? In the first place, as we know, he does not mean things in themselves: he sometimes speaks of these as 'objects *per se*' and even as 'objects of the understanding (*Noumena*)'; but in calling them by either name he is usually careful to explain that we can know nothing at all determinate about them. 'Object' in the sense in which it is used in the Analytic—especially if used in connexion with 'objective'—is always 'object of possible experience.' The objects of which Nature is the complex are solely such empirical objects. But what are objects of experience? In the first place, Kant does not include under this term all that in a wider sense we are accustomed to call objects of thought or knowledge.[1] I hardly think that Kant bears this limitation always in mind, when he expressly restricts the application of his categories to objects of experience: but his language leaves no doubt about it, and it seems to me very important to make it clear. There are two kinds of objects of Knowledge expressly excluded: (1) Forms of thought, considered as not applied to things; (2) Elements of sensation, considered otherwise than as elements of material things. As regards the first,

---

[1] Kant uses 'knowledge' (*Erkenntniss*) in a narrower sense. Cf. *Critique*, 2nd edn.; *Analytic*, § 24, end.

Kant's language is quite decisive. "General Logic," which deals with the forms of thought and reasoning *in abstracto*, "abstracts from all distinction of objects" and "from all relation of knowledge to its objects."[1] The forms of thought, therefore, with which Logic deals are not to be considered objects for the purposes of the present discussion: though they must be not only objects of thought, but— as Logic is a *Wissenschaft*—objects of scientific knowledge. And in fact the forms of judgment and reasoning of which logicians treat obviously admit of being compared and classified, made the subjects of judgments universal and particular, affirmative and negative. Indeed, if we are to think about thinking, as the logician does, we must apply the forms of thought, the fundamental categories of thought, to the forms of thought themselves: and Kant himself does this here very definitely when he presents us with a table of *twelve* categories divided into two groups, each group subdivided into two classes, and explains that the third category in each class arises from a union of the second category with the first.[2] All this, as I shall hereafter point out, seems to me difficult to reconcile with Kant's view of Number as a Time-determination. However, the forms of thought are not 'objects' in the sense in which Kant's Transcendental Analysis employs the term. The object in this signification must have elements supplied by Sense.

But again, we cannot say that any feeling, or

[1] Watson's *Selections*, pp. 41 f.   [2] Watson's *Selections*, pp. 51-53.

kind of feeling, or even any combination of feelings thought under one notion, can be an 'object' in this narrower Kantian meaning. It is true that in one place he defines 'Object' as "that in the conception of which the manifold of a given intuition is united."[1] But he explains in more than one passage that such judgments as "the room is warm, sugar sweet, and wormwood bitter"[2] are merely subjectively valid: adding in a note that "because they refer merely to feeling which can never be attributed to the object," such "judgments can never become objective, even though a concept of the understanding were superadded." So again he speaks of the "fine flavour of the wine as not belonging to the objective characteristics of the wine, even considered as a phenomenal object."[3] But obviously sweetness, bitterness, and flavours generally—like the forms of thought—may become objects of thought, be compared and classified, and otherwise subjected to the application of the categories and forms of judgment. Thus I may judge that some or all flavours of wine are agreeable, that the flavour of whisky is pronounced but not delicate, that if the flavour of port is combined with that of olives the pleasure is heightened, that the flavour of champagne is either sweet or dry, etc.:—and thus apply in turn all the logical functions of judgment and the pure concepts of the understanding in Kant's table. Still, as I take it, the judgment would not be objective

---

[1] *Prolegomena*, § 19, pp. 70, 71. [2] Watson's *Selections*, p. 58.
[3] *Kritik der reinen Vernunft*, Hartenstein, p. 63, M. Müller, p. 25 [a passage omitted in the 2nd edition].

or relate to objects in the signification Kant here uses. And in Kant's view this would be true also of combinations of sounds and colours.[1]

How then are we to distinguish the kind of sensible manifold of which the combination constitutes an object for Kant? So far as I can see, we might sufficiently distinguish it by the characteristic that in ordinary thought, or ordinary thought rectified by physical science, it is conceived to exist as we perceive it independently of our perceptions. This is what we commonly mean by a 'thing' or 'reality' when we use the word carefully: and it is such a 'thing' that Kant means by his 'object' here.[2] But this characteristic, as we know, Kant declares to be illusory: what I call objects are nothing but modificatious of my—or some other man's—sensibility, they are merely 'in us': and yet in thinking of them, we inevitably think of them as independent of the sensibility of which they are modifications.

I do not think that Kant is definitely aware that his 'implicit' definition of objects attributes to them a characteristic which his system withdraws from them, and declares to be illusory. Indeed, in important parts of his argument he appears to me to forget that it is an illusion, in spite of the explicit language in which he has elsewhere characterised it as such. For we find among the characteristics of

---

[1] Cf. Transcendental Æsthetic, *l.c.* Hart. p. 63, M. Müller, p. 25. Sensations of colours, sounds, heat do not in themselves help us to know any object.

[2] Cf. Second Analogy of Experience, Hart. pp. 175, 176, M. Müller, pp. 166 f.

empirical objects laid down as *a priori* cognisable, that they must contain a (phenomenal) substance that is thought of as remaining unchanged amid all phenomenal change : but it seems impossible to think this and at the same time to think of all phenomena as merely modifications of my sensibility. Yet Kant nowhere seems conscious of this *prima facie* contradiction, or makes any effort to explain it. It seems to him absurd that "the thing-in-itself" should "wander into my consciousness"; yet, so far as I can see, neither he nor his English expositors find any difficulty in conceiving the phenomenal thing to wander out of it. Both he and they seem to hold that I can know objects to be merely modifications of my sensibility, combined in certain ways by my understanding; while at the same time I also conceive them as different from the modifications of my sensibility and as perduring when the latter cease. Indeed, this unconscious contradiction seems to run through Kant's use of his cardinal term 'presentation' (*Vorstellung*): the '*Vorstellung*' is now identified with its object, and now again contrasted with it, without any attempt at reconciling the two incompatible views. At one time we are told that "outward things are nothing but mere *Vorstellungen*,"[1] while again it is declared that "the determination of my existence in time is only possible through the existence of real things which I perceive outside me, and not through the mere *Vorstellung* of a thing outside me."[2] Will it be said that these really

[1] "Æsthetic," § 3, p. 64. [2] In the "Refutation of Idealism," p. 198.

existent phenomenal things, though independent of *my* consciousness, are implicitly thought by me to be in relation to 'consciousness in general,' and that it is this relation which gives them their permanence, when they cease to be modifications of my sensibility? This—which resembles the Berkeleyan mode of reconciling Idealism and Common Sense—is an explanation certainly suggested by some passages in our recent English expositors of Kant. Thus (*e.g.*) Mr. Caird says,[1] that by the recognition of the data of sense as objective "the data of sense are taken out of their mere singularity as feelings, and made elements in a universal consciousness, in 'consciousness in general'; or, to put the same thing in another way, they are related to a consciousness, which the individual has, not as a mere individual, but as a universal subject of knowledge." But whatever happens to the data of sense in Kant's psychological laboratory, it is at any rate certain that they do not cease to be modifications of sensibility. Hence in order to explain how phenomenal things can be conceived to exist independently of my —or any other man's—sensibility, we should have to suppose not merely a rational consciousness which all men share, but a universal quasi-human sensibility, modified similarly to the human; and I need hardly describe the emphasis with which any such chimera would be repudiated by Kant.

[1] *Philosophy of Kant* [1st edn.], c. viii. p. 341. [The latter part of this lecture is taken from an article "A Criticism of the Critical Philosophy" (*Mind*, 1883, O.S. viii. pp. 318 f.), written before Dr. Caird's second edition had appeared.]

LECTURE V

THE MATHEMATICAL CATEGORIES AND PRINCIPLES

AT the close of the last lecture I was discussing Kant's use of the term 'object'—in the sense in which the word is commonly used by him, when it is used without qualification—*i.e.* for the empirical or phenomenal object as distinct from the 'object *per se.*' On the one hand, it is 'altogether in me,' consists of modifications of my sensibility unified by my understanding; on the other hand, its elements have to be somehow distinguished from other data of sense—colours, flavours, sounds, heat—which, as Kant says, cannot form part of an object even though a concept of the understanding were superadded. It seems to me that the sensible elements of the object can only be distinguished by the characteristic that in ordinary thought duly instructed by science they are conceived to exist apart from my sensibility, *i.e.* by a characteristic which Kant's Philosophy regards as illusory. This is a serious objection.

We have now to observe that one result of the view Kant takes of objects is a change in the meaning of 'objective'; and herein is to be found one explanation of his unconsciousness of the peculiarity in his implied definition of 'object' which I have pointed out—namely, that an object of experience is *prima facie* distinguished from what is not an object of experience, by the characteristic of being commonly believed to have an existence independent of the mind, an existence which, however, the philosopher knows it not to have. The change is expressed in the following passage of the *Prolegomena*:—"All our judgments are at first mere perceptive judgments, they hold good merely for us (that is, for our subject), and we do not till afterwards give them a new reference (to an object), intending that they shall always hold good alike for us and for every one else; for if a judgment agrees with an object, then all judgments [our own and those of others] concerning the same object must likewise agree among themselves; and thus the objective validity of the judgment of experience signifies nothing else than its necessary universality."[1] And this, accordingly, is the meaning that in Kant's philosophy is chiefly attached to the terms 'object,' 'objective,' except when the former is qualified by *per se*. Thus, while in the more ordinary use the signification of the noun is prior and that of the adjective secondary, in this new Kantian meaning the relation is reversed and the notion of 'object' is now determined by reference to this new meaning of 'objective.' Objective, that is to say, means what is necessarily thought by all

[1] *Prolegomena*, § 18, p. 69.

minds. Object means that the existence of which is so thought, even though the elements of such object are only in us. In fact, the antithesis of subjective and objective is quite changed. Subjective as opposed to objective is now *not* used of elements of thought derived from the judging minds, for these so far as they spring from the nature of the mind have objective validity. It is now used of what belongs only to the thought or feeling of particular subjects. In consequence of this new antithesis, the same notions and judgments—for example, the notion of Space and the synthetic judgments of Geometry, are sometimes spoken of as subjective—when their *source* is the point considered; and sometimes as objective—when stress is laid on their universal validity. Still there often seems to me a hopeless confusion in what Kant says of objectivity and object, owing to the conceptions of object *per se* and empirical object falling into one in his mind.

We now pass to examine in detail the contribution of Pure Thought—that is, of Thought considered apart from the data of sense and the forms in which the human mind receives them—to our conceptions of empirical objects. In virtue of this contribution we are able to lay down *a priori*—independently of particular experiences—the fundamental laws to which the complex of empirical objects which we call Nature must conform. The ascertainment of this contribution, in an abstract form, is, in Kant's view, not difficult: for the work, in the main, is found already performed by the science which, as 'common' or 'general' or 'formal' Logic, he distinguishes from Transcendental Logic, as the science that deals with the manner in which these forms determine our conceptions of empirical objects and their connexion. The general function of the Understanding, as we have seen, is Synthesis or Combination. In our conceptions of empirical objects and their connexion in experience, the results of this Synthesis are implicit or latent, and only discoverable by analysis. But the forms implicit in our conceptions of objects become explicit and manifest in our judgments about them. Accordingly Common or Formal Logic, concentrating attention on the formal rules of judgment and reasoning, and abstracting altogether from the content of knowledge (the objects about which we judge and reason), has already classified and systematised the universal forms of thought made explicit in judgments.

The acceptance by Kant of the results of Formal Logic is—with one or two qualifications to be presently noticed—complete and noteworthy. He considers that Logic—so far at least as the forms of judgment are concerned—was created in substantial completeness by Aristotle,[1] and that from his time it has not had to retrace a single step, of material importance, nor has it from his day been

---

[1] Aristotle did not, he thinks, find the right principle for making a system of fundamental categories, and consequently mixed in spatial, temporal, and empirical notions.

able to make one step forward. Indeed it is, I think, the example of this completeness attained at one stroke by Formal Logic which encourages Kant to hope that the work of Transcendental Analysis, and the true metaphysic in which it is ultimately to result—the systematic exposition of the *a priori* elements in our thought about the world—may attain completeness and fixity with almost equal rapidity.[1] Now, as I have before said, Kant's historical knowledge is seldom distinguished by thoroughness and accuracy: but in the present case his misconception of historical facts is very remarkable. If we look at his Table of Judgments, classified according to logical form and the strictly corresponding Table of pure concepts or categories,[2] we see that there are twelve forms classified under the four heads of Quantity, Quality, Relation, Modality. Under the head of Relation we find the concepts of Substance and Cause: we have already seen that the principles based on these are selected by Kant himself as examples of strictly *a priori* principles in the science of Nature. I think his exposition of these is the most interesting and important part of his account of these *a priori* principles; for, as we saw,[3] it was the new view of Causality, attained by meditation on Hume's penetrating criticism of the older view, which was the historical starting-point of Transcendental Philosophy. We may say, then, that the categories of Relation have a special importance

[1] Cf. *Prolegomena*, p. 177.
[2] Watson's *Selections*, pp. 48, 51; *Prolegomena*, § 21, pp. 76 f.
[3] Cf. above, p. 65 n.

in the Transcendental system: and, as we see, the three categories under this head, Substance, Cause, Community (or Reciprocal Action), are derived from the logical classification of Judgments as Categorical, Hypothetical, and Disjunctive. It is, therefore, really remarkable that this triple classification is not Aristotelian: Aristotle does not analyse the hypothetical form of judgments nor *expressly* the disjunctive, though he lays down the general formula for strict disjunctions in the principle of the excluded middle, but he only worked out a scheme of categorical syllogisms.

Here, then, Formal Logic, as conceived by Kant, has taken a step forward since Aristotle. But this is not all: in respect of the fourth class—judgments and categories of modality—Logic *has* had, in Kant's phrase, to "retrace the step" taken by the founder. I do not mean that modern logicians are agreed to exclude the topic of modality altogether: but there is certainly no *consensus* in favour of including it, still less as to the view which Formal Logic ought to take of modal distinctions.[1]

My aim now is to show that the two last out of the four heads in Kant's tables represent one a step forward, and the other a step, if not exactly backward, at least on one side, from the Aristotelian view of the forms of judgment: and if so, Kant's confidence in the completeness and fixity of his systematic tables is certainly not justified on the historical ground on

---

[1] Cf. Keynes, *Formal Logic*, 3rd edn. pp. 76-78; taking the discussion in Sigwart's *Logic*, pt. i. ch. vi., as a basis.

which he is inclined to base it. But has he any other ground for this confidence? He seems to think that because he has shown the Understanding to be essentially a faculty of Synthesis or Combination, having its root in the transcendental unity of conscious experience as referred to a self-conscious subject, therefore its fundamental forms have been obtained from a common principle, and therefore systematically, and therefore completely. But I cannot see that he has established any rational relation between the unity of a self-conscious intelligence and the multiplicity of the recognised logical forms of judgment: he has not shown—I do not see that he has even tried to show—that there must be just these forms and no more: the categories are no more systematised by being referred to one understanding or faculty of synthesis than beads are systematised by being strung on one string.

But having signalised this defect in Kant's demonstration, I pass on. Our general view of philosophy and its problems is very different from Kant's, recognising the slow and gradual evolution of human knowledge in the past, and not expecting any part of Thought to be free from it. Logic did not spring from Aristotle's brain, like Pallas from the brain of Zeus, as Kant seems to have supposed: but we will assume that the labours of formal logicians have had some result and that it is worth examining, without making any assumption as to its completeness and finality.

And in this examination, in the present lecture,

I shall confine myself to the first two heads of the table, Quantity and Quality : as the distinctions here taken are certainly Aristotelian, and have been accepted substantially unchanged by succeeding generations of scholastic and formal logicians. We still distinguish judgments as Universal, Particular, Singular, Affirmative, Negative; and the third distinction under the head of Quality for which Kant uses the not very happy term 'Infinite,' the distinction between negative propositions and affirmative propositions with negative predicates, is also of course recognised, and the species of immediate inference called obversion is based upon it. Well, then, there are two questions: (1) Are these characteristics and conceptions *a priori* forms of the thinking mind, not derived from experience? (2) What can be done with them in explaining the fundamental constitution of empirical objects and laying down *a priori* universal laws to which such objects are to conform?

Now, as I have said, I hold that the first question is not answerable in the sense in which Kant asks it. The human mind and its knowledge have been gradually developed through long ages in which minds have known, or seemed to know, things; and the old conception of the mind as created with a certain constitution independent of the empirical world that admittedly supplies the matter of its knowledge, seems to me arbitrary and unwarranted. But we can ask whether these conceptions appear to us, reflecting on them here and now, to be *necessary*, to be conceptions that the mind *must* apply in knowing or thinking about whatever it knows or thinks about. Now, as regards the conceptions 'universal' or 'general' and 'singular' or 'individual,' and also as regards the conceptions made explicit in the affirmative and negative forms of judgment, it seems to me that there can be no doubt on this point, so far as it can be determined by reflecting on our actual thought and trying what we can conceive and cannot conceive. These notions are necessary, and necessarily applicable throughout the whole range of our knowledge of reality, or what we take for such. Suppose them absent, and knowledge would become inconceivable: the matter of knowledge would be reduced to a vaguely felt diversity, incapable of being distinctly thought. Reality, as we think it, is an aggregate or system. We begin by thinking of it as an aggregate, but the more we know of it, the more we find it a system, of individual things. And when we concentrate attention on any one of these, we find that our whole knowledge, our whole definite conception, of it consists of universal conceptions: in judgments affirming these its likenesses to other individual things is made distinct, and in judgments denying them, its unlikeness. Only through such universal notions made definite by such judgments, can we classify and grasp the endless diversity of things.

I do not say that these conceptions of universality and individuality are the only fundamental conceptions or even the most fundamental: indeed, as what I have said implies, I conceive them as necessarily involving the even more fundamental conceptions of likeness and difference. But as to their fundamental and necessary character there can be no doubt.

I have spoken of the 'universal' and 'individual' but not of the *particular* judgments, designated in ordinary logic by the use of 'some.' For, though judgments of the form 'some A is B' not only occur in ordinary thought but seem indispensable, they are only required because knowledge is progressive, and only represent a stage through which it has to pass in the making. In fact, the relative importance attached to them in current formal logic seems to me a survival from the pre-scientific era of Logic, when its aim was to reduce debate to rational rules, rather than to advance knowledge. For the purposes of science, the judgment that some members of a class have an attribute—even if we take 'some' in its most definite sense, to mean more than one but less than all (as Kant seems to do)—immediately suggests the question, By what other characteristic is this portion of the class distinguished? We then seek at once to turn the 'some' into the 'all' of a sub-class, by ascertaining their common characteristics. And pending this ascertainment, the impulse to make our cognition as definite as possible prompts us at any rate to ask, How many? and so convert the indefinite 'some' into a definite number or definite ratio of the whole. This tendency of 'particularity' to greater definiteness is partly suggested by Kant's substitution of 'plurality' for it in his Table of Categories.

Granting, then, the necessity of these fundamental notions,[1] how do they come into the special problem of Kant's Analytic—*i.e.* the construction of empirical objects out of the data of sense, and the establishment of *a priori* principles with regard to them? We remember that, according to Kant, the categories do not enter into the conception of empirical objects and their connexion by being directly applied to empirical data: they are applied indirectly through a determination of the pure form of time which is conceived as having affinity at once with the category and with the data of sense. In the case of the categories of Quantity—Unity, Plurality, Totality—the 'schema' or time-determination is said to be the 'series of time.' In the case of the categories of Quality[2]—which Kant gives as Reality, Negation, Limitation—the 'schema' is said to be the 'content of time.'

Now, before I examine this in detail, I may as well say frankly that the whole of this part of Kant's philosophical construction appears to me palpably unsound—a forced and violent imposition of an apparently symmetrical form on matters of thought to which such form does not properly belong. I dwell on it, partly because it seems to me to reveal with unmistakable clearness the weak side of this great thinker. Kant has a genius for system-

---

[1] [Kant's categories of Quantity and Quality.]
[2] Cf. below, pp. 93 ff.

making: and—as the business of philosophy is to systematise knowledge, to find system in the world apparently known to us through experience and in the wider world of man's reasoned thought—to say this is to say that Kant has a genius for philosophy. But a man's *forte* is often also his *foible*: and Kant's genius for finding true system, discovering true relations and connexions of fundamental thoughts, carried with it a temptation to invent false system, and impose a fictitious and misleading appearance of symmetry on thoughts the true relations of which are only obscured by it.

And this, I think, is what has happened in the case of this doctrine of 'schematism,' *i.e.* of the limitation by time-determination of forms of thought which the forms of judgment exhibit as independent of time. As I have said, this part of Kant's philosophical construction started with the categories placed under the third head—the categories of 'Substance' and 'Cause'—first 'Cause' then 'Substance': and here the notion of schematism shows a philosophical insight which appears the more brilliant and penetrating, the more we study the efforts of previous thinkers to grasp the true significance of these fundamental notions. The relation of the notion of Subject in a categorical judgment to the predicate affirmed of it is clearly the relation of the substance of material things, that we conceive to remain unchanged amid the changes of their phenomenal attributes, to those changing attributes: only that in the thought of Substance we have added to, blended with, the logical notion of subject the time-determination of 'permanence.' So again the relation of dependence between two judgments expressed in the mere form of the hypothetical judgment "If A is, B is," is quite apart from any reference to time: when we judge "If virtue is involuntary so is vice," reference to Time does not come in at all: while, again, in scientifically judging physical phenomena to be connected as cause and effect, we have this same relation of thought applied to, blended with, limited by, a time-determination: the cause on which the effect depends must come before it in time: it is that phenomenon or complex of phenomena *after* which, as we conceive, the effect must come. In both these cases, the blending of time-determinations with thought-relations that have a wider scope is clear and unmistakable, however we may ultimately interpret it.

Well, then, Kant, having, as I said, by a brilliant and original stroke of philosophic insight, found this connexion between logical forms of judgment and time-determinations in the case of these fundamental notions of substance and cause, is irresistibly tempted to system-making on the strength of this discovery. He thinks that he has here the key to the whole matter, the explanation of our whole conception of empirical objects and their connexion, and of the principles that can be laid down *a priori* with regard to them: and therefore he determines to find a similar 'schematism' everywhere, to drive it through the whole table of logical forms and categories. Let us now examine the fallacious results of this mistaken system-making: and in so doing, re-establish the true relations and distinctions of thought which Kant is forced to pervert or ignore, in order to obtain his false appearance of symmetry.

I begin with Quantity. The 'schema' of Quantity —the time-determination by which the application of the logical category of Quantity to empirical phenomena is supposed to be regulated—Kant declares to be Number, which is said to be the "generation (synthesis) of Time itself in the successive apprehension of an object."[1] And on this application of the logical category to Time is said to depend the *a priori* principle that "all perceptions (objects of perceptions *qua* perceived) are extensive magnitudes."[2] Now there is, no doubt, an important difference between logical quantity and number: in passing from the former to the latter we pass from the merely indefinite plurality, involved in the relation between a class-notion and the individuals included in the class, to a perfectly definite plurality. But I cannot see that the transition introduces a time-determination. A number, as I conceive it, is the conception of a whole of like parts, considered simply as at once like and distinguishable. It does not matter in what their likeness consists; and, as we can apply the category of unity to any fact or aspect of fact which we make an object of thought, we can similarly apply number everywhere—counting

---

[1] [Watson's *Selections*, p. 90; *Critique*, M. Müller, p. 128.]
[2] [Watson, p. 92; M. Müller, p. 143.]

v MATHEMATICAL CATEGORIES & PRINCIPLES 89

together objects of thought that are only alike in being objects of thought—though we apply it most naturally and easily to things markedly alike and so naturally classified together. But it seems to me quite arbitrary, to limit the primary application of Number to successive phenomena, regarded as successive, and to regard Number accordingly as a Temporal notion. Kant's only argument for this seems to be that it takes time to count. I do not think this true of very small numbers where the things numbered are markedly alike: looking at my bookshelves, I perceive the volumes of different works to be two, three, or four respectively, by apparently single acts of attentive perception. But granting that it always takes time to count—as it certainly does in forming or applying the notions of larger numbers—it also takes time to draw a logical conclusion from premises: but it would be obviously absurd to say that therefore the thought of the conclusion involves a time-determination.

Indeed, I cannot see how this view of Number can be made consistent with Kant's fundamental distinction between forms of pure thought and the data and forms of sense. He tells us that the categories, the pure conceptions of the understanding have their origin in the understanding alone, independent of all sensibility: and he expressly says that these pure conceptions are, considered in themselves, free from all limitation by human conditions of sensibility:[1] and potentially applicable to perception

---

[1] Cf. "Transcendental Analytic," § 22, Watson's *Selections*, p. 75.

of any kind, whether like or unlike ours, if only it is sensuous: only that such an application must be *for us* empty and fruitless. But if this be so, the system or table of categories must surely be conceivable apart from any reference to Time; and if conceivable at all, it must surely be conceivable as a table of *twelve* categories: the characteristic of being *twelve* must therefore be as independent of time as any other characteristics of the categories. In short, the parts of any whole, whether logical or physical, to which we apply the idea of number, are commonly conceived so far as numbered, without any reference to time: and though the parts of a physical thing must be conceived as coexisting in time, this is not the case, according to Kant's express and repeated statement, with the parts of a logical whole or system.

And this leads me to another point, which Kant overlooks and which is inconsistent with his view of number: viz. that the notion of number does not necessarily involve any notion of extensive magnitude; the scientifically fruitful and important application of number is, of course, to such magnitudes: but it is not necessarily involved in the very idea of number. If I judge that there are four cardinal virtues and seven deadly sins, I do not in so judging even suggest to myself that there is more deadly sin than virtue in the world—though this may be an unhappy fact.

This brings us to the *a priori* principle or law of the empirical object, which Kant connects with the 'schema' of quantity, namely, that "all intuitions, or all phenomena as far as perceived, are extensive magnitudes."[1] Now, firstly, we observe that this principle, so far at least as its more obvious application to spatial magnitude is concerned, follows at once as an immediate inference from the propositions maintained in the Æsthetic. It was there maintained expressly (1) that Space is the form of all the phenomena of the outer sense, *i.e.* of all objects externally perceived; and (2) that Space is an unlimited given magnitude: all phenomena or objects perceived in Space must thus have the characteristic of being spatial magnitudes. The introduction of the notion of number is, then, not required for this conclusion. On the other hand, its introduction leads Kant into serious errors. It leads him to ignore the important distinction between the discreteness of the parts of number and the continuity of spatial magnitude. Number, in fact, is not applicable to spatial magnitude simply and immediately, but only through the medium of the assumption that the magnitude is divisible into equal parts: and, consequently as we know, some of the most familiar relations of spatial magnitudes — *e.g.* the relation between the magnitude of the circumference of a circle and the magnitude of its diameter — are not perfectly expressible by definite numbers.

But [secondly] Kant does worse than ignore this distinction and relation between the notions of *discrete*

---

[1] [The principle is differently stated in the two editions: the two statements are here combined.]

and of continuous quantity. He is led by ignoring it into the serious error of saying that "an extensive magnitude is one in which the idea of the parts necessarily precedes and makes possible the idea of the whole."[1] He expressly applies this to *all* the parts. "I cannot," he says, "have the idea of a line, however small it may be, without producing all its parts one after the other": and "similarly with any, even the smallest, portion of time." Now in the very same passage he lays stress on the infinite divisibility of spatial magnitudes. Surely Kant's acumen could not have failed to see—had he not been temporarily obfuscated by his unhappy schematism—that it is impossible to hold at once that a spatial magnitude is infinitely divisible, and that a distinct idea of the parts of this magnitude as parts has necessarily preceded the idea of the whole. For of however many parts we may be definitely conscious in forming the idea of a given line or a given portion of time, as all these parts are themselves extended magnitudes, they must be conceived as in their turn divisible into parts of which no definite consciousness can have preceded.

I have laid stress on this palpable inconsistency, because it affords a clear illustration of what I regard as erroneous in Kant's general assumption that the understanding "cannot separate what it has not previously bound together,"[2] especially in its application to phenomenal objects. In my view there is no foundation for this assumption: the essential function of thought, in all its departments, is not primarily

---

[1] [Watson's *Selections*, p. 92.] [2] [Cf. Watson's *Selections*, p. 64.]

or mainly the binding together into a whole of elements previously separate: but rather a process by which we pass from the consciousness of a vague manifold, of which the elements are obscurely thought, and even may have a merely potential existence, to a consciousness of the same manifold as not only more connected, but also more distinct in its parts or elements, and not only more distinct but fuller.

The schematism of the categories of Quantity, therefore, seems to me a mere illusion that leads Kant into a quagmire of fallacies. But if the schematism of the categories of Quantity breaks down, that of Quality fares no better: indeed, I think that the forced and fictitious character of the construction is even more palpable in this case. For, first, the *a priori* principle at which he arrives is more startlingly aloof from the logical forms he professes to apply. 'Quality' of a judgment or proposition in common Logic signifies the distinction between affirmative and negative judgments. Now there is nothing more evident about this logical antithesis, when abstractly contemplated, than its absoluteness, and the apparent absence of any possible mediation or transition between the two. And this is a point on which Logic had been clear and decisive from Aristotle's time to Kant's: the Law of the Excluded Middle 'that A must be either B or not B' is the one germ of the subsequently developed topic of disjunctive judgments and reasonings that we do find in Aristotle. The one fact, therefore, which is most alien to this antithesis is the continuity of transition from non-existence to

94 THE METAPHYSICS OF KANT LECT.

existence which we actually find in sensible experience. But Kant is determined to balance his *a priori* principle that all phenomena have extensive magnitude, by a corresponding principle relative to intensive magnitude or degree; and symmetry requires him to connect this with logical Quality. He has therefore to invent a 'schema' for Reality and Negation, and he accordingly invents the notion of a "continuous and uniform generation of reality from nothing to a definite degree"[1]—reality being conceived as that in phenomena which corresponds to sensation.

Now, in the first place, the notion of continuity in the gradations of intensity manifested by the sensible qualities of empirical objects is not a time-determination. No doubt, as sensations and empirical objects must exist in time, the continuity in variations of intensity which they exhibit must be manifested in time, but the notion itself has nothing to do with time. Secondly, we suddenly find here a new meaning given to reality. So far we have come across a Transcendental Reality which we cannot know, and an empirical reality which Kant repeatedly attributes to Space and Time: but now we are suddenly told that "reality is that in phenomena which corresponds to sensation . . . the transcendental matter of all objects."[2] Why should reality be thus equated to matter alone, instead of to form and matter combined? Only, I venture to think, from the unfortunate necessities of symmetrical schematism:

---

[1] Cf. Watson, *Selections*, p. 88.
[2] [Watson's *Selections*, p. 88; M. Müller, p. 126.]

for only this would have turned Quality into Intensive Quantity. But, thirdly, how are we to reconcile this correspondence of Reality to Sensation with Kant's view before quoted, that colours, sounds, etc., "being merely sensations and not intuitions, do not help us by themselves to know any object"?[1] How then can even empirical reality correspond to them? Surely Kant here gets confused between the popular and the scientific conception of an object.

But turning to the philosophical question raised, Can we lay down *a priori* that every sensible quality must have a definite degree? Observe, degree belongs also to spatial magnitudes, but not to all. There are degrees of curvedness of lines but not of straightness; of obtuseness and acuteness of angles but not of rightness; of oblongness in rectangular figures but not of squareness; of ellipticality but not of circularity. In the case of the material world, we do commonly assume that sensible qualities vary continuously upwards from the lowest perceptible degree.

Not less remarkable is the deduction which Kant makes from his principle of the 'Anticipations of Perception,' viz. that we cannot have experience of a vacuum. We are first told that reality corresponds to sensation, and negation to absence of sensation; and the possible continuous diminution of the real down to zero is inferred as corresponding to a similar diminution of sensation. But then we suddenly find that we somehow know *a priori* that

[1] Cf. above, p. 71.

"every sense *must* have a definite degree of receptivity,"[1] and accordingly that below the point at which any kind of sensation stops—below what we may call the sensible zero—the transcendental matter corresponding to such sensation must be still conceived as possibly existing, in any one of an indefinite number of continually diminishing degrees. Thus "we see that experience can never supply a proof of empty space or empty time, because the total absence of reality in a sensuous intuition can never be perceived, neither can it be deduced from any single phenomenon, and from the difference of degree in their reality; nor ought it ever to be admitted in explanation of them":[2] and thus the schematism of the category of Negation seems to end by demonstrating its strict inapplicability to phenomenal reality.

I hardly know where to begin to criticise this singular argument. (1) If the matter of all phenomenal objects consists of mere modifications of our sensibility, how can we consistently suppose a phenomenal object to exist corresponding to modifications which, by the very nature of our sensibility, cannot possibly occur? And (2), if we could suppose this, by what transcendental intuition do we know that our senses *must* be incapable of perceiving phenomenal reality below a certain degree? And (3), even granting that we must suppose as possibly existent a phenomenon that cannot possibly appear, and therefore that we can

---

[1] [Watson, p. 99; M. Müller, p. 151.]   [2] [M. Müller, p. 152.]

never have direct experience of void space and time, it still is not clear why the assumption of such a void can never be admitted as an explanation of phenomena: for, granting that an apparent void cannot be known to be real, it does not surely follow that it must be known to be merely apparent. And, finally, it seems to me that this corollary from the 'Anticipations of Perception' must land us in serious difficulties when we try to make it consistent with Kant's express interpretation of the first 'Analogy of Experience'—to the discussion of which I will now proceed.[1]

[1] [The last two paragraphs are from the article "A Criticism of the Critical Philosophy," *Mind*, O.S. 1883, vol. viii. pp. 333 f.]

LECTURE VI

SUBSTANCE

WE have now discussed the two first heads of Kant's table of forms of judgment and thought, regarded as applied in the constitution and connexion of empirical objects—the concepts and principles, that is to say, which come under the heads of Quantity and Quality. In passing from this I propose that we dismiss the forced and fallacious schematism, and merely carry with us the *a priori* principles that all objects of sense-perception must have extensive magnitude,[1] and intensive magnitude or degree. Kant calls these *mathematical* principles, " to indicate that they justify the application of Mathematics to objects of sense-perception."[2]

---

[1] This seems to me to follow from the Transcendental Æsthetic.

[2] Watson, *Selections*, p. 102. I may observe—what Kant indeed sees—that in respect of this application of Mathematics the first principle is of more fundamental importance than the second: since we can only apply Mathematics to the intensive magnitude of sense-percepts by interpreting it in terms of extensive magnitude. Thus we measure weight, which has empirically only intensive magnitude, by its tendency to produce motion, which has extensive magnitude. But I cannot see the *a priori* certainty that every quality of an empirical thing has a degree. Feeling we do assume to have a degree: also sensible qualities. But then, what of the objectivity of these according to Kant? To matter, according to the common view, degree is *not* ascribed.

These principles he also calls 'constitutive' of phenomena: through them we know *a priori* what phenomena will be like in certain important respects. The principles, on the other hand, which Kant connects with the forms of judgment and thought classified under the head of Relation,—the forms explicit in the categorical, hypothetical, and disjunctive judgment respectively,—he distinguishes as *regulative*: *i.e.* they do not tell us what phenomena must be like in any respect, but only give us rules that determine their relations of existence. Thus the *a priori* principle that every event must have a cause does not tell us in the least what the cause will be like, but only directs us to find something antecedent to the event in time, after which it must follow.

This distinction between 'constitutive' and 'regulative' *a priori* principles is, I think, quite clear in the case of the Principle of Causality. The distinction is not quite so clear in the case of the Principle of the Permanence of Substance, which I will take first. If we can say *a priori* of every empirical or phenomenal thing that there must be somewhat in it which remains permanent while other phenomenal elements of the thing change, why is not this principle 'constitutive' of the object? I confess that I am rather inclined to think Kant would so have regarded it, if the requirements of symmetry had not forced him to class it with the principle of Causality. However, passing from this for the present, let us consider how the principle is established.

First let us note that in establishing this principle Kant uses, in at least a clearer form than in the previous cases, the transcendental method of proof, of which he is the inventor. He distinguishes this method carefully and emphatically at once from the *demonstration* of mathematics and from the metaphysical method previously current, which, not adequately distinguishing synthetical from analytical universals, confusedly tried to derive from mere abstract conceptions propositions really synthetical.[1] Thus 'substance is permanent' is such a proposition, if we mean by substance that in a thing or things which cannot be thought as predicate or attribute of some other subject. And if this proposition is not to be merely explicative ('permanence' being already thought as part of the meaning of Substance) we must mean this by Substance. Now this proposition taken abstractly is not self-evident and cannot be demonstrated: we can only, Kant holds, establish its truth by showing that experience and objects of experience are only possible, if we assume this principle, and not otherwise. This is the Transcendental method. Let us examine carefully its application to the Principle of the Permanence of Substance.

Briefly, the argument is that our common conception of experience, as the apprehension of a complex of things as undergoing change or alteration in time, requires the notion of a permanent somewhat of which the phenomena—in the succession of which

[1] Cf. Watson, *Selections*, p. 105.

change as merely perceived consists—must be thought as successive attributes, or modes of its existence. Indeed Kant goes so far as to say that without this conception of a permanent somewhat the relations of change and coexistence would not be possible, that is to say, they could not be attributed to the manifold as object of *experience*; for in mere perception the manifold of phenomena is always merely successive. 'Substance,' in fact, stands in our thought for the unchangedness of Time; for Time itself does not change, but all change has to be thought in it. As Time by itself cannot be perceived, there must be in objects something to represent Time, something unchanging, and of which all change can only be thought as a determination. This is 'Substance'; and as it cannot change, its *quantum* cannot be decreased or increased.

Now, first, it does not seem to me true—I mean not truly to represent our common thought about Time as expressed in common language — to lay down in this unqualified manner that "Time does not change." For motion is a form of change; and Time is certainly thought to move: it seems to us as true to say that "Time flies" as that "Time abides." In short, as I have said, change and permanence, succession and duration, seem to be inextricably combined in our common notion of Time: which, therefore, can only be properly imaged not by a line but by a point, the Present, passing along a line.

However, I will not dwell on this, as I am quite

prepared to admit that I cannot conceive change, at least of an object or thing, without the conception of somewhat that perdures in or through Time. But I do not see that this perduring somewhat need be conceived as absolutely unchangeable. Suppose a manifold presented consisting of elements A B C D : it seems to me perfectly possible to conceive change to go on in it, in respect of one element after another, so that ultimately an entirely new manifold E F G H is found to have substituted itself for the other : and yet I can at any point of the process conceive the manifold as a changing thing, provided B C D remain unchanged while A is turning into E, etc.

It may be said that my supposition assumes a presentation of coexistent elements, whereas Kant declares that "our apprehension of the manifold of phenomena is always successive," and that "*as contained in a single moment*, each presentation cannot ever be anything but an absolute unity."[1] However, I do not know how Kant supposes himself to know this 'synthetic *a priori* judgment': so far as my experience goes, I should say that I am continually conscious of a quite simultaneous manifold of sensations and sense-perceptions. But even granting that apprehension strictly speaking is always serial, it is enough for the purposes of the above objection, if I am allowed to be somehow conscious of a simultaneous manifold, whether strictly presented or

---

[1] Cf. Watson, *Selections*, p. 57. [M. Müller, p. 88. The italics are Kant's, though omitted by Watson and M. Müller.]

partially represented, and this seems to me quite undeniable.

The notion, then, of an absolutely permanent substance does not appear to me necessary for the conception of change in empirical objects, as the transcendental argument requires: relative permanence would suffice. There are, however, other difficulties in the argument. The necessity of finding substance in objects seems to be regarded as following from the fact that "Time cannot be perceived by itself":[1] but the consequence would seem to fail unless substance *can* be 'perceived by itself': and yet the whole argument implies that this characteristic cannot be attributed to Substance—'the substratum of all the real'—any more than to time. According to the argument, what we perceive is what is attributed to the substance, not the substance itself: the changeable in things, not the unchangeable. But again: in the statement that "the quantum of substance in nature neither increases nor decreases," we seem to have a synthetic *a priori* proposition not warranted either by the logical category 'subject that is never predicate' or the time-determination of permanence. There seems to be a gulf not bridged over between the transcendental explanation and the fundamental assumption of physical science that has to be explained. Granting that we must think the known (mutable) qualities predicated of empirical things as qualities of a subject that cannot itself be thought as a predicate, and granting that this subject

---

[1] *Für sich wahrgenommen.* Cf. Watson's *Selections*, p. 107.

must be thought as permanent, why must it also be thought as having definite quantity? No doubt we do think thus of the matter which we conceive as identical throughout the processes of change occurring in inorganic things: but when we turn from these and examine our thoughts of organic things or of persons, we find no similar need of quantifying, no disposition to quantify, that which we conceive to remain identical amid change. Take the idea of an animal—a dog: we have in the notion of a dog the conception of something that remains identical from birth to death, through a varying complex of phenomenal change to which it furnishes the bond of unity: but we do not in this case *quantify* the identical somewhat: the idea of a quantum of 'caninity' that is not increased or decreased is absurd to us. Take, again, the idea of a person: contemplate a life in its psychical aspect. We have a stream of consciousness varying in volume, and in parts varying markedly in intensity: and we conceive the mind that is the subject of all this experience as having faculties and emotional susceptibilities that grow and decay: but to the person, the self-conscious self that remains identical through these varied changes, we cannot without absurdity attribute quantity. I submit therefore that this notion of an 'unchangeable quantum' must not be allowed to slip in, as involved in the notion of a permanent subject of mutable phenomenal predicates: it demands a transcendental explanation on its own account, and I cannot see that Kant tries to give this, or where his system could get it. Nay, could he conceivably show this consistently? For it was 'subject that cannot be thought as predicate' that was argued to be necessary, but by quantifying we surely give it a predicate! Other difficulties arise, when we ask which kind of quantity Kant means to attribute to his permanent substance, extensive or intensive, or both. There seems no doubt that he conceives his Substance as extended in space, for he identifies it with the Matter which physicists assume to be permanent. It remains, therefore, to ask whether the parts of this extended substance differ in their intensive quantity or not. He has already, in discussing the 'Anticipations of Perception,' rejected the assumption that "das *Reale* im Raume allerwärts einerlei sei":[1] hence we must suppose that the parts of his Substance have different intensive quantities. But thus his Substance turns out to be an aggregate of heterogeneous substances: and yet, as the ground for assuming its existence was that we might have something to represent, in Mr. Caird's words, the "unity or self-identity of time itself," this heterogeneity is surely a very singular and inappropriate characteristic.

[1] [M. Müller, pp. 152 f.: "The *real* in space must always be the same."]

LECTURE VII

CAUSALITY, COMMUNITY, MODALITY

I PASS to the Second Principle under this head, that "all changes take place in conformity with the law of connexion of cause and effect." I have already explained the 'schematism of the category' here involved, by which the abstract notion of 'dependence in thought' of 'Reason and Consequent' is at once limited and rendered applicable to phenomena by the time-determination of sequence: so that 'Cause' as applied in physical science means not only "that on which the effect depends," but "that antecedent phenomenon or complex of phenomena after which the effect must follow." It is certainly with this definite temporal meaning that modern science has investigated causes;—since final causes, in accordance with Bacon's witty suggestion, have been consecrated to heaven, as holy virgins, unfruitful through their very holiness. I took this [principle of causality] as the leading illustration of Kant's Schematism,[1] because in this case the distinction and relation of category and schema is as intelligible, natural, and

---
[1] [Cf. above, pp. 65 f.]

helpful as in some other cases it appears to me forced and misleading. In what I have now to say, therefore, I shall concentrate attention on the transcendental proof offered of the principle. This is at once simple and ingenious: and if it is—as I hold it to be —unsound, it is only on account of the fundamental error of the whole attempt to explain our apparent knowledge of Nature as a complex of changing things, while denying the Common Sense assumption that things other than the mind knowing, if rightly known, are known as they are independently of such cognition.

Kant starts with the assumption, before referred to, that the reception and apprehension of the sense-percepts, through which we know or seem to know material things, is always successive—whether the phenomenal characteristics of the object are known as coexisting with (relative) stability, or as objectively successive, following each other in the object. Thus the apprehension of the various elements of the manifold contained in the perception of a house is successive, no less than the apprehension of a ship moving down stream: although in the former case the successive perceptions correspond to objective characteristics conceived as (for the time) stably coexisting, whereas in the latter case an objective succession of phenomena corresponds to the subjective succession. This being so, a further comparison of the two cases shows that in the case of the house the succession of perceptions is arbitrary, need not conform to any fixed order: "my apprehension might begin with a perception of the roof and end with the basement, but it might just as well begin from below and end above; or again the units of my empirical observation might be apprehended from right to left or from left to right."[1] But in the case of the ship moving down stream, the order in which the perceptions follow one another in my apprehension is unalterably fixed and determined: I first perceive it higher up the stream and then lower down, and the order of these perceptions is inconvertible.

Here, then, we see the conception that we must apply—what we must think—in order clearly to conceive the difference between the merely subjective succession of perceptions, which is universal in our apprehension of any phenomenal fact, and that succession of perceptions by which we apprehend objective changes. We cannot find the difference in the phenomenality of the subjective succession, as contrasted with the reality of the objective changes —if we mean by 'reality' that the changes occur in things as they exist apart from their perception by human minds : for the notion of change cannot, any more than the notion of time which it involves, be applied to this extra-phenomenal existence. We can therefore only find it in the fixed and determinate order which, as we have seen, must characterise the succession of phenomena when thought as objective. That is, the objective sequence of the phenomena A, B, C, must be distinguished from their merely sub-

[1] Watson's *Selections*, p. 113.

jective sequence as perceptions by the characteristic that A must be thought as necessarily antecedent to B, and B to C, and B as necessarily coming after A, and C after B. But in this thought of necessary sequence, we have the thought of causality: for the idea of a phenomenal cause is the idea of a phenomenon after which another phenomenon which we call the effect must come. If therefore we are to conceive of Nature on the one hand as phenomenal—which sound philosophy requires—and on the other hand as a complex of objects undergoing objective changes —as Common Sense and Physical Science do and must conceive it—we must think all phenomena of change, all events, as subject to a fundamental law of necessary sequence: a law by which any event B is thought as necessarily coming after an antecedent event or group of events A.

If it be asked, " Will it not suffice if an objective change must be thought as occurring at a definite point of time, without connecting it with events that have previously happened?"—the answer is that in pure Time there are no points to which anything can be attached: the difference between one part of Time and another lies solely in the changes that take place in time. If therefore you are to fix the occurrence of a phenomenon to a definite point of time, you can only do this by attaching it to antecedent phenomena and thinking it as necessarily coming after them: there is no other way of fixing. In order, therefore, that the conception of objective change—experience of objective change—may be possible, a universal principle of necessary connexion of all events with events antecedent in time must be admitted. And this is the principle of Causality.

The argument that I have just given in outline is, I think, the most brilliant and persuasive example of the transcendental method that the constructive part of Kant's treatise affords. There seem to me, however, to be important reasons for not accepting this exposition of Causality, as an adequate explanation of the conception as used in modern physical science;—still less as establishing its validity if questioned by empiricists or sceptics.

Firstly, the necessity of a connexion between an event and its antecedents, which it is thus argued is implied in the conception of objective change—that, being objective, must be fixed at a definite point of time—does not carry with it any explanation of the *uniformity* which is found in our common conception of empirical causation. Yet this uniformity is indispensable if the scientific ascertainment of causes is to be practically serviceable for the relief of man's estate. To ensure any practical result, the ascertainment of causes must enable us to predict: but, as a basis for prediction, we require not merely the principle that every event must have a cause in the sense of necessary connexion with antecedent events, but also the principle that similar causes will have similar effects. It may be said that this is implied in Kant's statement of the principle—as it no doubt is in the common statement of it. In saying that every event has a cause, we commonly mean to imply that the complex of antecedent conditions with which we thus connect the event may recur, and that if it recurs the event will follow: we mean, in short, to signify a uniform connexion of similar pairs of phenomena. And it may be said that Kant no doubt means this, and has a right to assume it, so far as there are recurrent phenomena in nature: for if at any point of time, a given event is conceived to follow necessarily from a certain complex of antecedents, we cannot conceive that if the complex of antecedents recurred, its necessary consequent would not recur. The necessary connexion, it may be said, cannot be affected by a mere consideration of the point of time or space at which the events in question happen; since there can be nothing in mere time [or space] that can affect it.

But we may, I think, turn the point of this defence against itself. Position in mere time cannot affect any necessity of connexion between two kinds of phenomena that we have any ground for laying down *a priori*: but then—as we have just seen— there is no such thing conceivable as position in mere time. The connexion with antecedents that we necessarily give to any objective change by fixing it to a point of time, is a connexion with the whole aggregate of immediately antecedent changes, not with any one part of this antecedent complex of change more than any other part: and we have no ground, empirical or *a priori*, for supposing that this whole complex antecedent will ever recur. And any special connexion that we have empirical grounds for conceiving between the event in question and any particular part of its immediate antecedents can have nothing to do with the necessary fixity involved in objectivity of change. In fact, in fixing the position of any event in time we most commonly connect it with antecedents to which we do not conceive it to be causally related: *e.g.* we fix the death of a murdered man at a particular point in the series of continuous and repeated revolutions of the earth round its axis and of its continuously repeated revolutions round the sun: but we do not usually regard the antecedent part of the earth's movement as having any causal connexion with the murder.

It would seem, therefore, that these special causal connexions cannot be deduced from or subsumed under the principle of causality as stated by Kant: this may explain the general necessity of conceiving a causal connexion, but not the complex uniformities that Physical Science is believed to have ascertained. It may indeed be said that as science recognises that every portion of the physical world is connected through gravitation with every other portion, the concept of every event as necessarily connected with the whole complex of antecedent events must be admitted by science to be strictly speaking the true conception. I grant this, but my point is that the principle as so conceived, however incontrovertible, is useless for the discovery of the more special uniformities, by which alone the predictive power of Science is attained: not only cannot these subordinate laws of Nature be laid down *a priori*, but the more general fact that there are such laws cannot be thus laid down: at least Kant's transcendental proof has not shown the possibility of knowing it, apart from specific experience.

This last consideration affords a transition to the third 'Analogy of Experience,' [the 'Principle of Reciprocal Action':—] "All substances, in so far as they can be observed to coexist in Space, are in thoroughgoing reciprocity."

Now, when we consider this principle in relation to Kant's systematic explanation of the *a priori* element in our knowledge of phenomenal objects— *i.e.* as resulting from the application, through a time-determination or schema, of one of the forms of thought manifested in the logical table of judgments, to the empirical data given in sense-perception—we fall back again into the bad system-making of which the earlier mathematical principles supplied unmistakable instances. But in this case we may say that the forced schematism is harmless: that is, I cannot see that Kant even attempts to make it plausible. His ingenuity is not stimulated to invent fallacies such as that of regarding Number as a time-determination, and extracting continuous variation in intensive quantity out of the simple logical opposition between affirmation and negation. But in the category of 'Community' (interpreted as reciprocal action) there is a violent leap of thought from the form of disjunctive judgment. For the predicates of a disjunctive judgment (A is either B or C) are not mutually dependent in any positive way, they are mutually exclusive : the affirmation of either B or C involves the simple negation of the other as a possible predicate of A. The analogy between this relation, and the mutual dependence of two objects in respect of certain positive characteristics—which is involved in the idea of reciprocal action—is surely faint and far-fetched.

The transcendental proof of the principle may, however, be examined apart from this forced and invalid connexion with the form of the disjunctive judgment. The first paragraph of the proof runs thus:—"Things are coexistent which exist at one and the same time. But how do we know that they exist at one and the same time? Only if in the synthesis of apprehension the order in which the various determinations arise in consciousness is indifferent, or can go either from A through B, C, D, to E, or conversely from E to A. Were the determinations actually to follow one another in time, that is, in an order that began with A and ended with E, it would be impossible for apprehension to start with E and go backwards to A; for A would in that case belong to a time that was past, and therefore could no longer be an object of apprehension."[1]

From this it would seem that the fact that if, in any apprehension of sense-data, the order in which we pass from one to another of a group of sense-percepts A, B, C, D, E, is so far indifferent that we can either have them so or reversely E, D, C, B, A, then we can know that they coexist. But the proof seems

[1] Watson's *Selections*, p. 118.

obviously inadequate: for we can experience a series of sounds in one order, and then of similar sounds in the reverse order, without making, or having a right to make, this inference of coexistence. So of pains— *e.g.* if different parts of the body are pricked first in one order and then in the reverse order. We must take the proposition with the restriction that the percepts in question are regarded as objective; and being so regarded are assumed to have existed in the interval between the perception (*e.g.*) of A in the first series and its perception in the second. Suppose we make this assumption explicitly. Then it would seem that coexistence—and, therefore, relative permanence—*prima facie* is proved by the two series of experiences. And it does not seem that, so far as coexistence in time is concerned, there is any necessity to assume that the substance to which percept A is referred is in a relation of reciprocal action with the substance to which percept B is referred. The notion of 'action' seems only to come in when *change* is experienced: but in the case supposed we seem to assume an absence of change. And in fact it will be seen, from the statement of the principle, that Kant is obliged to introduce the condition of coexistence in *space*: and the argument to prove that coexistence involves reciprocal action requires this condition.

"Now suppose"—Kant's proof continues—"that a number of substances could be observed, each of which was so completely isolated from the rest that none acted upon any other or was itself acted upon; then I say that these objects could not possibly be observed to *coexist*, and that there is no way in which by empirical synthesis we could pass from the existence of one to the existence of another. If the objects are assumed to be separated by a space that is quite empty, no doubt the existence of each might be presented in turn in a series of observations; but this would not enable us to say whether the different phenomena themselves followed one another or existed at the same time."

But the argument does not seem to me logical. I agree that any material thing must be thought as having a definite position in space: and this means that it is spatially related to other things in space. But I do not see that any further mutual determination need be thought. I do not see why things cannot be thought to coexist which do not determine each other's existence further than by each occupying a place which the other cannot occupy at the same time. If we can—as Kant assumes—observe two things coexisting in space at all, I do not see that we require, in order to observe them, that the one must act on the other. His proof, in short, seems to break down.

[We still have to deal with the categories of Modality,] Possibility, Actual Existence, and Necessity, [and with 'the Postulates of all Empirical Thought' to which they lead].

In *ordinary* thought 'may' and 'must'—apart from the legal or quasi-legal meaning of 'permission' and 'coercion'—are used in two ways, which we may distinguish as respectively subjective and objective:

VII CAUSALITY, COMMUNITY, MODALITY

but, for a reason I will explain, I use 'factual' rather than 'objective.' The two meanings are not always easily distinguishable; but the subjective meaning is quite clear as regards 'may' in statements relating to particular *past* or *present* fact: *e.g.* if I say that Hannibal 'may' have crossed the Alps by the Mont Cenis Pass in his famous invasion of Italy, but that he 'may' have crossed by the Col d'Argentière, I do not of course mean that there are in fact two alternative possibilities, but that my belief is uncertain and suspended between the two alternatives. But I do not mean merely that my *individual* belief *is* thus uncertain, but that it is reasonably so, that there are not sufficient data for deciding. The subjectivity, therefore, of this meaning of 'may' does not exclude objectivity in the Kantian sense of universal validity. If, however, a man makes a similar statement with regard to the future—if he says of a future event that it may happen or may not—in ordinary thought I conceive that the statement commonly has a 'factual,' not merely a subjective import: it is intended to affirm that the two alternatives are in fact open. But scientific reflection — putting free-will out of account as it commonly does—leads us to regard the future as the determinate consequence of the present, and thus the *scientific* meaning of 'may' comes to be the same with regard to the future as it is regarding the past or present—when we say that a thing 'may happen' we mean that we have no reasonable grounds for affirming that it will not.

The 'possible' thus would seem to be that of

which we have no sufficient reason to deny the existence, past, present, or future. But what then, upon this line of thought, is the 'necessary,' what is the difference between asserting that a thing '*is*' and that it *must* be? This is not so easy to explain, when, applying the idea of 'must' to a particular fact, we try to get an explanation analogous to that just given of 'may.' For if I have adequate reasons for affirming categorically that A was B, what further degree of conviction can I imply by the assertion A must have been B? As Sigwart urges,[1] any categorical judgment claiming—as any such judgment ordinarily does claim—objective validity is 'necessary' in the sense that I feel compelled to make this judgment and no other if I wish to speak the truth, and also believe that any other mind, wishing to judge truly, *must* judge similarly. Indeed, when I say 'This must have happened so,' I do *not* ordinarily express a stronger conviction than when I say 'This happened,' but rather a conviction attained after questioning and trying alternative belief and failing. One may say, it is the assertoric judgment confirmed by Spencer's test, 'inconceivability of the opposite.' This view of Sigwart's seems to me true: it seems impossible to find any more definite progress in certainty of conviction between 'is' and 'must be,' so long at least as we give a merely subjective interpretation to modality or so long as we confine ourselves to assertions about particular facts as such.

We may, however, give the distinction an important

[1] [*Logic*, § 31.]

significance if we pass from the subjective to the objective view of modality, and take the distinction to relate to the difference between an empirically ascertained and a demonstrated connexion of a given predicate with a given subject. This is the interpretation that Kant gives of the distinction in one passage in his *Logic*. He tells us that "rational certainty distinguishes itself from empirical, through the consciousness of necessity bound up with it: it is therefore an *apodeictic* while the empirical is only an assertoric certainty. . . . We are rationally certain of what we should have seen to be true *a priori*, even without experience, though we may with regard to objects of experience have both rational and empirical certainty."[1] This is an intelligible view: but it obviously relates to the *content* of the judgment, though Kant does not seem clearly to see this here. For experience, as he elsewhere is never tired of telling us, cannot demonstrate a universal: whereas what we see to be true *a priori* must be a universal truth. In a particular case, indeed, the content of the two judgments may not vary in their application to *actual* experience. I may know by experience that all A are B, in which case the knowledge that A must be B can give me no further information concerning empirical objects. But this coincidence is accidental and precarious. If I discover a new A, I know nothing about it in the one case, while in the other I know as soon as it is discovered that it must be B.

[1] [*Werke*, Hartenstein's ed. viii. p. 71.]

I think, therefore, that this interpretation of the difference between 'is' and 'must be' cannot really be reconciled with Kant's statement elsewhere in the *Logic* "that the distinction between merely possible, or actual, or necessary truth relates solely to the judgment itself and not to the matter judged of,"[1] which brings us back to the subjective point of view.[2] On *this* line of thought, as I have said before, we get a definite distinction between 'may be' and 'is' and a definite progress in the value of the judgment, when we pass from the one to the other. On the other line of thought we get a progress from 'is' to 'must be' equally definite and important. But to put the two together as an explanation of modality involves an incoherence of thought.

And this incoherence Kant has not, I think, completely avoided in his *Critique*. He begins by laying down as regards the categories of modality that they "merely express the relation of the conception to which they are attached to our faculty of knowledge." Accordingly the Postulates of Empirical thought ought, in view of the general problem of the *Analytic*, to answer the question, 'What can we know *a priori* in relation to empirical objects' by applying the categories of possibility, actuality, and necessity? And this is what, at first sight, they seem to define clearly. "Granting," says Kant, "the conception of a thing to be quite complete, I may yet ask whether

---

[1] [*Op. cit.* p. 106.]
[2] Kant's meaning is clear from his illustration: "In making the problematic judgment 'the human soul may be immortal' I decide nothing as to the truth or falsehood of the proposition 'the human soul is immortal.'"

the object is possible or actual, and if actual, whether it is also necessary. Such determinations are not conceived to belong to the object itself; the only point is how the object, together with its determinations, is related to the understanding in its empirical use, to empirical judgment and to reason as applied to experience."[1] But when we look closer we find serious difficulties and ambiguities. These postulates as here given do not seem to be attained by the method which Kant uses in the rest of the Transcendental Logic. There is no 'schematism' manifest in them: none of the postulates apparently involves a time-determination. But I need not say that the great system-maker has no intention of abandoning his schematism here. "The scheme of possibility," he tells us, "is the harmony of the synthesis of different ideas with the conditions of time in general. . . . The schema of actuality is existence in a determinate time. The schema of necessity is the existence of an object at all times."[2]

Now here the schematism of actuality and necessity is clear and definite. 'Actual' as applied to empirical objects must denote what exists or has existed at *some* definite time. 'Necessary,' what exists at all times. This does not quite exhaust the meaning of 'necessity,' since, if we are speaking of objects of external perception, the 'universality' which is the meaning of 'necessity' as applied to empirical objects must be extended to space no less than to time. For in judging mathe-

[1] Cf. Watson's *Selections*, p. 122.   [2] Watson's *Selections*, p. 89.

matical truths to be necessary—*e.g.* that two straight lines cannot enclose a space—we mean that they do not enclose it anywhere, not merely that they do not enclose it at any time. This is, of course, not so with actuality.

But when we turn to possibility the schematism seems to me again forced. What symmetry would really require is that the 'possible' should be interpreted as what exists or has existed or will exist at *some time or other*: but that is obviously not the meaning of the word, and, in fact, so interpreted the 'possible' would be 'actual,' save that its actuality would not be completely known. Kant has to say that it is the "harmony of the synthesis of different notions with the conditions of time in general," the "determination of the notion of a thing at any time"[1]—which means no more than that the possible is what *may* exist at any time. Now, of course, if an empirical object—or connexion of empirical attributes—is conceived as possible at all, it must be conceived as possible in time: but that is not giving 'possibility' an exclusively temporal determination. For if the attributes are derived from external perception or its form, it is equally necessary that their connexion should conform to the conditions of spatial intuition. Indeed, Kant's statement of the first postulate makes no special reference to time, and his illustration of it is taken from space:—he says that there is no contradiction in the *conception* of a figure enclosed by two straight lines, but the

[1] Watson's *Selections*, p. 89.

conditions of space prevent our constructing it in imagination.[1] The schematism, then, of possibility seems to me forced. It does not give us any new notion which 'possibility' carries with it in relation to time as 'necessity' carries with it universality. And in fact the principle is a mere corollary from the conclusions of the Æsthetic. Empirical objects can only exist in time, and if objects of external perception, in space: we can, therefore, obviously know *a priori* that there can be no conception of such an object except under conditions of time; and also of space if it be an object externally perceived. Indeed, Kant says—in a passage that Professor Watson has *not* translated—that "the principles of modality are nothing further than explanations of the concepts of possibility, actuality, and necessity in their empirical use, and herewith at the same time restrictions of all categories to their empirical use."[2] This latter restriction, of course, does not follow from a mere explanation of the meaning of these terms in their application to empirical objects: but from the general view of the function of the understanding put forward in this part of the treatise.

I now pass to a point of some interest as to the scope of this category of 'Possibility.' Looking closer at the first postulate, we find a certain ambiguity in it. At first sight, it seems to mean that *anything* is rightly thought as possible, which agrees with the formal conditions of experience. But

---

[1] [Watson's *Selections*, pp. 122-3.]
[2] *Kritik*, Hartenstein's edition, p. 193; [M. Müller, p. 191].

subsequent discussion—not translated by Professor Watson—shows that Kant means that *only* this can be known *a priori* to be possible : *e.g.* as his illustrations indicate, the possibility of spatial figures, of continuous magnitudes, of permanent substances, of causal connexions, etc. Such things we can affirm to be possible : though (except in the case of spatial figures) it would be an understatement for Kant, who claims to have proved them to be necessary. But as regards any other connexion of ideas in thought, we cannot lay down *a priori* that it is possible in fact, but only *a posteriori*, that is to say, on empirical grounds. Thus the notion of a faculty of prophecy, and of what we now call telepathy, are in Kant's view " concepts the possibility of which has nothing to rest on, because it is not founded on experience and its known laws."[1] Kant, however, does not seem to say that he has thus given us two distinct conceptions of 'possibility' in its empirical use : (*a*) that which agrees with the formal conditions of experience; (*b*) that which accords with empirical analogies.[2] Of course prediction and telepathy in no way disagree with the formal conditions of experience. They are only not, according to Kant, founded on empirical laws scientifically ascertained.

We certainly require a distinction between the idea of contradiction (or non-contradiction) of necessary *a priori* laws of Nature and the idea of

[1] [M. Müller, p. 194.]
[2] I say 'analogies,' because if the object in question was something of which the existence could be strictly *inferred* from empirical facts, it would be actual.

VII CAUSALITY, COMMUNITY, MODALITY

correspondence (or non-correspondence) to merely empirically ascertained uniformities; and I should have thought it more in accordance with Kant's system—and the words of the first postulate—to limit 'impossibility' to the former. And indeed he does not exactly say that telepathy, etc., is impossible, but only that its possibility has nothing to rest on and cannot be tested. So that it is not to be called possible. It may be admitted that there is no scientific use in discussing conceptions to which only possibility in the wider sense attaches: *i.e.* for the actuality of which no empirical evidence is adduced. But then, as Kant quite well knew, that was *not* the case with prophecy or telepathy.[1] I cannot but think that some other word than 'impossible' would be more appropriate to signify things or processes which have no analogy in scientifically ascertained empirical effects. And when this was recognised it would be seen that this narrower notion of 'empirical possibility' is necessarily vague and indeterminate. Who is to say what is 'possible' in the narrower sense?[2]

I now turn to the other two postulates. It would appear from the second postulate that the two notions 'actual' and 'necessary' involve each other (so far at least as the larger part of the application of the notion 'actual' is concerned). For we are told that " what is *bound up* with sensation is actual," but what does 'bound up with' (*zusammenhängt*) mean? If anything is rightly judged to be 'actual' which is not a datum of sense-perception, what can

[1] Swedenborg!   [2] Cf. Mr. Wells's *War of the Worlds*.

it be except something of which the existence is cogently inferred from such data? And Kant himself says that, in order rightly to judge anything to be actual, "we must be aware of its connexion with some actual perception according to the analogies of experience which represent all real connexion in an experience."[1] But the third postulate defines the necessary as "that which, in its connexion with the actual, is determined in accordance with universal conditions of experience." It is rather difficult to see how the two can be distinguished : and, in fact, the distinction Kant seems to draw between them does not seem to me satisfactory. He says that no existence can be known to be (even 'conditionally') necessary, "except the existence of effects following from given causes in conformity with laws of causality. It is, therefore, not the existence of things or substances that we can know to be necessary, but only the existence of their state. . . . Substances can never be regarded as empirical effects."[2] On the other hand, he seems to hold that we may know that a *thing*[3] actually exists, though it cannot be perceived, when it is inseparably "related to certain perceptions (*mit einigen Wahrnehmungen zusammenhängt*). . . . Thus from observation of the attraction of iron filings we know that a magnetic matter pervades all bodies, although our organs of sense are so constituted that we cannot perceive it." But how can this be known except by inferring a causal connexion, and if the

---

[1] Watson's *Selections*, p. 124.   [2] Watson's *Selections*, pp. 125 f.
[3] Substance, I suppose.

connexion is not necessary, why are we said to *know* "that a magnetic matter pervades all bodies"?[1] It seems evident that Kant accepts as certain inferences that are based on a connexion not necessary but only empirical: but how he would justify this I do not know.

[1] In fact, it *was* a somewhat hasty inference.

LECTURE VIII

THE TRANSCENDENTAL DIALECTIC

So far I have been examining, impartially but closely, the main constructive part of Kant's philosophy, *i.e.* his account of the *a priori* elements in our commonly accepted knowledge of the physical world. I turn now to consider that part of his work which is primarily, though not solely destructive: destructive, that is, of the 'bad metaphysics' which attempts to attain, professes to expound, 'rational' as contrasted with empirical knowledge—knowledge, that is to say, going beyond the limits of possible experience.

Before we examine Kant's destructive work, it will be well to have before us in outline the *soi-disant* system of knowledge that it was designed to shatter. The detail of it I propose to reserve in order that it may precede, in each case, the detail of the criticism. But it will be well to have the general plan of it before our minds, before considering the general plan of Kant's attack.

From the starting-point of modern metaphysics in Descartes a definite triplicity of Being had always occupied the thought of the metaphysician. The nature of minds, of the world of matter, the relation between the two, the relation of both to God, and the philosophical conception of God, as distinct from the revelational conception—these were throughout the main topics of speculation. The centuries of mediæval social life in which religious conceptions had swayed men's thought with overwhelming predominance had —in spite of the new sway of intellectual interest towards the comprehension of the laws of the physical world—still left the Christian conception of the soul, the world, and God, as that which ordinarily determined the ground-plan of the metaphysician's thought. For him, as for the vast majority of his educated contemporaries, the idea of the world with which he started was that of an aggregate or system of material things, created by the primal and eternal Intelligence for a finite existence. In this world men, composites of soul and body, were placed, but to it they only partially and temporarily belonged in respect of their souls, which, unlike the world, were created for endless existence. As a philosopher, he sought to obtain reasoned convictions independent of revelation, on the matters to which these Christian beliefs related : but, however sincere his love of truth, he was—especially in Germany up to Kant's time—under strong moral pressure to arrive at conclusions in harmony with the established religious beliefs : at any rate, he could hardly think without serious regard to them, or diverge from them without anxious consideration. Now it soon appeared that the questions prominently suggested from this point of view were not questions which experience alone, however systematised, enabled the thinker to answer.

As regards the primal Divine Being, and his relations to the world and to human souls, this conclusion [as to the insufficiency of experience] seems to have been accepted unhesitatingly. The philosopher found current a Revelational Theology, based on the statements of Scripture and the decisions of ecclesiastical authorities; but he did not find an experimental theology. There was no body of systematic knowledge, professing to be derived from observation of the Divine nature and action. The philosopher's Theology, therefore — however important the data it might draw from experience,—must be in the main worked out by processes of abstract reasoning. But even in the case of Minds and the Material world, though empirical study supplied him with a mass of knowledge of particular facts and laws, it did not take him far towards an answer to the fundamental questions above indicated. Could man know, apart from revelation, that his soul was naturally immortal, and therefore fundamentally independent in existence of the material organism with which it was temporarily so mysteriously connected? At any rate, experience could not tell him this directly or taken alone: since, however complete the diversity between psychical facts—thoughts, feelings, etc.—and the movements of organic matter that seem to be causally connected with them, we have no experience of the former except as accompanied by the latter. Similarly as regards the material world, when we seek to penetrate its ultimate constitution, we have to go beyond experience. We know, indeed, from experience, the compositeness of ordinary empirical things, because we have experience of their breaking up into parts: but we soon convince ourselves that these parts are not ultimate, and that if we are to attain a true conception of the ultimate constituents of the physical world, it must be by processes of abstract reasoning. And it is still more evident that if we raise the obvious questions as regards the physical world as a whole, whether it had a beginning or has always existed, whether it has bounds or is infinitely extended, experience cannot furnish answers. As little can experience help us, if we raise questions as to the ultimate explanation of what I may call the particularity of the material world. In the view of Physical Science, through the work chiefly of Copernicus, Galileo, Kepler, and Newton, the particular state of the material world at any time had come to be definitely and scientifically thought as the necessary consequence of the particular state at any preceding time, the changes between the two times being explained by the operation of the universal laws of matter in motion. But however far back we trace this sequence in thought, the collocation of the parts of matter with which we leave off seems as arbitrary and contingent—something that might just as well have been otherwise,—as much, therefore, needing a reason for its existence, as the present state. Could philosophy acquiesce in conceiving the process of the world as an endless chain of arbitrary and contingent facts? If not, what explanation could be found? The explanation suggested by traditional theology referred the original collocation of matter in space to the wise creative choice of the primal Being, God. And the purposes determining this choice were usually taken to relate to the life of humanity. Could philosophy convert this into a cogently reasoned explanation; and if so, could it deal with the question lying behind, as to the existence of the primal Being, God, by conceiving his existence as intrinsically necessary? Or if not, what other system of thought on the subject could satisfy reason?

However these questions were answered, it seemed obvious that they carried the thinker beyond the limits of experience. In this way the subject-matter of metaphysical inquiry came to present itself—especially to the orderly and systematic mind of Wolff—as naturally divided into three branches, Rational Psychology, Rational Cosmology, and Rational Theology. In the two former cases a distinction was drawn between the Rational and Empirical methods as applied to minds and to the material world respectively. Not that Wolff aimed at an absolute separation between the two, as in both cases important data for the rational studies are derived from experience: but it was the rational studies as distinct from the empirical that supplied answers to the (metaphysical) questions above indicated.

What these answers were, we will consider more closely in later lectures. It is enough now to say that the mind was conceived as a substance, simple not composite, and therefore naturally indestructible and imperishable,—since only the composite is destructible.[1] The material world was conceived as an aggregate of simple substances, which were not actually extended so as to fill space—since what is extended must, it seemed, be divisible — but were arranged in an order which is confusedly perceived as continuous extension. This world was conceived as having come into existence through the creative act of a supremely perfect Being, whose existence is necessarily 'involved in its essence,' *i.e.* a supremely perfect non-existent Being was held (as by Descartes) to be a contradiction in terms.

These, then, are the chief metaphysical conclusions —or at any rate leading examples of the conclusions— which Kant in this third, destructive part of his Transcendental Philosophy set out to expose, as attained by an illegitimate and illusory exercise of the reason. For his general negative conclusion we are, I think, fully prepared, if we have followed with assent the arguments contained in the two first parts. If Time does not belong to reality, as it exists apart from our consciousness, but is only a form in which things appear to the human mind, it is clear that the very question (*e.g.*) whether the world—the real world—had or had not a beginning in time is as unmeaning as (*e.g.*) the question whether the soul is square or oblong.

---

[1] Experience seemed to show that 'destruction' was really changing relation of parts, 'breaking up.'

But Kant is not content to cut off bad metaphysics by such a simple and sweeping inference as this. He desires to exhibit in detail the fallacies into which the human reason is inevitably led, when it seeks knowledge beyond the limits of possible experience; partly because, as he tells us, these transcendental fallacies do not vanish when once refuted—as ordinary logical or formal fallacies do, should we happen (*e.g.*) inadvertently to perpetrate a syllogism with an undistributed middle term. The 'transcendental illusion' continually recurs and has continually to be corrected. But why are we thus condemned to this continual recurrence of error? The explanation according to Kant is this: Deep in our reason lie fundamental rules for its use, of the highest value in its empirical employment, but having inevitably a tendency to present themselves as objective principles for determining the characteristics of 'things in themselves,' though their proper application is merely to produce a certain systematisation of our conceptions, to aid our intellect in a comprehensive grasp of experience.

What, then, are these ideas of the Reason, and how are we to obtain a systematic view of them? We shall expect, from the method used in the second part to obtain a systematic view of the pure concepts of the understanding, that common logic will again furnish the plan of the system, *i.e.* that the ideas of the pure Reason will be correlated with the logical forms of reasoning. For the ordinary operation of Reason—in the narrower sense, in which it is distinguished from understanding and sensibility, regarded as forms of *a priori* knowledge—is shown in reasoning on empirical matter, that is, in processes of mediate inference, in which rational conclusions are drawn by a combination of judgments in syllogisms or, in most cases, in a series of syllogisms. Now as Kant found in common Logic three forms of reasoning, categorical, hypothetical, and disjunctive; and as the illusory Metaphysics which he set out to criticise—the professed knowledge transcending possible experience—was divided, as we have seen, under three heads, Psychology, Cosmology, and Theology, the correlation of the two triplicities was irresistible.

But here—as in the case of the more elaborate system of the pure understanding—the correlation is not equally satisfactory throughout: the symmetry is partly forced, and so far as it is forced, it obscures rather than illuminates the matter on which it is imposed. This I shall try to show more clearly in the sequel: but it is needful to state it, in giving a preliminary view of the system. The general function of the understanding is, as we saw, combination or synthesis of phenomena, constituting empirical objects and connecting them as possible objects of experience. But it does not aim at putting together these objects of experience into a whole. The idea of an absolute totality of possible experience—which the mind finds itself compelled to form—is an idea of the Reason in the special sense in which its function is distinguished from that of Understanding and that of Sensibility. In this special sense the *logical* function of the Reason is to combine the judgments of the understanding, as the understanding combines the percepts of sense. Now the absolute totality of all possible experience cannot itself be experienced: and therefore in seeking to know this absolute totality Reason inevitably aims, and must aim, at transcending Experience.

In speaking of 'absolute totality of experience' I have used the phrase of the *Prolegomena*. In the *Kritik* Kant makes the idea more definite :—" A transcendental conception of reason is . . . just the conception of the *totality of conditions* of anything that is given as conditioned. Now the *unconditioned* alone makes a totality of conditions possible, while conversely the totality of conditions is always itself unconditioned: hence a pure conception of reason may be defined generally as a conception of the unconditioned, in so far as it contains a ground for the synthesis of the conditioned."[1] Now, what is the exact meaning of the "unconditioned which alone makes a totality of conditions possible and is itself unconditioned"? The example of Kant's meaning which is certainly most easily intelligible is to be found in the cosmological ideas. Let us take the case of the synthesis of cause and effect— which we have already seen reason to regard as supplying the germ of Kant's system of concepts of pure understanding. The principle of causality is that any event presupposes an antecedent event

[1] Watson's *Selections*, p. 141.

as its necessary condition or cause, but this cause, according to the same law, must have an earlier antecedent cause, and this again a still earlier, and so on, through a retrogressive series.

Now reason demands that the totality of this series should be, not indeed specifically known—reason is not so exacting—but thought as a reality. It must therefore admit of being thought without contradiction. The demand that the series be completed, that is to say, forces reason to the conception of an uncaused or free cause, which yet—we find—cannot be thought without violating the principle of causality that leads to the series: and thus we get an 'Antinomy.' Similarly, a material thing existing in space is conditioned (determined in its position) by the coexisting matter with which, according to Kant, it is necessarily connected by reciprocal action and reaction. And here again Reason passes through the series of conditions to the unconditioned, and raises the question of the relation of the material world as a whole—which is necessarily unconditioned by any coexisting matter—to Space, and asks whether the world is finite or infinite in extension.

But it is not so easy to apply this idea of the totality of conditions, involving the idea of the unconditioned, to the principles and reasonings either of Rational Psychology or of Rational Theology. I think that in both these cases the conception of a totality of conditions or unconditioned is somewhat strained. And I am confirmed in this view by comparing the *Pro-*

legomena with the *Kritik* :[1] it will be observed that in the *Prolegomena* 'conditions' are only spoken of in the case of the cosmological idea. I do not mean that Kant's view was altered, or that he had abandoned the extended conception of the *Kritik* when he came to write the *Prolegomena*, but only that the more limited use of the notion of 'totality of conditions' as equivalent to 'unconditioned' is the narrower use. He therefore naturally fell back to it in what was designed to be a more popular exposition of his view. However, no doubt, we must take, and try to understand, Kant as extending the conception of conditioned and unconditioned to include all three cases. In the case of Rational Psychology he considers that the psychological idea is an 'unconditioned of the categorical synthesis in a subject,' or otherwise 'the absolute or unconditioned unity of the thinking subject.' To understand this, we must examine more closely what he calls the 'Paralogisms' of Rational Psychology.

One disadvantage of the forced symmetry of this part of Kant's system—the correlation of the three branches of fallacious Metaphysics, Rational Psychology, Cosmology, and Theology, with the three logical forms of reasoning, categorical, hypothetical, and disjunctive—is that too complete a separation

[1] In the former we find "first, the Idea of the complete subject (the substantial) ; secondly, the Idea of the complete series of conditions ; thirdly, the determination of all concepts in the Idea of a complete complex of [all] possible [being]" (Mahaffy's edition of the *Prolegomena*, § 43, p. 119). In the latter "we have, first, the unconditioned of the *categorical* synthesis in a *subject* ; secondly, the unconditioned of the *hypothetical* synthesis of the members of a series ; thirdly, the unconditioned of the *disjunctive* synthesis of the parts of a system" (Watson's *Selections*, p. 141).

VIII   THE TRANSCENDENTAL DIALECTIC   139

is established between the three branches. This will, I think, appear clearly hereafter, as regards the relation of the cosmological ideas to theology: *i.e.* it will appear that the questions raised in the two later of Kant's four antinomies—the question (1) whether to explain the whole series of caused changes of which the world-process consists, we have to suppose a free causality; and (2) whether to explain the same series of contingent facts, regarded as contingent, we have to suppose an absolutely necessary Being—are *prima facie* theological questions. I do not mean that Kant is not justified in giving them a cosmological form: that we will hereafter consider. But certainly the affirmative answers given to these questions in the pre-Kantian metaphysics, which Kant is attacking as fallacious, were theological answers: the free causality supposed at the beginning of the causal changes of the (supposed) created world was the causality exercised by the primal Being God, and it was this primal Being who was conceived to be absolutely necessary.

A somewhat similar forced separation occurs between the Rational Psychology and the Rational Cosmology: and it is noteworthy that this forced separation increases the difficulty of accepting Kant's account of the transcendental idea corresponding to categorical reasoning.

"We have," he says, "firstly the unconditioned of the categorical synthesis in a subject"; and soon after he identifies this idea with "the absolute or unconditioned unity of the thinking subject."[1] But, if we regard the idea thus defined as representing what reason tries to find in empirical objects—rather than what she professes to succeed in finding—and that is the aspect in which the Transcendental Philosophy presents the ideas of reason, why should she confine her attempt to Minds or Thinking Subjects? Every material thing, no less than every thinking person, presents to our thought, when logically analysed, the synthesis of predicates or qualities inhering in a subject or substance. Why should not reason seek for the real substance at bottom—the subject pure and simple that cannot be thought as a predicate—in the case of material things, no less than in the case of persons. And, indeed, was it not evident that Reason—the reason of metaphysicians—had occupied itself with this question.[2] And in fact, in the *Prolegomena*, Kant fully recognises this: and thus begins his account of the Psychological idea:—"It has been long since observed, that in all substances the proper subject, that which remains after all the accidents (as predicates) are abstracted, consequently that which is itself *substantial*, is unknown. . . ."[3] Here we have, I conceive, the critical view of the proper use and application of what I may call the categorical idea, the idea of the absolute subject in anything : *i.e.* that in it which cannot be thought as a predicate.

---

[1] Watson's *Selections*, pp. 141, 142.
[2] Cf. Locke, *Essay concerning Human Understanding*, Bk. ii. ch. xiii. § 19 ; ch. xxiii. §§ 1, 2.
[3] *Prolegomena*, § 46, Mahaffy's ed. p. 123 *fin*.

The only reason for confining his treatment of it to the Thinking Subject, is that only in this case did Reason appear to him to have deceived itself into thinking that it had *found* the absolute subject it sought for.[1]

But the fallacious Metaphysics that Kant goes on to attack, here and in the *Kritik*, does not content itself with affirming that in the Ego we find an absolute *subject*—*i.e.* a subject which cannot be thought as a predicate: its fallacy rather lies in a further assumption that the Ego is a simple substance and therefore indestructible. But similar simple, indestructible substances had also been not only sought but (believed to be) found by the reason of metaphysicians in the material world: and the search for such permanent indestructibles was by no means identical with the effort to find a subject which could not be thought as a predicate.

For the simple elements of which Wolff, for example, supposed material things to be composed must, if definitely conceived at all, be conceived not as subjects without, but as subjects with predicates. In popular physics and by physicists generally, these ultimates were conceived as having extension, involving size, shape, and absolute incompressibility (*i.e.* absolute resistance to any forces tending to annihilate their extension). And if, to avoid the difficulty of conceiving anything extended and yet not composed of parts, we follow Wolff in supposing the ultimate elements of matter to be unextended and without size and shape, still the unextended alone

---

[1] Cf. *Prolegomena*, Mahaffy's ed. p. 124 *fin.*

must have some predicates : and in fact Wolff's atom had not only an essential force or principle of activity by which it was distinguished from other atoms, but also some passive force by which the phenomenon of inertia in composite bodies was explained.

Now the question of the ultimate elements of matter Kant treats under the head of Cosmology, and the symmetry of his system requires this. But by thus separating the question whether the soul is a simple indestructible substance entirely from the question whether such substances are to be found as elements of the material world, he certainly divided questions which had been connected in the thought of the philosophers he was attacking : and it is important to notice this because it is, I think, this previous connexion of the questions which furnishes the real explanation of what Kant calls a Paralogism. Had Wolff and others merely considered the Ego from a psychological point of view, and merely found in it the 'subject incapable of being thought as predicate' which Reason is said by Kant to seek, I cannot see why they should have immediately attributed to it the predicates of permanence and indestructibility : the inconsistency would have been too palpable. It was because their Rational Cosmology influenced their Ontology, and, through this, their Psychology, that they were misled into attributing to the Ego the characteristics which a cosmological line of thought led them to attribute to the ultimates of matter.

LECTURE IX

RATIONAL PSYCHOLOGY

THE general view that I take of the part of Kant's discussion which he calls the 'Paralogisms of the Pure Reason' may be briefly and simply expounded. I am convinced of the truth of this general conclusion, that the propositions of the older Rational Psychology which he attacks—viz. that the human soul is a simple substance, in its nature indestructible and therefore naturally immortal, and having relations, represented in our thought as spatial, with the other simple substances which are the elements of the material world—that these doctrines, regarded as synthetic propositions *a priori*, are invalid and illegitimately assumed. And further, that they must be known *a priori* if at all, *i.e.* by considering the general notion of a self-conscious being: they cannot be proved from our experience of human minds, as known to us from introspection, or what Kant calls the 'inner sense.' These conclusions I accept as true: and of their negative importance there can be no doubt. But the reasoning by which Kant tries to prove them seems to me only partially sound: I think it contains a fundamental misapprehension of the knowledge of self which we obtain through self-consciousness.

My grounds for this double conclusion I will now briefly state. But first, I would again point out that (as explained at the close of the last lecture) the separation which the plan of Kant's system—his correlation of the triplicity of the transcendental ideas of the Reason with the triplicity of the logical forms of reasoning—leads him to make between Rational Psychology and Rational Cosmology, puts us at the wrong point of view for understanding how the doctrines that he is assailing were arrived at. It was precisely because Leibniz, Wolff, and their followers did *not* completely separate Psychology from Cosmology, did not regard the investigation of the nature of mind as quite apart from the investigation of the ultimate nature of the material world with which we find minds mysteriously connected, but on the contrary regarded minds as subject to the fundamental laws of the material world as rationally comprehended—it is, I say, just because of this that they inferred from the essential unity of the self-conscious self its substantial simplicity and therefore its natural permanence and indestructibility.

I have said that the threefold division of Metaphysics into Psychology, Cosmology, and Theology is adopted by Kant from Wolff—by whom, I think, it was first explicitly introduced. But Wolff prefixed to these three branch-studies a general study of the characteristics of Being and our knowledge of Being, which he calls Ontology. The conceptions and propositions of Ontology he regards as applicable, from their general character, to all the branch-studies: and it is here that we find the conception of a simple being, contrasted with a composite as essentially indivisible, and therefore — in contrast with composites — as incapable of coming into existence except by creation or ceasing to exist except through a correspondingly supernatural fiat of God. This notion, then, he and his followers applied to psychical as well as to physical facts. The self is recognised as such a simple being, unextended and therefore without parts, and so naturally indestructible. It accordingly takes its place among the ultimate elements of the physical world, which are similarly conceived to remain, indestructible and physically immutable,[1] through all the processes of physical change in which the composite matter that we empirically know is continually being broken up into parts which enter into new composite substances.

The validity of this inference from mutable and destructible composites to indestructible and physically immutable elements, we shall presently have to examine in its application to the material world: for this, in fact, constitutes the second of Kant's cosmological problems, that lead, according to him, to antinomies. My point now is that the

[1] In saying that these substances were physically immutable, I mean that if they changed they changed from an inner necessity of development, not from the operation of external forces.

separation, which Kant's system imposes on him, between the question as to the simple substantiality of Mind and the question as to the simple substances underlying Matter, is a forced separation. And I may add that I find striking evidence of this in a passage—which Watson has not selected—as to the 'interest of reason' in these antinomies. For in speaking of the antithesis in the second antinomy [1] he characterises the antithesis as apparently hostile to morality "if our soul shares the same divisibility and perishableness with matter"[2]—thus fusing the fundamental question of Rational Psychology with the cosmological question relating to completeness of division of a material object. Of this more presently. In any case I agree with Kant in regarding as illegitimate the transfer of the predicate of natural indestructibility to the self-conscious mind, as though it were somehow necessarily connected with the notions of unity and identity of the self-conscious self. I find no such necessary connexion and therefore find any reasoning in which it is assumed fallacious:—you may call it, if you like, a paralogism.

At the same time, Kant's exhibition of the fallacy does not seem to me exactly to hit the right point. He admits, of course, the essential unity of the self-conscious mind, as a perceiving and knowing subject: indeed we may say that it is the special characteristic

---

[1] In this antinomy the thesis is: "Everything in the world consists of simple parts"; and the antithesis: "There is nothing simple, but everything is composite."

[2] [Max Müller's translation, p. 408.]

of his system of philosophy to lay stress on this. The unity of self-consciousness is for him the source of all unity, all synthesis or connexion in the objects of empirical knowledge, as constructed by the understanding out of the data of sense. The essential function, as we saw, of the understanding, in the application of all its forms or categories, is synthesis, unification: and the root of this synthesis, what renders this unification of sense-perceptions possible, is the necessity that every sense-perception should be referrible to a self, and *capable* of being thought —if not always actually thought—as *its* perception. It is because all objects of experience are thus necessarily objects of the possible experience of a single conscious percipient mind, that Kant holds us to have the *a priori* knowledge of their constitution and relations set forth in the second part of his treatise. But it is just because of this startling extension of the meaning and function of self-consciousness in Kant's Philosophy, that he is disposed to draw a sharp line between the unity and identity of self as a subject of knowledge and its unity and permanence as an object of knowledge: and to regard as a paralogism the inference of the latter from the former. He does not deny that 'I' stands in our ordinary thought for Self as an object of thought, no less than for Self as a necessary subject of thought. He expressly says that the transcendental conception 'I think'—the common 'vehicle' of all transcendental conceptions—though as transcendental it is free from all empirical elements, "yet serves to distinguish between two different kinds of objects, from the different ways in which they are related to consciousness. *I*, as thinking, am an object of the inner sense."[1] Admitting this, he argues, *in the Kritik*, that Rational Psychology is bound to obtain its alleged synthetical truths strictly *a priori, i.e.* without reference to the inner experience in which I know myself as an object: and that if we examine its propositions with this strict condition in our minds, we find that it has made an illegitimate transition from the characteristics of the self as subject to characteristics which can only belong to self as object. I partly agree with this: but I think that in his exhibition of the paralogism Kant does not state the illicit transition quite correctly: I think the illegitimate inference of the Leibniz-Wolffian metaphysics is not simply from 'subject' to 'substance,' but from '*one* subject' to '*simple* substance.' In short, the Wolffians might answer truly that this rigid separation between Rational and Empirical Psychology was Kant's and not theirs, and was an unthinkable separation. For identity amid change, and therefore relative permanence, appears to me essential to the thought of a subject: and if Kant says 'permanence belongs to it *qua* object,' the answer is that it is essentially an object to itself. And Kant's argument seems to me self-contradictory in its subtlety of division of 'subject' and 'object.' "The conception of a thing that can exist by itself as a subject," he says,

[1] Watson's *Selections*, p. 145 *fin.*

"does not carry with it objective reality . . . because we cannot understand how an object of that sort could exist at all."¹ "We cannot understand" —but the 'we' are existent 'we's,' subjects that must conceive themselves as existing objects.

But if the Wolffians were to make this answer, if they were to admit that the conception of Self as substantial was derived—and must be derived—from that empirical cognition of Self as an object of introspection or inner sense, which is necessarily involved in the most purely speculative thought, I should then urge that from this empirical cognition of Self as object of introspection we can only be justified in attributing to it permanence during the psychical life of the individual: and not in attributing to it the absolute permanence and indestructibility—unless annihilated by creative fiat—which constitutes *the* important dogma of the Rational Psychology here assailed.

And this line of argument *is* adopted by Kant in the *Prolegomena*.² But in the *Kritik* he seems to go further and expressly deny the application of the predicate of permanence—even to the limited extent to which experience justifies it—to the Self or Ego.³ Kant seems to have been led to this view

---

[1] Watson's *Selections*, p. 152 *fin*.

[2] Cf. § 48 *init*. (Mahaffy's trans. p. 126):—"If therefore from the concept of the soul as a substance, we would infer its permanence, this can hold good as regards possible experience only, not [of the soul] as a thing in itself and beyond all possible experience."

[3] "Now in inner perception there is nothing permanent, for the *I* is merely the consciousness of my thinking. So long, therefore, as we limit ourselves to mere thinking, we are without the necessary condition for the application of the conception of substance to the self as a thinking being; we are unable, in other words, to say that the self is an independent subject."— Watson's *Selections*, p. 153.

by the remarkable barrenness of content of the notion of Self. "The simple idea *I*," he says, "is so completely empty of all content, that it cannot be called even a conception, but merely a consciousness which accompanies all conceptions. This *I* or he or it, this thing that thinks, is nothing but the idea of a transcendental subject of thought $= x$, which is known only through the thoughts that are its predicates, and which apart from them cannot be conceived at all."[1] He afterwards speaks of it as "the very poorest of all our ideas (*Vorstellungen*)."[2] Now perhaps this language is justifiable if the 'I' of the thought 'I think' is treated as strictly transcendental and examined in rigorous abstraction from experience. But in saying that "in inner perception there is nothing permanent, for the 'I' is simply the consciousness of my thinking,"[3] Kant has abandoned the transcendental ground; and here I think he is guilty of a transition as illegitimate as that which he rightly attributes to his opponents, although in an opposite direction. That is, he tries to reduce the notion of Self as object of inner experience to the meagreness of the 'I' of transcendental thought. Now of the self which introspection presents to us as a thinking thing, introspection doubtless tells us little enough: all the particularity of the mind, all that interests us in our thought of ourselves and other minds as relatively permanent objects of thought in contrast with the more transient

---

[1] Watson's *Selections*, p. 148.   [2] [*Ibid.* p. 150.]
[3] [*Ibid.* p. 153.]

states of consciousness, we only know by inference from the transient and ever-varying element of inner experience. But still it is going too far to say that the self presented in inner experience is merely thought as a logical subject *without* predicates. However little 'I' know of 'myself' in introspection, I still know myself as *one* and *identical*, perduring through the empirical stream of thoughts, feelings, and volitions.

This cognition may be liable to error—I find infallibility nowhere in human thought—or again it may seem unimportant: but it is presented as immediate and is as certain as any empirical cognition, and in it I certainly find 'given'—if anything is ever 'given'—the empirical permanence which Kant—in the *Kritik*—denies.

LECTURE X

THE MATHEMATICAL ANTINOMIES

I NOW pass to the Cosmological Idea and the Antinomies of Pure Reason.

The Antinomy, as Kant sometimes calls it, subdivides itself into four antinomies correlated—not without something of the violence to which we are now used—to the four logical categories of Quantity, Quality, Relation, and Modality. In the present lecture I shall confine myself to the first two antinomies, and shall begin with the second, because it refers to the inference from the composite to the simple, of which I have already had to speak. And not only for this reason: but also because the dogma of Wolff's metaphysics, that the ultimate elements of the physical world are simple substances—which Kant here presents as in irreconcilable conflict with an equally tenable opposite dogma—was the cardinal doctrine of Wolff's Rational Cosmology, so far as it is distinguished by him from Theology. The questions raised in the first antinomy, as to the finity or infinity of the world in Time and Space, are, as I shall presently explain, less inevitable and fundamental from Wolff's point of view.

LECT. X THE MATHEMATICAL ANTINOMIES 153

But before we proceed to the particular case, let us contemplate for a moment the Cosmological Idea, and the Antinomy or conflict to which it leads, in a general form. For here in the symmetrical exposition of the fourfold conflict to which the human reason is reduced, if it clings to the illusion that it can know things in themselves, and in the double solution that the Critical Philosophy affords of the conflict—explaining the two first cases by showing that *neither* of the conflicting conclusions is true, and explaining the two last by showing that both may be true—we have not only the most brilliant product of Kant's genius for system-making, but also, as he claims, the most persuasive.[1] This is, I think, true. If anything can persuade a man that the proper task of man's understanding and reasoning is not to know reality as it is, but to systematise the impressions it makes on our sensibility, this will persuade him. For if he takes the sensible world—the world of things as Sense and Understanding, in their ordinary empirical operation, present it—to be a *real* world, and tries to form a consistent conception of it as a whole, he finds himself environed on all sides with overwhelming and inevitable contradictions: whereas if he will only be content to regard it as a *phenomenal* world, Kant assures him that the contradictions all vanish, and his reason, accepting its limitations, is at peace with itself.

To illustrate the conflict let us take first, as I proposed, the second case; in which the human mind

[1] Cf. *Prolegomena*, § 50 *init.*, Mahaffy, p. 131.

attempts to grasp completely and conceive consistently the constitution of matter, by reasoning from the composite substances presented in experience to the ultimate elements of which they are composed. Take any portion of sensible matter, we can usually break it into parts and these again into further parts. Even if we find it too hard actually to break up, we can alter it by pressure, heat, or chemical methods, so as to convince ourselves that it is actually composed of a vast number of insensible parts that change their relative position when the whole is thus modified. But these parts as we commonly conceive them are not absolutely ultimate elements: when we reflect on any such part, we find that, since we conceive it as occupying space, we must conceive it as extended, and therefore as ideally divisible into further parts. Such a part, then, is not the ultimate reality of which we are in search, that would still exist if all composition were removed. But where then is this ultimate reality? Yes, says the Transcendental Philosopher, who is contemplating this metaphysical process from his position of critical aloofness, where is it indeed? You cannot find it, and yet you must find it, unless you will consent to learn the lesson of criticism. You cannot find it, because however far you go in your process of imaginary division, the ideal result of division at which you stop must still be extended or it is no longer matter; and yet if it is extended it must consist of parts, and the division has to begin again. At the same time you must find it, if you cling to your belief that your reason in this process is dealing with a real and not a phenomenal world. For if you once admit that you cannot find it and that the division has to go on for ever, then the answer to the question what matter ultimately consists of must be "nothing at all." For, in Kant's words, "assume that composite substances are not made up of simple parts. Then, if we think all composition away, no composite part will be left. And, by hypothesis, there is no simple part. Hence nothing at all will remain."[1]

The dilemma is effectively pressed home: and there is no doubt a strong temptation to relieve our minds of it by adopting the critical position, and accepting it as the business of our understanding and reason, in their empirical and scientific use, to systematise the phenomenal data of sense, and the business of the metaphysician merely to understand the way that the understanding and reason do this and must do it.

For from this point of view the dilemma vanishes. A merely phenomenal object must indeed be conceived as infinitely divisible, but this does not mean, in the case of the phenomenon, that it actually consists of parts infinite in number. For the parts of the phenomenal object do not exist as parts prior to our thinking them: they are constituted for our thought through our thinking them; in short, the phenomenal object is infinitely divisible but not infinitely divided. And this illustrates the general

[1] Watson's *Selections*, p. 160.

explanation which Kant gives of the *critical* solution of these antinomies: viz. that we have to conceive as merely regulative the idea of the reason, which demands completion in a rational process through a series of conditioned objects to an unconditioned—in this case demands that the series of parts of parts of parts of a material thing, each part being found by reflection to be necessarily composite, be brought to a termination somehow. In saying that we have to conceive the idea as merely regulative, I mean, as Kant says, that "the principle of reason serves as a rule which postulates what must take place, if we make the regress"—from the conditioned object or event to its condition, which we find also conditioned, and then to a further condition lying behind that and so on,—" but does not anticipate what is present before the regress is made, in the object as it is in itself."[1] For example, in the case we are contemplating the unsatisfiable demand of the uncritical reason for the unconditioned, for an absolutely partless atom of matter, becomes for the reason duly self-critical a postulate of infinite *divisibility*, which carefully avoids any affirmation of actual infinite dividedness. In this way it claims room for *any* degree of fineness of division, which Science, working on the data of sense, may find needful for a consistent theory of the phenomenal world: and at the same time shows us why we must not trouble ourselves, have no rational ground for troubling ourselves, with the question whether the smallest atom, which

[1] Watson's *Selections*, p. 174.

science requires to suppose, consists of parts and how these parts are to be conceived.

The escape thus offered from our dilemma is, as I said, certainly attractive. But the dilemma was not a new one: and Leibniz and Wolff had found a way out of it, which Kant does not *here* adequately deal with [1]—though what he would have said about it may be inferred from a general criticism of the Leibniz-Wolffian philosophy appended to the second part of his work. But we ought briefly to notice this other way out of the dilemma of the second antinomy, because it is perhaps the *only* other way out of it, if we insist, as Kant insists, that Reason is to answer somehow all the questions that Reason finds itself disposed to ask about the world—*i.e.* all the questions that refer to the possible and the necessary, for the actual could of course only be learnt in detail from experience. Briefly, the reason of Leibniz and Wolff found ultimately simple elements of the composite matter which experience presented: but the ultimates were unextended. "The elements," says Wolff, "of material things, are not extended, have no shape or size, and fill no space." The question of course arises: How then can they exist in Space, if they do not fill any part of it, and how can solid matter be composed of them? The answer that Leibniz and Wolff gave to this was that though the things which sense perceived as spatial were not ultimately phenomenal but real, their spatiality and

---

[1] He makes a contemptuous reference to the 'Monadists' in his remarks on the second Antithesis: but does not appear to me to deal adequately with their position. [Cf. M. Müller's translation, p. 381.]

continuous extension were phenomenal. Space as an object of the understanding was an order of coexistence of unextended entities, confusedly apprehended in external sense-perception, and its apparent homogeneous unbroken continuity is due to this confusion. For Wolff then externality or outsideness has two meanings, viz. (1) real externality as diversity or otherness of existence; and (2) spatial externality as the confused appearance of this. Real extension is the union, the coexistence as united, of a number of different things, which, as different from each other, are mutually external.[1] Our notion of pure space, however, as an extended continuous immovable entity, in which real things are and move, is imaginary: real space is the order of things coexisting, regarded as coexistent: but our imaginary notion of space may be usefully taken as representative of real space, when we are only considering and comparing bodies in respect of magnitude. Similarly, real time is the order of continuously successive things.

Now what is Kant's argument against this? We see at once that it seems to him a confusion between the thing as it is apart from our apprehension and the phenomenal thing. The thing in itself was rightly conceived as unextended, but the phenomenal thing must be conceived as extended, and Wolff's process from the composite to the simple appears to him to jump from the one to the other. But suppose Wolff were to answer: Certainly there is such a

[1] Wolff accordingly, as Kant after him, but with more systematic consistency, rejects the Idealism that denies all reality to the matter we perceive.

jump somewhere. Reason, arriving at the end of the regress from the composite empirical object to its ultimate element, has somewhere dropped the characteristics of continuous extension, size and shape. But that is because, in arriving at this conclusion, it has got out of the disturbing influence of sense. What would Kant have answered? I imagine he would have pointed to Geometry as a proof that the pure notion of space as continuous and extended was not confused but remarkably clear. I admit the force of this, but if it is admitted, is not the whole success of physical science in understanding the laws of the physical world similarly an argument against the complete phenomenality attributed by Kant to the empirical object?

Let us turn back now to the first antinomy. In the conflict that we have just discussed, the series of conditioned objects which Reason tries to carry in thought beyond experience to the unconditioned is a series of continual division and diminution—we try to pass from the thing made up of parts which themselves are made up of parts, to the ultimate element, whose existence is not conditioned by the prior existence of parts that make it up. In the conflict to which we now pass—and that Kant puts first—the series, on the contrary, is one of addition and enlargement. We find that the existences of which we have experience have things existing beyond them in space, and have had previous states of existence in time: and our Reason asks: When in thought we put these existences all together into a world, are we to conceive this world as unlimited or limited in extension and in past duration?

Now according to Kant we seem able to prove, with equal irresistibility, on the one hand that the world had a beginning in time and is limited in space, and on the other hand that the world had no beginning in time and has no limits in space. But, though the *conclusions* are thus symmetrically opposed, this is only partially the case with the reasonings: and it will conduce to clearness to take the question as to time apart from the question as to space.

One difference is that in the case of time, but not of space, theological considerations naturally come in. (And this is another reason why I took the second antinomy first: because of all the cosmological conflicts, it is the only one that can be quite separated from theology.) For traditional theology conceived the world as coming into existence through a creative act of God: and this, for ordinary thought, involved the conception of the Creator as existing before the creative act, and therefore of the world beginning in time. Again, the conception of the creative act as wise seemed to require, and experience seemed to confirm, the conception of the process of the world in time as not merely a process of change but a progress towards perfection: and this seemed to exclude the notion of an eternity already past in the process. Even Leibniz, the creator of the differential calculus, says "if the nature of things in the whole is to grow uniformly in perfection, the world of created things must have had a beginning."[1]

[1] Fifth Letter in the Correspondence with Clarke, § 74.

However, Kant's argument for the thesis that the world has had a beginning in Time, keeps clear of theology. It is, simply, that a series of changes at once past and infinite—a completed unending series, —is inconceivable. The series cannot be thought as both endless and over and done. I admit the difficulty of thinking this: but it seems to me to depend on the nature of time, and not on the nature of an infinite series—as Kant suggests. For I find no difficulty in the case of space in conceiving infinite extension—*e.g.* of a line—limited at one end: so far as I can think of infinity at all, I can conceive an infinite number of infinite lines in different directions starting from a given point in space. Nor, as we shall see, does Kant urge the inconceivability of a bounded infinite in spatial extension as a reason for regarding the world as limited in space. In the case, however, of space, I also find the argument for the thesis devoid of cogency.

Kant argues that if I think the world infinite in space, I must suppose "the successive synthesis of the parts of an infinite world to have been completed," and that "this is the same as saying that an infinite time must have elapsed during the summation of the totality of existing things," which "is impossible."[1] I deny this necessity. It is true that I cannot conceive myself as *experiencing* the boundlessness of space except in an infinite time: but I require no such time to negate the idea of a limit of space.

[1] Watson's *Selections*, p. 159.

LECTURE XI

THE 'DYNAMICAL' ANTINOMIES

WE come now to the two later Antinomies—or conflicts in which speculation is involved when it tries to pass through the series of conditioned objects or events, which experience as grasped by the understanding presents, to the unconditioned ultimate which seems needed to satisfy the reason. These Kant distinguishes as 'dynamical' from the two 'mathematical' antinomies which we considered last time.

But first, I must complete what I had to say on these earlier antinomies; and in so doing I shall point out a difficulty which attaches to Kant's separation between the two pairs. In examining the first pair, I inverted Kant's order. I did so for two reasons. First, in the metaphysical view which Kant is primarily assailing, the positive conclusion of the second antinomy is intimately connected with the conclusions of Rational Psychology. The simple subject of psychical predicates, the permanent thing with which the varying elements of psychical life were connected as attributes, was not, in the view of Leibniz and

LECT. XI THE 'DYNAMICAL' ANTINOMIES 163

Wolff, an entity disparate and to be kept apart in thought from the simple substances grasped by thought as the ultimate realities underlying empirical matter. On the contrary, the former was conceived so far as possible as analogous to the latter. I say 'so far as possible' because the extent of analogy varied: Wolff's common sense declined to follow Leibniz in attributing appetition and perception to the ultimates of inorganic matter. Still, for Wolff no less than for Leibniz, Minds took their place side by side with the elements of material things among the simple substances of which the world was composed.

Secondly—We have now to observe that the argument of the first antinomy, so far as it relates to the past duration of the world, is not in Kant's own treatment clearly separated from the argument of the third. This does not appear in the argument for the thesis—that the world has a beginning in time—which rests on the inconceivability of an endless series over and done. But the argument for the contradictory proposition (the antithesis) that the world cannot have begun in time appears to me not quite distinctly separated from the argument against an uncaused event in the third antinomy. For what Kant here argues is that "nothing can come into being in an empty time, because no part of an empty time has in it any *condition* decisive of existence rather than non-existence, which distinguishes it from any other part."[1] That is to say, he seems to argue that nothing can come into

[1] Watson's *Selections*, p. 158 *fin.*

being in empty time, because there can be no *cause* for its coming into being at one time rather than another. But this seems to assume that it cannot come into being through the *free*, uncaused volition of the Creator: that is, it assumes the question argued in the third antinomy. Now if we keep the questions distinct—as the articulation of Kant's system certainly seems to require—the argument must take a somewhat different form; and I cannot find any form in which it appears conclusive.

It may be said—as Leibniz urges against Clarke [1] —that if we are to conceive the world as beginning in time we must conceive it beginning at some definite point of hitherto empty time, and that this is impossible, because there is nothing in empty time to distinguish one point of time from another. But the first premise cannot be granted: the conception of the beginning of the world in time does not necessarily involve a dating of the beginning in relation to empty time. It is quite sufficient if we date it in reference to the time with which we are familiar. Suppose the process of the physical world is like that of a clock running down: and that physicists could time it so exactly as to know that a hundred millions of years ago some initial event must have occurred analogous to the winding up of the clock. We can obviously conceive this initial event to have occurred a hundred millions of years ago, and to have begun the particular process in which we now are, without defining further its relation to antecedent time: and

[1] Fifth Letter, §§ 55, 56.

if we can do this as regards this relative beginning, I do not see—apart from the *causal* difficulties connected with beginning—why we cannot similarly conceive an absolute beginning of the world, without dating it in reference to pre-mundane time. I think, therefore, that the argument for the antithesis in the first antinomy, if rigidly separated from the argument of the third, lacks cogency.

And the same may be said of the similar argument as regards limits in space. Kant argues that a bounded world in an unbounded space must be related to empty space, and that there is nothing in empty space to relate it to, no means of distinguishing one part of space from another. I quite admit that we cannot assign to the world a definite position in space, and that such questions as Where is it in space: is it moving or at rest? are questions to which we can conceive no answer having any relation to possible experience. But I do not think that this applies to the mere question whether it has or has not limits: we can conceive it limited, and therefore having empty space beyond it, without raising the question where it is in space.

I have said that the argument of the first antinomy, so far as it relates to the past duration of the world, is not, in Kant's own treatment, clearly separated from the argument of the third. I must now point out that it is hardly possible to separate the two questions, so long as we accept the principle of causality with the interpretation which Kant has given to it in the second part of the treatise. For if every event must have a cause, *i.e.* an antecedent event after which it must come—and if, as Kant has argued, we cannot conceive an event as objective and therefore happening at a fixed point of time, without conceiving it as in this sense caused—then we clearly cannot ask whether the world has had a beginning in time, without seeing at once that an affirmative answer brings us into conflict with the principle of causality.

Why, then, does Kant separate the two questions so decisively in his arrangement, if not in his argument? Partly, I think, on account of the entirely different *answers* which his philosophy leads him to give to them. The same confusion of thought between empirical or phenomenal objects, and things as they exist independently of human perception, occurs in all the antinomies: but the confusion leads to quite different results in the case of the first pair and the second pair respectively.

In the case of the two first antinomies the apparently contradictory conclusions are found to be both false, when we get rid of the confusion of thought which has led to them. They are false equally—though for different reasons—whether we regard the conclusions as relating to the phenomenal world or to the world of independent realities. If I inquire about the extension in space or duration in time of the phenomenal world (the world constituted by putting together the objects of sensible experience), it is, Kant says, "equally impossible to declare it infinite or to declare it finite"; because "experience either of an *infinite* space or of an infinite time elapsed, or, again, of the *limitation* of the world by a void space or antecedent void time, is impossible."[1] Similarly, it is false to say of phenomenal matter—matter as an empirical object—*either* that it actually consists of an infinite number of parts, or of a finite number of indivisible parts. What we ought to conclude, according to the Critical Philosophy, is (1) that the magnitude of the world may be extended indefinitely in space and time, so far as we have empirical grounds for conceiving it extended : it can never be a rational objection to any physical hypothesis adequately supported on other grounds, that it requires too much time or too much space. And similarly (2) that any given quantity of matter is indefinitely divisible, though not infinitely divided : we may assume molecules or atoms as small as we please, so far as we have scientific grounds for assuming them. In short, the true Metaphysics, according to Kant, gives Physical Science a licence to assume the material world as large and the parts of matter as small as it likes, on the simple conditions of calling the world phenomenal and never pretending to have reached a maximum or a minimum. As we saw, Kant does not maintain that Physical Science *required* the licence; and, in fact, it is pretty certain that it would go on just the same, if the licence were not granted. But the vogue of Kantism is partly due to the fact that many students of physical science, with a philosophical turn, have considered

[1] *Prolegomena*, § 52 c, Mahaffy, p. 137.

the licence cheap at the price, and accepted the terms. So much for the solution of the mathematical antinomies.

But in the case of the dynamical antinomies, though the fundamental confusion from which the apparent contradictions spring is the same, the solution is of an opposite kind. When the questions are raised (1) whether or not there is a 'free causality,' besides the natural causality (interpreted as necessary sequence); and (2) whether or not there is a necessary being, the affirmative and negative answers are, when the confusion between phenomenon and independent reality is removed, found to be both possibly true. That is to say, if we take the 'cause' to be a *phenomenal* cause—an event in time—then we can admit no other kind of causality. For even extending the notion of 'cause' to the phenomenal thing that is conceived as 'agent' or 'efficient,' it still must remain true, as Kant says, that "the determination of the cause to act must have originated among phenomena, and must consequently, as well as its effect, be an event which must again have its cause, and so on: hence natural necessity must be the condition on which efficient causes, so far as phenomena, are determined."[1]

Thus the conclusion of the antithesis "that all that comes to be in the world takes place entirely in accordance with the laws of Nature"[2] is true, if the world be understood as phenomenal. But at the

---
[1] *Prolegomena*, § 52 c, Mahaffy, p. 140.
[2] [Watson's *Selections*, p. 162 *fin.*]

same time the argument of the thesis that the phenomenal world as an effect is not adequately accounted for by an endless series of causes which must themselves be regarded as effects, is not answered. We may, however, find the answer in the relation between phenomena and things *per se*—when we have once clearly distinguished the two: and there is nothing to prevent us from applying to this relation the conception of Freedom. Thus, as Kant says: "Nature and Freedom can without contradiction be attributed to the very same thing but in different relations, on one side as a phenomenon, on the other as a thing *per se*."[1] Observe that Kant does not affirm that we *must* attribute free causality to the thing *per se*, just as we must think all the changes in phenomenal objects as necessary consequences of antecedent changes. All that he regards as established by the critical solution of the antinomy in which the Speculative Reason is involved by trying to reach through the series of conditioned causes a cause that is unconditioned and not in turn an effect, is (1) that the principle of Natural Causality cannot completely satisfy our demand for an adequate cause of the phenomenal world; and (2) that there is no reason why free causality should not be attributed to a 'thing in itself,' if we have other grounds for attributing it. Now in the case of human beings he holds that our moral consciousness gives us practical grounds for attributing to ourselves such free causality: that

[1] *Prolegomena*, § 53, Mahaffy, p. 141.

our apparent cognition that something in the eye of reason 'ought to be' necessitates the assumption that what ought to be can be, and that reason therefore can have causality in respect to phenomena.

This part of Kant's doctrine, so far as it relates to human freedom, I have already examined in a lecture of the ethical course.[1] Here I have only to point out that we must distinguish the 'practical freedom' which rests on ethical data, from the 'transcendental freedom,' or 'freedom, in the cosmological sense,' by which, as Kant explains, is merely meant 'the faculty' or 'power' of 'beginning a state spontaneously'[2]—a kind of causality which is not subject to the necessity imposed by the principle of natural causality on all phenomenal causes : *i.e.* of being also effects.

I have said that Kant's critical explanation, distinguishing phenomena from extra-empirical or transcendental realities, shows both affirmative and negative answers to the third—and fourth—Antinomy to be *possibly* true. He does not intend to prove the actual *truth* of both the [seemingly] contradictory conclusions. With regard to freedom this is most emphatically stated. "We have had no intention of proving that there *actually* is freedom, and that it is one of the faculties which contain the cause of the phenomena of our world of sense. . . . All that we have been able, or wished, to prove is that nature does not contradict the causality of freedom."[3] The

---

[1] [Cf. *Methods of Ethics*, 6th edn. Bk. i. chap. v., and App.]
[2] Das Vermögen, einen Zustand von *selbst* anzufangen. Cf. Watson's *Selections*, p. 182.   [3] Watson's *Selections*, p. 190 *fin.*

critical solution therefore does not treat the thesis and the antithesis similarly. When the confusion between the phenomenon and the thing in itself is done away with, the argument and conclusion of the antithesis are completely validated so far as phenomena are concerned: it is entirely true that "all that we conceive to happen in the phenomenal world we must conceive as entirely conformed to the law of natural causality." But the argument and conclusion of the thesis are not similarly affirmed as valid with regard to the real world. The critical philosophy does not warrant us—so far as the cosmological argument goes—in laying down that there *must* be a free causality attaching to, exercised by, things in themselves; but only that there may be. This 'lopsided' result is quite natural: since in Kant's view our faculties are made to know phenomena and are not made to know things in themselves.

But the question still may be raised, Is not the negative argument in favour of the thesis still valid, in a sense? Does it not remain true that 'natural causality' does not afford a complete explanation of phenomena? and if so, must we not find that explanation in the realities of which the objects of experience are the phenomena? Yes, answers Kant, "phenomena must have their source in that which is not a phenomenon."[1] That step beyond experience Kant definitely affirms. There must be Reality if

---

[1] [Watson's *Selections*, p. 184. Kant, however, says not 'source' but 'grounds.']

there are Appearances: and in Reality, if we only knew it, we should find the explanation of experience. But we cannot know it, and therefore can form no positive conception of the explanation. The world is rational: but not for us: it is not theoretically knowable as such.

We have now to observe a flaw in the symmetry of Kant's system. His interest in the question of human freedom has led him to make the freedom of *man* prominent in the discussion of the third antinomy. But the kind of Transcendental Freedom which the argument for the thesis naturally suggests is not human freedom, an uncaused beginning of the various particular series of effects that we attribute to human volition: but an uncaused beginning of the whole complex process of cosmical change. Human freedom is certainly not enough, as the effort to find an unconditioned cause to explain Nature can certainly not be satisfied by finding a free causality for human volition. And since, in Kant's view—by the application of the category that he calls 'community'—the whole aggregate of empirical objects that make up the physical world must be conceived as connected by actions and reactions, reciprocally determining each other's changes, the complex of natural change has to be thought as one connected whole. Hence a spontaneous causality adequate to satisfy the demand of Reason, and enable us to think the regressive series of natural causes as a completed whole, must, it would seem, be a single causality for the whole united complex of change. But a causality of this scope and extent would seem to be indistinguishable from the Divine creative act to which traditional theology referred the origin of Nature as a whole. Hence the Transcendental Freedom of an unknown reality, which the critical solution of this conflict maintains to be possible, though not actual, would seem to be Divine Freedom. And if we admit Divine Freedom: *i.e.* a Primal Being outside the world, to whom the whole series of phenomena connected by natural necessity may be referred as transcendental cause, then human freedom is, from a cosmological point of view, superfluous. I think Kant would have made this more plain: only that (1) the problem of human freedom has a special interest for him, from its fundamental importance for the ethical basis on which his theology ultimately rests; and (2) the articulation of his system prompts him to separate as much as possible the cosmological ideas of Reason from the theological. But the separation is forced: and this is also true of the fourth Antinomy, to which I now pass.[1]

When, however, we compare the argument for the thesis in this case, with that of the thesis of the preceding antinomy, it seems at first sight as if the same series of conditioned events were pursued by Reason to diverse conclusions in the two cases respectively. For in either case it is, apparently, the series of causally connected changes in the empirical world that Reason is tracing back: but in

[1] Watson's *Selections*, p. 165.

the third antinomy, the difficulty of finding completion in the series of natural causes is held to drive the Reason to the supposition of an absolutely free causality, in the fourth the same line of thought is supposed to drive the Reason to the assumption of an absolutely necessary Being.

In short, it would seem that, if Kant's system had only permitted, he might have represented the thesis of the third and that of the fourth antinomy as together forming a single antinomy, of which the two conflicting conclusions were the affirmations of Freedom and Necessity. Reference, however, to the solution of the fourth antinomy shows that there is in Kant's view a difference in the lines of thought pursued in arguing the third and fourth thesis respectively, which he certainly has not clearly expressed in expounding the antinomies. "In what immediately precedes," he says, "we have considered the changes of the world of sense in their dynamical series—a series each member of which stands under another as its cause. We shall now take this series of states as our guide in the search for an existence that may serve as the supreme condition of all that changes; that is, in our search for the *necessary being*. Here we have to deal not with an unconditioned causality, but with the unconditioned existence of substance itself."[1] That is, in the third antinomy attention is fixed on the changes in empirical things; in the fourth, on the changing things.

The reason why the two arguments look so much

[1] Watson's *Selections*, p. 191.

alike is that, in Kant's view, the 'contingency' of the empirical thing seems to depend on its changeability. He says: "It is easy to see that, as every object in the totality of phenomena is changeable, and therefore is conditioned in its existence, no member of the series of dependent existence can possibly be unconditioned: in other words, we cannot regard the existence of any member of the series as absolutely necessary."[1] It is because it is changeable that it is 'conditioned in its existence,' and therefore, however far back we retrace in thought the existence of phenomenal things, we cannot find necessity: though, when we have clearly distinguished phenomena from things in themselves, the existence of such a necessary Being is seen to be possible, but only as an 'extra-mundane being' entirely outside the series of the sensible world.

I think, however, that Kant is wrong in thus connecting the contingency of the things that constitute the sensible world, as ordinarily conceived, with its mutability. To show this, suppose we assume—what we ordinarily do assume in trying to conceive physical and chemical changes—that the ultimate parts of matter only change in their relations to other parts, and remain in other respects unchanged. Kant must admit this conception, according to the 'first analogy of experience': viz. that 'Substance is permanent and its *quantum* in nature neither increases nor decreases.' Then let us trace back in thought the changes in the physical world-processes:

[1] Watson's *Selections*, p. 191.

at any point at which we stop, the positions in which we leave the ultimate parts of matter seem to us no less arbitrary and contingent than the positions in which we now find them. That is, we see no reason why their collocation in space should not have been different.

But, it may be asked, with regard either to my supposition or Kant's, how does the introduction of a Necessary Being help the matter? For if we conceive it in time, as the argument for the thesis contends,[1] we have still to understand *how* a Necessary Being in time can be the cause of a contingent: and I know no way in which this transition can be made to appear rational, nor does Kant's argument suggest any. But again, if we take the critical solution, and suppose the necessary, uncaused Being, out of time, the difficulty still remains: how comes a Necessary Being to cause a contingent being? It seems to me impossible to conceive the contingent as the necessary consequence of the necessary.

I draw attention to this difficulty, because it appears to me that the solution of the third antinomy has to be combined with that of the fourth, in order to afford to the Speculative Reason that moderate amount of satisfaction which is all that the critical philosophy professes to afford to it. That is, we have to suppose, in order to explain the series of the sensible world—whether we regard that as a series of changes or a series of changing and contingent

[1] "The causality of the necessary cause of the changes, and *therefore also the cause itself*, must belong to time and to phenomena in time."—Watson's *Selections*, p. 166.

existences — not only a transcendental and free causality, but also a necessary Being to which this free causality is attributed. We have to suppose this, in the case of the third antinomy no less than in that of the fourth; for the transcendental causality which is supposed to explain the series of natural phenomena must be the causality *of* something: and if the being that exercises it is not conceived as necessary and therefore uncaused, its existence will require a cause no less than the series of phenomenal existence.

It may be said, that on the principles of the Critical Philosophy, we cannot thus apply the conception of causal dependence to things in themselves, since that conception has only a legitimate application to empirical objects. I admit the force of the argument: and can only answer that Kant repeatedly applies it so himself.[1] Further, if the Critical Philosophy rigidly abstains from this extended application of the category of Causality, its so-called critical solution of the conflicts of reason becomes illusory. That is, it amounts only to saying that besides the necessary sequence of natural or phenomenal causality, by which we can never really explain any phenomenal effect, because the series cannot be completed, we may also suppose an unknown relation to an

---

[1] For example, his refutation of Idealism (as expounded in the *Prolegomena*, § 13, Remark ii. Mahaffy, pp. 53 ff.) involves this 'transcendent' application of the notion of cause. And also expressly his solution of the third antinomy: "phenomena must have their source in that which is not a phenomenon." [Watson's *Selections*, p. 184. For a fuller discussion of this topic by Professor Sidgwick the reader is referred to *Mind*, O.S. iv. pp. 408 ff.; v. pp. 111 ff.]

unknown entity which is not a phenomenon, which *might* afford the required explanation if we only knew it. Surely, having got so far towards Agnosticism, it would be simpler to say that we might be able to give a satisfactory answer to the question of Reason, if we only knew more: but that is an attitude towards the unsolved problems and unreconciled contradictions of thought which it does not require the elaborate apparatus of the Critical Philosophy to adopt.

In any case, it is evident from Kant's solutions that he has theology within his purview in both these later antinomies, though he tries to keep it in the background as far as possible. It is, in fact, to the Divine Being and the Divine Causality of traditional theology that the solutions of both Antinomies really lead us: though in the case of the third this result is obscured by the prominence of the question of *human* freedom. In any case, it is a very narrow and restricted conception of the Divine Being and Causality to which this general cosmological consideration of the empirical world seems to lead. To the fuller view of the Divine Nature and Causality, which since Descartes had occupied a permanent and prominent place in modern philosophy—though undergoing important changes—we have now to turn.

LECTURE XII

RATIONAL THEOLOGY

WE now come to the last part of Kant's attack on the illusory metaphysics which his Criticism aims at destroying—the examination of Rational Theology. We may confidently say that for Kant as a man—and the man in Kant is never lost in the philosopher—this is the most important part of his destructive work: and in considering it, we must always bear in mind that the destruction is intended to clear the ground for construction. For, in Kant's view, the belief in God is absolutely indispensable to morality, rational human action is impossible without it. This he declares, with uncompromising emphasis, in a chapter near the end of the *Critique*—called 'The Canon of Pure Reason'—in which he deals with the relation of the practical to the speculative reason. "Without a God," he says, "and without a world not visible to us now but hoped for, the glorious ideas of morality are indeed objects of applause and admiration, but not *springs of purpose and action.*"[1] In each, indeed, of the three branches of illusory meta-

[1] [M. Müller's trans. p. 697.]

physics against which the three parts of his Transcendental Dialectic are respectively directed, Kant finds that practical interests have been predominant in stimulating the effort to obtain, and supporting the illusion of having obtained, knowledge transcending experience. "The highest aim," he says, "to which the speculation of Reason in its transcendental employment is directed, comprehends three objects: the freedom of the will, the immortality of the soul, and the existence of God."[1] Accordingly, when he is discussing the doctrine of Rational Psychologists, as to the substantial simplicity of the Ego, he knows that what they and he are interested in is the possibility of proving the immortality of the soul: similarly, in dealing with the conflicts to which cosmological ideas lead, his long digression on human free-will—which is, as I said, somewhat misleading as regards the conclusion of the speculative argument against the sufficiency of natural causality—shows again the predominance of Kant's practical interests. And this is very clearly expressed, as regards the whole of the antinomies, in a section on the "Interest of Reason in these Conflicts," in which he sums up separately the propositions of the theses in each of the four cases of conflict, and the propositions of the antitheses. In the case of the latter there seems to him a "perfect uniformity in the mode of thought and a complete unity of principle, namely, the principle of pure Empiricism, not only in the explanation of the phenomena in the world, but also in the

[1] [*Critique of Pure Reason*, Max Müller's trans. p. 684.]

solution of the transcendental ideas of the world as a whole."[1] These antitheses were, it will be remembered: "That the world had no beginning in time and has no limits in space: that there is no such thing in the world as an absolutely simple, partless substance: that all that happens takes place in accordance with natural causality, so that there is no freedom: and that there is no absolutely necessary being either in the world or outside of it." This is Kant's idea of pure Empiricism. It will be seen at once that the Empiricism with which we are familiar is decidedly purer. Our Empiricism, indeed, would make substantially the same answers to the two last questions, though in a somewhat different form. It would affirm that experience gave no ground for regarding human volition as an exception to the general law—itself only an empirical generalisation —of uniformity and sequence in natural phenomena; and that similarly experience gave no ground for regarding any thing or event, in the world or out of it, as absolutely necessary. But of beginnings of the physical world in time, limits in space, and indivisible substances, our pure Empiricism would simply say nothing, having no empirical grounds for forming any conclusion, positive or negative.[2]

However, the 'practical interest' of which I am now speaking is, as Kant says, on the side of the theses; which, put together, form the view that he calls Dogmatism. I give it in his words. "That

[1] [*Critique*, M. Müller's trans. p. 406.]
[2] This is why English Empiricism fitted in so easily with the Critical Solution.

the world has a beginning: that my thinking self is of a simple and therefore indestructible nature: that the same self is free in all his voluntary actions, and raised above the constraint of natural causality: that, finally, the whole order of the things, which make up the world, is derived from an original being from which all receives its unity and purposive connection —these are so many foundation stones of morality and religion."[1]

Here are two points to notice: first, how theology, kept as much as possible in the background when Kant is *arguing* the cosmological antinomies, comes to the front when we consider the practical aim of the theses. Creation by God was what the first meant to establish; a Creative God is the necessary Being of the fourth; the two intermediate yield the Immortality and Freedom which seemed indispensable to the moral government by God of the human world. Creation as a temporal event, and the natural indestructibility of human souls, the critical solution has to throw over; for when the distinction between phenomena and things in themselves is clearly apprehended, the supposed cosmological proof of them is seen to be illusory. But for Freedom and God and Creation non-temporally conceived, the critical solution finds a place, though it does not profess to prove them: the adequate proof of them—or rather the demonstration of their necessity as practical postulates—must rest on ethical considerations.

My second point is an incidental illustration of

[1] *Critique*, M. Müller's trans. p. 406.

the occasionally forced character of Kant's system-making. I noticed before how his separation of Rational Psychology from Rational Cosmology led him to ignore the close connexion, in the metaphysical view that he is describing, between the substantial simplicity of the soul and the simplicity of the real substances which Leibniz and Wolff held to underlie empirical matter. Owing to this separation, he ignores the Soul altogether in his *cosmological* discussion of the idea of simple substances. Yet here, in summing the theses as Dogmatism, he seems to regard the simplicity and indestructibility of the thinking self as *the* question at issue in the second Antinomy. And, in fact, it *was* the question of practical interest: but it is startling to find how entirely Kant seems to forget that he has carefully kept it out of the Cosmological discussion.

But however much theology and morality are really in the philosopher's mind in dealing with Rational Psychology and Cosmology, still, in these parts of the discussion, the relation of the ideas of the Reason to the concepts and principles of empirical science necessarily occupied his first attention. Whereas in the part to which we now pass in considering the conception and arguments of Rational Theology, we are from first to last beyond the range of empirical science: and here for Kant the sole important question is, Can the theorising reason of man prove, what a rational man, who has to act in the world no less than to know it as completely as possible, must believe? But, though this is for Kant the main issue at stake, his discussion begins a long way off it. The reason is that the metaphysical idea of God—especially in the form in which the latest system, Wolff's, presented it—though intended to support and blend with the traditional theological idea—was materially different from it in its metaphysical construction and aspect; at any rate, in the aspect that it assumed for the metaphysician, when he tried to demonstrate its validity.

To get familiar with this idea, and understand Kant's treatment of it, it will be well briefly to trace its development through Descartes, Leibniz, and Wolff—the three thinkers whom, as I before said, Kant has chiefly before his mind in his assault on illusory metaphysics. Descartes' exposition of the idea of God is, in the final and most systematic statement of his philosophy (*Principia Philosophiae*), bound up with his famous proof of the existence of God—that which Kant attacks as the 'Ontological proof'—a line of argument derived from mediæval thought.[1] The point is, to put it as logically as may be, that the proposition *God does not exist* necessarily contains a contradiction in terms, when we have defined God as a supremely perfect being: because a non-existent God is a supremely perfect being without a certain perfection (viz. existence), and is therefore a contradictory conception.

Leibniz criticises this proof as formally insufficient. Descartes has not proved that the idea of a most

[1] Cf. Descartes' *Principles of Philosophy*, i. § 14, Veitch's ed. p. 199. The argument, however, is perhaps made more clear in the Fifth Meditation (Veitch, pp. 145, 146).

perfect being is not self-contradictory, or, to put it otherwise, that the existence of God so defined is possible. The two propositions are mutually inferrible according to the assumption of Leibniz—also implicitly made by Descartes—as to the relation of thought to reality: what can be thought without contradiction is in reality possible, though not therefore actual. He agrees, however, with Descartes in holding it to be a unique characteristic of the idea of God, that to prove God possible is to prove that he exists. And he holds further that this proof can be given: and so adopts Descartes' demonstration as substantially valid though formally incomplete.

Proof is wanted, beyond the mere finding of the idea in our minds: for we are liable to find in our minds ideas of which the elements seem at first sight harmonious, but prove to be really incompatible. Thus a man might say that he had in his mind the ideas of a 'greatest possible number' and a 'swiftest possible motion': but 'greatest possible,' says Leibniz, is really incompatible with the idea of number and 'swiftest possible' is really incompatible with the idea of motion. For we can always conceive a number greater than any assigned number, and a velocity greater than that of any definitely conceived swift motion.

Proof is wanted, then, of the real conceivability of the idea of God: but proof, Leibniz thinks, can be simply and briefly given. The proof puts in a more precise and logical form what is more vaguely suggested by Descartes' words that "the infinite perfections of God are conceived more clearly and distinctly than material objects, being simple and unobscured by limits."[1] As put by Leibniz the proof is as follows :—

The conception of God, the primal being and source of all other being, contains all reality or positive quality without limitation. Imperfection always involves limitation of some kind, and limitation imperfection: so limitation of all kinds must be excluded. That is, there are no negative attributes: not-A, whatever positive quality A may be taken to mean, cannot possibly be predicated of God. Hence the conception cannot be self-contradictory: for contradiction when made explicit must appear as negation. God, therefore, as the Being in whom all infinite reality is included, is possible, because the conception does not involve a contradiction; and therefore, as Descartes argues, God must exist; for existence is included in the notion of all reality.

Similarly Wolff, who adopts the argument of Descartes with Leibniz's addition: introducing, however, a careful definition of 'reality' so as to distinguish it from phenomenon. His argument runs: —The most perfect—or most real—Being is the sum of all realities, taken without limitation. This Being is possible, because no element of the concept can negate or contradict any other: and being possible it must exist, because existence, whether necessary or contingent, is Reality and not phenomenon.

[1] *Principles of Philosophy*, i. § 19, Veitch, p. 201. In the Reply to the Second Objection to his *Meditations*, Descartes is more precise (cf. *Œuvres de Descartes*, par L. Aimé-Martin, p. 117).

This, then, is the conception of God which Kant calls the Transcendental Ideal. Before discussing the metaphysical proofs of the existence of God, so conceived, he connects the idea, in an ingenious and original way—which, as a bit of system-making, must be called brilliant—with the logical form of disjunctive reasoning, as the ideas of Rational Psychology and Cosmology were connected respectively with the categorical and hypothetical forms of reasoning. In exhibiting this connexion, he passes from the *real*, empirically real, determination of things in time and space, by their necessary connexion with antecedent and coexistent things and events, to consider the *logical* or conceptual determination of an *individual* thing as such. Every individual thing, as we conceive it to exist, must be thought as having or not having each one of all possible predicates: by the logical law of the excluded middle we must be able to predicate of it that it is either A or not-A, either B or not-B, etc.: if we do not know whether it is A or not-A, we do not know it completely: the determinateness of our thought is not adequate to the determinateness of its existence. In other words, if we could apply to it in thought all possible predicates, by a series of disjunctive syllogisms—and only so— our thought of it would be completely determinate: but this complete determination is a mere idea of the reason, which cannot be completely carried out in our thought of any empirical thing, since we do not know all possible predicates. Now, in this idea of complete determination is involved, as we have seen, the idea of a sum of all possible predicates: and if, examining this idea closer, we exclude from this all that is derivative and therefore negative or limitative notions, which must be derived from the corresponding positive, we get the notion of a sum of all possible positive simple predicates. And this—in accordance with the reasoning just given—gives us a completely determined thought, the thought of an individual being, including all reality. And as the thought of any finite being is, so to say, logically made out of this 'Ens Realissimum' by negation and limitation—this Ens Realissimum comes to be thought as the Primary Being from which all finite beings are derived, the Supreme Being to which all else is subordinate. Thus, according to Kant, the Transcendental Ideal becomes the God of the Dogmatic Metaphysician.

But how does the Metaphysician prove its existence? By different methods, one of which, the Ontological Proof, argues that the predicate existence cannot be denied of the subject 'Ens Realissimum' without a contradiction. This I have already explained. But the natural course of Reason is rather that which Kant distinguishes as the Cosmological Proof: that is to say, we reason from the finite and contingent existence, of which we have experience, to the existence of an absolutely necessary Being, which we identify with the Ens Realissimum, the primal Being that contains all reality, from which all that is finite must, we think, be derived.

In this procedure, it will be observed, we abstract from all characteristics of empirical objects except their finite and contingent existence. This cosmological proof has therefore to be distinguished from the physico-theological, in which the inference is from the design and purpose manifest in the world to a Designing Intelligence as its cause.

The Physico-theological proof, says Kant, "will always deserve to be mentioned with respect. It is the oldest, the clearest, and the simplest of all, and it imparts life to the study of nature."[1] On the other hand, in the cosmological proof he finds so many fallacies brought together "that it really seems as if speculative reason had exhausted its dialectical skill in producing the greatest possible transcendental illusion."[2] But neither proof, in his view, is really independent of the ontological proof. In fact, according to Kant, if you arrange the three proofs in order, beginning with the most popular, which is the physico-theological, we shall find — in his view — that the physico-theological has, when we press it closely, to fall back on the cosmological, and similarly the cosmological has to fall back on the ontological.

Let us trace the process by which the reasoner, endeavouring to prove the existence of God by Reason apart from Revelation, finds himself, according to Kant, irresistibly driven back upon the highly abstract metaphysical argument which I before explained. He begins with the argument from design.[3] A man finds a watch and he infers a watchmaker: he finds a world exhibiting manifest marks of a vast and complex

---

[1] [*Critique*, M. Müller's trans. p. 535.]
[2] [*Op. cit.* p. 530.]   [3] Cf. Watson's *Selections*, pp. 219 ff.

adaptation of means to a definite end: the more he knows of the natures of finite things and the uniformities of their behaviour, the more difficult it seems to regard this adaptation as the unpurposed result of natural laws. He cannot but refer the unmistakably planned result to designing intelligence: he cannot but infer from the systematic unity of the plan the unity of the intelligent cause. But, granting all this, the argument proves, as Kant says, an Architect, not a Creator of the world: it is the origin of the form and order in the physical world that it explains, not the origin of its matter or substance. For in the human adaptation of means to ends on which the argument rests, the matter is always *given* to the designing mind, not *made* by it: not an atom of the material of the watch derives its existence from the watchmaker. To justify us in conceiving the matter of the world as created by God, we have to introduce a new argument: we have to fall back on the *contingency* of every finite thing and all finite things. The physical world, in all its parts and all stages of its process, presents itself to our thought as something that might have been otherwise, *i.e.* granting that we find necessary connexions in the coexistence and sequence of its parts, the necessity thus found is always a conditioned necessity and leaves the whole still contingent; our reason therefore still demands a cause why the whole physical world and its history is and has been what it is and has been. Even if, under the guidance of speculative astronomy and physics, we suppose our world and planetary system as it is to be the necessary result of the nature and collocation of material particles in an original nebula, that nature and collocation still present themselves to thought as no less contingent and arbitrary than the particularities of our actual globe and planetary system. Our reason must still seek for an explanation, a cause of this contingency and particularity: and we can only find it in a necessary being, something of which we cannot think that it might have been otherwise, because it is inconceivable that it should not exist as we conceive it. And this necessary being must be the Ens Realissimum: for we must conceive it as completely determined from a logical point of view: *i.e.* it must be either A or not-A, B or not-B, and so on through the whole series of possible predicates, and in each case we must think it as having the positive predicate—for if any real positive quality were denied of it, the manifestation of that quality in the world of finite things would remain unexplained.

Now we already know from the fourth antinomy that Kant cannot regard this line of argument as valid: the solution of the fourth antinomy was that while nothing in the world of phenomena can be thought as unconditionally necessary, there *may* be an absolutely necessary Being in the world of things as they are apart from our sense-perceptions; but we cannot affirm that there must be: our ignorance of things in themselves is too complete to allow of this assertion. But, even if we grant the inference from the contingent to the necessary, he holds that our reason cannot identify this necessary being with the Ens Realissimum, unless we can prove in some other way that the Ens Realissimum must necessarily be. For, without this, we cannot be certain *a priori* that the existence of finite things *may* not be unconditionally necessary, although we could not infer this necessity from our conception of finite things. Thus the cosmological proof, when strictly examined, is found to require the ontological proof for its validity. Here, then, lies the final and central issue for rational or speculative theology. Is this proof cogent?

Well, allow me to suspend for a moment this great question, and answer a somewhat easier one: Is Kant's argument against it, which appears to have convinced many generations of thoughtful persons, itself cogent? To give it in Kant's words. "If," he says, "I take the term God, and say, *there is a God*, I do not enlarge the conception of God by a new predicate, I merely *posit* the subject itself with all its predicates, as an object corresponding to my conception. The content of the object and of my conception must be precisely the same: the real contains no more than the possible. A hundred real dollars do not contain a halfpenny more than a hundred possible dollars:— If the object contained more than the conception, the conception would not express the whole object, and would therefore be an inadequate conception."[1]

I have tried, by selection of phrases, to put the argument as plausibly as possible: I must regard

---

[1] Cf. Watson's *Selections*, pp. 208 f. [The translation is amended.]

it as plausible, as it has satisfied so many people.
But I confess it seems to me to involve an intolerable
paradox. That my conception of anything—say 100
dollars—which I do not think as actually existing
is precisely the same as my conception of it as
actually existing seems to me quite unthinkable.
Kant says that 100 real dollars do not contain a
halfpenny more than 100 dollars not thought as
existent: but the remark seems to me an unconsciously crafty suggestion to throw the reader's mind
on a wrong track. Certainly the difference is nothing
like a halfpenny: the question is whether it *may*
not amount to 100 dollars! Look at it thus. If
the predication of existence makes no difference to
the conception, it must be equally true that the
predication of non-existence makes no difference
to it: therefore there can be no difference between
the thought of a hundred dollars as non-existent
and the thought of a hundred dollars as existent.
Is it not, on the contrary, palpable that there is just
a hundred dollars difference? It is not, therefore,
because the conception of a thing as existing is not
different from the conception of a thing precisely
similar but not thought to exist, that I fail to find
cogency in the Ontological proof: but rather because
the two conceptions seem to me not only distinguishable, but when distinguished equally possible, in the
case of the Ens Realissimum, no less than in the case
of other objects. So far as I am able at all to
conceive an individual being having all positive
predicates, I am able to conceive it as including all

o

positive predicates except existence: and when I have so conceived it, I am conscious of no rational necessity compelling me to add the predicate of existence rather than the predicate of non-existence. The proposition that the Ens Realissimum thus conceived exists seems to me no more necessarily true than the proposition that it does not exist,— so long as I try to settle the question by mere reflection on my abstract ideas.

But I have a prior difficulty, as regards the formation of the notion of an Ens Realissimum: viz. I do not know that all positive predicates are really compatible, as attributes of the same being. For this is certainly not the case as regards objects of empirical thought: positive predicates are frequently incompatible, as straight and curved of a line, square and round of a figure, blue and yellow of the same surface.[1]

And this is especially important, when I consider that this notion of Ens Realissimum is to be identified with the theological notion of God, and to have all the moral attributes of Deity. For thus viewed, we see that the assumption of the compatibility of all positive predicates, made in the formation of this transcendental Ideal, requires us to hold—what Leibniz, of course, did hold—that 'Evil' moral and physical is a merely negative attribute. But I can see no reason to suppose this. Physical

---

[1] Wolff's exclusion of 'phenomena' is meant to get rid of these analogies; but I do not know that the same incompatibility is not true of the qualities without limit attributed to the Ens Realissimum.

pain seems to me as positive as pleasure: and, though much moral evil is no doubt analysable into mere *defects* or negations of positive quality, I do not find this conceivable in all cases, as, for example, in the case of pure malevolence.

APPENDIX TO LECTURE XII

INFINITE AND ABSOLUTE OR UNCONDITIONED
(INFINITE-ABSOLUTE)

THESE terms for nearly half a century—second and third quarter of the nineteenth century—were leading terms in English metaphysical controversy. The period begins with Hamilton's article on the "Philosophy of the Unconditioned,"[1] and it may perhaps be taken to end gradually with the decline of the influence of Mill and Spencer on English metaphysical thought, which I place about forty years later, attributing it primarily to the teaching of Caird and Green.

In the current controversy between Empiricism and Transcendentalism these notions have somewhat fallen into the background: I think partly from policy. Transcendentalism, endeavouring to persuade a world largely dominated by Empiricism, thought it best to come forward in an Epistemological rather than an Ontological garb: and to transcend experience—if I may so say—without the waving of flags so conspicuous as these words had come to be.

But it still remains, I think, important that we should obtain as clear and complete a grasp of them as we can: and for this purpose we may still derive some instruction from the controversy to which I have referred.

First, I ought to say that in this controversy, as regards the main question at issue, the English writers—keenly as they

---

[1] *Edinburgh Review*, Oct. 1829 [republished in *Discussions on Philosophy and Literature*, 1852].

disputed with each other—were all on one side. The common enemy was the post-Kantian philosophy of Germany. This philosophy—especially as taught by Schelling and Hegel—was held to maintain the cognisability of what Hamilton called the 'Infinito-Absolute' or the 'Unconditioned.' In Hamilton's language, "Kant had annihilated the older Metaphysic, but the germ of a more visionary doctrine of the Absolute (Infinito-Absolute) than any of those refuted, was contained in the bosom of his own philosophy. He had slain the body, but not exorcised the spectre, of the Absolute; and this spectre has continued to haunt the schools of Germany even to the present day. . . . The theories of Reinhold, of Fichte, of Schelling, Hegel, are just so many endeavours to fix the Absolute in knowledge."[1] And indeed this knowledge is conceived by them as the special aim of Philosophy. As Hamilton says, expressing Schelling's view, "While the lower sciences are of the relative and conditioned, *Philosophy*, as the science of sciences, must be of the *Absolute*—the *Unconditioned*."

This view, then, the leading English thinkers for the half century indicated—however widely they differed—agreed in rejecting. They argue that "the Absolute cannot in any manner or degree be known, in the strict sense of knowing":[2] though Hamilton holds that "we are, in the very consciousness of our inability to conceive aught above the relative and finite, inspired with a *belief* in the existence of something unconditioned beyond the sphere of all comprehensible reality";[3] and Mr. Spencer holds that we necessarily affirm its existence as logically implied in the existence of the relative and the finite, and have an indefinite consciousness of it: though at the same time it is rightly described as unknowable. Indeed he goes so far as to say that this indefinite consciousness of the Absolute and Unlimited itself exists absolutely in our minds.[4] And Mill, too, speaking as then the leading representative of English Empiricism —though disagreeing entirely with Hamilton's arguments—has no doubt that he has "established the futility of all speculations

---

[1] [*Discussions*, p. 18.]

[2] [Spencer, *First Principles*, 3rd edn. § 27, p. 98. Omitted in the last edition.]

[3] [*Discussions*, p. 15.]   [4] Cf. his *First Principles*, chap. iv.

respecting those meaningless abstractions 'the Infinite' and 'the Absolute,' notions to which no corresponding entities do or can exist."[1] The grounds on which Mill holds this may be briefly summed up as the acceptance of the doctrine of the 'Relativity of Human knowledge' in its widest sense :—"the entire inaccessibility to our faculties of any other knowledge of Things than that of the impressions which they produce in our mental consciousness."[2]

On the whole, then, we may say that the prevalent view of English Philosophy in the middle half of the nineteenth century, in spite of all its internal controversies, was in conscious, uncompromising antagonism to the doctrine that the Absolute or Unconditioned or the Infinite-Absolute was knowable, and that it was the special business of Philosophy, as distinguished from empirical sciences, to know it. At the same time it recognised that in holding this view it was in opposition, not only to the post-Kantian philosophy of Germany, but to the general drift and aim of metaphysical speculation from its earliest appearance in the development of European thought—as Hamilton puts it —"from the dawn of philosophy in the school of Elea," at the end of the sixth century B.C. "Metaphysic," he says, "strictly so denominated is virtually the doctrine of the Unconditioned. From Xenophanes to Leibnitz [before Kant, no less than from Fichte to Hegel after Kant] the Infinite, the Absolute, the Unconditioned, formed the highest principle of Speculation"; but, he adds, "until the rise of the Kantian Philosophy, no serious attempt was made to investigate the nature and origin of this notion."[3] But in saying this last, Hamilton does not go far enough. Speaking of Modern Philosophy,[4] from Descartes onward, we may say that though 'Infinite' is an essential attribute of the primal Being which the metaphysician calls God, the notions of 'Unconditioned' and 'Absolute' are not applied by them to this Being. They speak of God, the source

[1] [*Examination of Sir W. Hamilton's Philosophy*, 3rd edn. p. 70.]
[2] [*Op. cit.* p. 13.]
[3] [*Discussion on Philosophy*, etc., 3rd. edn. p. 15.]
[4] And especially excluding Plato, as I have no time to digress into a discussion, how far the first principle, the 'something not hypothetical,' which philosophy, according to Plato, seeks, may be properly interpreted as 'Unconditioned' or 'Absolute.'

of all finite Being, as original Being, most real Being, Highest Being, Infinite and All-perfect, comprehending all realities or perfections, perfections which are thought as Infinite : but they do not apply to this original or primary Being the conceptions of 'Absolute' or 'Unconditioned.' On the other hand, in the post-Kantian philosophy of Germany, 'the Absolute'—though conceived in a fundamentally different way by Fichte, Schelling, and Hegel respectively—is undoubtedly throughout the rapid and remarkable evolution of thought which these names represent the leading conception of the chief object of philosophical inquiry. It may be said that the difference is merely one of words : but to discuss this would involve a discussion of the whole course of Modern Philosophy, which is necessarily beyond my scope. I am concerned with making as clear and precise as possible the conceptions in which the great issue between English and Germans was formulated in the century now closing; and in order to do that, I must confine myself to the thinkers in whose exposition the terms in question are leading terms. But I am not undertaking to give a summary account even of post-Kantian philosophy. I am only trying to help towards an answer to the questions :—What do the post-Kantian thinkers mean by the terms Absolute, Unconditioned (I take these rather than Infinite, as that, as we have seen, is equally characteristic of pre-Kantian thought); What place does the notion Absolute or Unconditioned occupy in their philosophy; and How came it there?

Well, the answer to the third question is pretty evident from what I have said. Comparing pre-Kantian with post-Kantian philosophical terminology, it undoubtedly comes there through the epoch-making influence of Kant. 'Absolute,' however, is not a leading notion in Kant's philosophy, except as *qualifying* the *necessity* of the Necessary Being sought in the fourth Antinomy—he only uses the term in the subordinate manner of pre-Kantian thinkers; but 'Unconditioned,' as we know, is a very important term in his system, and I think that the post-Kantian term Absolute, whatever else it means, always has a certain correspondence to Kant's term Unconditioned. Let us, then, examine the Kantian use of this term. "The Unconditioned," as we have seen, is a general term for what the Reason seeks but cannot find, when it aims, on different lines of thought, at putting together into a complete whole that connected knowledge of empirical objects which understanding and imagination, combining the data of sense, supply, and the physical sciences present in a systematic form.

Trying to think the empirical world as a whole, Speculative Reason asks questions which experience obviously cannot answer, but which a natural and inevitable confusion between objects of experience and "things-in-themselves" misleads Reason into supposing answerable *a priori*. Whether the world had or had not a beginning in time, has or has not limits in space : whether the substances that make it up have or have not indivisible ultimate elements : whether the necessary sequence of causal events which we must find everywhere in tracing back the world-process, terminates anywhere in an uncaused event—such as a 'free' volition would be—or must be thought as endless : whether,—from the contingency which belongs to all empirical facts, which, though necessary results of other facts, are only conditionally necessary,—we can or cannot infer the existence of an absolutely and unconditionally necessary Being :—if valid answers to these questions were really attainable, they would, according to Kant, give us under each head knowledge of the Unconditioned.[1] But, as we know, valid answers cannot be obtained; so long as we confound phenomenal things with realities existing independently of our sensibility and thought, the contradictory answers under each head are found equally untenable, and yet there is no conceivable third answer. When, however, we get rid of this confusion, we find that under the first two heads the questions are such as ought not to be asked : for they cannot relate to real things existing out of Time and Space; while, as regards phenomena, they are meaningless in the form originally asked. For, *e.g.* even to ask whether a merely phenomenal world had or had not a beginning in time implies that Time is real, otherwise than as the form of our

---

[1] According to Hamilton's use of Absolute, one of the alternatives in each case is the Unconditioned Infinite, another the Unconditioned Absolute. 'Absolute,' he notes, is used in a wider sense='aloof from relation, condition, dependence,' and a narrower='finished, perfect, completed': in the narrower. the Unconditioned is a genus of which the Absolute is a species. I shall not use the term in the second sense except I so state.

Sensibility. All we can reasonably ask is, 'How far back may we go in time, in our scientific synthesis of phenomena': to which the answer is: 'As far back as you have empirical grounds for going'; and similarly as regards spatial extension and divisibility. That is the idea of the Unconditioned, under these heads, has a merely *regulative* use, in that synthesis of objects of experience which is Reason's proper task.

On the other hand, under the last two heads both answers may be true. Here again, so far as experience and the empirical world are concerned, the use of the idea of the Unconditioned is purely regulative: it entitles and directs us to seek without limit empirical causes and conditions for all empirical facts. At the same time the free causality and the necessary existence affirmed in the theses may be attributed to the extra-cognitional Reality or Thing-in-itself.

The conclusion of the Speculative Reason is thus that there *may* be in the world of Noumena a free causality and *may* be an unconditionally necessary Being: but we cannot know positively that they are. But though this is the conclusion of the Speculative Mind, you must never forget that it is *not* the conclusion of the Kantian Philosophy. For, on the basis of ethical conviction, and for the purposes of practice, we have to *postulate* the free causality of the human will, and the existence of God. For man, as a rational agent in the world, must (1) recognise the moral law as 'absolutely' and 'unconditionally' binding; (2) aim at realising his 'highest good.' But this 'highest good,' in Kant's view, does not consist in Virtue only. "Virtue or the worthiness to be happy is the 'supreme good,' 'the supreme condition' of a rational pursuit of happiness: but it is not the whole or complete good; . . . in the highest good which is practical for us, that is, which is to be realised through our will, virtue and happiness are conceived as necessarily united."[1] But "a rational agent who is also a part of the world of nature and dependent on it," and has "no power to bring nature into complete harmony with his principles of action," has no reason to expect that nature *as such* will realise the required connexion between morality and happiness: still, since as a rational being he ought to seek to promote the highest good, the highest good

[1] Watson's *Selections*, pp. 291 f.

must be attainable. "He must therefore *postulate* a cause of nature as a whole, distinct from nature, with at once power and will to connect morality and happiness in exact harmony with each other":[1] *i.e.* God, as God, is conceived in what Kant distinguished as Moral Theology.

But now, when we try to put together the results of the criticism of the Speculative Reason,[2] with the results of the examination of the Practical Reason, we find that the negative results of the former are importantly modified. For the Speculative Reason, though it could not prove the existence of an original, unconditionally necessary Being, yet was not critically barren of valid results. It showed the possibility of such a Being outside nature and its Supreme cause : it showed how God must be conceived if a proof of the reality of His existence could be obtained on any other line of thought. "The Supreme Being," said Kant, "is for purely speculative reason a mere ideal, but still a *perfectly faultless* ideal, which completes and crowns the whole of human knowledge. And if it should turn out that there is a moral theology, which is able to supply what is deficient in speculative theology, we should then find that transcendental theology is no longer merely problematic, but is indispensable in the determination of the conception of a Supreme Being, and in the continual criticism of reason, which is so often deluded by sense and is not always in harmony even with its own ideas. Necessity, infinity, unity, existence apart from the world (not as a soul of the world), eternity as free from conditions of time, omnipresence as unaffected by conditions of space, etc., are purely transcendental predicates, the purified conception of which, essential as it is to every theology, can be derived only from a transcendental theology."[3]

Having given this brief summary of Kant's complex view, let us now consider it in relation to the issue before-mentioned raised between English philosophy of the central half of the nineteenth century and the post-Kantian philosophy of Germany. Does Kant hold that the Absolute or Unconditioned can be cognised or conceived, and if so, what is it, what are we to say of it ? Now to these questions very various answers have been

---

[1] Watson's *Selections*, pp. 296 f.
[2] Cf. Watson's *Selections*, p. 221. [3] Watson's *Selections*, p. 222.

given; and it will be instructive to compare them, not merely for the light they throw on Kant's system, but also for the difference of meanings which they show to exist in the use of the term 'Absolute.'

According to Hamilton the Unconditioned, for Kant, is not an object of knowledge: but its notion, as a regulative principle of the mind, is more than a mere negation.[1] Now this answer is not wrong, in my view; but it is not luminous: it does not give Kant's view, because it does not introduce his distinction between phenomena and Things in themselves—things as they are apart from human apprehension. When we take this distinction, we see that a double answer is required, because there are two questions—one relating to phenomena, the other to things in themselves.

As regards the phenomenal world, the Unconditioned is not to be found, in any of the cases in which the uncritical reason seeks to find it, not on account of the limitation of our faculties of cognition, but simply because it is *not there*.

But if this is what becomes of the idea of the Unconditioned in its application to the phenomenal world, what are we to say of its application to Things in themselves? Now, if I understand Hamilton, his view of Kant's answer to this question, simply *identifies* 'the Unconditioned' with 'Things in themselves,' and declares it unknowable, because the human mind can only know, not the things themselves, but their effects on our senses. To quote Hamilton's words: "Things in themselves, Matter, Mind, God—all in short that is not finite, relative and phenomenal, as bearing no analogy to our faculties, is beyond the verge of our knowledge. . . . Thus . . . a knowledge of the Unconditioned is declared impossible."[2] I think this entirely misrepresents Kant's view. Kant certainly does not hold that Things in themselves, realities as existing out of relation to human experience, are one and all Unconditioned: nay, he does not even know speculatively that any of them are Unconditioned. I will not speak of Things in themselves other than thinking beings: because, though in the *Prolegomena*, repudiating "Idealism," Kant certainly affirms the existence of this class of Things in themselves, in the *Critique* he seems to treat their existence

[1] [Cf. *Discussions*, p. 27.]   [2] [*Op. cit.* p. 16.]

as problematical.[1] Let us then confine ourselves to thinking beings: these certainly are for Kant Things in themselves. Kant expressly says of the human subject that he is "conscious of himself as a thing in himself"; and, on the basis of the postulates of the Practical Reason, he conceives such subjects as creatures, created indeed timelessly in a timeless act, but still created by an Original Being of Infinite Power, Wisdom, and Goodness. It is true that he attributes to them, as rational beings, a free causality: and it is important to lay stress on this, because this is the main starting-point in the Kantian system for Fichte's doctrine of the Absolute Ego, which begins the evolution of the post-Kantian Metaphysic of the Absolute. But though he conceives them as having a free causality, he conceives them as essentially finite and imperfect: indeed it is on this conception that the postulate of immortality depends, because a "finite rational being is capable only of an infinite moral progress from lower to higher stages of moral perfection."[2] Well, then, beings whom we cannot but think as created finite, imperfect, we obviously cannot but think as conditioned; even though we can have no speculative knowledge of the conditions of their existence, except on its moral side.

How far, then, does Kant apply the idea of the Unconditioned to Things in themselves? Well the answer, from what has been just said, is surely clear. He can apply it only to God the Original Being; and the postulates of the Practical Reason compel us to think of God as a First Being all-wise, all-good, all-powerful, the cause of nature but not a part of nature. To such a being we *must* apply in practical thought, and in theology (in which practical thought and speculative thought blend, though the former is predominant), the conception of unconditioned necessity of existence, which the critical discussion of the fourth antinomy left as *possibly* applicable in the world of things in themselves though not in the phenomenal world.

Here, then, according to my view, is Kant's final answer to the questions, 'Can the Absolute be known, and how far can it be known'?—meaning by the Absolute, 'Unconditioned Reality.'

---

[1] Cf. Watson's *Selections*, "On the Distinction of Phenomena and Noumena," pp. 129-134.

[2] [Watson's *Selections*, p. 295.]

Kant's 'Absolute' is God: His existence cannot be speculatively known, but for practical reasons He must be thought to exist, as the First Cause of the World, with infinite power, wisdom, and goodness; and being so thought, He cannot but be identified with the unconditionally necessary Being which the critical solution of the fourth antinomy showed to be *possible*, though it could not prove it to be actual.

We have examined two views of Kant's Absolute, the difference of which depends on the difference of meaning attached to the term. (1) If "Absolute" = non-relative = non-phenomenal (according to a prevalent view of Relativity of Human Knowledge), then, no doubt, Kant's Absolute = Things in themselves. (2) But 'Absolute' is not an important Kantian term:[1] its importance, as I have said, is post-Kantian: and if we take Absolute = Reality, that is, Unconditioned (this latter *being* a leading term with Kant), Kant's answer to the inquiry concerning our knowledge of the Absolute must, I think, be that I have given.

But there is another view of Kant's Absolute that is given by Fichte, the first and nearest to Kant of the three leading Teutonic thinkers who worked out the doctrine of the Absolute against which the English mind rebelled; it is thus important as throwing light, if not on Kant, at any rate on these further developments. In a remarkable passage in a course of lectures delivered towards the close of his life—in 1813, not more than a year before his death—Fichte says that though Kant comprehended the Transcendental Ego as the union of inseparable Being and Thought, he did not comprehend it in its pure independence, but only as the common fundamental characteristic of its three for him original modes x, y, z: and thus he "had really three Absolutes, while the one true Absolute was reduced to their common characteristic."[2] These 'three Absolutes,' according to Fichte, are to be found in the three *Kritiken*, the Critique of Pure Reason, the Critique of Practical Reason, and the Critique of Judgment. With the fundamental doctrines of the two former we are already familiar; with regard to the third, I will only say that it only aims at a kind of Mediation, through the notion

---

[1] It does not occur, for example, in Watson's index.
[2] [Fichte's *Nachgelassene Werke*, ii. pp. 103 f.]

of End, between the conclusions of the Speculative Reason in the first Critique as to the world of Experience or Nature, and the view put forward in the second Critique as to the supersensible world of free rational beings.

Fichte's account of the 'three Absolutes,' then, is as follows: "In the *Critique of Pure Reason* sense-experience was for him the Absolute (x): and of the Ideas—the higher, purely Spiritual World—he speaks in truth in a very deprecatory way. One might conclude from his earlier works, and from certain hints thrown out in the *Critique* itself, that in his own view the matter could not be left so: but I would undertake to prove that these hints are only one more inconsistency: for if the principles there laid down were carried to their logical conclusions, the Supersensible world must entirely vanish, leaving as the only Noumenon the 'is' to be realised in experience."[1] But the lofty morality of the man "corrected the error of the Philosopher, and the *Critique of Practical Reason* appeared. In it was manifested, through the indwelling notion of the Categorical Imperative, the Ego as something in itself, which it could not be in the Critique of Pure Reason, where its only basis is the Empirical 'is': so we get a second Absolute, a moral world = z." He then goes on to say that in the Critique of Judgment it was acknowledged that the Supersensible and the Sensible Worlds must have some common though quite inscrutable root, which would be the third Absolute = y.

Overlooking this third, let us ask what Fichte means by the two distinct Absolutes found respectively in the *Critique of Pure Reason* and the *Critique of Practical Reason*.

First, I must explain that Fichte's development of Kantism —ignoring or overriding, as Modern English Transcendentalists ignore or override, the Refutation of Idealism in the *Prolegomena* —discarded altogether the conception of Things in themselves other than Thinking beings. Accordingly the points in Kant's doctrine that are fundamentally important for Fichte are (1) the conception of self-consciousness as making nature in the Critique of Pure Reason, *i.e.* as the source of all Synthesis and all form in the world of Empirical objects; and (2) the conception of

[1] Fichte means the bond of Synthesis between sensible data, supplied by the Transcendental Ego, and expressed by the copula "is."

independent rational activity in the moral world, the essence of all thought of duty and moral action. But these two, he considers, Kant ought to have conceived as essentially one and brought into intelligible relation : he ought to have seen that it is the same rational self-conscious activity that makes nature and makes duty and is at once the source and explanation of all knowledge and all duty: and he ought to have effected a rational systematisation of the two functions—which in his system as expounded by him are apparently so diverse, and deduced them from a common principle, a primary activity of the Transcendental Ego. Had he done this, the 'one true Absolute' would have been revealed in this primary activity, the first source and condition of all else in consciousness, therefore of all else in the universe. But as he did not do this, we are left—so far as the two treatises on the Pure and Practical Reason go—with two different Absolutes.[1]

In the *Critique of Pure Reason* — according to Fichte's trenchant but one-sided account of it—if its line of thought were consistently carried out, the higher spiritual world would have no place. The only Noumenon, the only Reality as distinct from appearance or the phenomenal (the sham Noumena, *i.e.* all Things in themselves other than Self-conscious Egos, being abolished) would be merely the Transcendental Ego as the source of Synthesis of Empirical elements, of such Synthesis as is expressed in the copula 'is' in any Empirical judgment.

In the Moral World shown us in the *Critique of Practical Reason*, on the other hand, the Reality is the Activity of rational, free, self-determining Will.

I think that this application of the notion of Absolute to Kant's system is quite legitimate, when we regard the system from Fichte's point of view, and as partially transformed by his mind; though it is certain that no such application was ever made, or would have been admitted by Kant himself.

---

[1] 'Absolute,' I think, means here primarily Reality as contrasted with phenomena (but also with the attribute of being unconditioned).

THE METAPHYSICS OF T. H. GREEN

LECTURE I

SUMMARY ACCOUNT

I CAN perhaps most easily show the difference between my point of view and that of Green by examining closely the language of the first page of his *Metaphysics of Knowledge*.[1] Now what we are supposed to admit is, I presume, the general conclusions of Psychophysiology, the dependence, that is to say, of the series of feelings, thoughts, etc., which constitutes our mental life, on another series of changes, viz. changes in the nerve-matter of our brain. The question still remains: "how there come to be for us those objects of consciousness, called matter and motion, on which we suppose the operations of sense and desire and thought to be dependent." Now the phrase '*be for* us' is ambiguous. It may mean (1) how we come to conceive, (2) how we come to conceive *rightly* or to *know*, those objects called matter and motion. The first question would be purely psychological or psychogonical: it would not raise any question as

[1] *Prolegomena to Ethics*, vol. i. ch. i. § 9, p. 13.

to the validity of the notions. But it seems clear that the second meaning is what we require. For when we admit the functions of the soul to be dependent on material processes, we mean on the really occurring processes of really existing matter, not on our thoughts of these processes. In the vast majority of cases these processes occur when no one perceives or thinks of them: and they occurred, as we believe, in just the same way in the ages when no one thought of them, or when they were wrongly thought of—for example, when the heart, not the brain, was supposed to be the seat of emotion or intelligence.

This is important when we come to the next sentence: "If it could be admitted that matter and motion had an existence *in themselves*, or otherwise than as related to a consciousness, it would still not be by *such* matter and motion, but by the matter and motion which we know, that the function of the soul, or anything else, can for us be explained. Nothing can be known by help of reference to the unknown." Now in this sentence there is a certain danger of confusion between the view of Kantian or Spencerian Agnosticism and the view of Common Sense and ordinary physical science. If by 'existing otherwise than as related to a consciousness' Green means 'existing so as to be incapable of being known' it is obviously true that matter and motion as so existing cannot furnish an explanation of the functions of the soul or anything else. And, according to Kant, 'matter in itself' is essentially unknowable: according to Spencer, *qua* agnostic: "the reality underlying appearances is totally and for ever inconceivable to us." If, then, when we say that the functions of the soul are materially conditioned, we mean that they are conditioned by an unknown $= x$, I agree that the affirmation is certainly not an explanation. But if by 'existing otherwise than as related to a consciousness' we mean 'existing when no one is conscious of them'—that is obviously what taught by physiology we do hold. The movements of nerve-particles on which we believe thought and feeling to be dependent are movements that we believe to have gone on for long ages before any one knew anything about them. In this sense we must and do conceive matter as existing in itself—capable of being known but not known. But the phrase 'otherwise than' is confusing. For knowledge implies that the thing known exists as it is known: so far as our conception of a thing is different from the reality, that thing is not truly known.

"But," Green goes on, "matter and motion, just so far as known, consist in or are determined by relations between the objects of that connected conciousness which we call experience." Here again we have to disentangle and distinguish incontrovertible truth from mentalistic paradox. No doubt our common conception of matter and motion is a conception of related fact: the extension, even the position in space of a thing, involves relation to all else that is extended or placed in space. The effort to conceive of anything not related to something else would be a futile effort. But the words 'consist in relations' seem to imply the absurdity that relations are conceivable without things related. And the first question that we have to put is, Does Green mean this? This question we must put, because his language repeatedly seems to mean it: yet I think we must answer in the negative: and understand the next sentence accordingly. He does *not* mean to reduce matter and motion—the physical world generally—to relations alone, but to relations and related feelings. "If," he says, "we take any definition of matter, any account of its 'necessary qualities,' and abstract from it all that consists in a statement of relations between facts in the way of feeling, or between objects that we present to ourselves as sources of feeling, we shall find that there is nothing left."

Now so stated—apparently as a result of direct reflective analysis—I have to meet this proposition by a simple denial. But a simple denial is uninstructive: let us try to explain it. The source of the error, in my opinion, lies in the fact that imaginary sensation accompanies conceptions when we dwell on them, just as sensation accompanies perception. In ordinary perception of an object external to my body I appear to cognise—and, according to Common Sense and Science, in most cases really do cognise—a portion of matter really existing (though not precisely as I conceive it) in the world known to me in experience. But along with, empirically inseparable from, the perception occurs feeling of various kinds: and in ordinary thought about matter elements of feeling (colour, etc.) are undoubtedly mixed. According to me, however, reflection aided by science separates these elements, and the notion of matter in space, as used in scientific thought, is *not* reducible to feelings.[1]

Here I would ask those who hold the other view to state what feelings and relations the motions of nerve-particles conceived as concomitants of our states of consciousness mean to them: and what they mean by regarding such feelings as having existed, or to what substitutes for such feelings they attribute reality. I have never seen an answer to these questions that will stand examination. Mentalists commonly avoid the difficulty by saying that in speaking of nerve-particles and nervous processes, or any other kind of matter in motion, they use, and have a right to use, popular language—as an instructed person does in speaking of the sun rising and setting: he knows all the time that the earth moves round the sun, and misleads no one. Similarly, they know all the time that what is called matter is really analysable into feelings and relations, and therefore with this explanation should be allowed to use the language of Common Sense freely. Now I quite admit that it would be absurd to dispute the mentalists' right to use popular terminology in merely popular discourse or writing: just as it would be pedantic to object to a modern astronomer for talking

[1] Cf. *Philosophy, its Scope and Relations*, pp. 63 ff.

of the sun rising or setting, though such language, strictly taken, implies the geocentric view. But my objection is not to the mentalist's using in ordinary discourse language that implies assumptions contradictory of his express conclusions, but to his using such language in the professedly scientific reasonings by which the conclusions are reached. What would be thought of an astronomer who in a scientific treatise began by apparently assuming that the sun went round the earth, and carried the apparent assumption through the very arguments by which he leads us to the conclusion that the earth goes round the sun? Surely we should require that he at least altered his terminology: we should challenge him to throw his argument in a form which avoided assumptions contradicted by his conclusions. That, then, is my challenge to the mentalists who trace psychophysiologically the process by which the notion of matter in space is alleged to be compounded of feelings visual and tactual.

Having said this much, I now propose to accept, for the sake of discussion, Green's mentalistic starting-point, and see how he proceeds to work out his system.

The argument has two steps, one dealing with knowledge and one dealing with nature. First, we are told that 'the knowledge of nature' can only be explained by a principle which is not part of nature. For knowledge of nature is knowledge of the relations of the content of experience, through which alone that content possesses a definite character and becomes a connected whole. The source of this knowledge of relations, of this connected experience which thus combines, unifies, organises these relations, cannot itself be conditioned by them. It is commonly granted that we can only know phenomena: that what we call an 'objective' world is only a phenomenal world. Still we make, and have to explain, the distinction between 'appearance or illusion' and 'reality' in this phenomenal world. We shall find that the terms 'real' and 'objective' have no meaning except for a consciousness which conceives a single and unalterable order of relations determining its experiences, an order with which, as each experience occurs, the temporary presentation of the relations determining it may be contrasted. When we make a mistake—*e.g.* of vision—we conceive phenomena as related in a manner incompatible with this single system of relations.

This conception of a system of relations is presupposed in all conscious experience: for conscious experience involves consciousness of change; and consciousness of change involves 'consciousness of events as a related series.' Now a consciousness of events as a related series cannot be one or any number of the series of events, nor a product that supervenes after some of the events have elapsed—since "it must be equally present to all the events of which it is the consciousness."[1] Nor will it solve but only throw back the problem to say that such consciousness is a product of previous events; unless we say that it is

[1] [*Op. cit.* § 16, p. 21.]

produced by a series of events of which there is no consciousness. And that is inconceivable.

In short, then, experience, in the sense of 'a consciousness of events as a related series'—experience as the source of a knowledge of the order of nature —cannot itself be explained by any natural history. "It would seem to follow that a form of consciousness, which we cannot explain as of natural origin, is necessary to our conceiving an order of nature, an objective world of fact from which illusion may be distinguished. In other words, an understanding—for that term seems as fit as any other to denote the principle of consciousness in question— irreducible to anything else, 'makes nature' for us, in the sense of enabling us to conceive that there is such a thing."[1]

Let us assume, then, that in order to conceive experience — the very experience to which the naturalist appeals as the basis of *his* knowledge— we must conceive a continuing and unifying principle that is not natural, but that distinguishes itself from nature, and in knowing nature, knows itself other than nature, a consciousness which cannot be conceived as the product of nature, or explained by any natural history; because it is implied in the experience through which our conception and knowledge of nature is attained. The next question is, whether 'Understanding' can be held to 'make nature' in the further sense that it is a source or condition of *there being these relations*—not only of our conceiving

[1] *Op. cit.* § 19, p. 22.

them. Can we hold that "the understanding which presents an order of nature to us is in principle one with an understanding which constitutes that order itself?"[1] The common sense objections to this are not really valid.

Briefly it comes to this. 'Common Sense' is supposed to hold that the relations—say of order in space, causation, resemblance—by which the mind puts together its notions of things into a coherent system, are merely notional and not real: fictions of the mind not in the things. Against this view it is easy for Green to show that if we try to conceive the things without this relation, we fail: the things vanish.[2] I pass over this for the present, because I cannot follow Green[3] in accepting Locke as a representative of the 'traditional philosophy of Common Sense.' Locke no doubt did not intend to diverge from Common Sense; but he did diverge from it fundamentally, and thus led—as all histories of philosophy recognise—to the mentalistic paradoxes of Berkeley and the sceptical paradoxes of Hume. It was the task of Reid to trace this divergence to its source, get rid of the radical error in analysis that led to it, and thus found the Philosophy of Common Sense. But to discuss this adequately would take us too far afield. [Let us pass then to the second step in the argument.]

Here Green takes as a point of departure that Nature means to us a single, unalterable, all-inclusive

---

[1] [*Op. cit.* § 19, p. 23.]   [2] *Op. cit.* § 23, p. 26.
[3] *Op. cit.* § 20, p. 23.

system of relations.[1] It means, even acccording to him, something more and different: a system not of relations only but of related facts (say feelings)—facts not 'unalterable' but in continual change, though, no doubt, such change is subject to invariable laws. But of the latter point more presently: let us now assume provisionally, and concentrate attention on, the 'single unalterable system of relations.' What is implied in such a system? What is the condition of its possibility? I must quote Green's answer at length, because I must confess my inability to follow his argument:—" Whether we say that a related thing is one in itself, manifold in respect of its relations, or that there is one relation between manifold things, *e.g.* the relation of mutual attraction between bodies —and one expression or the other we must employ in stating the simplest facts—we are equally affirming the unity of the manifold. Abstract the many relations from the one thing, and there is nothing. They, being many, determine or constitute its definite unity. It is not the case that it first exists in its unity, and then is brought into various relations. Without the relations it would not exist at all. In like manner the one relation is a unity of the many things. They, in their manifold being, make the one relation. If these relations really exist, there is a real unity of the manifold, a real multiplicity of that which is one. But a plurality of things cannot of themselves unite in one relation, nor can a single thing of itself bring itself into a multitude of relations.

[1] *Op. cit.* § 26, p. 29.

It is true, as we have said, that the single things are nothing except as determined by relations which are the negation of their singleness, but they do not therefore cease to be single things. Their common being is not something into which their several existences disappear. On the contrary, if they did not survive in their singleness, there could be no relation between them—nothing but a blank, featureless identity. There must, then, be something other than the manifold things themselves, which combines them without effacing their severalty."[1]

I grant that "relation involves the existence of many in one"—that what we conceive as one thing we, in so conceiving it, necessarily conceive as having many relations, and that any one relation must be a relation which connects a plurality (two at least) of objects related. But what is the meaning of saying that "a plurality of things cannot of themselves unite in one relation, nor can a single thing of itself bring itself into a multitude of relations"? I thought the aim of the preceding argument was to show that they *are* in the relation and cannot be conceived out of it. What, then, is the meaning of the phrase 'cannot of themselves unite'? In order even to ask the question, Can they of themselves unite? etc., we must conceive them out of the relation: whereas Green's point is they cannot be so conceived. This, indeed, he dimly sees [as is evident] from what he goes on to say: "It is true . . . that the single things are nothing except as determined by relations which are the

[1] *Op. cit.* § 28, p. 31.

negations of their singleness, but they do not therefore cease to be single things. . . . On the contrary, if they did not survive in their singleness, there could be no relation between them—nothing but a blank, featureless identity." But the fact that they survive in their singleness does not show that they need something other than themselves to make them so survive.

However, let us grant that unless we "deny the reality of relations and treat them as fictions of our combining intelligence" we must suppose them to be held together by something other than themselves. Then, as in the world of experience, the world as presented to sense and represented in thought, we find on reflection that the unifying principle is a conscious intelligence, so we must suppose that in the world of reality there is an analogous principle. "If we suppose them (the relations) to be real otherwise than merely as for us, otherwise than in the 'cosmos of our experience,' we must recognise as the condition of this reality the action of some unifying principle analogous to our understanding."[1]

At this point Green takes some pains to deal with the doctrine of Kant which distinguishes [between 'phenomenal reality' and] 'reality in some absolute sense.' Into this argument I do not now propose to enter. I have already given my own criticism of Kant; and the doctrine of 'unknowable things in themselves,' though I will not say that it is not held by scientific men,[2] is at any rate not one in which

[1] *Op. cit.* § 29, p. 32. [2] Mr. Spencer in a sense holds it.

scientific men as such take much interest. If there is a world of such unknowables, it is at any rate not the world of past and present reality into which science is ardently inquiring—with a firm conviction of its power of distinguishing the real from the unreal, truth from error, with regard to it. Let us keep ourselves to this world, and ask what is required to make it conceivable.

LECTURE II

THE SPIRITUAL PRINCIPLE IN KNOWLEDGE AND IN NATURE

I PROPOSE to begin the present lecture with a brief examination of the fundamental points of the doctrine of Green's chap. i., so far as I gave a summary account of them in the last; and then to proceed with the critical exposition from the point where I left off.

The conception of *Knowledge* we all agree requires a knowing mind: the main drift of the chapter is to show that the conception of *Nature* involves it equally. The argument might be put in two sentences:—(1) Nature as known and as knowable is a system of objects related to a subject or knowing mind, and related to each other through their relation to the subject. (2) No other Nature is conceivable. Materialists — and Common Sense so far as the physical world is concerned—think of Nature as matter in motion. But Matter means "relations between facts in the way of feeling, or between objects that we present to ourselves as sources of feeling," and Motion similarly "has no meaning except . . . as expressing relations of what is contained in experience."[1] Also "it is an accepted doctrine of modern philosophy" that "knowledge is only of phenomena," and that "nothing can enter into knowledge that is unrelated to consciousness,"[2] which Green takes as meaning that "relation to a subject is necessary to make an object, so that an object which no consciousness presented to itself would not be an object at all." But the last two propositions are not necessarily identical: since the former may be held, and has been widely held, by Mentalists of a different type from Green: those whom in previous lectures I distinguished as Sensationalists.[3] There is in fact an ambiguity in it depending on an ambiguity in the word 'consciousness.' This word is sometimes used as equivalent to, or definitely including 'self-consciousness,' the reference, *i.e.*, to a permanent identical self or subject of the stream of transient changing psychical fact which constitutes the varying element of the mind's empirical life; but sometimes again it is used for this varying element itself. In this latter sense, the proposition that "nothing can enter into knowledge that is unrelated to consciousness" may be held by a Sensationalist, who agrees with Hume that when he observes himself he cannot find anything but a changing complex of transient facts, ultimately analysable into Sensations or Feelings.

I note this, because Green's polemic appears to be primarily directed against this view, and not

---

[1] [*Op. cit.* § 9, p. 13.]   [2] [*Op. cit.* § 10, p. 14.]
[3] Cf. *Philosophy, its Scope and Relations*, p. 52.

against the philosophy of Common Sense or Natural Dualism. But no philosophy can ever ignore Natural Dualism. The result is that there is a kind of 'triangular duel': a contest in which three distinct views are involved; each of the two opposed to Green's partially agrees and partially disagrees with his view. The Sensationalist and the Idealistic Spiritualist (Green) agree in being mentalistic: *i.e.* in reducing the material world, at least as known and knowable, to mental fact of some kind: the Natural Dualist and Green agree as against the Sensationalist in recognising reference to an identical self as an essential and permanent element of consciousness. Availing himself of this division of his opponents, Green puts together the views in which each agrees with him, and takes the world as known to, and believed to exist by, each individual, as a world of essentially mental fact, every part and element of which is necessarily related to a conscious subject.

But this does not yet bring us to Green's characteristic doctrine. The elements of this empirical world of each individual are not only essentially related to a conscious subject: they are essentially related to each other, each to all,—related through position in time, position in space, resemblance, causal connexion, reciprocal action. No object of experience is conceivable apart from a whole complex of such relations. Nature then, no less than the experience of each individual, is for Green a connected system of objects of consciousness, which are what they are—when we rightly conceive them—through the relations that connect them. I have said 'objects of consciousness.' This appears to be for Green equivalent to related 'feelings,' with the proviso that the difference between one feeling and another consists in its different relations. This appears from his analysis of *error* in empirical cognition. The question "whether any impression is or represents anything real or objective" is a question "whether a given feeling is what it is taken to be," that is, "whether it is related as it seems to be related," for "a particular feeling is [merely] a feeling related in a certain way." Error in empirical cognition, accordingly, consists in a mistake as to the relations of what is felt—in conceiving a certain set of relations so that they are incapable of combining into a system with other recognised relations. Or, as the Table of Contents says, "The question, Is anything real or not? means Is it, or is it not, *related* as it seems to be related?" It thus "implies the conception of reality or nature as a single unalterable order of relations."[1] Thus the essence of 'Nature' is for Green 'an order of Nature.' On the other hand, "Nature with all that belongs to it is a process of change: change on a uniform method, but change still. All the relations under which we know it are relations in the way of change, or by which change is determined."[2] The question, How can Nature be at once 'unalterable' and a 'process of change' seems to require more consideration than Green vouchsafes it; but what he means is that the real world, though perpetually changing, is changing

---

[1] [*Op. cit.* p. x., pp. 16 ff.]   [2] *Op. cit.* § 18, p. 22.

according to unchanging laws. On this more presently. However, taking this view of Nature as essentially a single connected all-inclusive system of relations, in a sense unalterable, let us now examine the non-natural principle which it necessarily implies.

(1) Why is this 'non-natural,' and (2) what is its relation to Nature? In the earlier part of the chapter, in which Green is considering the "Spiritual Principle in [empirical] knowledge," his answer seems clear. 'The relations of the experienced' must have a 'source,' a 'principle of union,' from whose 'combining and unifying action' they 'result': and this Principle "being that which so organises experience that the relations . . . arise therein," cannot "itself be determined by those relations."[1] But why do the relations want a source? Why cannot they get on without one? These questions are answered in a passage (§ 28) to which I directed special attention at the close of the last lecture.[2] As I said, the argument appears to me invalid on Green's premises; because, according to him, we cannot even conceive the manifold things out of the relations: and, therefore, cannot even raise the question whether, if we could conceive them out of the relations, they would be seen to require something other than themselves to bring them into the relations. We must conceive the real world as a system, having unity and connexion as well as manifoldness and diversity; but I cannot see why we should therefore suppose a special source for the unity; or why "either we must deny the

---

[1] [*Op. cit.* § 9, p. 14.]   [2] Cf. above, p. 219.

reality of relations altogether and treat them as fictions of our combining intelligence," or we must suppose the manifold things to be held together by something other than themselves.[1] But still, granting the fundamental assumption of Mentalism, I admit the force of the argument which Green urges, from the analogy between the world of each one's experience and the 'real' world, common to us all, of which the world of each one's experience and thought is an indefinite fragment. If the aggregate of thoughts and feelings into which the world as empirically known to me is analysable has every element of it connected by reference to a self-conscious subject, we may argue from analogy that there must be such a subject similarly related to the Universe.

Before I proceed to examine further Green's conception of this universal principle or non-natural subject, I must say a word on his relation to Kant, as explained by himself (§§ 31-41). It will be seen that he is arguing for some time on Kant's side (§§ 31-37) in favour of the doctrine which they agree in holding, viz. that what Green calls a 'principle of consciousness,' Kant a 'synthetic unity of apperception,' is the source of form, relation, and connexion in the world of empirical reality. Observe that Green does not in this argument distinguish forms of sensibility from forms of thought: and that he abstracts from the difference between Kant's phenomenalism and his own mentalism. For the 'Nature,' that in Kant's view is made by the Understanding and

[1] [Cf. *op. cit.* § 29, p. 32.]

Imagination determining the form of time in which the data of sense are apprehended—this is merely the systematised appearance of a really real world not existing under the conditions of Time and Space. The *objective* empirical world, in Kant's view, is therefore only a world common to human subjects, and gives no ground for Green's supposition of a Universal Subject of the Universe of Reality, being, as I said, for Kant independent of the forms of human sensibility and understanding.

Then (§§ 38-41) Green argues against Kant's unknowable world of things-in-themselves. In § 38 he states fairly the difference between Kant's view and his own,—though keeping in the background the complexity of the Kantian psychology, the threefold distinction between forms of sensibility, forms of thought, and ideas of reason. But in his argument against this view there seems to me a certain misapprehension of Kant. Green says that Kant's distinction between 'form' and 'matter' implies "that phenomena have a real nature as effects of things-in-themselves other than that which they have as related to each other in the universe of our experience. And not only so, it puts the two natures in a position towards each other of mere negation and separation, of such a kind that any correspondence between them, any dependence of one upon the other, is impossible. As effects of things-in-themselves, phenomena[1] are supposed to have a nature of

---

[1] By the way, 'feelings' or 'sensations' is more appropriate than 'phenomena' for Kant's view of the matter of empirical objects.

their own, but they cannot, according to Kant's doctrine, be supposed to carry any of that nature with them into experience."[1]

(1) The first sentence and the last suggest that in Kant's view the data of sense, by synthesis of which empirical objects are formed, could actually exist apart from the forms (of sensibility and thought) due to the constitution of the human mind. But I know no ground for attributing this view to Kant. (2) The second sentence altogether ignores Kant's view that the forms of the Understanding were applied to the data of Sense through the *schemata* or time-determinations due to the exercise of pure or productive imagination. These schemata, *e.g.* 'permanent,' 'mutable,' for *subject*, predicate; *antecedent*, temporally consequent, for *reason*, logically consequent, bring about, in Kant's view, just the correspondence required for the synthesis of form and matter in knowledge of empirical objects.

But the criticism of Kantism in the following passage seems to me to hit the mark, still with the partial misunderstanding in one sentence that I have just indicated :—" The ' cosmos of our experience ' and the order of things-in-themselves will be two wholly unrelated worlds,[2] of which, however, each determines the same sensations. All that determination of a sensible occurrence which can be the object of possible experience or inferred as an explanation of experience — its simple position of antecedence or

---

[1] *Op. cit.* § 39, p. 41.
[2] *Op. cit.* § 39, p. 42. ' Unrelated '—in the one causes, effects in the other.

sequence in time to other occurrences, as well as its relation to conditions which regulate that position and determine its sensible nature—will belong to one world of which a unifying self-consciousness is the organising principle: while the very same occurrence, as an effect of things-in-themselves, will belong to another world . . ."[1]

So again, the objection in § 41 to the causal relation which Kant assumes to exist between 'things-in-themselves' and their effects on sensibility seems to me sound; as according to Kant we have no warrant for extending the application of the category of causality, *in any positive way*, beyond the limits of experience. The assumption, therefore, that 'things-in-themselves' (other than thinking beings) *are* causes of phenomena contradicts the principles of Kant's *Analytik*.

I have said enough on Green's relation to Kant: I return to the exposition of his own system. Dropping 'things-in-themselves,' he conceives the real world, the only real world, the Universe, as a connected order of knowable facts, and therefore essentially a 'single, unalterable, all-inclusive system of relations.' This real world, therefore, presupposes, just as the experience of each finite mind presupposes, a combining, unifying, self-distinguishing principle or subject which by its synthetic action constitutes the relations that determine phenomena. It is a principle other than nature; for "the relations by which,

[1] '*Belong to another world*'—according to Kant it only belongs to this in respect of its *causation*, not in respect of its quality. Otherwise Green's objection to the *double* determination of the phenomenon seems to me sound.

through its action, phenomena are determined are not relations of it—not relations by which it is itself determined. They arise out of its presence to phenomena, but the very condition of their thus arising is that the unifying consciousness which constitutes them should not itself be one of the objects so related."[1] This principle, therefore, is not in time, nor in space. It is not material, nor subject to motion, for matter and motion are merely names of relation; it is not a substance, for 'substance' is only a correlative of change, has no meaning or conceivable existence apart from change. This One Subject, therefore, is not to be conceived as the substance of the world, for "that connexion of all phenomena as changes of one world which is implied in the unity of intelligent experience cannot be the work of anything which the substance qualified by those changes."[2] Such a non-natural self-conscious subject is what Green means by a Spiritual Principle.

Let us look a little closer at this strange entity. It is not, as Green has before explained (§ 41), a cause of which nature is the effect, for "causation has no meaning except as an unalterable connexion between changes in the world of our experience."[3] But what then is meant by saying that this non-natural principle is a 'source' of relations, that they "result from its combining and unifying action"?[4] Surely this is only saying in other words that they are effects of which it is a cause. Green seems to

---

[1] *Op. cit.* § 52, pp. 54, 55.
[2] *Op. cit.* § 53, p. 56.
[3] *Op. cit.* § 41, p. 44.
[4] [*Op. cit.* § 9, p. 14.]

admit the difficulty, and to answer by saying that this language is 'metaphorical.'[1] But surely it is a weak position when such fundamental notions as 'source,' 'action,' 'agency,' etc., are admitted to be used 'metaphorically,' and yet no attempt is made to justify or explain the 'metaphor' by some clear and precise statement of the truth it adumbrates. But let us suppose that these terms, apparently implying a causal relation, really mean something else.

The fundamental difficulty is not removed. Green's argument was that this principle of union cannot be conditioned by *any* of the relations that result from its combining and unifying. How then are we to obtain a conception of its relation to nature? for any such conception must have a 'unifying' effect: it must enable us to form a coherent view of Nature and Spirit taken together.

There is, indeed, one conception which is at least free from the special objections urged against the notions of 'action,' 'agency,' 'source,' 'results,' etc., as applied to the relation between Spirit and Nature: and this is the conception which the main line of Green's argument suggests. That is the relation of subject and object in knowledge, in its simplest form —the cognition of an object by a subject, or the presentation of an object to a subject. For this relation is disparate from, unlike any relation among objects; and thus this relation comes to the front in the next chapter *On the Relation of Man, as Intelligence, to the Spiritual Principle in Nature*, to which I pass.

---

[1] *Op. cit.* § 54, p. 57 *init.*

Here we are led to analyse more closely the fact of human knowledge. Man, as a being that knows, is not a mere series of events: human consciousness is not a mere stream or succession of changing states. Knowledge is of related facts: it is essential to every act of knowledge that the related parts of the object known should be present together to the knowing mind. "The acts of consciousness in which the several members are apprehended, as forming a knowledge, are a many in one. None is before or after another. This is equally the case whether the knowledge is of successive events or of the 'uniformities' which are said to constitute a law of nature."[1] As an instance Green takes "a man's knowledge of a proposition in Euclid. This means a relation in his consciousness of certain parts of a figure determined by the relation of these parts to certain other parts. The knowledge is made up of those relations as in consciousness. Now it is obvious that there is no lapse of time, however minute, no antecedence and consequence, between the constituent relations of the consciousness so composed"—in this I quite agree. But Green goes on—"nor between the complex formed by these constituent relations and anything else."[2] If 'the complex formed,' etc., means—as the words seem to mean—the whole state of consciousness, this statement cannot be accepted. It seems clear, on the contrary, that there is the most definite time-relation of 'antecedence and consequence' between the complex consciousness which constitutes the knowledge

[1] *Op. cit.* § 56, p. 61.   [2] *Op. cit.* § 57, pp. 61, 62.

of a demonstrated conclusion and the intellectual apprehension of the successive steps of the demonstration.

This is so plain, that when Green draws the inference that this knowing consciousness is not a 'phenomenon,' not an 'event in the individual's history,' he seems to be confounding the knowing consciousness with the object known. It is no doubt true that when we consider the object of any one's knowledge—say a proposition of Euclid—the system of relations of which it consists is independent of time. Though complex, there is no succession, no lapse of time between its parts: and it is—so far as it is true knowledge—unalterable, the same at one period as at another. It is not affected by the fact that A knew it yesterday, B knows it now, and C will know it to-morrow. And this is also true, as Green points out, when the knowledge is of successive events. Take, *e.g.*, the knowledge that I have gone through half a dozen steps of reasoning in learning a proposition of Euclid. It is true of this knowledge, no less than of knowledge of a demonstrated conclusion, that it does not itself consist of successive steps, but is a single apprehension of such successive steps; and it is no less true that so far as this complex fact is truly known, it may be equally well known by any one else at any subsequent time. All this is true: but it does not justify the inference that this single apprehension of a complex truth—whether geometrical or biographical—is not an event in my mental history. If, as Green says, in learning a proposition of Euclid, a series of events takes place, surely we must recognise the conscious knowing of the proposition as the final event of the series.

We cannot allow him to pass from the "consciousness which constitutes a knowledge" to "the content of such consciousness" as though they were identical conceptions. We may admit the content not to be an event in time, but we cannot admit that the knowing of it is not an event in time. Indeed when Green tells us that "a known object is a related whole, of which . . . the members are necessarily present together," he seems to mean that they are present simultaneously; his argument, in fact, has no force unless he means this. But what is simultaneously present must be present at some particular instant—or during some particular period—to some particular knowing subject. And if so, surely what thus happens or begins to happen must be an event in the history of this person!

The truth appears to be that Green is so concerned to lay stress on the points (1) that knowledge is not a succession of states of consciousness, and (2) that the complex relations that make up the extent of any act of knowledge are present together, in this act, to the knowing mind, that he allows himself to be carried along to the paradox of asserting that the *act* of knowledge itself is not an event in the mental history of this mind. Now a knower who knows, but does not know at any point of time or through any period of time, is absolutely inconceivable to me, and nothing in my experience helps me towards conceiving it.

Here I may conveniently develop another criticism, briefly noticed before. In several passages of Book I. Green speaks of the real in human experience as a "single *unalterable* system of relations." I let this pass provisionally, because there is a sense in which the epithets may stand. If we assume that all events are completely determined by their antecedents, then the whole process of change in which our minds live, and which it is the effort of the study of nature to know, is in a sense unalterable :—*i.e.* from a *complete* knowledge of the [physical] world at any point, including all physical laws of change, we could infer the past, as far back, and the future, as far forward, as we choose to follow it.

But because the process of cosmic change is determined, and in this sense unalterable, it does not therefore cease to be a process of change, of which it is an essential condition that it takes place in time. Accordingly when Green concludes that any act of knowledge—even the "ordinary perception of sensible things or matters of fact"—involves "the determination of a sensible process which is in time by an agency which is not in time," we have to point out that this sensible process must be a part of the whole cosmic process—of the "single and unalterable system of relations," and must as a part of this be completely determined; so that there would seem to be no room for any other determination. To this I shall return. However, Green's conclusion is that the knowledge we arrive at through sensation and sense-perception is not itself in time—though the sensation is—and implies the presence of an agent not subject to the conditions of time, an 'eternal' and 'spiritual' principle.

LECTURE III

THE RELATION OF MAN TO THE SPIRITUAL PRINCIPLE IN NATURE

BEFORE passing to the end of chap. ii. and chap. iii. let us review the ground so far traversed, and try to make clear to ourselves the results attained. First, I may again remark that the controversy between Green's Idealism and the Philosophy of Common Sense or Natural Dualism—to which I provisionally adhere—is never prominent or important in Green's argument. As we saw, he treats this line of thought so slightly that he takes Locke as a representative of what is called Common Sense and does not even allude to Reid, and obviously knows nothing of his work. His chief controversy accordingly is not with Natural Dualism which maintains the current distinction between mind and matter, accepted by Common Sense and Physical Science, including Psychophysiology. It is not this view which he conceives his opponent to hold, but rather a species of what I call Mentalism—the philosophical view that resolves matter altogether into mental elements. The species is that which I think it convenient to distinguish from Idealism as

Sensationalism—which resolves matter into Feelings, and is mainly English. He also has in view what I may perhaps distinguish as Phenomenalism, the doctrine that resolves *matter as known* into elements of feelings while recognising an unknown external matter whose action on us causes these feelings. To this view he naturally opposes, in a great measure, the same arguments that he opposes to the more paradoxical Sensationalism; but he has to add, in dealing with Phenomenalism, a confutation of the supposed unknown substratum of matter, the 'thing by itself,' that has the support of Kant's authority. Into this dispute between schools, to neither of which I belong, I have entered but slightly: my concern has been with Green's own system and its construction. This construction, however, is influenced by the system of thought that he conceives to be opposed to him. The adversary is supposed to hold that the world is composed of feelings as elements. Against this Green's point is that "feelings without relation are nothing to us as thinking beings," and that the concatenation of objects which make up for each mind its experience or its empirically known world consists essentially of relations, of which as thought-relations some principle other than any or all objects, some thinking principle, must be conceived as the source. The source of these thought-relations, that which combines, unifies, organises experience, cannot be conditioned by the relations, and therefore cannot be conceived as a part of the empirical object world that exists for each. Then passing from the world of each one's experience to the larger common object world that each conceives to exist for all, we find ourselves led to postulate a similar non-natural principle for Nature.

Nature is thus conceived as essentially a single unalterable all-inclusive system of relations, by which all phenomena are combined into a systematic whole: and the source of connexion, the combiner, the unifyer, must be a non-natural or Spiritual Principle. Here I made one criticism. How, as no element of Nature is conceivable out of relation, can we conceive it as requiring a non-natural principle to bring it into relation? It seems that in order to exhibit the evidence for a non-natural principle Green has first to conceive Nature as analysed into elements; yet this in the same breath he declares to be irrational and inconceivable! Surely this will not do. But further difficulties appear when we examine Green's fundamental doctrine that the relations by which through the action of this non-natural principle "phenomena are determined are not relations *of* it—not relations by which it is itself determined."[1] First, it is difficult to understand how this universal Principle is, on Green's premises, conceivable. He has laid down that everything which is an object of thought to me must be determined by relations which my thought supplied: and that this eternal self-distinguishing consciousness cannot be conceived as determined

[1] [*Op. cit.* § 52, p. 54.]

SPIRITUAL PRINCIPLE IN NATURE

by the relations of which its activity is a source: "the very condition of their thus arising is that the unifying consciousness which constitutes them should not be one of the objects so related."[1] But if it cannot be thought under its own relations, surely it can no more be thought under the relations which are the product of my intellectual activity—since, as we noted last time, I am *qua* thinker, a mere limited reproduction of the eternal consciousness. But if so, how can this eternal consciousness be an object of thought at all to me, consistently with Green's general view of thought and its objects? Similarly, how can other human beings, conceived as self-conscious selves, be such objects? Finally, how can I myself be properly an object of my own thought?

The difficulty takes another form when we examine the relation of the non-natural principle to Nature. It is not in Time, not in Space, not a Substance, not a Cause—for "Causation has no meaning except as an unalterable connexion between changes in the world of our experience."[2] But then what is meant by saying that it is a source of relations, and that they 'result from' its combining and unifying action? To this, as we have seen,[3] Green only gives the singularly weak answer that this language must be taken to be 'metaphorical.' I do not debar a philosopher from the use of metaphor by way of illustration: but I think he is bound also to state his meaning in unmetaphorical language:

---

[1] [*Op. cit.* § 52, p. 54 *fin.*]   [2] [*Op. cit.* § 41, p. 44.]
[3] Cf. above, p. 232.

242 THE METAPHYSICS OF T. H. GREEN LECT.

and this Green does not seem ever to do as regards the important point that we are discussing.

There is another inconsistency in his conception of Nature. It is a "single, unalterable, all-inclusive system of relations."[1] But why not 'related feelings'—granting the negation of things other than feelings—surely relation must relate something! Green's only answer is that "feelings without relations are nothing to us as thinking beings." But that is his answer. The question is whether thought-relations are not equally inconceivable without feelings. Green to our surprise ultimately admits this: he is as willing to deny that there can be 'mere thought' as 'mere feeling,' he declares "feeling and thought to be inseparable and mutually dependent": and yet, having admitted this, goes on speaking of Nature as *essentially* a "single, unalterable, all-inclusive system of relations"; and throughout his discussion, seems to ignore feelings completely in his account of the real world. I cannot refrain from conjecturing that in this Green has been unconsciously influenced by the desire to avoid attributing feelings to his universal self-distinguishing consciousness; as this would clash with the traditional philosophical conception of the Divine Mind as Rational but not Sentient.[2] However, we seem to be left with (1) Nature as a single unalterable—though, by the way, continually changing—system

[1] [*Op. cit.* § 29, p. 30.]
[2] This difficulty seems to me to attach to all Neo-Kantian attempts to reconstruct the Kantian view of the world without 'Things in themselves.'

of thought-relations, with feelings admitted to be somehow inseparable from thought, though ignored in the definition; and (2) with a spiritual principle which 'acts' without causality, unifies and combines what is inconceivable otherwise than in combination, and, in short, of which we can form no distinct conception except that it is a subject related to the world of objects as each one's intellect is related to the objects of his own experience.

The one positive conception which he does give of spirit is more closely contemplated in chap. ii., in which the relation of man as intelligence to the Spiritual Principle in nature is considered. Here again it should be observed that Green's antagonism is primarily to a sensationalist explanation of knowledge which professed to resolve an act of cognition into a series of feelings. Against this he urges well and forcibly that in the knowledge of any complex object—whether a succession of past events, or the uniformities of nature, or a geometrical proposition—all the relations of the parts of the object known must be apprehended by the mind in a single act. He also urges truly that the *content* of any cognitive consciousness—so far as it is truly knowledge—is unaffected by the time at which (or the knower by whom) it is known. It is the same yesterday and to-morrow, for me and for you—otherwise it would not be true knowledge. This is the part of the argument which I consider most sound and constructively important.

But from these sound premises Green draws the

startling conclusion that this cognition is not 'an event in the individual's history.' If, however, learning a proposition of Euclid is—as Green says—a series of events in the individual's history, it is absurd to refuse to recognise the conscious knowing of the proposition as the final event in the series. Also, when he says that the members of a known object are "necessarily present together . . . none before or after another," he in effect says that they are present simultaneously. But simultaneity is a time-determination as well as succession: what is simultaneously present must be present at a particular point of time, or through a period of time—through all time if we like.

In fact, however, Green recognises that 'our perceiving consciousness' has itself apparently a history in time. The solution [of this seeming inconsistency] I must give again[1] in his own words, as it is one of the cardinal points in his teaching: "Our consciousness may mean either of two things: either a function of the animal organism, which is being made, gradually and with interruptions, a vehicle of the eternal consciousness; or that eternal consciousness itself, as *making* the animal organism its vehicle and subject to certain limitations in so doing, but retaining its essential characteristic as independent of time, as the *determinant* of becoming, which has not and does not itself become."[2] He afterwards speaks of the eternal consciousness as a "system of thought and knowledge which realises

[1] Cf. above, p. 235 *fin.* [2] *Op. cit.* § 67, p. 72.

or reproduces itself" in the individual.[1] Let us consider these 'two meanings' of consciousness. They seem to be two very different things: (1) a function of an animal organism; (2) an eternal consciousness limiting itself and making the animal organism its vehicle. The conceptions seem as clearly distinct as can be; but what then becomes of the 'self' in this doubleness? Oh! Green assures us " our consciousness is one indivisible reality "[1] of which these are two aspects, the same thing regarded from two different points of view. But then there would seem to be a third meaning of 'consciousness': it is the (3) "indivisible reality" of which (1) and (2) are aspects, but it is also both of these. I confess I find it difficult to conceive God as an aspect of myself, and yet God existing already and eternally as all-knowing. Green adduces the old simile of the two sides of a shield. But we can see clearly how the two sides of a shield are united into a continuous surface by the rim; we surely cannot similarly see how 'one indivisible self' should result from an eternal consciousness limiting itself and using the animal organism as its vehicle.

[1] *Op. cit.* § 68, p. 74. Observe the alternatives offered, 'realises' or 'reproduces.' If 'realises' is the right word, then the eternal consciousness is only potentially, if 'reproduces,' then it is actually, existent apart from the finite individual. Surely a little more ought to be said on these alternatives, as the difference is, from a theological point of view, immense. It is, in fact, the issue between Hegelian Theism [Right] and Hegelian Atheism [Left] that is thus slurred over. But I think Green must be taken theistically: and therefore to mean 'reproduces' rather than 'realises,' as he holds (§ 69, p. 75) that "there is a consciousness for which the relations of fact, that form the object of our gradually attained knowledge, *already* and eternally exist"—though how anything can exist *already* for a subject out of time, he does not explain.

The explanation is: "The consciousness which varies from moment to moment, which is in succession, and of which each successive state depends on a series of 'external and internal' events, is consciousness in the former sense. It consists in what may properly be called phenomena; in successive modifications of the animal organism, which would not, it is true, be what they are if they were not media for the realisation of an eternal consciousness, but which are not this consciousness. On the other hand, it is this latter consciousness as so far realised in or communicated to us through modification of the animal organism, that constitutes our knowledge, with the relations, characteristic of knowledge, into which time does not enter, which are not in becoming but are once for all what they are."[1]

But does not this, Green supposes his reader to ask, "involve the impossible supposition that there is a double consciousness in man? No, we reply, not that there is a double consciousness, but that the one indivisible reality of our consciousness cannot be comprehended in a single conception. In seeking to understand its reality we have to look at it from two different points of view . . ."[2] Here and elsewhere Green is so much occupied with distinguishing intellect and knowledge from mere feelings that he is led to obliterate the distinction between 'psychical' and 'physical' phenomena. He seems to say that the "consciousness that varies from moment to

[1] *Op. cit.* § 67, p. 72.   [2] *Op. cit.* § 68, p. 73.

moment . . . consists in successive modifications of the animal organism," but surely my consciousness which varies from moment to moment is a stream of psychical facts, distinct from modifications of a material organism, however these may be mentalistically interpreted.

But I will not dwell on this. Let us assume with him that the important distinction is between 'knowledge' and 'sentient life,' and not between 'feeling' and 'matter in motion.' The difficulty is not the least reduced. One of the things I am most certain of is the unity of myself. Green says that (1) I am really two things, so disparate as an eternal consciousness out of time, and a function of an animal organism changing in time; and yet at the same time that (2) I am one indivisible reality contemplated from two different points of view. I submit that Green is bound to reconcile this contradiction, which he does not do by simply stating that both contradictory propositions are true. As it is, his doctrine is rather like the theological doctrine of the Athanasian Creed, only the Athanasian Creed does not profess to give an intelligible account of the mysteries that it formulates.

But apart from this there is a further difficulty, or rather the old difficulty of chap. i.—the difficulty of conceiving the eternal subject, according to Green's view of it, as a cause of which anything in the world is the effect. For it will be observed that, in the later pages of chap. ii. (§§ 67-73), these causal terms recur. The eternal consciousness "makes the animal organism its vehicle," it is the "determinant of becoming": it is "operative" throughout the succession of events which constitute the growth of the individual mind: it "acts on the sentient life of the soul" and "uses it" as its organ.

These are all terms which imply the causality of the eternal subject, in special relation to a certain part of the world in space and time, in the most definite and unmistakable way. They are just as irreconcilable as the terms used in chap. i. with the statement repeatedly and emphatically made that the relations by which the non-natural subject unifies Nature are not predicable of *it*, the subject: and in particular with the statement that "causation has no meaning except as a connexion between changes in the world of our experience."[1] Are they also 'metaphorical,' and if so, what becomes of the whole view if metaphor is discarded? This question may perhaps find an answer in chap. iii., to which I now pass.

It is in virtue of this "self-realisation or reproduction in the human consciousness of an eternal consciousness not existing in time, but the condition of there being an order in time, and an intelligent experience," that we are entitled to say that "man is a free cause."[2] The term 'cause' is, indeed, not strictly appropriate, since, though this 'eternal consciousness' or 'unifying principle' distinguishes itself from the manifold which it unifies, it must not be supposed that it has "another nature of its own apart from

[1] [*Op. cit.* § 41, p. 44.]   [2] [*Op. cit.* § 74, p. 79.]

what it does in relation to the manifold world."[1] But what is meant by calling it a cause and what does it cause? Green says that "but for our own exercise of causality" in knowing the statement would have no meaning.[2] We know the action of our own minds in knowledge, we infer thus the action of the self-originating mind in the universe. How we can apply the notion of causation in any sense *consistently* with what is stated in chap. i. as to the impossibility of applying thought-relations to the source of these relations is not explained. But I will not dwell further on that. Let us try to get a clear idea of what the action is. The agent is said to give the world its character:—that would seem to mean creates it. But then the agent must have a determined character apart from the world; and that, as we have seen, is denied: "it must not be supposed that the unifying principle has another nature of its own apart from what it does in relation to the manifold world." It seems, in short, to be a cause that is nothing apart from its effect.

Green is perhaps aware of the obscurity of his statement, for he takes pains to repudiate any notion of explaining with any detail what the work is as a whole.[3] Perhaps if this declaration of philosophic impotence had been made at the outset, the reader would have read with less ardour. But however little Green offers an explanation of the world, at any rate he offers an account of it: and it seems not unreason-

[1] *Op. cit.* § 75, p. 80.
[2] [*Op. cit.* § 77, p. 82 *init.*]   [3] Cf. *op. cit.* § 82, p. 86.

able to demand that the account should not contain inconsistent conceptions. What are we to make of a subject out of Time, to which objects are already present—a subject to which we cannot apply any thought-relations, because it is the source of all such, yet which we must think as making, determining, openly acting: a subject which gives the world its character, and yet has no nature of its own apart from it? And what again of a world composed of thought-relations, admitted to be inseparable from feelings related, and yet of which the thought-relations are given by a subject to which feeling is never attributed?

However, let us take it that this agent is a free cause, and man, as knowing, is similarly free so far as his consciousness is "identified by this eternal consciousness with itself, or made the subject of its self-communication,"—so far, in short, as it is a 'reproduction' of the eternal mind. It is true that "man's attainment of knowledge is conditional on processes in time and on the fufilment of strictly natural functions." But even these functions, "which would be those of a natural or animal life if they were not organic to the end consisting in knowledge, just because they are so organic, are not in their full reality natural functions, though the purposes of detailed investigation of them—perhaps the purpose of improving man's estate—may be best served by so treating them. For one who could comprehend the whole state of the case, even a digestion that served to nourish a brain, which was in turn organic to knowledge, would be essentially different from digestion in an animal incapable of knowledge."[1] This seems to me a bold assertion. Why should it be 'essentially' different? No doubt brain affects digestion. But why 'essentially'? By this Green means a great deal, as we see from what follows. For we may say, he holds, that "in strict truth the man who knows, so far from being an animal altogether, is not an animal at all or even in part." He has only to add that he is not an eternal consciousness at all: and the fasciculus of contradictions would be symmetrical and complete. However, we need not pause on this hard saying. At any rate, in Green's view the "inquiry as to what man in himself is, must refer... to the character which he has as consciously distinguishing himself from all that happens to him."[2] "We are entitled to say," he tells us, "that in himself, *i.e.* in respect of that principle through which he is at once a self and distinguishes himself as such, he exerts a *free* activity—an activity which is not in time, not a link in the chain of natural becoming, which has no antecedents other than itself but is self-originated." Or—which Green apparently regards as a convertible statement—is originated "by the action of an eternal consciousness, which uses them ['the processes of brain and nerve and tissue, all the functions of life and sense'] as its organs and reproduces itself through them."[3]

Now, in order to examine closely this attribution of

---

[1] *Op. cit.* § 79, p. 84.
[2] *Op. cit.* § 80, p. 85.   [3] *Op. cit.* § 82, p. 86.

'freedom' to human intelligence, let us grant—what I have above strenuously denied—that an act of human knowledge is not an event in time, and also that the relation of knowledge to its object is entirely unlike any other relation within the known world, and incapable of being developed out of any concatenation of such relations. But it must remain true that in human minds knowledge is partial and changing: some know some things, others other things, and the knowledge that any one has at one time of his life is different from the knowledge he has at other times. I suppose Green does not intend to deny that of these differences and variations there is a natural explanation to be given, since he says "why any detail of the world should be what it is we can explain by reference to other details which determine it";[1] and surely the exact degree of finiteness, the limitations, the particularity, in the knowledge of any finite mind at any particular time is a 'detail of the world,' and its variations must come into and form part of the process of cosmic change. If so, we must conclude that the 'freedom' of intelligence has no particular or practical application. For if intelligence is 'free,' still the particularity of the intelligence of any particular mind must be as much caused as anything else in the world. That it knows at all may defy a natural explanation: but that it knows this or that, so much and no more, must be completely so explicable. We may remember that the same statement was found to apply to Green's

[1] [*Op. cit.* § 82, p. 86.]

'freedom' in the ethical sense.[1] But there is a want of complete correspondence between the two which it is desirable to note.

Green, it will be seen, treats the notion of Freedom under two heads in chap. iii. of Book I. and in chap. i. of Book II.—as the "freedom of man as intelligence" and as the "freedom of the will." It is fundamentally important, in understanding Green's 'freedom,' to keep this double use of the notion in mind. For in his view 'free' simply means 'not natural,' not explicable by natural causality; and that, in either case, means only that in human intelligence and human volition alike—so far as the two are distinguishable—a self-distinguishing, self-objectifying consciousness is necessary. At the same time, there is a considerable difference between Green's treatment of the two cases. For in considering the "freedom of man as intelligence" I do not find that he gives any explanation of—or even takes any notice of—the fact of *Error*. He has, as we saw, previously given an account of error as conceiving a phenomenon in relations inconsistent with the single unalterable system. But he does not consider how man's 'free intelligence' can do this. The self-distinguishing consciousness in chap. iii. to which 'free causality' is attributed is always (so far as I can see) conceived to exercise its freedom so as to attain or produce *knowledge*—real knowledge—not illusion and error. But in the case of the 'free will' the distinction between 'virtuous' and 'vicious' choice—choice of

---

[1] Cf. the author's *Ethics of Green, Spencer, and Martineau*, pp. 16 ff.

true good and choice of mere pleasure—appears in the forefront of the discussion.

Still, equally in both cases, the deflection from truth and right on the part of the self-distinguishing consciousness is inexplicable. Why does the eternal spirit, reproducing itself so many million times in connexion with so many organisms, produce so much error and so much vice? I find no serious attempt to answer this in Green. But he seems practically to admit in both cases that the *particularity* of the individual's cognition or volition—the difference between A, who discovers truth, and B, who produces chimeras, between A, who makes a right choice and seeks his true good, and B, who makes a wrong choice and seeks his self-satisfaction in pleasures that do not satisfy—these particularities and differences are to be explained by differences in the previous *histories* of A and B. For he says—as already quoted—"why any detail of the world is what it is, we can explain by reference to other details which determine it":[1] and the ignorance and errors of some, the particularities and limitations of the knowledge of others, are certainly 'details' of the world. So again "the form in which the self or ego at any time presents the highest good to itself—and it is on this presentation that its conduct depends—is due to the past history of its inner life . . . The particular modes in which I now feel, desire, and think, arise out of the modes in which I have previously done so."[2] He lays stress, indeed, on the fact that in all cases a self-distinguishing

---

[1] Cf. above, p. 252.   [2] *Op. cit.* § 101, p. 105.

consciousness has been operative throughout this history: but as this is a similar element in all the different cases—for it is the eternal consciousness reproducing itself in all—it cannot possibly furnish an explanation of the differences.

Summary of Green's Metaphysical View

(1) Everything that is or can be an object of thought is constituted by relations :—relations of its elements to each other, of itself to other objects, and to the whole of nature; it also involves a self-conscious, self-distinguishing thinker or subject, apart from which any object is inconceivable.

(2) If it be said " but besides relations there must be feelings related "—the answer is that feelings without relations are nothing for us as thinking beings.

(3) Relations are results of the activity of thought, combining and unifying: thus the world of each man's experience is in some sense produced by the activity of each intelligent self.

(4) But the distinction between truth and seeming, between impressions that correspond to objective reality and mere subjective illusion, involves the conception of a single unalterable system of relations —for error and illusion lie merely in conceiving relations wrongly, *i.e.* otherwise than they are in this single system.

(5) This single unalterable system of relations must therefore be referred to a universal self or

ego: and its partial apprehension by human minds must be explained by supposing this universal ego to ["realise or"] reproduce itself in individual human beings gradually, making the function of an animal organism its vehicle.

(6) The acts of knowledge of human beings—acts in which the knowledge eternally possessed by the universal ego is reproduced in the human mind—are "out of time," though the process of attaining knowledge is, no doubt, a process carried on in time.

APPENDIX TO THE LECTURES ON THE METAPHYSICS OF GREEN

[The chief part of a lecture entitled "The Philosophy of T. H. Green," which Professor Sidgwick delivered at Oxford shortly before his death, is here reprinted from *Mind*, N.S. vol. x. 1901, pp. 18 ff. The lecture was never revised, but—as it was written some time after those that now precede it—it is inserted as supplementary to them.]

I can now, I hope, state both briefly and clearly my view of Green's Metaphysical System. First, it is a species of Mentalism. Nature, or the world of space and time, is conceived as a single, unalterable, all-inclusive system of relations: and these relations are thought-relations; they result from the activity of thought. So again, so far as this conception of Nature goes, the system is clearly the species I have called Idealism. If Nature is essentially a system of thought-relations, Reality is—so far—Thought. And if Thought was conceived as simply *für sich bestehend* [1]—as Green had conceived it some years before—the whole system might have been purely Idealistic. Thought would then not only have made Nature, but have completed itself—its system of relating and related notions—in Spirit: so that the Universe of Reality would have been truly thought as Thought itself.

But this is not Green's view in the *Prolegomena*: on the contrary, it is a view that he decidedly and emphatically excludes. The single all-inclusive system of thought-relations which constitutes nature, "implies something other than itself, as a condition of its being what it is." [2] It presupposes the activity of a thinking being, a "self-distinguishing, self-objectifying, unifying, combining consciousness" whose synthetic activity is the source of the relations by which the knowable

[1] Cf. *Works*, vol. ii. p. 11 note.   [2] *Prolegomena*, § 52 f.

world is unified : and we are entitled to say of this entity, that the relations which result from its synthetic action are not predicable of it. "They arise out of its presence to phenomena, or the presence of phenomena to it, but the very condition of their thus arising is that the unifying consciousness which constitutes them should not be one of the objects so related." This consciousness is therefore "not in time, not in space," etc., not "above or beyond or before nature," nor a "substance of which the changing modes constitute nature," nor "a cause of which nature is the effect": and "causation, indeed"—we are told—"has no meaning except as an unalterable connexion between changes in the world of experience." The most distinctive term for it—as "consciousness" and "mind" have wider meanings—is Spirit.

Briefly, then, a spirit's thinking activity is the source of a system of notions, by which the world is constituted, but it cannot itself be thought under any of these. It is the former proposition that leads me to call Green's view Idealistic: it is the latter which leads me to call it Spiritualistic, according to the definition before given.

For it is not only the Divine Spirit, that constitutes the world, which is affirmed incapable of being itself conditioned by any of the relations that result from its combining and unifying action : this is no less true of human minds so far as they have knowledge, and understand the world, to however partial and limited an extent. Indeed, finite minds are not merely similar in this respect to God, and analogously active—in unifying and combining—each within the limits of his own experience : this likeness, this analogy of action is, in Green's view, an adequate ground for inferring *identity*, between God and finite minds, so far as the latter are not merely sentient but intelligent. 'Man' is for Green, as for Common Sense, a composite or dual being : but the duality seems to be different. For modern Common Sense, at least, man is composed of Mind and Matter, and feelings no less than thoughts—as contrasted with cerebral nerve-processes—are regarded as mental facts. For Green, on the other hand, sentiency, and even consciousness in a certain sense, belongs to the nature constituted by thought-relations : but so far as knowing, each man's consciousness is nothing but the eternal consciousness itself, reproducing or realising itself in a limited form in connexion with the man's animal organism which it makes its vehicle, and whose sentient life it uses as its organ. It is as such a reproduction or realisation of the one Divine Mind that a man is also a "self-distinguishing, self-objectifying consciousness," a "self-conscious personality" or briefly a "spirit."

"Realise or reproduce." The alternatives are rather startling: so vast an issue appears to be left an open question by the disjunction thus quietly suggested. For if we say "realise," God and his complete knowledge, and Nature, the single all-inclusive system of relations appear to lapse into potential existence; reality being restricted to finite spirits and their partial and imperfectly understood experiences. We should thus get an Idealism curiously correspondent to the sensationalism of J. S. Mill; possibilities of thought taking the place of the latter's possibilities of sensation. Can we infer from the alternative phrase that Green recognised this or something like this as a tenable metaphysical position? I cannot say: but one who has read the *Prolegomena* through can hardly doubt that he decisively adopted the other alternative. The conception of One Divine Eternal Spirit, who really *is* all that the human spirit is capable of becoming, is essential to his ethics: God is the ideal of the human spirit, but he is an ideal completely realised.

This then is Green's 'Spiritualism' as distinguished from his Idealism. There is, of course, an essential connexion between the two: my point is that there is also, in a certain sense, an essential opposition. The Spirit makes nature: but it is and must be a non-natural principle. That is, it constitutes nature by a system of relations which result from its action as thinking: but for that very reason these thought-relations "are not relations of it, not relations by which it is itself determined." For, once admit it to be otherwise, once suppose that any of the thought-relations resulting from its thinking activity are applicable to it, then it becomes *pro tanto* a part of nature: its non-naturalness can no longer be maintained, and the *pivotal* notion of the whole system is removed.

We come, then, to the questions which I primarily offer

for discussion. Is this combination of Idealism and Spiritualism —as I have distinguished them—really thinkable? and does Green really succeed in thinking it? I am compelled to answer both questions in the negative, but I shall devote my own discussion chiefly to the second question.

Let us first take Green's positive account of Spirit, and ask, point by point, whether we can definitely think the qualities or functions he attributes to it, without, in so thinking, predicating of it some of the relations which, according to Green, result from its combining and unifying activity, and are therefore not properly predicable of it.

First, he conceives it as *one* and *many*: one Divine Mind and many reproductions of it; here we have relations of number.

Secondly, the human spirit is identical with the Divine:—the latter is said to be a "spirit which we ourselves are": yet again it is a "reproduction" of it and a reproduction is different from the original. Here we have a peculiar and difficult combination of the relations of identity and difference.

Again, a Spirit is a "self-distinguishing" consciousness: that means, I suppose, that it attributes to itself unity, identity, difference from nature and, I suppose, from other spirits. But again it is a "self-objectifying" consciousness: that is, it conceives itself as an object: and therefore in a relation of similarity with nature, so far as both spirit and nature must be thought as having whatever attributes are connoted by the word "object." Finally, it is a "unifying" and "combining" consciousness: but by each of these terms its function is conceived in a relation of similarity to processes that we conceive as occurring in Nature; Nature is continually presenting to us combinations and unifications, as well as separations and divisions.

In short, taking Green's descriptive terms, and endeavouring to think by means of them, we find that we are inevitably conceiving Spirit as conditioned or determined by the very same relations that we use in determining phenomena.

Turn now to the negative characterisation that he gives of Spirit, to emphasise and impress on us its non-naturalness. It is, he says, not in time, not in space, not a substance, not a cause. But can he really think it thus? Let us see.

First, the Spirit is "not in Time." If so, we are to understand not merely that it does not change but that it does not perdure; since changing and perduring are equally time-determinations. Hence when Green speaks of the Divine Spirit as "eternal," we must understand him to intend to mean not "everlasting," but merely the same as when he speaks of it as "not in time." But can we conceive this to be his meaning when he speaks of it as "a consciousness for which the relations of fact that form the object of our gradually attained knowledge *already* and *eternally* exist"; or when he speaks of the "best state of man as *already* present to a divine Consciousness"? Must we not think of the divine Consciousness as "in time" if we think of it as "already" such and such. So again, when speaking of the problem suggested by the constant spectacle of unfulfilled human promise, he says "we may content ourselves with saying that the personal self-conscious being, which comes from God, is for ever continued in God":—surely here God is conceived as eternal in the sense of abiding "for ever." Again, it is because the divine mind reproduces itself in the human soul that that soul is said to have a "spiritual" demand for an "abiding satisfaction of an abiding self"; but how could this be legitimately inferred unless the Divine Mind itself were conceived as abiding and perduring through Time?

But if "in time," why not a substance, since substance is for Green the permanent correlate of change? and can we avoid thinking of the Eternal Mind as the permanent correlate of the processes of change and development essential to finite minds?

Finally, can we conceive the Eternal Consciousness—following Green's thought—as not a cause? He tells us that it is a "source" of the relations which constitute Nature; that they "result from" its combining and unifying action; that it "makes the animal organism its vehicle"; that it "is operative" throughout the succession of events which constitute the growth of the individual mind; that it "acts on the sentient life of the soul" and "uses it" as its organ. Are not these all terms implying causality? And yet he says—arguing against Kant—that "causation has no meaning except as an unalterable connexion between changes in the world of our experience."

Green ultimately sees the inconsistency,—though I think he carries the exposition of the Metaphysics of Knowledge much too far without hinting at it. But I will not digress on this point. Let us rather try to understand the explanation that he ultimately gives. It is, I think, the most difficult passage in the *Prolegomena* :—

"When we transfer the term 'cause' from the relation between one thing and another within the determined world to the relation between that world and the agent implied in its existence, we must understand that there is no separate particularity in the agent, on the one side, and the determined world as a whole on the other. . . . The agent must act absolutely from itself in the action through which that world is—not as does everything within the world, under determination by something else. The world has no character but that given it by this action ; the agent no character but that which it gives itself in this action." [1]

It should be added that the "action," in the same passage, is stated to be "that inner determination of all contained in the manifold world by mutual relation, which is due to the action of the unifying principle."

It appears, then, that Green ultimately attributes to God Causality : but endeavours to establish an essential difference between Divine and Natural Causality : viz. that the Eternal Consciousness, as unifying principle, has "no separate particularity" apart from the manifold world, "no character but that which it gives itself in 'its unifying' action"—although it "must act absolutely from itself in the action through which the world is." Now I cannot myself conceive these characteristics united: I cannot conceive anything "acting absolutely from itself" and yet having "no character but that which it gives itself in this action." But, waiving this objection now, I admit that this negation of "character other than that which it gives itself in the action" differentiates the Causality of the Divine Mind profoundly from Natural Causality : but I think it does this at great cost to the system as a whole.

For, first, if God is thus reduced to a mere unifying principle, having no character except that which it gives itself in synthesising the manifold of nature, I do not see how the conception can be made to include the content which the ethical

[1] *Prolegomena, Metaphysics of Knowledge,* p. 81.

part of Green's doctrine requires. It is because there is a Divine Consciousness realising or reproducing itself in man that the true good of man is argued to be not Pleasure, but Virtue or Perfection, and Perfection is held to consist in the realisation of capabilities already realised in the Divine Existence: briefly put, man's true good is development in the direction of becoming liker to God. But this whole conception implies that God has what Mr. Balfour calls a 'Preferential Will' in relation to human life and action; and that this Will is realised in man's choice of Virtue in a sense in which it is not realised in his choice of sensual pleasure. Well, I do not see how this conception can be maintained if God is also conceived as having no character except that self-given in unifying the manifold of nature: for this unification is surely equally effected in the lives of sinners and in the lives of saints, as both are equally capable of being scientifically known. In short, this conception of the relation of God to the world seems to me to constitute a gulf between Green's Metaphysics and his Ethics which cannot be bridged over.

If, on the other hand, we leave Ethics aside, and confine ourselves to the conception of the Divine Spirit regarded as belonging to the *Metaphysics* of *Knowledge*, it seems to me that this eternal consciousness, characterless apart from its unifying action, is a rather insignificant entity: whose existence is not only difficult to establish logically, but not much worth establishing. The conception, indeed, of the world as a systematic whole, having unity and order through the complex relations of its parts, as well as infinite plurality and diversity; and the conception of the progress of knowledge as consisting in the continual discovery of order, system, and unity in what at first presents itself as an almost chaotic diversity—these are conceptions of the highest value. But when they are grasped, what is the further gain to knowledge in referring the unity and system to a unifying principle as its source, if that principle is to have no other character except what it gives itself in its unifying action. Is there any hope that such a conception can in any way help us to *grasp* the unity, the system of relations, more fully and truly? Nay, must not the notion of a Divine Mind if reduced so far, inevitably dwindle still further, and reveal itself as merely a hypostasised logical element or aspect of the knowable world regarded as a systematic whole?

And this view, I think, will be confirmed by a rigorous examination of Green's main argument for establishing the existence of a spiritual principle in nature. It is the source of the relations that constitute experience a connected whole: but where lies the logical necessity of assuming such a source? Green answers that the existence of the relations involves "the unity of the manifold, the existence of the many in one. . . . But," he says, " a plurality of things cannot of themselves unite in one relation, nor can a single thing of itself bring itself into a multitude of relations . . . there must "—therefore— "be something other than the manifold things themselves which combines them." The argument seems to me unthinkable, because, as Green has emphatically declared, I cannot even conceive the manifold things out of the relations: and therefore I cannot even raise the question whether, if I could so conceive them, I should see them to require something other than themselves to bring them into the relations.

But [secondly] Green has another line of argument. He can—he does—appeal to self-consciousness. "The action of our own Mind in knowledge," he says, gives us a positive conception of the action of the Divine Mind in the universe. Now for myself, in attaining knowledge, I seem to *find*, not to *originate*, truth. But, granting the human consciousness of "action absolutely from itself" in knowledge, can we infer from this the action of the Universal Mind, consistently with Green's theory of the human spirit? For if my self-consciousness is to be the *causa cognoscendi* of the causality of the *unifying* principle in the world, that self-consciousness must surely include an indubitable cognition of the essential unity of the self: but in trying to think Green's conception of the human spirit, I find the notion of its essential unity vanishes. "Our consciousness," he says, "may mean either of two things: either a function of the animal organism, which is being gradually made a vehicle of the eternal consciousness; or that eternal consciousness itself, as making the animal organism its vehicle." He then assures us that our consciousness is still "one indivisible reality": and that the two things just distinguished are merely two aspects of it, the same thing regarded from two different points of view. I cannot think myself thus; I cannot think God as one aspect of me, and my body as another aspect; and it seems to me that if I did succeed in thinking this, the essential unity of self would have vanished. Green adduces the old simile of the opposite sides of a shield: but it seems to me inapt. For I see clearly that a shield not only *may* but *must* have two opposite sides, united into a continuous surface by the rim: whereas I cannot see how one indivisible self can possibly have as its two sides an animal organism and a self-limiting eternal consciousness.

I have already detained you long, and yet treated too briefly vast topics; but before I conclude, I should like to say a word on the polemical aspect of Green's Metaphysic. He does not seriously trouble himself with Materialism, and Volitionism does not seem to have come within his ken. Nor, again, is his controversy in the main with Common Sense or Natural Dualism —of which, indeed, his notions are so vague that he speaks of good old Locke as a representative of the "traditional philosophy of Common Sense." It is rather Sensationalism or Phenomenalism which Green regards as his natural opponent, and to the refutation of which he directs much attention. And yet his attitude towards that element of the knowable world which either of these metaphysical views is disposed to take as ultimate, seems to me somewhat fluctuating and obscure.

He repeatedly speaks of Nature as merely a system of thought-relations, and affirms that "if we exclude from what we have considered real all qualities constituted by relations, we find that none are left"—thus apparently resolves all particular qualities in the manifold of experience entirely into relations. Yet elsewhere he seems to admit that "we cannot reduce the world of experience to a web of relations in which nothing is related"; and merely argues against the Sensationalist that in the world of knowable facts there is no such thing as "mere sensation, a matter wholly unformed by intelligence." "A fact consisting in mere feeling is an impossibility."

He is equally willing to admit that there is "no such thing as mere thought"; and in fact only to contend that feeling and thought are inseparable and mutually dependent. And he expressly affirms this mutual dependence of thought and feeling, not only in the case of our empirical consciousness, but in the case also of "the world-consciousness of which ours is a limited mode." But if this be so, I do not see how Green is justified—or thinks himself justified—in making the thought element so prominent, and the feeling element so subordinate in his account of Nature; or in speaking of Nature as a system of relations, instead of related feelings; or in resolving—as we saw—the particularity of a feeling entirely into relations. And finally, if "mutual independence of thought and feeling has no place in the world-consciousness," difficult questions arise to which Green suggests no answer. For instance, if any feeling is attributed to the world-consciousness, must not all feeling in the world be so attributed? or how are we to distinguish? Does God then feel the pleasure and the pain of the whole animal kingdom? And if so, is not the ground cut from under the anti-hedonistic positions of Green's Ethics? But I perceive that this topic will introduce so great a wave of discourse—as Plato says—that I must reluctantly abandon it, and apologise for the extent to which I have already tried your patience.

THE PHILOSOPHY OF MR. HERBERT SPENCER

INTRODUCTORY:

KANTIAN INFLUENCE IN ENGLAND

AGNOSTICISM AND RELATIVISM

IN the lectures on Green I have endeavoured to characterise and to criticise elements of actual philosophical thought derived from Kant's Transcendental Philosophy *viewed on its constructive side*: *i.e.* viewed as an attempt to exhibit systematically those factors of our conception and knowledge of the empirical world which are cognisable *a priori*, either as forms of sensibility or as forms of intellectual synthesis, otherwise termed fundamental concepts or categories.

But this is only one side or aspect either of the Kantian system itself or of its influence on English thought; nor is it the side or aspect which was at first clearly the most prominent. It is true that, as I say in my *Outlines of the History of Ethics*,[1] the thinker who in the first third of the nineteenth century was commonly regarded as the representative of German tendencies in philosophy—namely, Coleridge—transmitted the influence [2] of Kant as apprehended through the medium of post-Kantian thought and especially the thought of Schelling. Thus, as I have said (*Outlines, l.c.*), "the Kant partially assimilated by Coleridge was a Kant who could not be believed 'to have meant more by his Noumenon or Thing in itself than his mere words express';[3] who, in fact, must be believed to have attained,

[1] P. 271.
[2] Cf. J. S. Mill's essay (1840), "Germano-Coleridgian doctrine," "Coleridge and the Germans."
[3] Coleridge, *Biographia Literaria*, vol. i. pp. 145 f.

through his practical convictions of duty and freedom, that speculative comprehension of the essential spirituality of human nature which his language appeared to repudiate. Thus viewed on its metaphysical side, the German influence obscurely communicated to the English mind through Coleridge was rather post-Kantian than Kantian, though the same cannot be said of its strictly ethical side." [1]

But the Kantism transmitted through Coleridge was but very partially assimilated. And in the more important examples of Kantian influence in the second third, or rather more, of the century, we find Kant's doctrine assimilated more on its negative and destructive than on its positive side. The two main points of the doctrine so assimilated may be characterised respectively as *Agnosticism*, or the unknowableness of the Absolute or Unconditioned; and *Relativism*, that is, the 'relativity of human knowledge.' The Agnosticism, however, in the case of the two leading examples of this influence—Sir W. Hamilton and Dean Mansel—was combined with theological orthodoxy; and the Relativism is somehow reconciled with Natural Dualism.

Before I pass to examine the form which each of these two doctrines assumes in the philosophy of Mr. Spencer, I will explain them briefly in the form in which they are presented by Hamilton—since the influence of Kant comes to Spencer entirely through Hamilton and his disciple Mansel, and not directly. I begin with Hamilton's 'Philosophy of the Conditioned' as Mansel calls it. Briefly the 'Law of the Conditioned' is: "All positive thought lies between two extremes, neither of which we can conceive as possible; and yet, as they are mutual contradictories, we must recognise the one or the other as necessary." [2] Or, as Hamilton more fully explains, taking as an illustration our quantitative notions of space and time, all that we positively conceive lies between two poles [the maximal and the minimal], and at either pole—where our thought comes upon the unconditioned—we find two pairs of contradictory inconceivables, one of which must be true, though we can conceive neither. So again, we cannot conceive the will to be free, as that would involve an uncaused event, an absolute commence-

[1] *l.c.* p. 277.
[2] [Hamilton's edition of Reid's *Works*, p. 911.]

ment of existence; at the same time, we cannot conceive an infinite regress from effect to cause.

Here we have obviously a reproduction of the three first of Kant's cosmological antinomies; but it is a reproduction with important modifications. For Kant does not argue that infinite time or infinite space is inconceivable. On the contrary, he makes in the Æsthetic the remarkable statement that space is presented as an 'infinite given magnitude' (*unendliche gegebene Grösse*); and in arguing the thesis of the first antinomy it is not infinite time but infinite *past* time which he argues to be inconceivable: for "the infinity of a series consists just in this, that the series can never be *completed* in a successive synthesis," hence we cannot conceive an "infinite series of states to have passed away in the world."[1] Similarly, Kant argues—ingeniously—that we must think the world limited in space, because "in order to think the world which fills all space as a whole, we must suppose the successive synthesis of the parts of an infinite world to be *completed*." Finally, Kant never questions the infinite divisibility of *Space*; it is infinitely divisible *Substance* which seems to him an unthinkable notion: because if we suppose that any composite substance is not ultimately resolvable into simple parts, "then, if we think all composition away, no composite part will be left; and as by hypothesis there is no simple part, nothing at all will remain."[2]

The difference, it will be said, is that in the case of Substance —as Kant with those he is arguing against assumes—the simple is necessarily thought as *prior* to the composite; but we cannot similarly conceive the parts of Space as prior to the one Space of which they are parts. So again Kant has no difficulty in conceiving Infinity as an attribute of the Divine Being; indeed he thinks it an indispensable notion; what he questions is the possibility of giving a speculative proof of the existence of such a being.

Hamilton's Philosophy of the Conditioned, therefore, diverges widely from Kant, in respect of the notion of the Infinite. And here I agree with Kant: I find no difficulty in conceiving Infinite Time or Infinite Space as such; but there certainly is a difficulty in conceiving a completed Infinite and therefore a

[1] [Watson's *Selections*, pp. 158 f.]   [2] [*Op. cit.* p. 160.]

past Infinite. It is partly true that, as Hamilton says, the notion of Infinite Quantity is negative; that is, when we try to conceive Infinite Magnitude positively otherwise than negatively, we can only conceive it as "greater than any assignable magnitude"; and it is with that meaning that we employ the notion in mathematical reasoning. The notion of Infinite, so far as it means more than this—and it certainly seems to mean more—is no doubt negative—negative of limit: but that does not seem to me to justify the assertion that the Infinite is inconceivable.

But there is another fundamental difference between Hamilton's and Kant's method of dealing with the dilemmas which Kant calls antinomies. Their solutions are entirely different. Hamilton's conclusion is agnostic. "One or other of two alternatives is true, but we cannot say which" (except in the case of Free Will, when he follows Kant in deciding for Freedom on *moral grounds*).[1] But Kant's critical conclusion is a solution of the difficulty by means of the distinction between phenomena and things *per se*. For example as regards Time: once grasp that Time is not a form of real existence but only of human perception, and the difficulty of an infinite Past vanishes: the series of past Time is not a series that really has existed, but only one that we must think. The true critical conclusion is that in systematising experience we may carry back the regress of Time as far as we like; and similarly of Space. But Hamilton is too much of a Natural Realist to accept the transcendental Ideality of Time and Space. With regard to Space, he expressly maintains that "we at once must and do think Space as a necessary notion, and do perceive the extended in Space as an actual fact": and if he makes no corresponding assertion with regard to Time, I think it is only because it seems superfluous.

This leads me to the 'Relativity of Human Knowledge.' For, as I have said, it is characteristic of Hamilton's Metaphysic to endeavour to combine—on the question on which Natural Dualism, Materialism, and Mentalism diverge—or to effect a compromise between, the position of Natural Dualism and the position of Kant as defined in the *Prolegomena*; *i.e.* Kantism, taken in its Realistic attitude, its attitude of opposition to "all Idealism."

[1] [Cf. *Metaphysics*, ii. pp. 410 ff., 542 f.]

On the one hand, Hamilton, developing the old distinction of Primary and Secondary Qualities of matter into a threefold classification of Primary, Secundo-primary, and Secondary, gives as the characteristic of Primary Qualities—of which the most fundamental are 'Trinal extension' and 'Ultimate incompressibility'—that we "apprehend them as they are in bodies," "as modes of the non-ego, . . . clearly conceive how they must exist in bodies, in knowing what they are objectively in themselves"; while the Secondary Qualities—colour, sound, flavour, etc.—are apprehended "as they are in us," "as modes of the ego," as "subjective cognitions" or "sensations proper," and "not in propriety, qualities of body at all." This is the old distinction of Locke. But Hamilton's development, as I said, includes also an intermediate kind of qualities, "Secundo-primary"—such as the various modes of gravity, cohesion, and the like, known as heavy, light, hard, soft, rigid, flexible, rough, smooth, etc.—which also fall under the 'category of Resistance or Pressure,' and have the metaphysical characteristics of both the other classes. That is, we apprehend them both as they are in bodies and as they are in us: both "immediately in themselves" and "mediately in their effects on us"; "in their Primary or objective phase they manifest themselves as *degrees* of resistance opposed to our locomotive energy," and are so far quasi-primary: but this "objective element" is always accompanied by a secondary quality or affection of our sentient organism. Well, all this—developed at great length by Hamilton [1]—is or appears to be 'Natural Dualism' pure and simple. If we had only this part of his doctrine before us we should never dream of attributing to him the view explicitly stated by Kant (*Prolegomena*) that "the qualities of body which are called primary"—no less than the secondary—"belong not to the things in themselves but to their phenomena," and "have no proper existence outside our representation." [2]

Yet elsewhere Hamilton's language seems thoroughly Kantian. "Our whole knowledge of mind and matter is relative; . . . of things in themselves, be they external, be they internal, we know nothing or know them only as incognisable"; . . . "all that we

[1] [Cf. Dissertations in his edition of Reid's *Works*, pp. 845 ff.]
[2] [Cf. *Prolegomena*, Mahaffy's trans. p. 55.]

272 PHILOSOPHY OF HERBERT SPENCER

know is phenomenal, and phenomenal of the unknown."[1] At an early stage of his lectures on Metaphysics he states and explains "the great axiom that all human knowledge is only of the relative or phenomenal." He explains that "Matter, so far as it is a name for something known," is "a common name for a certain series or aggregate of appearances or phenomena manifested in coexistence," which by the constitution "of our nature we are compelled to think conjoined in and by something"; . . . but this something absolutely in itself, *i.e.* considered "apart from its phenomena, is to us as zero."

Similarly "in so far as mind is the common name for the states of knowing, willing, feeling, desiring . . . it is only the name for a certain series of connected phenomena." But "so far as it denotes the subject in which the phenomena of knowing, willing, etc. inhere, it expresses what in itself or in its absolute existence is unknown. . . . Our whole knowledge of mind and matter is thus only relative: of existence absolutely and in itself we know nothing."[2]

It is somewhat surprising to find these two lines of thought so vigorously pursued and expressed by the same thinker; and certainly when one now reads the lectures and articles of the most distinguished academic teacher of Philosophy in Great Britain in the first half of the century, it does seem that the two streams of metaphysical thought which meet in him—the traditional Scottish Philosophy of Common Sense, and Kantism—do not properly blend. The explanation is that 'Relativity of Knowledge' is a complex and ambiguous term: there are various significations which it may bear, and which it does bear for Hamilton: some elements of its meaning are quite compatible with the Natural Dualism to which his doctrine of Primary Qualities belongs, while other elements are not; and Hamilton's defect lies in not clearly distinguishing these different elements.

1. The assertion that knowledge is relative *may* mean no more than that it is a *relation* between the knower and the known: and therefore between two things distinct in existence. This meaning is, of course, quite compatible with knowing qualities of matter as they are in bodies. In fact knowledge,

---

[1] [*Discussions on Philosophy*, p. 639.]
[2] [*Lectures on Metaphysics*, ii. pp. 136-138.]

true knowledge, as we commonly conceive it, is a relation which does not modify the qualities of the known. In this sense, however, the assertion that we can only know the relative is insignificant: for it simply means that we cannot know anything without knowing it; and similarly the assertion that we cannot know the Absolute—if 'absolute' is understood as meaning 'out of the relation.' For this proposition again simply means that we cannot know anything without knowing: and this would be equally true if we had suddenly revealed to us the most perfect knowledge of God and the Universe as they were independently of our knowledge.

2. A more important meaning, but still perfectly compatible with Hamilton's theory of Primary Qualities, is that which refers to relations among objects known, not to the relation between knowing subject and known object. It is undoubtedly true, and epistemologically important, that we never cognise, nor can we really conceive ourselves cognising, an object that is not in relation to other objects: especially in perceiving any part of matter, or the *non-ego*, we perceive it in spatial relations to other parts; and again, in judging that it possesses such and such qualities, we attribute to it implicitly relations of resemblance to other things having the same qualities, and relations of difference from other things having different qualities. Relativity in this sense is of course quite consistent with our knowing—objectively, and as they are in the real things—the size, shape, divisibility, incompressibility, density, rarity, situation, and change of situation of matter.

3. But there is a third meaning. Though we cannot, speaking generally, resolve 'quality' into 'relation,' yet many qualities are found by reflection to be essentially relational; and this is the case with the Primary Qualities of Matter. They are all, as Hamilton says, "evolved from the two universal conditions of occupying space and being contained in space." But reflection shows each of these to be *relational*: for *e.g.* what does "occupying space" mean except that if another portion of matter moves in the direction of the space said to be occupied, it will at a certain point of its course find an obstacle to its moving further. 'Occupation,' in fact, in its physical as well as its general meaning, implies a relation, actual or potential,

to something else that attempts to — or might similarly — occupy.

But (4) the *relations* thus implied in the very conception of Primary Qualities are—in the case of Primary Qualities *actually perceived*—in part relations to the percipient organism. And, in Hamilton's view, my 'immediate knowledge' of matter must be knowledge of matter actually in contact with my organism, and so in definite spatial relation with it. This he expressly says in one passage. "The Primary are the qualities of body in relation to our organism as a body simply,—the Secundo-primary are the qualities of body in relation to our organism as a propelling, resisting, cohesive body," etc.[1]

5. Finally, there is the Relativity *of* Qualities to Substances and Substances to Qualities.

I think that all these different meanings were more or less in Hamilton's view when he affirmed Relativity of Knowledge; but *not* adequately distinguished from the meaning which the phrase ordinarily carries with it in Philosophy—a meaning incompatible with Natural Dualism or with his view of Primary Qualities, *i.e.* the meaning which involves denial of our knowledge of things as they are independently of our cognition.

[1] [Reid's *Works*, Dissertations, p. 857.]

LECTURE I

METAPHYSICAL DOCTRINES

I PROPOSE to give a critical exposition of Mr. Spencer's metaphysical and epistemological doctrines—his view of the Universe, so far as known and knowable, and his theory of the criterion or method for distinguishing truth from error. I ought to say that he does not himself use either of these technical terms to denote any part of his doctrine. He does not seem to have heard of 'Epistemology,' and he employs the term 'Metaphysician' exclusively to designate a class of thinkers who have followed an erroneous method to untenable conclusions. Still he has a very definite epistemology, which he regards as fundamentally important. And he has a metaphysical system—a systematic view of the nature and relations of finite minds to the material world, and to the Primal Being or Ultimate Ground of Being—of the coherence of which he is strongly convinced.[1]

---

[1] This 'system' indeed is nowhere systematically expounded: the exposition of it is to be found only in fragments scattered through the three volumes of his *First Principles* and *Principles of Psychology*—chiefly in Part I. and the earlier chapters of Part II. of the former, and in Part VII. of the latter; also in chap. x. at the end of vol. i. of the *Psychology*, and in the closing paragraphs of the *First Principles*.

I take first that part of Mr. Spencer's philosophy in which the influence of Kant through Hamilton and Mansel is most manifest—his doctrine of 'the Unknowable.'[1] His avowed object, in this part of his work, is to reconcile the 'antagonism between Religion and Science,' which is, he tells us, "of all antagonisms of belief, the oldest, the widest, the most profound and the most important." With this aim he proposes to "contemplate the two sides of this great controversy," preserving an "impartial attitude." Accordingly, in chap. ii., he gives us a discussion of 'Ultimate Religious Ideas.' But what are 'religious ideas'? A little discussion of religion would have been in place in this part of Mr. Spencer's treatise. He appears to assume that inquiries concerning "the origin and hidden nature of surrounding things" are as such religious. But though the answers to such questions may be religious—if they affirm that the existence of surrounding things originated in and is sustained by the Will of a Being to whom worship is due—it does not appear that the questions as such are religious any more than scientific or philosophical. When Thales taught that "water is the original source of all things," when Epicurus taught that earth and stars were formed by the collisions and combinations of primordial atoms, they were surely speculating about the 'origin and nature of surrounding things,' but it would be absurd to call their doctrines religious. And we remember that in Kant's system, the question whether the world has had a beginning is classed as

[1] *i.e. First Principles*, Part I.

primarily a cosmological, not a theological question. It especially concerns us to note this, because it is by arguments—to an important extent—derived from Kant through Hamilton as well as from the line of English Empiricism that Mr. Spencer proves his agnostic conclusion that "no tenable hypothesis can be formed as to the origin or nature of the Universe regarded as a whole."

He takes the 'origin' first. There are, he says, three verbally intelligible suppositions: we may either assert that the Universe is self-existent, or self-created, or created by an external agency.[1]

Now I submit that it is only the third of these hypotheses that can be called 'religious,' and even this only if the external agency is a Divine Mind. The general question, therefore, is philosophical, not theological: accordingly, in the present discussion I shall treat Mr. Spencer's agnostic conclusion as *philosophical* agnosticism, reserving the specially theological or religious aspect of it for consideration later. His conclusion is that none of these verbally intelligible suppositions is really conceivable. As regards the first—'Self-existence' can only mean existence without a beginning, and we cannot conceive existence without a beginning: for we cannot conceive infinite past time. This, in Mr. Spencer's view, appears to be simply because "unlimited duration is inconceivable"[2]—an argument whose apparent force seems to me due to a want of distinction between imagina-

---

[1] *First Principles*, § 11, p. 30. [Quotations throughout from the 3rd (stereotyped) edition.] [2] *Op. cit.* § 11, p. 36.]

tion and conception—it is not based on the certainly more forcible argument of Kant that infinite past time involves a contradiction, because it is the essence of an infinite series that it should *not* be completed.[1] The second hypothesis—self-creation—need not detain us long. *Prima facie*, the notion involves a contradiction, and I know no thinker of importance who has maintained it. But, for a reason that will subsequently appear, it is worth while to note Mr. Spencer's method of disposing of it. He says that "really to conceive self-creation, is to conceive potential existence passing into actual by some inherent necessity": but we cannot do this, as "we cannot form any idea of a potential existence of the Universe,—as distinguished from its actual existence." For "if represented in thought at all, potential existence must be represented as an actual existence."[2] Noting this, let us pass to the third—"the commonly conceived or theistic hypothesis—creation by external agency." Here, however, it is at once obvious, Mr. Spencer holds, that, even if the hypothesis be accepted, the question is only pushed a step backward: we shall have to inquire into the origin of the existence of the external agency, and the alleged impossibility of conceiving infinite past time must apply equally to that. Besides this, Mr. Spencer urges that no analogy with a human artificer enables us to conceive the production of matter out of nothing: and even

[1] Kant does *not* affirm, as Spencer seems to do, that infinite *progress* is an impossible notion: and I find no inconceivability in it, though I admit it to be unimaginable.

[2] [*Op. cit.* § 11, p. 32.]

if we could conceive this, there would remain the impossibility of conceiving space so produced.

Mr. Spencer then turns to the question as to the nature of the world. "When we inquire," he says, "what is the meaning of the various effects produced upon our senses . . . impressions of sounds, of colours, of tastes, and of those various attributes which we ascribe to bodies, we are compelled to regard them as the effects of some cause . . . and we cannot carry out an inquiry concerning their causation without inevitably committing ourselves to the hypothesis of a First Cause."[1]

But, since the common notion of 'cause' implies antecedence in time, the inquiry after a *first* cause of the effects on our consciousness, would seem to carry us back to the inquiry into the origin of the world. It seems, however, that Mr. Spencer means not merely something prior in time to the states of consciousness in question, or to the matter in motion which now apparently operates on our senses; but something on the present existence of which this consciousness or this matter in motion depends for its existence. And this so-called First Cause, as there can be no cause limiting it, must be Infinite and Absolute. Here Mr. Spencer—largely with the aid of arguments derived from Hamilton and Mansel's Philosophy of the Conditioned—arrives at the conclusion that while we cannot but assume a First Cause for the phenomena of our own consciousness, and "regard this first cause as Infinite and Absolute,"

[1] [*Op. cit.* § 12, pp. 36 f.]

still the arguments which force on us these inferences are illusive, and the conclusions themselves consequently fallacious.

I will not examine the argument in detail, but will only say that it seems to me confused and vitiated by the ambiguity of meaning of 'First Cause.' Let me briefly explain this. Mr. Spencer starts with a plurality of finite minds—his own and his readers'—each knowing immediately the transient facts of his own consciousness. He finds that he must suppose 'some cause' of these facts in the sense of some presently existing entity not himself, on which these facts depend for their existence. Then, he argues, this entity must either be the first cause or "have a cause behind it which thus becomes the real cause of the effect." But this can only mean that the entity in question must either be dependent on something else or independent: and if we grant that it is dependent on something else and so on, it does not follow that we shall ever come to a part of the whole universe which is not dependent for its existence on some other part; for the parts may be mutually dependent (as the parts of an organism) and only the whole independent. But if we take this view the difficulty of conceiving the whole as Absolute and Infinite would seem to be avoided; unless we assume that whatever exists in independence of anything else *can* have no necessary relation *within* itself. This, however, Mr. Spencer does assume : but surely it is an arbitrary assumption. He seems to think that a 'necessary' relation within the whole *must* be "inspired by something else": but I find no such implication. What I conceive to exist necessarily I simply conceive as something that could not be otherwise. The idea involves no relation to anything outside.

However, Mr. Spencer's conclusion is—as before stated—agnosticism both as regards the origin and the nature of the universe: and these being in his view the chief 'religious questions,' the only religious truth that Mr. Spencer can recognise is that there is a Power manifested to us by the universe, but that that Power is utterly inscrutable.

But this conclusion he also arrives at by an examination of 'Ultimate Scientific Ideas,' which forms the latter half of his professedly impartial examination of Science and Religion. (The consideration of this I defer for the present.) And this identical result of the two examinations he offers as the 'Supreme Verity' in which the reconciliation of Religion and Science is to be found, viz. that "The reality underlying appearances is totally and for ever inconceivable to us . . . but we are obliged to regard every phenomenon as the manifestation of an incomprehensible power, called Omnipresent from inability to assign its limits, though Omnipresence is unthinkable."[1] And this agnostic conclusion is proclaimed not only finally and decisively but solemnly and triumphantly. A 'high merit' is attributed to Religion for having dimly discerned from the beginning, and continually insisted on this sublime verity: for the guardianship

[1] [*Op. cit.* § 27, pp. 98 f.]

and diffusion of which Humanity ever has been and ever must be Religion's debtor. At the same time Mr. Spencer feels bound to point out that Religion herself has been 'partially irreligious' through not being consistently and completely agnostic, but asserting that "the cause of all things possesses such and such attributes."[1] As to one part, then, of the fundamental questions of Ontology or Metaphysics in the narrower sense as I have defined them—the nature of the Divine or Primal being, and its relation to finite minds and the material world—Mr. Spencer's answer is simple. All we know is a Power totally inscrutable and unknowable, whose existence is apprehended by a consciousness which though indestructible is perfectly indefinite and undifferentiated. "Our consciousness of the unconditioned," he says, "is literally the unconditioned consciousness" or "raw material of thought to which in thinking we give definite forms."[2] This 'Supreme Verity' is the residuum to which Theology is reduced in Mr. Spencer's philosophical laboratory.

Let us now leave Theology aside, and turn to the chief metaphysical question or group of questions which remain—those presented by the nature and relation of finite human minds to the material world which is their common object. But even here we cannot leave on one side Mr. Spencer's 'Unknowable.' For, as I said, the existence of this is not only the Ultimate Verity of Religion: it is no less the Ultimate Verity for Science. When we try to understand

[1] [*Op. cit.* § 28, p. 101.]   [2] [*Op. cit.* § 26, p. 96.]

Time, Space, Matter, Force, Consciousness—no less than when we try to understand God and His relation to the finite world,—we are equally driven to the conclusion that the "reality underlying appearances is and must be totally and for ever inconceivable by us." Hence, in dealing with the conception of (finite) minds and matter, no less than in dealing with the conception of God, "he repudiates as impossible the Philosophy which professes to formulate Being as distinguished from Appearance." For him Philosophy, like the sciences which it systematises, is concerned throughout with 'appearances' or 'phenomena' or 'manifestations.'[1]

When, however, with this general characterisation of the object of philosophical knowledge, we apply to it the distinctions of metaphysical schools already discussed,[2] it would seem at first sight that the positive element of Mr. Spencer's metaphysics must be indistinguishable from mentalism. For what do we mean in ordinary thought and discourse by 'appearances' as distinguished from being or reality? We surely mean modes of consciousness, feelings, or thoughts, or combinations of the two produced in minds. And much of Mr. Spencer's language would support this view. The "manifestations of the Unknowable, considered simply as such," are, he says, "divisible into two great classes called by some *impressions* and

[1] This is the aspect of Mr. Spencer's system which led me to call it *Phenomenalism* in respect of its positive content, and 'Agnosticism' in respect of its fundamental negation.

[2] [Here, as in the note above, Professor Sidgwick is referring to unpublished lectures. But some account of his views concerning these distinctions will be found in *Philosophy, its Scope and Relations*, by consulting the index.]

ideas. The term *sensation*, too, [being also] commonly used as the equivalent of impression, and *state of consciousness* as signifying either an impression or an idea." And though he finds objections to all these terms, it is not on account of their purely mentalistic import: it is because they carry with them implications which he would avoid at the outset — implications of something impressing, of " a sensitive organism and something acting on it," of " something of which a state of consciousness is a state, and which is capable of different states." He therefore classes the manifestations as ' vivid ' and ' faint' respectively, using terms that obviously denote purely mental facts, modes of consciousness.[1] The vivid manifestations are sensations, or sensational feelings, or sense-percepts—either pains or sights, sounds, tastes and smells, or percepts of the tactual and muscular senses: the faint manifestations are images or thoughts which are, he tells us, "imperfect and feeble repetitions" of the vivid,— what we call ' ideal ' sights and sounds, etc., in contrast with real. He describes how the stream of vivid manifestations flows, in the conscious life of each of us, side by side with the stream of faint manifestations, sometimes one predominating, sometimes the other. Both streams appear to be never broken, the members of each cohere with one another: but the "great body of the vivid current is absolutely unmodifiable by the faint, and the faint may

---

[1] *Op. cit.* § 43, p. 143. Cf. *Principles of Psychology*, Part VII. chaps. xvi. and xvii.

become almost separate from the vivid."[1] The chief exceptions to this separation between the two currents are (1) that the vivid manifestations which we distinguish as sensations of muscular tension have as their conditions of occurrence ideas of muscular action; and (2) that the emotions, though vivid manifestations, are produced by and classed with faint manifestations.

Well, is not all this pure unadulterated mentalism, so far as the knowable world goes: *i.e.* an elaborate and emphatic reduction of the material world as commonly conceived, into mental elements? Sights, sounds, tastes, smells, sensations of pressure, muscular tension — these along with "intense pains" (and I suppose pleasures of sense) are described as making up the main stream of vivid manifestations: emotions though vivid being, as said, connected and classed with faint manifestations: and "all things known to us" being divisible into the two classes. These and the Unknowable Reality underlying them would seem to make up the universe, which might therefore be expressed by the formula: vivid consciousness + faint consciousness + X. The system thus presented might be called Mentalistic Agnosticism or Agnostic Mentalism. Nor is this impression of the system at first altered when we find how Mr. Spencer applies this view to the interpretation of Natural Dualism. I will give it in his own words:—"What is the division equivalent to? Obviously it corresponds to the division between *object* and *subject*. This profound-

[1] Cf. *First Principles*, § 43, p. 153.

est of distinctions among the manifestations of the Unknowable, we recognise by grouping them into *self* and *not-self*. These faint manifestations, forming a continuous whole differing from the other in the quantity, quality, cohesion, and conditions of existence of its parts, we call the *ego*; and these vivid manifestations, indissolubly bound together in relatively-immense masses, and having independent conditions of existence, we call the *non-ego*. Or rather, more truly — each order of manifestations carries with it the irresistible implication of some power that manifests itself: and by the words *ego* and *non-ego* respectively, we mean the power that manifests itself in the faint forms, and the power that manifests itself in the vivid forms."[1]

This is the ultimate division the affirmation of which, according to Mr. Spencer, is 'postulated' as the "primordial proposition which Philosophy requires as a datum."[2] I confess that these summary equations, " vivid manifestations " = Non-ego, " faint manifestations " = Ego, are by no means " obvious to me." Indeed it would rather have seemed obvious that—in ordinary thought—sounds, tastes, smells, sensations of muscular tension, etc., belong to the *Ego* no less than thoughts and emotions. But no doubt they are more difficult to disentangle from our ordinary conception of the material world: and we are familiar, from Berkeley and others, with the view that our common notion of matter is made up of and exhaustively analysable into elements of this kind.

[1] *Op. cit.* § 44, p. 154.   [2] *Op. cit.* § 45, p. 156.

METAPHYSICAL DOCTRINES

This passage, therefore, by itself would not have altered my view of Mr. Spencer's Mentalism; though it might perhaps have led me to doubt the rigour of his Agnosticism. For the last sentence seems to interpret our conceptions of Ego and Non-ego as implying not merely a duality in the manifestations of the Unknowable Power but also a duality in the Power itself. And as he immediately goes on to say that these conceptions "have for their explanation" an "ultimate law of thought that is beyond appeal" he seems to acquiesce in this dualism. But surely if, as we were before told, the deepest verity both of science and of religion is given by an indefinite consciousness of an utterly unknowable reality, it cannot also be right to have a definite conception of it as two powers, manifesting themselves respectively in vivid and faint consciousness.

And indeed—in spite of the "law of thought that is beyond appeal"—this dualism is expressly repudiated by Mr. Spencer in a later passage: "The true conclusion implied throughout the foregoing pages is that it is one and the same Ultimate Reality that is manifested to us subjectively and objectively."[1] The antithesis of Subject and Object, of Ego and Non-ego, belongs to Appearance and not to Reality. Indeed it is just the inevitability of this antithesis, combined with the philosophical conviction that it is *not* valid, if taken as representing Reality, that is the

---

[1] *Principles of Psychology*, vol. i. § 273, p. 627. [Quotations throughout from the 3rd edition.] In view of this sentence, and the preceding section, Külpe is doubtless right in regarding Spencer as a Monist of what he calls an 'abstract' type.

deepest basis of Mr. Spencer's Agnosticism. "The antithesis," he says, "of subject and object, never to be transcended while consciousness lasts, renders impossible all knowledge of that ultimate reality in which subject and object are united."[1]

But this does not meet the difficulty of consistently affirming knowledge of the utterly unknowable: since the affirmation that it is one imports just as definite a piece of metaphysical knowledge as the affirmation that it is two or more. But I will not dwell on this now: as we shall find later on that Mr. Spencer seems to have a much more extensive and complex knowledge of his Unknowable. I will rather point out that 'the ultimate law of thought' which he goes on to explain (*First Principles*, § 44) hardly seems to me to justify even his phenomenal duality. He says that the "primordial division of self from not-self is a cumulative result of persistent consciousnesses of likenesses and differences among manifestations." But though the two groups of manifestations are internally alike, and unlike each other, in being respectively 'vivid' and 'faint,' it hardly seems that the unlikeness is sufficient even to suggest their reference to different powers, when we consider that the 'faint' are said by Mr. Spencer to be copies or repetitions of the 'vivid.' If the copies called ideal sounds resemble the copies called ideal smells in being faint, they resemble on the other hand the vivid manifestations called real sounds in quality, and, so far as the latter resemblance goes,

[1] *Op. cit.* p. 627, end of § 272.

would be naturally referred to the same cause as the real sounds, operating more feebly.

However, according to Mr. Spencer the group of 'vivid' manifestations, carrying with it the implication of a manifesting power and excluding emotions (which are rather summarily thrown over to the 'faint' manifestations), is the *non-ego*. But our common notion of the *non-ego* implies existence distinct from and *independent* of the *ego*: indeed Mr. Spencer goes on to say that the primordial datum of Philosophy is "the postulate that the manifestations of the Unknowable fall into two separate aggregates constituting respectively the world of consciousness and the world beyond consciousness."[1] But how does the 'vivid' element, or aggregate of elements, in the stream of our conscious experience —our sensations and sense-perceptions, sights, sounds, tastes, smells, touches, pressures, muscular tensions —how does all this become a "world beyond consciousness"? He has admitted that we commonly think and speak of the 'vivid' manifestations as states of consciousness: and when he comes to the Principles of Psychology he gives these sensations— distinguished as 'feelings peripherally initiated'— a leading place among the elements of Mind or Consciousness. How then is it that, in *First Principles*, they come to be an "aggregate of manifestations constituting the world beyond consciousness"? Mr. Spencer's answer is as follows (pp. 155, 156):—

"We continually learn that while the conditions

[1] *First Principles*, p. 156.

of occurrence of faint manifestations are always to be found, the conditions of occurrence of vivid manifestations are often not to be found. We also continually learn that vivid manifestations which have no perceivable antecedents among the vivid manifestations, are like certain preceding ones which *had* perceivable antecedents among the vivid manifestations. Joining these two experiences together, there results the irresistible conception that some vivid manifestations have conditions of occurrence existing out of the current of vivid manifestations—existing as potential vivid manifestations capable of becoming actual. And so we are made vaguely conscious of an indefinitely-extended region of power or being, not merely separate from the current of faint manifestations constituting the *ego*, but lying beyond the current of vivid manifestations constituting the immediately-present portion of the *non-ego*."

It would seem from this that the manifestations that *properly* constitute 'the world beyond consciousness'—since it is too paradoxical to put beyond consciousness my present sensations of sight, sound, etc.—are merely 'potential manifestations capable of becoming actual'; *i.e.* sensations that we might have but actually do not have. At any rate these merely potential manifestations are a main part of the 'world beyond consciousness.' But how can we conceive merely *potential* manifestations existing as the conditions of occurrence of actual manifestations? Surely the conditions must be as 'actual' as the manifestations that they condition! Moreover, before, in dealing with the pantheistic hypothesis of self-creation, Mr. Spencer has laid down that "we cannot form any idea of a potential existence of a universe as distinguished from an actual existence: if represented in thought at all, potential existence must be represented as actual existence."[1] Well, what is sauce for Pantheism must be sauce for Phenomenalism: the potential vivid manifestations must be thought as actual: but if thought as actual, how can they be thought as beyond consciousness?

There seems to be a dilemma. If the "vivid manifestations indissolubly bound together which we call the *non-ego*" are *actual*, they cannot constitute a "world beyond consciousness." They must be within consciousness, elements of consciousness in the sense in which Mr. Spencer conceives consciousness when he distinguishes 'the thoughts and feelings which constitute a consciousness'—with which Subjective Psychology is concerned—from the existences with which the rest of the sciences deal. They must therefore belong to Mind, in the sense in which Mind is regarded as "something totally without kinship with other things":[2] that is to say, they must belong to the *ego*, not to the *non-ego*. If, on the other hand, the vivid manifestations are conceived as merely potential, they cannot constitute an *actual* non-ego, an *actual* world beyond consciousness; and it is an actual, not a potential world, which Common Sense and physical science require.

[1] *First Principles*, § 11, p. 32.
[2] *Principles of Psychology*, vol. i. § 56, p. 140.

In the face of this dilemma will Mr. Spencer ultimately decide to let the 'vivid manifestations' go to the Ego or subject? He certainly seems to do this in some passages: and is indeed led to this by another line of thought, developed in the Psychology (Part II. chap. iii.), in which he gives an elaborate psycho-physiological proof, in his best manner, of the proposition that "though internal feeling habitually depends upon external agents, yet there is no likeness between them either in kind or degree." The feeling, he argues, is an effect which varies, qualitatively and quantitatively, according to the specific structure of the sentient organism, its individual structure, the part affected, the condition and motion of that part, etc., while the cause all through remains the same. "Thus," he says, "we are brought to the conclusion that what we are conscious of as properties of matter, even down to its weight and resistance, are but subjective affections produced by objective agencies that are unknown and unknowable. All the sensations produced in us by environing things are but symbols of actions out of ourselves, the natures of which we cannot conceive."[1] And what is here said of 'Relativity of Feelings' is said in the next chapter of 'Relations between Feelings': it is similarly shown that no relation in consciousness can "resemble or be in any way akin to its source beyond consciousness," it can only symbolise something unknown beyond consciousness. Accordingly the conclusion that he calls Transfigured Realism is thus

[1] *Principles of Psychology*, vol. i. § 86, p. 206.

stated : "While *some* objective existence, manifested under *some* conditions, remains as the final necessity of thought, there does not remain the implication that this existence and these conditions are more to us than the unknown correlatives of our feelings and the relations among our feelings. The Realism we are committed to is one which simply asserts objective existence as separate from, and independent of, subjective existence. But it affirms neither that any one mode of this objective existence is in reality that which it seems, nor that the connexions among its modes are objectively what they seem."[1]

But, if this be so, if the 'vivid manifestations' are not properly thought as *elements* of the objective existence beyond consciousness, but only *symbols* of such existence, which they do not resemble and to which they are not in any way akin, what becomes of that differentiation of subject and object, elaborately expounded in *First Principles*, and expounded again more fully in *The Principles of Psychology*? For by this differentiation, owing to the accumulated differences between 'vivid' and 'faint' manifestations, the former are shown as aggregated into the Non-ego and the latter into the Ego: so that the fundamental antithesis between the two appears to be the necessary result of psychological laws. But this necessary result, this conclusion that we are irresistibly led to think, is surely the conclusion of Crude Realism, not of Transfigured Realism. In describing it Mr. Spencer continually talks of sights, sounds,

[1] *Principles of Psychology*, vol. ii. § 472, p. 494.

odours, pressures, sensations of cold, etc., as the leading examples of vivid manifestations: so that the 'non-ego' formed by the aggregation of these is constituted, it would seem, entirely of the subjective elements which can only symbolise and not resemble objective reality. It would seem, then, that this elaborate process of differentiation has led us wrong: it has led us to a material world—as Mr. Spencer elsewhere admits, finding in it an argument against 'the metaphysician'—in which " colours are regarded as inherent in the substances distinguished by them, sweetness is an intrinsic property of sugar, and hardness and softness supposed to dwell in stones and flesh."[1] These views, it would now seem, have to be given up: the colours, sounds, flavours, tactual feelings have to be abandoned to subjectivity, and to submit to be classed again with the 'faint manifestations,' in spite of the elaborate set of differences which Mr. Spencer has established between the two classes.[2]

And this would seem to apply even to one special feeling or state of consciousness which—both in his *First Principles* and his *Principles of Psychology*— Mr. Spencer singles out and regards as specially representative of objectivity: *i.e.* the sensation of muscular tension which gives us *resistance* as the primary attribute of Body. We find that each of the experiences from which space is generated "involves the resistance of an object touched, and the muscular

---

[1] *Principles of Psychology*, vol. ii. § 404, p. 372.
[2] Cf. *op. cit.* § 458, p. 463.

tension which measures this resistance,"[1]—in brief, it is an experience of Force; and that similarly the 'resistance-attribute of matter'—which distinguishes the conception of Matter from that of empty Space —"must be regarded as primordial." Thus "matter as opposing our muscular energies, being immediately present to consciousness in terms of force; and its occupancy of Space being known by an abstract of experiences originally given in terms of force; it follows that forces, standing in certain correlations, form the whole content of our idea of Matter."[2] Similarly Motion, as we know it, is traceable to experiences of Force. "Hence we come down finally to Force, as the ultimate of ultimates." By the 'indestructibility of matter' which Mr. Spencer holds to be knowable *a priori*, "we really mean the indestructibility of the *force* with which matter affects us":[3] and "similarly with the no less *a priori* conclusion that motion is continuous: that which defies suppression in thought is really the force which the motion indicates."[4] We thus arrive at the Persistence of Force conceived as "an ultimate truth of which no inductive proof is possible,: a principle which as being the basis of Science cannot be established by Science." And as the original experience of force is the particular 'vivid manifestation' which Mr. Spencer distinguishes as a sensation of muscular tension—sometimes called by him 'impression of resistance' or 'consciousness of something

---

[1] *First Principles*, § 47, p. 164. [2] *Op. cit.* § 48, p. 167.
[3] *Op. cit.* § 54, p. 179. [4] *Op. cit.* § 57, p. 184.

that resists'—he would at first sight seem to hold that in this manifestation at any rate we cognise an objective fact.

Even "when that which resists my grasp is something I call inanimate I am nevertheless," he says, "unable to suppress from my consciousness the representation of the pressure occurring in it as the correlative of the resistance offered by it to my muscular effort. There arises in me an idea of strain, caused in that which yields me these vivid feelings. I cannot by any possibility exclude this consciousness of a force in the vivid aggregate somehow allied to that which I distinguish as force in the faint aggregate—cannot break the link which association has produced between these states of consciousness."[1] Again, even more definitely: "on raising an object from the ground, we are obliged to think of its downward pull as equal and opposite to our upward pull"; and "it is impossible to represent these pulls as equal without representing them as like in kind."[2] But though this is impossible—and though in other passages (which I shall discuss in the next lecture) Mr. Spencer seems to hold that my highest warrant for accepting anything as true is that it is impossible not to think it—he does not apply this principle here.

This sensation of muscular tension—transformed into a 'consciousness of something that resists'— is indeed the 'general symbol for the independent

---

[1] *Principles of Psychology*, vol. ii. § 464, p. 476.
[2] *First Principles*, § 60, p. 189.

METAPHYSICAL DOCTRINES

existence' of the object: the "root-conception of existence beyond consciousness, becomes that of resistance *plus* some force which the resistance measures."[1] But, in the passage just quoted from *First Principles*, he goes on to say that the 'likeness in kind' between my pull and the *thing's* counter-pull—which I cannot help imagining—must be repudiated: "since their likeness in kind would imply in the object a sensation of muscular tension which cannot be ascribed to it, we are compelled to admit that force as it exists out of our consciousness is not force as we know it." Though the feeling of muscular strain furnishes us with the primordial attribute of matter, and in thinking of force in the object world we cannot help applying to it the idea of muscular strain, still we must admit that this application is erroneous and invalid. Sensations of muscular strain, no less than sensations of colour, sound, touch, etc., must be abandoned to subjectivity—be recognised as merely subjective symbols of an unknown Reality.

"Thus, by persistence of force," he ultimately explains, "we really mean the persistence of some Power which transcends our knowledge and conception. The manifestations, as occurring either in ourselves or outside of us, do not persist: but that which persists is the Unknown Cause of these manifestations. In other words, asserting the persistence of Force, is but another mode of asserting an Unconditioned Reality without beginning or end. Thus, quite unexpectedly, we come down once more to that

---

[1] *Principles of Psychology*, vol. ii. § 466, p. 480.

ultimate truth in which, as we saw, Religion and Science coalesce."

We seem then brought back to the Mentalism and Agnosticism which I before attributed to Mr. Spencer. In spite of the 'differentiation of subject and object,' all the 'vivid manifestations,' even the primordial consciousness of resistance, have to be recognised as subjective and altogether unlike anything in the 'world beyond consciousness'; in fact this world, as an object of Mr. Spencer's thought, is merely an Unknown Cause and Unconditioned Reality—though, as he affirms it to 'persist' and 'to be without beginning or end,' I suppose it must be conceived to be in time.

But still this mentalistic agnosticism does not express his final view, in spite of the vigour with which some of his arguments lead to it. He still holds to his phenomenal dualism—for reasons which I will presently examine—and he holds to a knowledge of the world beyond consciousness, which I at least find it difficult to reconcile with his agnostic utterances. Take, for example, besides all that is said of 'the differentiation of vivid from faint manifestations,' the interesting discussion of the scope of Logic which we find in his *Principles of Psychology* (§§ 302-305). Here, speaking as one of those who "acknowledge that subject and object are separate realities," he states as the distinctive characteristic of the science of Logic—as distinguished from an 'account of the process of reasoning'—that "Logic formulates the most general laws of correlation among existences considered as objective . . . contemplates in its propositions certain connexions predicated, which are necessarily involved with certain other connexions given : *regarding all these connexions as existing in the non-ego—not, it may be, under the form in which we know them, but in some form."* [1] Here we appear to know, as existing beyond consciousness, the *same connexions* which we know in the world of consciousness—*e.g.* relations of number—although we do not know that they exist 'under the form in which we know them.' This seems difficult to reconcile with the proposition that "no relation in consciousness can resemble or be in any way akin to its source beyond consciousness":[2] for in the passage describing the scope of Logic, there seems to be not only affinity but some sort of identity between the connexions we contemplate within consciousness and those that we may believe to exist really in the *non-ego*. And Mr. Spencer's whole view of Logic is difficult to reconcile with the position that the *non-ego* or object-world is strictly an unknown and unknowable reality, apprehended in an indefinite consciousness.

The final expression of Mr. Spencer's view is to be found in the chapter entitled Transfigured Realism, where he tries to illustrate it by a diagram, showing the projection of a cube on a cylinder, made by lines radiating from a point behind the cube. The cube represents the objective reality ; the cylinder "stands for the receptive area of consciousness"; the "pro-

---

[1] *Principles of Psychology*, vol. ii. § 302, p. 87. Italics mine.
[2] *Op. cit.* vol. ii. § 472, p. 494 *init.*

jected figure stands for that state of consciousness we call a perception of the object."[1] The illustration is worth studying to understand Mr. Spencer's metaphysical view; but it has a misleading element, since cube, cylinder, and projected figure have all in common the important attribute of extension: so that they are fundamentally more alike than Subject, Percept, and 'Reality out of Consciousness' are held to be by Mr. Spencer. I am not sure that Mr. Spencer sees this: still his application avoids the misleading suggestion. "We may understand," he says, "very clearly how it becomes possible that a *plexus* of objective phenomena may be so represented by the *plexus* of subjective effects produced, that though the effects are totally unlike their causes, and though the relations among the effects are totally unlike the relations among their causes, and though the laws of variation in the one set of relations differ entirely from those in the other; yet the two may correspond in such a way that each change in the objective reality causes in the subjective state a change exactly answering to it: so constituting what we call a cognition of it—a relative knowledge of it."

On this I will make now two remarks. First as to 'plexus of objective *phenomena*.' But what can 'phenomena' mean here? The cube, I understand, stands for what I call extra-cognitional fact, the world out of consciousness: 'phenomena,' then, must surely mean the effects on consciousness of such fact. I cannot help thinking that Mr. Spencer is here confusedly

---

[1] *Principles of Psychology*, vol. ii. § 473, pp. 496 ff.

carrying the antithesis of phenomenon and reality outside the sphere within which it belongs. Next it will be observed that we come ultimately to ' what we call a cognition of it [the objective reality]—a relative knowledge of it.' But how is this reconcilable with the assertion in *First Principles* of the utter inconceivability of the underlying reality?

Of this more in the next lecture, when we shall have to examine Mr. Spencer's epistemological principles.

LECTURE II

METAPHYSICAL AND EPISTEMOLOGICAL DOCTRINES

IN the last lecture, after explaining Spencer's philosophical Agnosticism and its grounds, I passed to the more difficult task of ascertaining the exact relation of this Agnosticism to the Natural Dualism which he regards as the primordial datum of Philosophy, as systematised or unified knowledge of the knowable. This affirms the profoundest distinction among phenomena or manifestations to be that between *ego* and *non-ego*, or perhaps rather between 'Mind' and 'Matter' (as Mr. Spencer contemplates throughout a plurality of conscious minds). I directed attention to the diversity and contradiction of the conclusions to which we seem to be led when we examine his conception of Matter or the *non-ego*. To this point I shall return presently. But first I propose to complete the discussion of the Metaphysical question (in the narrower sense) by trying to ascertain similarly his view of the Nature of Mind : I shall then pass to his *epistemological* doctrine.

As regards the Nature of Mind we find—as we found regarding the Nature of Matter—that results reached by different lines of thought are difficult to put together.

The process of differentiation of subject and object, which we have examined in considering Mr. Spencer's notion of matter, leads primarily to the conclusion that the Ego is a term for *one* of the two great aggregates of 'states of consciousness'—*i.e.* for the aggregate or series of 'faint states' (thoughts and imaginations) as *contrasted* with the aggregate or series of 'vivid states,'[1] which are distinguished as Non-ego. This, as I said, I find irreconcilable with the view of Common Sense—accepted elsewhere by Mr. Spencer—that sensations, colours, sounds, touches, etc. are among the feelings which constitute a consciousness or mind, and this, being 'a something without any kinship' with the nervous actions from which those feelings are inseparable, renders the Psychology which studies them a "totally unique science, . . . antithetically opposed to all other sciences whatever."[2] These vivid states of consciousness are also described as 'peripherally initiated feelings,' and as such form one of the primary divisions of "components of mind."[3]

So much for the varying and transient psychical facts which Mr. Spencer calls states of consciousness. But in ordinary thought Mind or Ego does not denote an aggregate of these states; but (1) a permanent identical something of which they are states,

---

[1] Vivid states, it will be remembered, are briefly sensations and sense-perceptions, because emotions, though 'vivid states,' are handed over to the 'faint aggregate.'

[2] *Principles of Psychology*, vol. i. § 56, p. 140. [3] *Op. cit.* § 66, p. 166.

and (2) is conceived to be differently related to different states, active in some, passive in others. Now, though Mr. Spencer allows himself to speak of the "faint aggregate which I call my mind,"[1] he does in his own way recognise that I do not apply the term to anything I conceive as merely an aggregate. Thus, as regards (2), he rather startles us by referring—as though it needed no explanation—to "the fact that the faint series has a power of changing its own order."[2] But surely that is unthinkable. How can the *series* have the power? The past states cannot be thought to have it, as being past they are not actual; still less the future; and even if we could think the present state of our consciousness as having the power of changing, it is not the series. This 'power of changing,' in short, if attributed to mind at all, must be attributed to it not as a series of changing states, but as something that remains permanent through the series. And in fact Mr. Spencer eventually gives us a new view of "the Subject as the unknown permanent *nexus* which is never itself a state of consciousness, but which holds states of consciousness together."[3] This would seem to be what we ordinarily call Self or Ego, considered as supplying the element of continuity in our conscious life.

[But then at an earlier stage of his work Mr. Spencer has demonstrated that the substance of Mind cannot be known[4]], and by this we should understand

---

[1] *Op. cit.* vol. ii. § 462, p. 472 *fin.* [2] *Op. cit.* vol. ii. § 455, p. 460.
[3] *Op. cit.* vol. ii. § 469, p. 484. [4] *Op. cit.* vol. i. § 59, p. 146.

him to mean that we can know no more about it than this—that it is not and cannot be known. Yet now, to our surprise, this permanent *nexus* is treated as material! Even 'self-analysis,' he says, would show the subject "that this *nexus* forms part of the *nexus* to that peculiar vivid aggregate he distinguishes as his body"; and psycho-physiology will enable him to see that it is a set of nervous plexuses. "For, . . . an idea," he continues, "is the psychical side of what on its physical side is an involved set of molecular changes propagated through an involved set of nervous plexuses. That which makes possible this idea is the pre-existence of these plexuses, so organised that a wave of molecular motion diffused through them will produce, as its psychical correlative, the components of the conception in due order and degree. This idea lasts while the waves of molecular motion last, ceasing when they cease; but that which remains is the set of plexuses. These constitute the potentiality of the idea, and make possible future ideas like it. Each such set of plexuses, perpetually modified in detail by perpetual new actions; capable of entering into countless combinations with others, just as the objects thought of entered into countless combinations; and capable of having its several parts variously excited, just as the external object presents its combined attributes in various ways, is thus the permanent internal *nexus* for ideas, answering to the permanent external *nexus* for phenomena." But what then becomes of the 'unknownness' of the substance of

Mind? Mr. Spencer is aware that he has to answer this question; and his answer seems to be that the set of nervous plexuses is itself only a mental symbol of an unknowable reality. For "our ideas of matter and motion, merely symbolic of unknowable realities, are complex states of consciousness built out of units of feeling."[1] Although the set of plexuses appears when we take a psycho-physiological view as the "permanent internal *nexus* . . . which continues to exist amid transitory ideas"—each idea being only the psychical side of an involved set of molecular motions propagated through the set of nervous plexuses—this relative permanence of the material substratum of mental phenomena vanishes again when we turn to analyse our concept of a nervous plexus. For then we see that our concept of this or any other complex modification of matter " is but the symbol of some form of Power absolutely and for ever unknown to us; and a symbol which we cannot suppose to be like the reality without involving ourselves in contradictions."[2]

"See then our predicament," he says: "we can think of Matter only in terms of Mind. We can think of Mind only in terms of Matter. When we have pushed our explorations of the first to the uttermost limit, we are referred to the second for a final answer; and when we have got the final answer of the second we are referred back to the first for an interpretation of it. We find the value of

---

[1] *Principles of Psychology*, vol. i. § 63, p. 150.
[2] *Op. cit.* vol. i. § 63, p. 159 *init.*

x in terms of y; then we find the value of y in terms of x; and so on we may continue for ever without coming nearer to a solution. The antithesis of subject and object, never to be transcended while consciousness lasts, renders impossible all knowledge of that Ultimate Reality in which subject and object are united. And this brings us to the true conclusion implied throughout the foregoing pages—the conclusion that it is one and the same Ultimate Reality which is manifested to us subjectively and objectively. For while the nature of that which is manifested under either form proves to be inscrutable, the order of its manifestations throughout all mental phenomena proves to be the same as the order of its manifestations throughout all material phenomena."[1] It would seem, therefore, that the 'power' which the 'faint series' has of changing 'its own order' is after all only the power of our old friend the Unknowable to produce faint manifestations; and that though by inevitable laws of thought we are led to *contrast* the power manifested by faint feelings = Ego, with the power manifested in vivid sensations = Non-ego, the 'true conclusion' is that the same power is manifested in both.

How are we to put together this complicated set of inconsistencies?

Mr. Spencer's agnostic conclusion doubtless seems to him sufficiently humble; but I am not satisfied with it.

To me it seems misleading for him to say that

[1] *Principles of Psychology*, vol. i. § 273, p. 627.

the antithesis of subject and object is "never to be transcended while consciousness lasts." If that were so we surely could not think of either in terms of the other; but, according to his argument, this is just what we can do, and we can do nothing else; even although at the same time we have to think of mind as something totally without kinship with matter in motion. And out of this medley of oscillating contradictions it seems to me to result not only that knowledge of the Ultimate Reality itself is impossible, but that philosophical knowledge even of its manifestations is—I will not say 'impossible'—but is as yet unattained by Mr. Spencer. For he has told us that the task of Philosophy is to co-ordinate, unify, systematise the results of the particular sciences; but a systematisation that leaves such fundamental inconsistencies ought surely to admit that it has failed to accomplish its task.

I now turn to Mr. Spencer's Epistemology as set forth in his *Principles of Psychology*, Part VII. chaps. ix.-xiii.

I must begin with a brief account of the earlier chapters. In the first he explains that, having "provisionally assumed certain fundamental intuitions," we have now to "prove their congruity with the other dicta of consciousness . . . in other words, we have to take up the vexed question of subject and object. The relation between these, as antithetically opposed divisions of the entire assemblage of manifestations of the unknowable, was our datum."[1] In chap. ii. commences an attack on 'Metaphysicians' continued through four chapters. The root-error attributed to metaphysicians is a faith in Reasoning 'greatly in excess of that which is its due,' an 'unbounded confidence in it.'[2] Reasoning, says Mr. Spencer, has done so much for us, that we have been led to a superstitious awe of Reason as against Perception, *i.e.* to an 'unwarranted belief' in the superiority of 'the deliverances of consciousness reached through mediate processes to the deliverances of consciousness reached through immediate processes.' He observes, however, that men of science are not apt to fall into this superstition: if experience (or 'reasoning so automatic as to be no longer called reasoning') conflicts with calculation, they prefer experience. It is metaphysicians who tacitly assume that 'beliefs reached through complex intellectual processes' are superior in authority 'to beliefs reached through simple intellectual processes,' and, "setting out with this as their postulate, seem unconscious that they have postulated anything."[3] But, asks Mr. Spencer, 'how can Reason claim superior trustworthiness in the trial of Reason *versus* Perception'?[4] But

---

[1] *Principles of Psychology*, vol. ii. §§ 386 f. pp. 310 f.

[2] As Hume is one of the metaphysicians contemplated, I may remark that it shows a curious ignorance of Hume to attribute to him an unbounded confidence in the reasoning process. I suppose Mr. Spencer has never read or has forgotten the first section in Part IV. of the *Treatise on Human Nature* entitled "Of Scepticism, with regard to Reason."

[3] *Op. cit.* § 391, p. 316.

[4] *Op. cit.* § 391, p. 317. Before going further, may I say that I rather object to all controversies carried on against a class of people holding such various doctrines as 'metaphysicians.' It reminds me of the vulgar view of Greek sophists; and indeed Mr. Spencer is not quite free from unworthy appeal to vulgar dislike of metaphysicians.

if we take English Philosophy, Locke has no idea that there is any conflict between his philosophical reasoning and Common Sense; and Berkeley, who sees the conflict, seriously puts forward his 'Idealism' as a mode of reconciling Common Sense and Philosophy. In fact, this reconciliation is what nearly every eminent English metaphysician (since it was seen that reconciliation was needed) has been trying to effect, Berkeley as much as Reid, and Brown no less than Hamilton. Hume is the conspicuous exception; but Hume, while declaring the conflict irreconcilable, does not sum up in favour of Reason: that is just what he does not do. Mr. Spencer's reply would be that he is defending 'Realism'; and that metaphysicians generally are opponents of true Realism, if they are not all Idealists and Sceptics.

Here it becomes obvious to ask: What does Mr. Spencer understand by 'Realism'? Well, he adopts the rather inconvenient course of going on for a long time without any definition; but in the course of the argument it gradually comes to be defined by implication. Thus in chap. iii., on the 'Words of Metaphysicians,' though the main aim is to show that "language absolutely refuses to express the idealistic and sceptical hypotheses," the final positive conclusion is that the words used by metaphysicians "separately and jointly imply existence beyond consciousness;"[1] e.g. that the word 'impression' only 'remains intelligible' when I understand it as connoting the 'independent existence' of something that impresses, as

[1] [*Principles of Psychology*, vol. ii. § 395, p. 335.]

well as something—mind—that is impressed.[1] But other conclusions appear to be arrived at, which are not expressly formulated in the final summary of the chapter. For example, that the "word *brown* is meaningless unless space of three dimensions . . . is simultaneously conceived."[2] So, in chap. iv. on 'the Reasonings of Metaphysicians,' arguing against the Kantian view that time and space are 'subjective forms,' his conclusion is that it is impossible to separate space from the objective world.

It would seem then inferrible from chaps. iii. and iv. that the Realism which Mr. Spencer is concerned to defend is the belief in the existence of an objective world in space of three dimensions. Of this belief he proceeds to give (chaps. v.-viii.) what he calls a 'negative justification': *i.e.* a "proof that Realism rests on evidence having a greater validity than the evidence on which any counter-hypothesis rests." This negative justification consists of three arguments, drawn respectively from the priority, the simplicity, and the distinctness of the realistic belief.

The argument from priority affirms that, in what we commonly regard as sensation or sense-perception of external objects, "the thing primarily known is not that a sensation has been experienced, but that there exists an outer object," and even that "the existence of a sensation is a hypothesis that cannot be framed until external existence is known."[3] By 'primarily known' Mr. Spencer seems to mean that

---

[1] [*Principles of Psychology*, vol. ii. § 394, p. 334.]
[2] *Op. cit.* § 392, p. 320. [3] *Op. cit.* § 404, p. 369.

the definite conception of an external object comes, in the development of the individual human mind, earlier than the definite conception of one's own feelings as one's own. And it is important to note how, according to his view, this external object was primarily conceived. "Even the metaphysician," he says, "will not fail to remember that originally he regarded colours as inherent in the substances distinguished by them; that sweetness was an intrinsic property of sugar; and that hardness and softness were supposed actually to dwell in stones and in flesh."[1] But this 'priority' to sensation of the cognition of matter as coloured, sweet, etc. is importantly qualified. For Mr. Spencer distinguishes 'having a sensation'—which he even calls 'the simple *consciousness* of sensation' (!) — from 'being conscious of having a sensation,' and admits not only that the former fact is prior to the cognition of the external object, but also that the 'conception of the outer agent eventually framed is framed out of such sensations' which are rightly regarded as the 'things originally given.' His point, in short, is simply that these sensations existed before there was "any consciousness of subject or object."[2] But, thus qualified, the 'argument from priority' has no force against that species of Mentalism which I have distinguished as Sensationalism: it concedes all the priority of Sensation to Perception which the Sensationalist—as distinct from the Spiritualist—is concerned to claim.

The 'argument from simplicity' affirms that "the

---

[1] *Principles of Psychology*, vol. ii. § 404, p. 372.   [2] *Op. cit.* § 405, p. 373.

deliverance of Consciousness which yields Realism," *i.e.* the apparent cognition of an external object, is either immediate or—granting it to be inferential—is reached by a single act of inference; whereas the conclusion of either 'Idealism or Scepticism'[1] is reached by a long complex process of inference: the latter, therefore, from its mere length and complexity, involves more danger of error.

Finally, the 'argument from distinctness' affirms that "the one proposition of Realism is presented in vivid terms";[2] while "each of the many propositions of Idealism or Scepticism is represented in faint terms."[3] Therefore the Realistic proposition is *prima facie* more trustworthy. Surely there is some confusion here, due to the fact that Mr. Spencer has not defined the 'proposition of Realism.' Doubtless the elements of the external object as perceived are 'vivid'; but the question at issue between Realism and Mentalism does not involve any difference as to these: the question is whether this object has an existence independent of consciousness; and surely 'existence independent of consciousness' which Realism predicates of the object is a term exactly as faint as 'existence dependent on consciousness.' In short, whatever else in the object as commonly apprehended is 'vivid and definite' it is certainly not its objectivity!

Coming now to the main Epistemological doctrine,

---

[1] Or, as I should say, 'Mentalism or Scepticism.'
[2] 'Vivid' is not the same as 'distinct.'
[3] [*Principles of Psychology*, vol. ii. § 410, p. 380.]

I pass over the characteristic endeavour to prove that there *must* be a Criterion of Truth and Error, *must* be an answer to the question, "What is it which makes one deliverance of consciousness preferable to another?" *must* be "somewhere some fundamental act of thought by which the validities of other acts are to be determined."[1] It seems to me that Mr. Spencer's attempt to demonstrate this necessity is manifestly fallacious: he tries to show that "a certainty greater than that which any reasoning can yield has to be recognised at the outset of all reasoning";[2] but as the demonstration is itself a process of reasoning, it could surely only establish its conclusion by a self-contradiction. With this preliminary remark I pass to the discussion of the criterion that Mr. Spencer actually proposes.

But before proposing it Mr. Spencer first shows by a loose induction that complex propositions are more liable to error than simple ones: he does this in order to lay down that, before applying the criterion, we must "resolve each complex proposition into the simple propositions composing it," and then test each simple proposition separately.[3] He next proceeds to classify propositions "according as their terms are real or ideal, or partly the one and partly the other." He shows how cognitions may be 'presentative,' 'representative,' and 're-representative,' or partly one, partly another of these: how they become 'constructively compound' when—remaining particular—they pass into the representative and re-representative; and

---

[1] *Principles of Psychology*, vol. ii. § 416, p. 389.
[2] *Op. cit.* § 417, p. 390 *fin.*   [3] [*Op. cit.* § 422, p. 399.]

'cumulatively compound' when they are generalised from particular cases.[1]

Finally, he passes to the *epistemological* classification to which this is preliminary.

The fundamental distinction is between (1) propositions "of which the predicates always exist [in consciousness] along with their subjects"; and (2) propositions "of which the predicates do *not* always exist [in consciousness] along with their subjects. Those of the first class express cognition such that the thing alleged continues before consciousness as long as the thing of which it is alleged continues before consciousness; and those of the second class express cognition such that the thing alleged may disappear from consciousness while the thing of which it is alleged may remain. These are respectively the cognitions we necessarily accept and the cognitions we do not necessarily accept."[2]

Class (1) is again subdivided into : (*a*) "Cognitions in which the coexistence of the two terms is but temporarily absolute," such as 'simple cognitions of the presentative order,' as "I perceive light as long as I gaze at the sun"; and 'certain presentative-representative cognitions,' such as the proposition that a body has extension as long as its resistance is being felt. (*b*) "Cognitions in which the union of subject and predicate is permanently absolute," such as the axioms of Mathematics, and other "cognitions which contain abstract relations, quantitative or

[1] *Principles of Psychology*, vol. ii. § 423, p. 400.
[2] *Op. cit.* § 425, p. 402.

qualitative," *e.g.* the "most abstract cognitions which Logic formulates."[1]

But "one more important distinction remains to be noticed." In the *simplest* propositions of any of these subclasses "the connexion of predicate with its subject is so close that its coexistence cannot be kept out of consciousness." In other cases—*e.g.* in the "cumulatively-representative cognitions which Logic formulates"—the "invariable coexistence predicated is often inconspicuous, and may be overlooked. . . . It exists in consciousness but implicitly, and not explicitly. It may not be sought for, and in some cases search may fail to disentangle it."[2]

In chap. xi. we come at length to the Criterion to which the previous discussion has been leading up. "The inconceivableness of its negation is that which shows a cognition to possess the highest rank—is the criterion by which its insurpassable validity is known."[3] Or, in the more psychological language of the preceding paragraph, "to ascertain whether along with a certain subject a certain predicate invariably exists," we have to try "to replace this invariably existing predicate by some other or to suppress it altogether without replacing it." If the negation of a proposition is inconceivable—*i.e.* if its "terms cannot by any effort be brought before consciousness in that relation which the proposition asserts

---

[1] *Principles of Psychology*, vol. ii. § 425, pp. 403 f.

[2] *Op. cit.* § 425, pp. 404 f. This very important remark seems to me to involve Mr. Spencer's view of necessary truth in something like a contradiction. For how can it be said that a relation between two terms exists in consciousness when we are not conscious of it, or that we are conscious of it when we overlook it and fail to find it.   [3] *Op. cit.* § 426, p. 407.

between them"—we are "at once under the psychological necessity of thinking it, and have the highest possible logical justification for holding it to be unquestionable."[1] This is, in Mr. Spencer's view, the simple and universal criterion of truth, the 'universal postulate,' on the validity of which the validity of all reasoning depends.

Before I examine the criterion, the meaning of the term "inconceivable" requires some discussion. In the controversy between Mr. Spencer and J. S. Mill, to which reference is made in Mr. Spencer's chap. xi. and Mill's *Logic*, Bk. II. chap. vii., we find both admitting that, in ordinary use, 'inconceivable' has two meanings, one of which is 'incredible': and both equally regard this latter meaning as improper. Mill, however, holds that Mr. Spencer has been somewhat hasty in repudiating the meaning so far as his use of the term is concerned. I have said Mr. Spencer intends the criterion to guarantee propositions that represent particular facts, no less than propositions of universal import—*e.g.* the proposition 'I feel cold,' or 'I perceive light' when I am gazing at the sun—and Mill urges that if I say that the opposite of such a proposition is inconceivable, I must mean incredible; for it would not be true to say, in the strict sense of 'conceive,' 'I cannot conceive myself not feeling cold.' We can say, "I cannot conceive that I am not feeling cold," but then we have passed from conception to belief. Mr. Spencer, as I understand, maintains that in this case the coexistence of the

[1] *Principles of Psychology*, vol. ii. § 426, p. 407.

predicate-notion 'feeling cold' with the subject-notion 'self' is 'temporarily absolute,' but only 'temporarily.' But is this so? Only, I think, in extreme cases of very intense sensation or conception. Shakespeare says—

> No man can hold a fire in his hand
> By thinking on the frosty Caucasus.

And though I have never tried this painful experiment, I think it probable that it would exclude even the imagination of Caucasian frost. But that would not be the case with a milder degree of disagreeable heat. I find, indeed, that disagreeable sensations, when not too violent, even tend to provoke the imagination of their opposites, *e.g.* great thirst continually excites the image of cool spring water gurgling down my throat, etc. I cannot, therefore, agree that the utmost certainty in a proposition representing a transient particular fact involves the *inconceivability* of its negation, except in the special sense of inconceivability, in which it is indistinguishable not from 'incredibility' unqualified, but from *intuitive* incredibility. This particular species of incredibility Mr. Spencer does not take account of in his distinction.

It is not 'intuitively incredible' that a cannonball should be fired from England to America; though, as Mr. Spencer says, it is 'unbelievable.'[1] But my refusal to believe it cannot be justified by a mere examination of the terms of the proposition: it requires me to recall what I know of the experi-

[1] [*Principles of Psychology*, vol. ii. § 427, p. 408.]

enced range of cannons. In this meaning I agree with Mr. Spencer in regarding 'inconceivability of negation' as a universal characteristic of propositions which present themselves as self-evident truths. But I do not hold this 'Intuitive Criterion,' as I call it, to be infallible—any more than the Cartesian form of the criterion.[1]

Let us now observe the limitations with which Mr. Spencer affirms the validity of his criterion: "That some propositions," he says, "have been wrongly accepted as true, because their negations were supposed inconceivable when they were not, does not disprove the validity of the test, for these reasons:—(1) That they were complex propositions, not to be established by a test applicable only to propositions no further decomposable; (2) that this test, in common with any test, is liable to yield untrue results, either from incapacity or from carelessness in those who use it."[2] These two qualifications surely reduce very much the practical value of the criterion. For how are we to proceed if philosophers disagree about the application of the criteria? How are we to test 'undecomposability'? For notions which on first reflection appear to us simple are so often found on further reflective analysis to be composite. Which conclusion, then, are we to trust, the earlier or later? This seems to me a serious dilemma for Mr. Spencer; whichever way he answers he is in a difficulty. If he says the earlier, then I do not see how he can meet Mill's example of the dis-

---

[1] Cf. below, pp. 461 f.   [2] *Principles of Psychology*, vol. ii. § 433, p. 425.

belief in the existence of antipodes, for the proposition that 'heavy things must fall downward' would certainly have seemed simple. If he says the later, then what becomes of the argument in previous chapters in which the metaphysician is condemned for trusting the long and complex process of thought more than a short and simple one; for the analytical process by which we find compositeness in what originally appeared simple is commonly long and complex?

Let us now examine the fundamental proposition of Realism, to which this discussion of the criterion is intended to lead up. He tells us that 'metaphysicians' illegitimately assume that "beliefs reached through complex intellectual processes" are more valid than "beliefs reached through simple intellectual processes"; that the common language they use refuses to express their hypotheses and thus their reasoning inevitably implies the common beliefs that they repudiate; and that the belief of Realism has the advantage of 'priority,' 'simplicity,' and 'distinctness.' But surely this first, simply, distinctly affirmed belief is that which Mr. Spencer calls Crude Realism: the belief that the Non-ego is *per se* extended, solid, heavy, even coloured (if not resonant and odorous). This is what common language implies; and the reasoning by which Mr. Spencer proves the relativity of feelings and relations, still more the subtle and complicated analysis by which he resolves our notions of extension and solidity into an aggregate of feelings, lead us away from our original simple belief that the green grass we see exists out of consciousness as we see it, just as much as the reasonings of Mentalism, Scepticism, or Kantism. He says himself in his chapter on the 'Relativity of Feelings': "The *primitive belief* that redness exists as such out of the mind . . . is *thus* rendered as hard for the psychologist to entertain *as its opposite is hard to entertain for the uncultivated.*"[1] But when the 'psychologist' (whom I suppose Mr. Spencer wishes us to distinguish from the 'metaphysician') has got rid of this 'primitive belief,' what becomes of the 'argument from priority'? And when by an elaborate analysis, difficult to follow, he has analysed our perceptions of order in space into perceptions of possible order in time 'symbolised' by coexistent feelings, what becomes of the 'argument from simplicity'? And when finally the Object is left as an 'indefinable' something, to whose nature we more or less vaguely approximate by faint feelings of muscular tension, what becomes of the 'argument from distinctness'? Really the long discussion in which Spencer first seems to be maintaining Natural Realism, and then proceeds to denaturalise it, has all the serious incongruity of a metaphysical dream!

[1] [*Principles of Psychology*, vol. i. § 86, p. 205. Italics Professor Sidgwick's.]

THE SOPHISTS

I

(Reprinted from the *Journal of Philology*, vol. iv. No. 8, 1872.)

GROTE'S account of the Sophists, in the 67th chapter of his *History*, seems to me to have the merit—in so far as it was not anticipated by Welcker—of a historical discovery of the highest order. Before it was written the facts were all there, but the learned world could not draw the right inference: but after the point of view has once been suggested, the main substance of Grote's conclusions appears to me as clear and certain as anything of the kind can possibly be. I am therefore surprised that it has not been more generally accepted. As far as I am aware, it has not had the slightest influence on German erudition. Certainly the view of the Sophists presented in Curtius' popular history of Greece (which is likely to become a manual in our schools and colleges) is altogether præ-Grotian. The state of opinion among English scholars is more difficult to ascertain precisely. Much of my present paper has been suggested or confirmed by passages in the essays of Dr. Thompson and Professor Campbell: and I should be glad to find that their general views agree more nearly with my own than I now suppose. But Professor Campbell seems, though with much moderation, to sum up substantially against Grote: and through Dr. Thompson's remarks are scattered satirical references to the language of the famous chapter which seem to indicate considerable disagreement. At any rate, Mr. Cope, in the *Journal of Philology*, directly attacked the new theory: and Sir A. Grant (in his edition of Aristotle's *Ethics*) substantially rejected it.[1] Lastly, Mr. Jowett, in his recent translation of Plato, has emphasised in his preface his disagreement with Grote on this point, and argued the question forcibly, though briefly, in his introduction to the *Sophistes*. I cannot help thinking that Grote, if he had lived, would have made some sort of rejoinder to the last-mentioned elaborate and influential work. And since the master's hand is still, and this reply can never be, it may seem not untimely that a disciple should attempt βοηθεῖν τῷ λόγῳ ὀρφανῷ ὄντι. εἴπερ γὰρ ὁ πατὴρ αὐτοῦ ἔζη, πολλά γ' ἂν ἤμυνε.

The line marked out for such a rejoinder will appear more clearly from a brief notice of the steps of the controversy. The old view of the Sophists was that they were a set of charlatans who appeared in Greece in the fifth century, and earned an ample livelihood by imposing on public credulity: professing to teach virtue, they really taught the art of fallacious discourse, and meanwhile propagated

---

[1] [In an edition published subsequently Sir Alexander Grant modified his view to some extent.]

immoral practical doctrines. That, gravitating to Athens as the Πρυτανεῖον of Greece, they were there met and overthrown by Socrates, who exposed the hollowness of their rhetoric, turned their quibbles inside out, and triumphantly defended sound ethical principles against their plausible pernicious sophistries. That they thus, after a brief success, fell into well-merited contempt, so that their name became a byword for succeeding generations.

Against this Grote argues: (1) That the Sophists were not a sect but a profession: and that there is no ground for attributing to them any agreement as to doctrines. That, in fact, the word Sophist was applied in Plato's time in a more extensive sense than that in which he uses it: so as to include Socrates and his disciples, as well as Protagoras and his congeners. So that, as far as the term carried with it a certain invidious sense, this must be attributed to the vague dislike felt by people generally ignorant towards those who profess wisdom above the common: a dislike which would fall on Plato and the Philosophers as well as on the paid teachers whom he called Sophists: though no doubt the fact of taking pay would draw on the latter a double measure of the invidious sentiment. (2) That as regards the teaching of immoral doctrines, even Plato (whose statements we must take *cum grano*) does not bring this as a charge against the principal Sophists, Protagoras, Prodicus, Hippias, Gorgias: that it is *a priori* improbable that any public teachers should propound doctrines so offensive to the common sentiments of mankind: that, therefore, we can scarcely suppose that Thrasymachus so propounded the anti-social theory of justice attributed to him by Plato in the *Republic*; and that even if he did, we cannot infer from this anything as to the other Sophists.

On this second point Grote is chiefly at issue with the German writers (with whom Sir A. Grant substantially agrees). It is on the first head that Mr. Jowett joins issue, and to this I shall at present restrict myself. Mr. Jowett urges that though the meaning of the word Sophist has no doubt varied, and has been successively contracted and enlarged, yet that there is a specific bad sense in which any intelligent Athenian would have applied the term to certain contemporaries of Socrates, and not to Socrates himself, nor to Plato. Wherever the word is applied to these latter, "the application is made by an enemy of Socrates and Plato, or in a neutral sense." In support of this he points out that "Plato, Xenophon, Isocrates, Aristotle" all give a bad import to the word: and the Sophists are "regarded as a separate class in all of them."

Now, first, I should have thought that we might say of any term denoting a man's walk in life, and connoting doubtfully an invidious sentiment, that it is either applied in a neutral sense or by an enemy, *i.e.* with polemical intent. Even the slightest flavour of dislike is enough to make the man himself, and his friends, avoid such a word: as we see in the common use of the terms 'attorney' and 'solicitor.'

Therefore, that disciples of the martyred sage, and those who learnt from them, never called Socrates a Sophist is very certain. But that the Athenian public considered him as such, whether intelligently or not, is surely undeniable. Mr. Jowett says that Aristophanes may have identified Socrates with the Sophists "for the purposes of comedy." But the purposes of comedy are surely not served by satire that does not fall in with common conceptions. The Athenians looked on Socrates as the most popular and remarkable of the teachers to whom young men resorted with the avowed object of learning virtue or the art of conduct, and the more evident result of learning a dangerous dexterity in discourse; and as such they called him a Sophist. The differences between him and such men as Protagoras would appear to them less important than the resemblances. The charges brought against him by his accusers express just the general grounds of suspicion felt against both alike. Whether a man corrupted youth rhetorically or dialectically, whether he made the worse case appear the better by Declamation or Disputation, would seem to them quite a secondary matter. That this view involved a profound misapprehension, I do not of course deny: but all evidence seems to me to show that the misapprehension was wide-spread and permanent. More than half a century afterwards, Æschines (who can scarcely be regarded as 'an enemy'), when pleading for another example of salutary severity, reminds the Athenians how they had put to death the Sophist

Socrates. Again, Xenophon tells us that when the Thirty Tyrants wished to silence Socrates, they ordained that no one was to teach λόγων τέχνη: Xenophon says, of course, that they did it to bring him into disfavour with the multitude: but the whole proceeding implies that this was the popular view of his function. And Xenophon's comment on the transaction is expressed in a way to confirm this. "They thus," he says, "brought to bear against him τὸ κοινῇ τοῖς φιλοσόφοις ὑπὸ τῶν πολλῶν ἐπιτιμώμενον" —φιλοσόφοις, observe, not σοφισταῖς.

Mr. Jowett, however, appeals to the evidence of Isocrates, who clearly, he says, regarded the Sophists as a separate class, and at the same time used the term in a bad sense. And other writers on the same side have laid much stress on the testimony of Isocrates, as standing outside the Socratic tradition, and so free from any suspicion that may be raised as to the impartiality of Plato or Aristotle.

It is therefore very important to ascertain accurately what this testimony is. It is to be found in three orations—the Encomium of Helen, the oration entitled κατὰ τῶν Σοφιστῶν, and the speech περὶ 'Αντιδόσεως in which the old man (82) enters into an elaborate defence of his own career. All these convey the same kind of notion of a species of public teacher who was generally viewed with suspicion: and whom he certainly calls Sophist. At the same time, the points of view of the two most important of these speeches, the κατὰ τῶν Σοφιστῶν and the περὶ 'Αντιδόσεως, are to some extent opposed. In the former he is censuring these public teachers : in the latter he is to some extent defending them, in so far as he is forced to class himself with them, as he does indirectly, though he never applies to himself the term Σοφιστής. When we look closer at the account he gives of them in the oration which is most directly concerned with them, we find that he distinguishes three classes, against each of which he brings a different kind of complaint. (1) Against the earlier rhetoricians who had composed treatises he makes the same objections as Aristotle, that they laid too much stress on the forensic application of rhetoric. From these he seems to distinguish (2) those who profess πολιτικοὶ λόγοι, among whom it is evident that he is himself to be ranked : though he expresses great contempt for the charlatanism of many of them, and is careful to guard himself from the charge (which he enforces with some severity against them) of claiming too great efficacy for professional teaching in the making of an orator, and attributing too little to practice and natural faculty. The passage, however, which reminds us most forcibly of the attacks of Plato and Xenophon (and to which Grote's opponents especially appeal) is directed against (3) another class, quite different from the last two. These Sophists attempt to persuade young men that if they associate with them they will learn the true art of life—ἅ τε πρακτέον ἐστὶν εἴσονται καὶ διὰ ταύτης τῆς ἐπιστήμης εὐδαίμονες ἔσονται. So far they resemble the Protagoras of Plato. But when we find them called "people whose business is disputation," and "who profess to search after truth," and when Isocrates adds that "private persons will soon find that their so-called ἐπιστήμη leads to less success in affairs than the δόξαι of other people," and will regard this employment of time as ἀδολεσχία and μικρολογία—the suspicion dawns on us that these Sophists are no other than the disciples of Socrates. And the suspicion becomes a certainty when we, remembering the *Gorgias* and the *Phaedrus* and the strained relations between Plato and Isocrates, find (in the περὶ 'Αντιδ.) that these disputatious people are in the habit of speaking ill of discourses of the public and useful sort (βλασφημοῦσι περὶ τῶν λόγων τῶν κοινῶν καὶ τῶν χρησίμων) : when Isocrates adds with insulting generosity that their disputations—which he associates with astronomy and geometry—may possibly do young men some good as intellectual exercises, if they do not spend too much time on them and so "get stranded among theories of the old Sophists (τῶν παλαιῶν Σοφιστῶν), such as Empedocles and Parmenides": and when we find Plato's works unmistakably alluded to in another discourse as the "Laws and Republics composed by Sophists." The testimony of Isocrates then comes to this: he attacks the Sophists in the same style as Plato: only Isocrates calls Sophists just those whom Plato and posterity call Philosophers, while the more honourable title of "Philosophy" he reserves for his own special industry, the Art of Public Speaking. When two antagonists, with vocations so sharply contrasted as those of Plato and Isocrates were, both claim for themselves the name of Philosopher and endeavour each to fix on the other the odious appellation of Sophist, we may surely conclude that either term is in popular usage so vague as easily to comprehend both, and that the two are varyingly contrasted according the temper of the speaker. This is confirmed when we look again at Xenophon. We have seen that Philosophy with him was a profession that the vulgar called λόγων τέχνη; we may notice in contrast with this that he speaks contemptuously of physical inquiries, into the nature of "what the Sophists call the κόσμος"—so far coinciding with Isocrates. No doubt the honest man's conception of Philosophy did not go beyond the dialectical ethics of his master. Plato again admits in the *Politicus* that one who wishes to introduce into politics any principles more scientific than the current maxims and prejudices is sure to be called by people in general μετεωρολόγος καὶ ἀδολέσχης τις σοφιστής: thus using the very words of Isocrates and seeming to allow that the latter's application of the term is in no way exceptional.

I think, however, that we may go further than this and argue that if we examine carefully Plato's own use of the term Σοφιστής, we can see clearly that it is applied to two distinct kinds of teacher, corresponding respectively to the two classes into which Isocrates divided his contemporaries and rivals. Plato of course does not include himself or Socrates in either of these classes, any more than Isocrates conceives himself amenable to the charges which he marshals κατὰ τῶν Σοφιστῶν. But just as Isocrates is obliged to admit that he would be commonly ranked in one of the two divisions: so Plato cannot deny that there is a strong family likeness between his master's method and that of the other kind of Sophist, and that it requires considerable subtlety to distinguish the two: and does not scruple to attack as sophistical teaching the favourite doctrines of his fellow-disciples.

As this point is one to which Grote does not expressly advert, and as it seems to me of considerable importance not only for the present controversy, but generally for the right understanding of Plato's dialogues, and even to some extent in the determination of their chronological order, I shall allow myself to dwell on it at some length.

It seems to me that those dialogues of Plato in which Sophists are mentioned fall naturally into two groups, and that in each of these the being called Sophist exhibits a strongly and definitely marked character, so different from that of his homonym in the other group, that if they had not been called by the same name, no reader would ever have dreamt of identifying the two.

Let us first take the Sophists with whom we are by far the most familiar—Protagoras, Polus, Hippias, Gorgias, Thrasymachus. What is the common characteristic of these persons, as presented by Plato?—besides that of receiving pay, which must surely be considered an accident rather than a property of any class of teachers. We cannot even say that all professed to teach virtue, for Gorgias expressly disclaims any such profession. The one attribute found in all of them is that they are rhetoricians and declaimers, in the habit of making long speeches, and quite unused to that interchange of question and answer which is the essence of the Socratic manner of discourse. It is true that they have reflected upon language and affect subtle verbal distinctions: but upon this, as on other subjects, they can only talk at length: they are not prepared to define their abstract terms (or use them with precision), and are perfect tiros in the art of argumentation. The contrast between Protagoras and Socrates in this respect is almost tediously emphasised in the dialogue that bears the former's name. Protagoras can scarcely be brought to the requisite brevity of answer: he will insist on 'orating.' And the unsuspicious innocence with which he and Hippias and Polus submit themselves at first to the Elenchus, their absolute incapacity to see whither the questions are leading, the swift and sudden shame of their overthrow, are the comic effects on which the dialogues rely for their lighter entertainment. Thrasymachus, in the *Republic*, is not quite so fresh: he knows somewhat more what Socrates is after, and thinks he can parry the invincible Elenchus: but still like the rest he is essentially a rhetorician, his forte lies in long speeches, and at the critical point of the discussion he wishes to make his escape, "having deluged our ears with a regular *douche* of discourse," as Socrates says.

Let us now turn to the other group of dialogues

and examine the Sophist as he is defined in the *Sophistes* and caricatured in the *Euthydemus*. The difference of type is most striking. The Sophist's manner of discourse is no longer sharply contrasted with that of Socrates: it is rather, as Professor Campbell says, "the ape of the Socratic Elenchus." A shifty disputer has taken the place of the windy declaimer of the other dialogues: instead of pretentious and hollow rhetoric we have perverse and fallacious dialectic. The Sophist of the *Protagoras* and *Gorgias* has close affinity to the ῥήτωρ and is with difficulty distinguished from him: in fact, Plato can only distinguish them by restricting the sphere of ῥητορική to forensic speaking: this, he tells us, is a quackery that simulates justice, while the Sophists are more ambitious quacks who mimic the art of legislation. These latter, then, correspond to the teachers of πολιτικοὶ λόγοι among whom Isocrates classes himself—strongly objecting to be confounded with those who merely wrote and taught for the law-courts—except that the latter carefully avoids the more vague and extravagant professions which Protagoras and others probably made: he still, however, maintains that in so far as Virtue, Practical Wisdom, and Political Science can be taught, the teaching of them is involved in and bound up with the art of public speaking, his own φιλοσοφία. This, he claims, does impart τὸ λέγειν εὖ καὶ φρονεῖν in so far as these are not gifts of nature and effects of practice: and as making this claim he is distinctly Plato's Sophist of the first type. Still this restriction of ῥητορική to its forensic application is somewhat forced: both Sophist and Rhetor would be popularly regarded as professing the art of declamatory or rhetorical discourse and so naturally classed together and confounded: as Plato himself tells us in the *Gorgias*, φύρονται ἐν τῷ αὐτῷ καὶ περὶ τὰ αὐτά.

But the Sophistes of the dialogue so called is expressly contrasted with both the Statesman and the Rhetor: he is the Professor of Disputation, of the art of question and answer according to rules, ἐριστική,—thus exhibiting exactly the character which Isocrates tries to fix upon Plato. Further, we are told that this Sophist claims to deliver men from groundless conceit of their own knowledge by cross-examining them and pointing out their inconsistencies: the special function of Socrates. Of course Plato does not admit that the Sophist is the true Dialectician: but he resembles him as a wolf does a dog. He is a tremendous argufier, and able to impart to others the argumentative art. The difference between him and Socrates is that his effect is purely negative: he begins and ends with captious disputation, his skill is simply to bewilder and perplex: he is not, as Socrates, a midwife of true knowledge.

It is just this difference which is dramatically exhibited in the *Euthydemus*, with much broad drollery of caricature. Here a couple of Sophists of the eristical sort are seen exercising their art on an intelligent youth. They put captious questions to him and entangle him in contradictions by means of verbal quibbles, until he does not know whether he is standing on his head or his heels. Socrates then takes him in hand and, by gentler questioning, ultimately draws out of him answers of remarkable point and pregnancy; and so the true Dialectic is contrasted with its counterfeit Eristic.

The difference is clear enough to us, who are accustomed to trace the whole growth of philosophy from the fertile germ of Socratic disputation. But we can see even from Plato himself that it would be much less clear to unphilosophic contemporaries: that the effect of the Socratic interrogations on a plain man would be just this bewilderment and perplexity and sense that he had been taken in by verbal quibbling, which Plato describes as the effect of Eristic Sophistry. At any rate, the Sophist of the *Sophistes* and the *Euthydemus* is much more like the disciples of Socrates than he is like the Sophist of the *Protagoras* and the *Gorgias*. And therefore, while the uninstructed public, as we have seen, would lump Declaimers and Disputers together as Professors of the Art of Discourse, I think Mr. Jowett's "intelligent Athenian" would be much more certain to grasp the distinction between the teachers of public speaking who more or less claimed to impart political wisdom on the one hand, and the teachers of disputation and ethics on the other, than he would be to appreciate the finer differences that separated Euthydemus and Dionysodorus from the Socratic Schools.

But we may go further than this. Plato himself does his best to obliterate these latter differences:

THE SOPHISTS 337

not of course as far as his own teaching is concerned, but certainly in respect of his brother Socratics.

Even the received Histories of Philosophy do not altogether conceal this fact from the student. It is true that he reads in one place of Sophistical Eristic, which he is led to look on as a part of the charlatan's stock-in-trade: and in another place of Megarian Eristic, which he regards as a development of philosophy. But he can get no clear notion of the difference between the two: and when he comes to the *Euthydemus* he finds them indistinguishably blended in the object of Plato's polemic.[1]

Not only is the whole manner and method of the Sophists in this dialogue a manifest caricature of the manner and method of Socrates—the Sophists profess εἰς ἀρετῆς ἐπιμέλειαν προτρέψαι by means of dialogue: they challenge the interlocutor ὑπέχειν λόγον: their examples are drawn from the common objects and vulgar trades, the frequent recurrence of which in the talk of Socrates was (as we learn from Xenophon) an established joke[2]—but further they maintain positions that we know to have been held by Megarians and Cynics, their fallacies and quibbles are just like those of Eubulides, and we may fairly presume that what we have here presented to us as "Sophistic" is neither more nor less than a caricature of the Megarian Logic.

[1] The identification is at least suggested in the *Sophistes*; cf. Campbell, p. liv., where indeed Prof. Campbell supports to some extent the view here maintained, though he does not contrast Plato's two uses of the term Σοφιστής in the manner that I have done.

[2] They talk of oxen and sheep, the cook, the smith, the potter.

Z

In short, there is only one kind of Eristic in Plato's view : and the only reason why historians insist on distinguishing two kinds is, that they have made up their minds that there must be a broad line of distinction between the Sophists and the disciples of Socrates.

The results so far obtained—that among the Sophists attacked by Plato we can distinguish two kinds,[1] corresponding to two classes distinguished by Isocrates : that in one of the Isocratean species Plato is polemically included, while with the corresponding Platonic Sophists Plato's fellow-disciples are inextricably commingled—all this seems to me certain, and quite sufficient to refute the received opinion that there was a broad and clear historical distinction between Sophists and Philosophers. The position which I shall go on to maintain is more hypothetical, and I am anxious to separate it from what I have so far tried to prove, in order that any doubts which may be felt with regard to the one may not extend themselves insensibly to the other.

I am disposed to think that the Art of Disputation which is ascribed to Sophists in the *Euthydemus* and the *Sophistes* (and exhaustively analysed by Aristotle in the περὶ Σοφιστικῶν Ἐλέγχων) originated entirely with Socrates, and that he is altogether responsible for the form at least of this second species of Sophistic.

Thus to turn the tables on the arch-antagonist of Sophistry, and charge him with sowing the sophistical

---

[1] It is not, of course, meant that Plato himself clearly distinguishes the two.

THE SOPHISTS 339

tares which his great pupil is so earnest to separate from his dialectical wheat, will seem a paradox. And I cannot prove it: but I think I can show that it is the most probable hypothesis.

My first argument is one of general historical probability. I do not see from whom else the method could have been derived—as far as the form is concerned: for no doubt its sceptical and destructive aim, and the logical puzzles and paradoxes which it uses, may be traced to Protagoras and Zeno. But as a method of conducting argument, it seems to me just an "ape of the Socratic Elenchus": a deliberate, artificial reproduction of the spontaneous and characteristic manner of the great sage, a manner which shared and expressed—and indeed seems to us inseparable from—his philosophic and personal originality, his Induction and his Irony.

I am aware that the authority of Diogenes Laertius stands in the way of this view. He states on Aristotle's evidence that Zeno was the originator of Dialectic, thus making no distinction between the Zenonian and the Socratic methods. More definitely he refers Eristic to Protagoras: πρῶτος ἔφη—he says —δύο λόγους εἶναι περὶ παντὸς πράγματος ἀντικειμένους ἀλλήλοις· οἶς καὶ συνηρώτα, πρῶτος τοῦτο πράξας: and afterwards enumerates among his writings a τέχνη ἐριστικῶν.

Now this last assertion is rather an awkward fact for me: and I thought at first that it was impossible in face of it to maintain my hypothesis. But on reflection there appeared to be fair ground for discarding it: for (1) we cannot really reconcile Diogenes and Plato, but are forced to choose between the two; and (2) we can suggest a very probable explanation of Diogenes' assertion, assuming it to be erroneous.

First, then, it seems to me quite incredible that if Protagoras had really not only practised, but actually invented, Eristic, as described in the *Sophistes*—methodical disputation by short questions and answers—he could ever have been represented as Plato represents him in the dialogue which bears his name. For here he is not casually or slightly, but emphatically and prominently contrasted with Socrates, as the master of the opposite method of long speaking. It is true that he professes to be able to speak at any length that may be desired: but this is only a bit of his brag: it is quite clear that he cannot. The Elenchus is quite new to him, and he falls a most helpless victim to it. Now the coarsest satirist would not describe a man as quite unskilled in an art which he had himself invented: and Plato is not a coarse satirist: and moreover, as Grote well observes, he is not here even a severe one, as far as Protagoras is concerned: he wishes to allow him such credit as he deserves, and so he does not put in his mouth (as in the case of Prodicus and Hippias) a piece of affected verbiage to make him ridiculous, but an able and interesting dissertation. He treats him with consideration and fairness, if not with esteem, as a master in his art such as it was.

It seems to me then that Plato could not have known what is stated by Diogenes, and at the same time that he must have known it, if the statement had been true. He was no doubt aware that Protagoras maintained the thesis, Οὐκ εἶναι ἀντιλέγειν, which was a favourite with the Eristics: indeed he himself traces this connexion in the *Euthydemus*. And I am inclined to think that it was on this reference that the statement of Diogenes was based; if so, we can conjecture exactly how he was misled. Protagoras, no doubt, was in a manner Eristic, just as Zeno was, but it was in a rhetorical manner: he very likely wrote a τέχνη ἐριστικῶν, as Diogenes says: but if so, we must suppose it merely to have contained instructions how to make speeches on both sides of a case, no doubt with the aid of logical fallacies. Diogenes finding the reference in the *Euthydemus*, and not thinking of any other Eristic than τὸ νῦν ἐπιπόλαιον γένος, as he afterwards calls it, naturally attributes this latter to the famous father of sophistry.[1]

But I should not rely on this hypothetical reasoning, if it were not supported by strong general probabilities. Surely the whole conception of Socrates and his effect on his contemporaries, as all authorities combine to represent it, requires us to assume that his manner of discourse was quite novel: that no one before had systematically attempted to show men their ignorance of what they believed themselves to

---

[1] I may observe that Diogenes goes on to say that Protagoras taught ψυχὴν εἶναι τὰς αἰσθήσεις, which is obviously derived from the *Theaetetus* misunderstood. It is not therefore very bold to conjecture that his other statement is simply derived from the *Euthydemus* misunderstood.

know. Suppose a society to which the "Art of Wrangling," as Locke calls it, is familiar, and the historical Socrates, whom we seem to know as well as we know Dr. Johnson, seems quite *dépaysé*: we feel that his philosophical originality and his moral earnestness must have expressed themselves in some quite different manner.

But Socrates once there, appearing to the public as the Arch-Sophist, who overcame all rivals in wordy fight, and by his greater impressiveness and attractiveness to youth threw them all into the shade, so that comedians naturally selected him to represent the class—what could be more natural than that he should have a host of imitators? Indeed Xenophon expressly tells us of such men who, from the free and abundant banquet of Socratic discourse, carried away fragments which they sold for money.

The question then is, Would Plato call such men Sophists?

It must be borne in mind that a Sophist, in Plato's peculiar use of the term, combined two attributes: he taught for pay, and he taught sham knowledge: and the term might seem to be applicable wherever these attributes were found in combination. If then there were among the disciples of Socrates men who taught for pay, not having private fortunes like Plato, and who taught sham knowledge, *i.e.* doctrines with which Plato disagreed: how was he to regard them? I imagine he would be puzzled, and would make distinctions among them. There might be some like Euthydemus and Dionysiodorus, in whom he would

THE SOPHISTS 343

feel an absolute want of philosophic earnestness: with these, whether they had or had not formed part of the — no doubt varying and irregular — circle who listened to Socrates, he would recognise no tie of brotherhood: and would not hesitate, if occasion offered, to satirise them under the invidious term. There would be others like Aristippus, who certainly took money for his teaching, and against whose theory and practice Plato would feel a strong aversion: but who was yet a man of convictions, and a man of speculative force and originality. He would be difficult to class. And in fact, though Aristotle speaks of him as a Sophist, Plato never does, never indeed mentions him personally, though he is understood to be directly controverting his theories in two dialogues. If, again, there were also members of the School of Megara, with which Plato had at first felt the closest affinity, and from which his divergence had been slow and gradual: if these undoubted Socratics had fallen away into the wickedness of taking fees, while their dialectical method degenerated more and more into captious and purely negative disputation: Plato, we may suppose, would be pained and perplexed. But he might gradually come to recognise that these men, even though they might be old friends and actual co-disciples of Socrates, were yet essentially Sophists, and their teaching Sophistry.

I conceive, then, that Socrates was seed and source of a new kind of Sophistry, the post-Socratic Sophistry, as we may call it: which it was extremely difficult for the subtlest mind to distinguish from the profession of Socratic philosophy. Or may we not say, that the distinction would be properly impossible, conjecturing that the proper positive and negative characteristics of the Sophist, presence of fees and absence of philosophic earnestness, would not be found together? It is clear that Plato's conception of a Sophist involves the—I trust—groundless assumption that "the man who takes fees must be a quack": and if he found men taking fees, whom he would shrink from calling quacks, though he might deplore their philosophic aberrations, he would be in a dilemma as to the employment of the term.

At this point, one wants to know exactly how far the Socratic principle of not taking fees was carried out in what we are accustomed to call the Socratic schools, intensively and extensively: how many acted on it, and how strictly. No doubt all true disciples of Socrates would be reluctant to abandon the principle, and to give for gold what gold should never buy.[1] But *il faut vivre*: and what were men to do who had neither the αὐτάρκεια of Antisthenes nor the fortune of Plato? To the latter, indeed, who is described to us as consuming his full share of τὰ ἔξω ἀγαθά, such men might fairly say, in the words of Euripides—

πρὸς τῶν ἐχόντων τὸν νόμον τίθης.

Then, again, there are different ways of effecting the transfer of commodities: one may veil or attenuate the repulsiveness of the transaction in various degrees. Even the virtue of Socrates is said to have gone out

[1] Cf. *Memorabilia*, I. c. vi. § 13.

frequently to dinner: Quintilian, indeed, reports a tradition that 'Socrati collatum sit ad victum.'[1] Plato was, as I have said, well-born, and probably well-to-do: but even he, if we may trust the *Epistles*, did not disdain presents from Dionysius and other friends. Poorer Socratics, one may surely assume, would take similar presents with less scruple, and the practice would gradually become regular. At this stage it would be difficult to distinguish presents from fees: especially from fees claimed in the magnificent manner of Protagoras. I observe that Dr. Thompson has no hesitation in identifying the disputatious Sophists of Isocrates, who imparted virtue for four or five minæ, with "some of the minor Socratics": and it seems probable that the number of such paid Socratics would increase as time went on and the personal influence of the master declined. In fact, the principle of gratuitous teaching was so impracticable, that it must be given up: until the community generally saw the propriety of supporting philosophers, as in Plato's model state, they must get a livelihood out of society somehow.

Meanwhile, I think, we may assume that the first type of Sophist was declining: or rather was gradually shrinking back into the rhetorician out of which he had expanded. The new dialectical method had the attraction of novelty: and at the same time all the nobler element of the strong and wide-spread influence which had thronged the lectures of Pro-

[1] The same authority adds that Zeno, Cleanthes, and Chrysippus *mercedes acceptaverint*: so that the principle appears to have been altogether abandoned by the severest of the post-Aristotelian schools.

tagoras and Hippias, the enthusiasm for wisdom and virtue, the fearless aspiration and the sublime credulity of youth, would be attracted and absorbed by the new teaching. Isocrates, no doubt, with his "philosophy" represents in a manner the old Sophists: but in his profession of practical wisdom there was but a meagre residuum of the magnificent promises of Protagoras. There were besides, as Aristotle informs us, teachers who gave systematic instruction in political science, using collections of laws and constitutions. But such moralists as Prodicus we may assume to have quite disappeared in the fourth century: they are in fact, to use Welcker's phrase, "forerunners of Socrates" and true ethical philosophy: they represent an earlier and ruder stage of moral reflection: when the Socrates has come their day is over. The time, then, would arrive when Eristic would be the only prominent rival of Dialectic: and when Plato, looking abroad for the quack teacher to contrast with the true philosopher, would discover him among his old friends and comrades, and find in his features an odious resemblance to the revered lineaments of his master. But this view of Eristic would not come to him all at once: there would be a clear interval between the time when he distinguished it as a perverse and mistaken dialectic from his own method, and the time when he actually identified it with Sophistic.

Now I think that just this appears if we arrange the dialogues of Plato in the chronological order which would on other grounds be most probable, and trace his employment of the two terms—Sophistic and Eristic—down the stream of time.

Take first the *Protagoras*. This is generally placed in the first group of the dialogues, chronologically arranged. I am inclined to place it among the very earliest. At any rate, I regard it as representing Plato's recollections of the actual collision between Socrates and the original Sophists. Here there is no mention of Eristic: nor does it appear in the *Gorgias*, which however must be placed at a considerable interval from the *Protagoras* in order to allow time for the complete change that has taken place in Plato's ethical view. This dialogue indeed is less directed against the old-fashioned sophistry than against rhetoric. It is true that Plato places σοφιστική, as "Quackery of Legislation," side by side with ῥητορική: but I think he is more concerned to attribute this quackery to Athenian politicians generally than to any professional teachers. A similar view to this is developed again in the *Republic*, in one of the most brilliant and effective passages that Plato ever wrote. "You, the Public," he rings forth, "are the Arch-Sophist, it is your Public Opinion that corrupts youth." It may be observed that Thrasymachus, who is the victim of Socrates in the prolusory dialogue that fills the first book of the *Republic*, is not called a Sophist, and does not profess the art of conduct: he is merely a rhetorician who maintains a popular immoral paradox. The *Republic*, though it has much affinity to the *Gorgias*, must be placed, I think, at a certain interval after it: because Plato's ethical view has been again somewhat modified. He is no longer in the extreme of reaction from the hedonism of the *Protagoras*: he submits to try the issue between Virtue and Vice by the standard of Pleasure. Now here for the first time we come across Eristic as a method. The word ἐριστικός has been used before in the *Lysis*. But there it is employed untechnically and quasi-eulogistically: it is implied that the youth called ἐριστικός has dialectical capacity. In the *Republic*, however (v. 454), we hear of an ἀντιλογικὴ τέχνη, into which many fall unwillingly, καὶ οἴονται οὐκ ἐρίζειν ἀλλὰ διαλέγεσθαι, because they are unable κατ' εἴδη διαιρούμενοι τὸ λεγόμενον ἐπισκοπεῖν and so they διώκουσι κατ' αὐτὸ τὸ ὄνομα τοῦ λεχθέντος τὴν ἐναντίωσιν. Here we have already a method or manner of reasoning, in no way connected with Sophistry, but obviously belonging to persons seriously engaged in the pursuit of truth.

In the *Meno*, again, which I should place between the *Gorgias* and the *Republic*, we have Sophistic and Eristic side by side and unconnected. The Sophists are still our old friends: they are not exactly attacked: they are even half-defended against Anytus, who is made to confess that he knows nothing about them, though it is possible that he may be right in despising them. But Eristic is noticed quite independently: it is contrasted with the method of Socrates as a perverse kind of Dialectic. "If he were one of the σοφοὶ καὶ ἐριστικοὶ καὶ ἀγωνιστικοί, I should say εἰ μὴ ὀρθῶς λέγω, σὸν ἔργον λαμβάνειν λόγον καὶ ἐλέγχειν": and again Socrates objects to the ἐριστικὸς λόγος that οὐκ ἔστι ζητεῖν ἀνθρώπῳ οὔτε ὃ οἶδεν οὔτε ὃ μὴ οἶδεν.

This latter position is examined at length in the *Theaetetus*, which I consider to belong to a group of dialogues later than any yet mentioned. This group is defined in my view by two characteristics. (1) The concentration on ethical and political interests, due to the influence of Socrates, has ceased: Plato's attention is fixed on questions from a social point of view more narrow and professional, from a philosophical point of view more central and fundamental—on knowledge: its nature, object, and method. He has passed definitely from the marketplace into the school; and as an indication of this (2) he is now engaged in controversies with other philosophers: an element absent from the earlier dialogues—even from the *Republic*. When he takes up ethical questions again, as in the *Philebus*, the more scholastic and technical treatment is striking.

Now in the *Theaetetus* perverse dialectic is noticed, though not by the name of Eristic, but by that of *Sophistic*, which here bears its later meaning. "If," says Socrates, "you and I were engaged in *Sophistic logomachy* (ξυνελθόντες σοφιστικῶς εἰς μάχην τοιαύτην) we should go on verbally confuting each other: a sort of confutation that produces no real conviction."

This, then, is the first identification of Sophistic and Eristic: that is, if I am right in connecting closely the *Euthydemus* and the *Sophistes*, previously discussed. I know that the *Euthydemus* has generally been placed earlier: but I think this is due to a mistaken inference from the style. The extreme difference of form has blinded readers to the substantial affinity of its polemic with that of the *Sophistes*.

I am aware that any argument which depends on an assumption as to the order of Plato's dialogues is insecure, on account of the difference of opinion that exists on the subject. In particular, many would dispute the place I assign to the *Theaetetus*. But most, I think, would allow at any rate that there was a time at which Plato attacked as Sophists rhetorical moralists and politicians, a later time at which he defined a Sophist as a perverse disputer, and a time between the two at which he contended against the same sort of perverse disputations without identifying it with Sophistry. And this seems strongly confirmatory of my view that this kind of disputatious Sophistry is post-Socratic and a degenerate offshoot of Socratic method.

THE SOPHISTS

II

(Reprinted from the *Journal of Philology*, vol. v. No. 9, 1873.)

In the last number of this *Journal* I argued in favour of the view put forward by Grote as to the common acceptation, in the age of Socrates and Plato, of the term Sophist. I tried to show, that even after it had partly lost its vaguer and wider signification—inclusive of Masters of any Arts, Poets and *literati* generally—it still was not restricted to teachers of a particular sect or school, having common doctrines, or even a similar philosophic tendency: but was applied to all whom the vulgar regarded as teaching λόγων τέχνην, whether they were rhetoricians and declaimers like Gorgias and Protagoras, or arguers and disputers, after the fashion that Socrates brought into vogue. It comprehended, therefore, several classes of persons besides the Professors of the Art of Conduct with whom Socrates is contrasted in the earlier Platonic dialogues. It included, for example, Rhetoricians generally, even though like Gorgias they disclaimed altogether the teaching of Virtue: in fact, it is evident from Plato's *Gorgias* that the distinction which he there tries to draw between Sophist and Rhetor is but vaguely apprehended by the popular mind. It included also (as I was chiefly concerned to show) Socrates and his disciples: who were considered—by all except themselves—as Sophists of the Disputatious, as distinct from the Declamatory, species. In fact, even Plato, in his later works, and Aristotle, show us, under the title of Sophist, a professor of quasi-Socratic argumentation: quite unlike the rhetorical lecturers on Conduct whom Socrates confutes in the earlier dialogues. We may perhaps distinguish three stages in the signification of the term: or rather (as they are not strictly successive) three areas of an application narrowing gradually, but not uniformly, so that at any time the class would be conceived with considerable vagueness, and very differently by different persons.

(1) Even after the σοφία which a Sophist professed was generally understood to be something higher than mere technical skill in any department, still an eminent specialist who made any pretensions to general enlightenment might easily be called a Sophist: and so the term would be applied, by many persons, to such professors of music as Damon and Pythoclides, to Hippodamus the architect and Meton the astronomer.

Then (2) I conceive that for about the period 450–350 B.C. the word was commonly used to denote all who professed, as Xenophon says, λόγων τέχνην: including both the rhetorical and dialectical professors of the Art of Conduct (which the vulgar would persist in regarding as an Art of talking about conduct), and also rhetoricians like Gorgias, Polus, etc., down to Isocrates: not that the line between the two was very clearly drawn, as Isocrates claimed that his 'Philosophy' really involved instruction in morals, and it was matter of debate down to the time of Cicero whether the true orator must not necessarily possess a knowledge of things in general. However, during the latter half of this period, after the death of Socrates, the appellation, being an invidious one, was probably repudiated with equal vigour and ultimate success by Rhetoricians and Philosophers.

But (3) we need not doubt that the still stricter manner in which Plato (in the *Gorgias*) conceives the class of σοφισταί, distinguishing them from the ῥήτορες, was at least partially current in the time of Socrates. For when once cultivated society in Greece had become persuaded that ἀρετή—excellence of character and conduct—could really be imparted in lectures, and were willing to pay large sums for obtaining it: naturally the professors of this Ars Artium would be regarded as in a special sense Professors of Wisdom, σοφισταί. And it is such men as these that the term always suggests to readers of Greek history, however they may be vaguely conscious of its wider usage. The fresh light in which he placed the ethical teaching of these men was the most important result of Grote's discussion. If his argument had appeared generally so overwhelming as it seems to myself, the present paper would not have been written: but since the contrary view is still supported by the whole prestige of German erudition, I shall endeavour to re-state Grote's case in such a manner as to show most clearly on what a curious combination of misrepresented historical evidences, and misconceived philosophical probabilities, the opposite theory rests.

But before doing this, I wish to notice one or two points in which I cannot follow Grote, and by which he seems to me to have prejudiced unnecessarily the general acceptance of his theory. Although one may fairly say that to a mind like Grote's scarcely anything could be more antipathetic than the manner of Protagoras and his followers: and although it is evident to careful readers of his *Plato*, that he had the deepest enthusiasm for the spirit that dwelt in Socrates, and reigned over the golden age of Greek philosophy: still the intensity of his historical realisation has made him appear as an advocate of the pre-dialectical teachers. He seems always to be pleading at the bar of erudite opinion for a reversal of the sentence on certain eminent Hellenes. Now with this attitude of mind I have no sympathy. There was at any rate enough of charlatanism in Protagoras and Hippias to prevent any ardour for their historical reputation—even though we may believe (as I do) that they were no worse than the average popular preacher, or professional journalist, of our own day. One might more easily feel moved to take up the cudgels for Prodicus, resenting the refined barbarity with which Plato has satirised the poor invalid professor shivering under his sheepskins. But justice has been done to Prodicus by the very German erudition against which I have here to contend. And as for the class generally—they had in their lifetime more success than they deserved, and many better men have been worse handled by posterity. It is only because they represent the first stage of ethical reflection in Greece, and therefore the springs and sources of European moral philosophy, that one is concerned to conceive as exactly as possible the character of their teaching. The antagonism to that teaching, which developed the genius of Socrates, constitutes really so intimate a relation that we cannot understand him if we misunderstand 'Sophistik.'

But again, in his anxiety to do justice to the Sophist, Grote laid more stress than is at all necessary on the partisanship of Plato. No doubt there is an element of even extravagant caricature in the Platonic drama: and the stupidity of commentators like Stallbaum, who treat their author as if he was a short-hand reporter of actual dialogues, is provoking. Still, one always feels that the satirical humour of Plato was balanced and counteracted by the astonishing versatility of his intellectual sympathy. And the strength of Grote's case lies in what Plato actually does say of the Sophists, and not in suggestions of what he may have said untruly.

Before examining the evidence, it may be well to state clearly the conclusions commonly drawn from it which I regard as erroneous. What does a writer mean when he speaks of 'Sophistical ethics,' 'Sophistical theories on Law and Morality'? As far as I can see, he always means speculative moral scepticism leading to pure egoism in practice. He means a denial of the intrinsic validity of all traditional social restraints, and a recommendation to each individual to do exactly what he finds most convenient for himself. That nothing is really proscribed or forbidden to any man, except what he chooses to think so: that Nature directs us to the unrestrained pursuit of pleasure, and that the seeming-strong moral barriers to this pursuit become mere cobwebs to enlightened reflection: that "Justice is good for others" than the just man, and that the belief that it is good for him to be just is kept up by these others in their own interest—this is supposed to be the teaching which the youth of Athens thronged to hear. Whatever speculative and rhetorical garnish the Sophists may have added, this was "der langen Rede kurzer Sinn."

I might have abstracted this statement from almost any of the German writers whose works are text-books in our universities: but I will choose as my authority the generally judicious and moderate Zeller. He speaks of "Sophistik" as "Moralische Skepsis": of the "Sophistische Theorie des Egoismus," the sophistical "Grundsatz dass für jeden recht sei, was ihm nützlich," the sophistical "Satz von der Naturwidrigkeit des bestehenden Rechts": to the Sophists, he says, "das natürliche Gesetz schien nur in der Berechtigung der Willkür, in der Herrschaft des subjectiven Beliebens und Vortheils zu bestehen ": " das Sophistische Ideal" was "die unbeschränkte Herrschermacht."

I need not multiply quotations : and perhaps even these are superfluous. In Schwegler's smaller treatise, in Erdmann's more recent handbook, in the popular history of Curtius, views substantially the same are put forward. Now I would not deny that licentious talk of this kind was probably very prevalent in the polite society of Athens during the age of Socrates and Plato. But the precise point which I, after Grote, maintain, is that such was not the professional teaching of those Professors of the Art of Conduct whom it fell to Socrates to weigh in his formidable balance : that it was not for this that he found them wanting : and that it is a grave misapprehension of his relation to them to conceive him as shielding morality from their destructive analysis, and reaffirming the objectivity of duty in opposition to their " Absolute Subjektivität."

The indictment thus sweepingly drawn against a profession proceeds upon two lines of argument. It appeals to the evidence of contemporary authority, especially Plato: and it is further supported on a presumption drawn from the metaphysical doctrines believed to have been held by the Sophists. It will be convenient to take the two arguments separately : accordingly, in the present paper, I shall confine myself entirely to the first.

The only testimony which it is worth our while to

consider at length is that of Plato. Aristotle's knowledge of the contemporaries of Socrates must have been entirely second-hand: and indeed what he says of the Sophists must be taken to refer chiefly to what I have ventured to call post-Socratic Sophistry —the Eristical disputation which I conceive to have been chiefly imitated from Socrates, and to have borne at any rate less resemblance to the rhetorical moralising of Protagoras and Prodicus than it did to the dialectic of Socrates.

Obviously we can make no use of the evidence of writers like Aristophanes and Isocrates, who lump Socrates and his opponents together under the same notion. And though Xenophon does not, of course, do this: still his conception of sophistical teaching is evidently of the vaguest kind. He probably would have included under the term physical theorists like Anaxagoras, for we find him speaking of "the Cosmos, *as the Sophists call it.*" So that we cannot refer with any confidence to his description of the class generally, but only to the notices that he gives of particular individuals. The most important of these is an account of a dialogue between Socrates and Hippias, which is noticed below: he further represents his master as borrowing from Prodicus the well-known fable of the Choice of Hercules: and this together with other testimonies has led to the general acquittal of Prodicus from the charges brought against his colleagues. But the main part of our historical investigation must turn upon the Platonic dialogues. Those in which the Professors of Conduct

THE SOPHISTS 359

appear or are discussed are chiefly the *Hippias Major* and *Minor* (if we admit the genuineness—or verisimilitude—of the former), and the *Protagoras*: the *Meno*, *Gorgias*, and *Republic*. I have tried to show that in the *Sophista* and *Euthydemus* the Sophist is a teacher of an entirely different type. And of the six dialogues above mentioned I think it may be fairly contended that the three former are most likely to represent the actual relation of Socrates to the ethical teachers of his age; for they are no doubt the earlier, and the obvious aim of each of them is to exhibit Socrates in controversy with Sophists: whereas in the *Meno* the Sophists are only mentioned incidentally; the polemic of the *Gorgias* is directed primarily against Rhetoricians, and the *Republic* is chiefly constructive and expository. Now suppose a person to know no more than that there were in Athens certain clever men whose teaching was dangerous, as being subversive of the commonly received rules of morality, and tending to establish egoistic maxims of conduct: and suppose that with this information he is set down to read the three first-mentioned dialogues. He is introduced to Hippias, Protagoras, and Socrates. Hippias has composed an apologue in which he makes Nestor recommend to Neoptolemus the different kinds of conduct that are considered Noble or Beautiful: Socrates, by ingenious questioning, reduces him to helpless bewilderment as to the true definition of the term καλόν. Again, Hippias has lectured on the contrast between the veracious Achilles and the mendacious Ulysses:

Socrates with similar ingenuity argues that wilful mendacity or wilful wrong-doing generally is better than ignorance and involuntary error: Hippias protesting against the dangerous paradox. Again, he finds Protagoras explaining how it is that any plain man is, to a certain extent, a teacher of Virtue, having knowledge of the chief excellencies of conduct, and being able to communicate them to others: a Professor of Conduct is only a man who knows and teaches what all plain men know and teach, in a somewhat more complete and skilful manner. Socrates, on the other hand, argues that all Virtue resolves itself into a method of calculating and providing the greatest possible pleasure and the least possible pain for the virtuous agent. Can any one doubt that such an unprejudiced reader would rise from his perusal of the three dialogues with the conviction that Socrates was the Sophist as commonly conceived, the egoist, the ingenious subverter of the plain rules of morality? And though perhaps even at this point of his studies (and certainly when he had read a little further) he would decide that Socrates was not really a "corrupter of youth," he would see no reason to transfer the charge to Protagoras or Hippias. He would see that Socrates attacked their doctrines not as novel or dangerous, but as superficial and commonplace. Impostors they might be, in so far as they pretended to teach men what they knew no better than their pupils: but if they knew no better, they knew no worse: they merely accepted and developed the commonly received principles. And thus—to come to the later dialogues to which I have referred —one finds that Socrates even half defends them in the *Meno* against the popular odium which he shared with them: Anytus is made to confess, that whatever blame they may deserve, his own abuse of them has been uttered in mere ignorance. So again in the *Republic*, where Plato's satire takes a bolder sweep, there is a sort of indirect and latent defence of the Sophists against the charge on which Socrates suffered as their representative. Plato clearly feels, that whatever quarrel Philosophy might have with the Sophists, Demos had no right to turn upon them: Demos himself was the arch-Sophist and had corrupted his own youth: the poor Professors had but taught what he wanted them to teach, had but conformed to the common manner and tone of thought, accepted and formulated common opinion. Nor is the view of 'Sophistik' presented in the *Gorgias* really different, though it has been differently understood. No doubt it is a 'sham Art of Legislation,' it does not give the true principles on which a sound social order is to be constructed: but that is not because it propounds anti-social paradoxes: rather, it offers seeming-true principles, which fit in with the common sense of practical men.

It is said, however, that there are other passages in Plato which clearly exhibit the anti-social tendencies of the Sophistic teaching: and that especially in the last two dialogues to which I have referred such evidence is to be found. Let us proceed to examine these passages in detail.

The most comprehensive and pregnant formula in which this anti-social teaching is thought to be summed up, is that τὸ δίκαιον, justice, or social duty generally, exists νόμῳ only, and not φύσει. It is clear from the references in his *Ethics*, etc., that Aristotle found this doctrine very widely held by his predecessors: and we should draw a similar inference from a well-known passage in Plato's *Laws* (x. pp. 889, 890), where he speaks of "the wisest of all doctrines in the opinion of many . . . that the honourable is one thing by nature and another thing by law, and that the principles of justice have no existence at all in nature, but that mankind are always disputing about them and altering them." The commentators do not hesitate to treat these passages as referring to the Sophists: in fact, they make the reference in such a matter-of-course manner, that one is startled to find how entirely unauthorised it is. Aristotle's allusions are quite general: and Plato simply says that these are "the sayings of wise men, poets as well as prose-writers." This no doubt does not prove that he is not referring to the Sophists: but when we consider that it is the great assailant of Sophistry who is speaking, it seems pretty strong negative evidence. It is said, however, that other passages in Plato show so clearly that the doctrine was actually held by the Sophists, that there was no reason why he should mention them by name in the *Laws*. It is said (1) that Hippias in the *Protagoras* draws precisely the same distinction between νόμος and φύσις, and that Plato's testimony is here confirmed

THE SOPHISTS 363

by Xenophon (*Mem.* iv. c. 4); (2) that Callicles in the *Gorgias* employs the same antithesis as a quasi-philosophical defence of his cynically avowed immorality; (3) that Thrasymachus in the *Republic* puts forward a view of justice coinciding substantially with that of Callicles, though not couched in the same language. This cumulative evidence seems at first sight very strong: but I think that on a closer examination every part of it will be found to break down.

In the first place, it must be observed that the mere adoption or bringing into prominence of the distinction between the 'conventional' and the 'natural' as applied to the laws and usages of society is no evidence of egoistic, anti-social disposition or convictions. Rather, we may say, is the recognition of such a distinction an obvious and inevitable incident of the first beginnings of philosophical reflection upon society, especially in an age of free and active mutual communication among a crowd of little States differently organised and mostly in a state of rapid change. And the natural effect of such recognition upon an ordinary mind, sharing in the ordinary manner the current moral sentiments and habits of its society, is rather an endeavour to separate the really sacred and stringent bonds, the fundamental and immutable principles of social behaviour, from what is conventional and arbitrary in positive law and custom. And it is just in this attitude of mind that Hippias appears in the dialogue with Socrates that Xenophon records. After some characteristic sparring, Socrates has defined the Just to be the Lawful. This surprises Hippias.

"Do you mean they are identical?" he answers, "I do not quite understand how you use the words . . . how can one attribute much intrinsic worth to laws, when their makers are continually changing them?" That is, Justice in Hippias' view is therefore not τὸ νόμιμον, because it must be σπουδαιότερον πρᾶγμα. And the few sentences in the *Protagoras* in which the Professor's style of lecturing is somewhat broadly caricatured are quite in harmony with Xenophon's account: and indeed would suggest this view rather than the other if taken alone.

With Callicles the case is quite different. His use of the antithesis of φύσις and νόμος is no doubt flagrantly immoral: an open justification of the most sensual egoism. The only lacuna in the argument here—and it seems to me a sufficiently large one—is that Callicles is not a Sophist, and has no obvious connexion with Sophists. "No matter," say Zeller and others, "he must be reckoned a representative of the Sophistische Bildung." Now here a distinction must be taken, the importance of which I shall presently urge at more length. If by 'Sophistische Bildung' is merely meant what German writers commonly call the 'Aufklärung,' or rather the frivolous and demoralising phase of the 'Enlightenment' diffused through polite society in this age, the negative and corrosive influence which semi-philosophical reflection upon morality has always been found to exert—this is no doubt represented in Callicles. But if it is meant that Plato intended to exhibit in Callicles the result, direct or indirect, of the teaching of our Professors of Conduct: then I can only say that he dissembled his intention in a way which contrasts strikingly with the directness of his attack in other dialogues. For Callicles is not only nowhere described as a friend or pupil of Sophists: but he is actually made to express the extremest contempt for them. "You know the claims," says Socrates, "of those people who profess to train men to virtue." "Yes, but why speak of these empty impostors (ἀνθρώπων οὐδενὸς ἀξίων)," replies Callicles. Certainly we have here a most unconscious 'representative.'

It is said, however, that Aristotle speaks of Callicles as a Sophist, or at least as a Sophistical arguer: and that, in respect of his use of this very antithesis. The passage referred to is *Sophist. Elench.* xii. 6. Both Sir A. Grant and Mr. Cope interpret it in this way: and as Aristotle's authority on such a point cannot be disregarded, we must consider the passage carefully. Sir A. Grant introduces it as follows:[1]—

"One of the most celebrated 'points of view' of the Sophists was the opposition between nature and convention. Aristotle speaks of this opposition in a way which represents it to have been in use among them merely as a mode of arguing, not as a definite opinion about morals. He says (*Soph. El.* xii. 6), 'The topic most in vogue for reducing your adversary to admit paradoxes, is that which Callicles is described in the *Gorgias* as making use of, and which was a universal mode of arguing with the ancients,—namely, the opposition of 'nature' and

---

[1] *Ethics of Aristotle*, vol. i. p. 107 [2nd edn. 1866 (p. 148, 3rd edn. 1874)].

'convention'; for these are maintained to be contraries, and thus justice is right according to convention, but not according to nature. Hence they say, when a man is speaking with reference to nature, you should meet him with conventional considerations; when he means 'conventionally,' you should twist round the point of view to 'naturally.' In both ways you make him utter paradoxes.'"

Now the words which are here rendered "that which Callicles is described in the *Gorgias* as making use of" are ὥσπερ καὶ ὁ Καλλικλῆς ἐν τῷ Γοργίᾳ γέγραπται λέγων. But what is "Callicles in the *Gorgias* described as saying"? Is he "reducing his adversary to admit paradoxes"? On the contrary, he is *complaining of this procedure on the part of Socrates.* ὡς τὰ πολλὰ δέ, he says, ταῦτα ἐναντία ἀλλήλοις ἐστίν, ἥ τε φύσις καὶ ὁ νόμος. ἐὰν οὖν τις αἰσχύνηται καὶ μὴ τολμᾷ λέγειν ἅπερ νοεῖ, ἀναγκάζεται ἐναντία λέγειν. ὃ δὴ καὶ σὺ τοῦτο τὸ σοφὸν κατανενοηκὼς κακουργεῖς ἐν τοῖς λόγοις, ἐὰν μέν τις κατὰ νόμον λέγῃ, κατὰ φύσιν ὑπερωτῶν, ἐὰν δὲ τὰ τῆς φύσεως, τὰ τοῦ νόμου. It is Socrates who is the Sophist, or at least is charged with Sophistry: and Aristotle, intent on his subject, and not thinking of the reputation of Socrates, has simply quoted the passage as a good illustration of a particular sophistical topic. This piece of evidence therefore turns out most unfortunately for our opponents. It incidentally illustrates that close affinity between the later, Eristic, Sophistry, and the teaching of Socrates, which it was the object of my former paper to exhibit: but it has nothing whatever to do with the morals of Callicles or their origin.

When we attempt to speak exactly of the relation of Callicles to 'The Sophists,' the necessity of distinguishing the different meanings of the term Σοφιστής makes itself strongly felt. Callicles may be fairly or at least plausibly called a pupil of Gorgias, but expresses utter contempt for Professors of Conduct (a class in which Gorgias expressly declined to be included). I think the explanation of this is not hard to find, if we bear in mind the circumstances under which the dialogue was written. It must be later than the execution of Socrates: and it was probably composed not long after that event:[1] at a time, therefore, when the orthodox-conservative reaction was at its height, and the odium attaching to the name of Sophist especially strong. The languidly contemptuous dislike and distrust with which old-fashioned persons had formerly regarded all this new-fangled lecturing and disputing on conduct was now changed into loud and menacing hostility. This new art that had attracted the leisured youth of Athens was not, they now saw, mere idle pastime and folly: it was a deadly seed from which aristocratic-revolutionary intrigues and the despotism of the Thirty had sprung. Hence every one was anxious to repudiate the invidious title: in particular, the teachers of Rhetoric would emphasise the distinction between them and the Professors of Conduct, which hitherto, in the view of the world in general, had scarcely been recognised.

[1] Cf. Thompson's *Gorgias*.

"We have nothing to do," they would say, "with the charlatans who pretend to impart virtue: what we profess is the harmless, practical, necessary art of Public Speaking." Thus Isocrates, who in the preceding age would have accepted the title of Sophist, and who at a later period [1] does not repudiate it, now insists on being called a Philosopher, and writes an oration κατὰ τῶν Σοφιστῶν. Under these circumstances the polemical aim of Plato in writing the *Gorgias* was somewhat complex. On the one hand, he endeavours to show the substantial identity of Rhetoric and Sophistic: they were both aimed at the production of Appearances, not Realities: the benefits of both were equally hollow and illusory. On the other hand, he has no sympathy whatever with the prevalent fury against the Professors of Conduct, the blind selfish impulse of the Athenian public to find some scapegoat to punish for the general demoralisation which had produced such disastrous consequences. He does not say—as posterity generally have understood him to say—"It is not Socrates who has done the mischief, but other teachers of virtue with whom you confound him." On the contrary, he is anxious to show that the mischief is not attributable to Professors of Conduct at all. It is with this view that he introduces Callicles, the 'practical man' who despises professors, and thinks that the art of private and public life is to be learnt from men of the world. This is the sort of man who is likely to hold egoistic and sensual maxims of conduct. His unaided reflection easily

---

[1] In the περὶ Ἀντιδόσεως, written not long before his death.

penetrates the incoherencies and superficialities of the popular morality: his immoral principles are weeds that spring up naturally in the social soil, without any professional planting and watering, so long as the sun of philosophy is not risen.

This latter view appears still more clearly in the *Republic*, especially in the fine passage at the outset of Book II. (compared with Book VI.). There the *naturalness* of the evolution of audacious unrestrained egoism from conventional morality is made still more prominent. "We find," says the youthful interlocutor, "that people in general praise justice and try to instigate us towards it, but we always find that they do so by speaking of the rewards it gets from gods and men. They admit too that justice is hard and irksome, injustice easy and pleasant. Again, we find that they honour rich men in public and private, even though wicked: and do not conceal their contempt for the virtuous poor. Nay the gods, since their forgiveness and favour is to be obtained by sacrifices, seem to do much the same. Hence a spirited young man naturally thinks that though successful lawlessness is no doubt difficult, and perhaps ordinary people had better keep to the broad road of law-observance, still the former path is the nobler of the two in its very difficulty, and he who can walk it successfully is truly fortunate in the eyes of gods and men." Surely here we may read between the lines an answer to the charge against Socrates. "You corrupt youth," said the Athenians to the sage, "and they make oligarchical revolutions." "Not so," retorts the disciple, "it is you who cause the demoralisation, by your low views of virtue and of the gods. An acute and spirited youth pushes these to their logical conclusions: he decides that consummate Injustice is one of the καλά which the proverb declares to be χαλεπά: and thus inspired he enters clubs and plots revolutions."

What has been already said will have indicated the view that I take of the cynical deliverances of Thrasymachus. I see no reason to class him among the Professors of Conduct whom we are now considering. Plato does not call him a σοφιστής: and though no doubt he might be called so, in the looser sense in which the term was applied to Gorgias, he does not fall within the class either according to the earlier or to the later of its more limited definitions. He does not define justice as a professed teacher of virtue, but as a rhetorician, possessing the cultivated omniscience to which ancient rhetoricians commonly laid claim, and so able to knock off a definition of Justice, as of anything else. That "Justice is the interest of the stronger" is a plausible cynical paradox which a cultivated person might naturally and prosperously maintain in a casual conversation: but we are not therefore to suppose that Hippias or any other Professor of Conduct would take it as a thesis for a formal lecture on Virtue. Indeed, even if we had not direct evidence to show that their discourses were much more conservative and commonplace, we might have concluded *a priori* that the Athenian youth would not have thronged to hear, with the simple earnestness described by Plato, such frivolous paradoxes as those thrown out by Thrasymachus.

We may now see with what justice Grote exclaims that the German writers "dress up a fiend which they call 'Sophistik,'" which exists only in their imaginations. Analysing the historical costume of this scarecrow, we find it to consist chiefly of unrelated fragments, illegitimately appropriated and combined. The framework, however, on which these fragments are hung is supplied by the general scheme of development of Greek philosophical thought, which seems to be accepted in Germany. If this framework be left unassailed, it will still be believed that the earliest professional teaching of morality in Greece *must have been* egoistic and anti-social: although there may be no evidence to prove that it *was* so. I shall therefore try to show in a subsequent paper[1] that Grote's view of the teaching of the Sophists is no less strongly supported by general historical considerations than by particular testimonies: and that the adoption of the opposite theory has led Zeller and others into serious misapprehension of the true drift and position of both Socrates and Plato.

[1] [This paper was never written.]

INCOHERENCE OF EMPIRICAL PHILOSOPHY

(Reprinted from *Mind*, vol. iii. O.S., October 1882.)

I USE the term Empirical Philosophy to denote a theory which is not primarily a theory of Being, but a theory of knowledge; nor, again, a merely psychological theory, considering the psychical fact called knowledge merely as a phenomenon of particular minds; but a doctrine that is concerned with knowledge in respect of its validity, laying down the general criteria by which true or real knowledge may be distinguished from what is merely apparent: what —using a convenient, though hardly current, term— I will distinguish as an *epistemological* doctrine. Admitting that any complete system of philosophy must include some reasoned answer—positive, negative, sceptical, or critical—to ontological questions, I still think that the term Philosophy may be fairly applied to what is primarily a doctrine of the criteria of knowledge, without reference to any ontological conclusions which such a doctrine may be held to establish. And if we try to give a precise and distinctive meaning to the term "empirical" or "experiential," as applied to existing schools of philosophy, without materially restricting its ordinary use, we must, I think, make it signify merely the *epistemological* doctrine that all cognitions that can be philosophically accepted as valid, whether universal or particular, must be based upon experience. In this sense we may say that Empiricism of some kind is the philosophy which students of Natural Science, at the present day, generally have, or tend to have; and also other persons who cannot be called students of Natural Science, but whose minds are impressed and dominated by the triumphant march of modern physical investigation. Such persons have a general, unanalysed conviction, independent of close reasoning of any kind, that the recent conquests of the human intellect over the world of concrete fact are mainly due to that precise, patient, and elaborate questioning of experience which has certainly been an indispensable condition of their attainment; that the extension and steady growth of these conquests constitute at the present time the most important fact for one who wishes to philosophise; and that any philosophy that is not thoroughly competent to deal with this fact has thereby a presumption against it that it is behind its age. And in order that my point of view in the remarks that follow may be understood, I should like to say at the outset that I fully admit the force of this general presumption in favour of Empiricism. Just as at the outset of modern philosophy in the age of Descartes (as well as earlier still, in the age of Plato), Mathematics naturally presented itself as the type of solid and definite knowledge, so, it seems to me, the type is now furnished by the sciences that rest on experience; to which Mathematics—in the natural *prima facie* view—stands in the subordinate relation of an instrument.

I am therefore as much disposed as any one can be to go to experience for a test of truth; but I find myself unable—with all the aid of the eminent thinkers who have recently maintained some form or other of Empiricism—to work out a coherent theory of the criteria of knowledge on an Empirical basis. The difficulties in the way of this attempt appear to me to be of a very fundamental character; and one important group of them—those which relate rather to the premisses of empirical philosophy than to the rational procedure by which its conclusion is reached — do not seem to me to have received sufficient notice from the leading empirical writers. It is, therefore, to this part of the argument that I chiefly wish to direct attention in the present paper.

Before, however, I proceed to state these difficulties, it will be well to define somewhat more closely the fundamental doctrine of Empiricism. I understand this to be that all trustworthy cognitions [1] are either immediate cognitions of particular, approximately contemporaneous, facts, or capable of being rationally inferred from these;—let us say, for brevity, either

---

[1] I ought perhaps to state that in this paper I use the term cognition to include intellectual states or acts which are, or involve, false judgments, as well as those which are, or involve, true judgments—or, to express it otherwise, *apparent* as well as *real* cognitions.

'immediately empirical' or 'mediately empirical.' It is only in this sense that the statement that all valid judgments are founded on experience appears to me to have a definite epistemological import, *prima facie* tenable.

To make this clearer, I will consider briefly certain other senses in which knowledge is currently said to be "founded on" or "derived from" experience. In the first place, by predicating this of any piece of what presents itself as knowledge, it may be merely meant that such apparent knowledge is *caused* by certain antecedent empirical cognitions, from which, however, it is *not* rationally inferrible; or rather, strictly speaking, that it has *among* its causes such antecedent cognitions—for no one would give a mere statement of these antecedents as a complete account of its causation. The vulgar induction of a universal rule from a few particular cases is an instance of this kind of derivation of a belief from experience. It is evident that the ascertainment of the empirical antecedents of such a universal judgment, however interesting psychologically, does not in itself help us to decide the question of its truth or falsehood; for (1) *ex hypothesi* it does not supply adequate grounds for regarding the cognition so caused as philosophically established, and (2) it is no less manifest that it does not disprove the belief so arrived at—since obviously a generalisation from a few cases may be true, though it cannot be proved by reference to these cases alone. The epistemological question we have to ask about it is not from what sources it was originally derived, but upon what grounds it is now deliberately held.

The result is similar if the ascertained psychical antecedents from which any judgment is said to be "derived" are not cognitions at all but merely feelings—sensations or emotions. The ascertainment of the invariable antecedence of any such psychical facts obviously cannot validate any cognition thus ascertained to be their consequent (unless it be the cognition of these facts themselves). And it seems to me equally evident that it cannot invalidate it;—it is only by a palpable confusion between "antecedents" and "elements," or by a quite unwarranted transfer of chemical inferences to psychical facts, that certain Associational psychologists claim to have "analysed into elementary feelings" apparent cognitions of what is not feeling, when they have merely shown these feelings to be invariable antecedents or concomitants of the cognitions in question. Any cognition, as introspectively contemplated, is essentially different from any mere aggregation of feelings; and I am aware of no tenable grounds for concluding that such cognition "really consists" of elements which careful introspection does not enable us to discern in it.

Still more is the ascertainment of the (so-called) "derivation from experience" of any piece of apparent knowledge *epistemologically* irrelevant, if the antecedents loosely referred to as 'experience' are neither cognitions nor feelings, but relations of the *bodies* of the cognising individuals (or their ancestors) to other material things: as for instance if by saying that a child can be shown to have had "experience of space," before it can judge that a straight line is the shortest line between its extremities, it is merely meant that its limbs must have been moved about, or other matter moved across portions of its body, etc. For no empirical science professes to explain the relation between the validity or invalidity of judgments and the antecedent motions of the organism of the judging individual; so that the mere knowledge of the antecedent motions in any such case, however complete, would not give us any presumption as to the truth or falsehood of the consequent cognition. All that the most confidently dogmatic of modern biologists claim is that the cognitions of any organism capable of cognition—or rather the organic movements accompanying them—will have a certain tendency to produce motions preservative of the organism under the external conditions that normally follow those that caused the cognitions in question; and it is obvious that a cognition may have this tendency without being true.

Finally, it should be observed that the phrase "empirical theory of the origin of knowledge" is often used to denote a doctrine which, like Locke's, is merely empirical (in a sense) as regards the *ideas* by comparing which knowledge is held to be constructed; but is essentially 'intuitional' or '*a priori*' as regards the actual synthesis of ideas that constitutes knowledge. However strongly Locke holds that ideas " come from experience "—*i.e.* from presentation to the mind of the realities which the ideas represent —he none the less holds that universal and immutable relations among these ideas admit of being intuitively known by abstract reflection, and that it is the apprehension of such relations that constitutes knowledge, in the highest sense of the term. And, clearly, it is the latter doctrine and not the former that must determine his *epistemological* position.

I may be allowed, however, to observe that even as regards the materials of knowledge, it does not appear to me that the ascertainment of the first origin of ideas can have any decisive effect; on account of the great changes which ideas gradually undergo, in the course of their use as instruments of scientific reasoning. We may find instances of such change in the nomenclature and terminology of almost any science. To begin with mathematics: I do not deny that my original ideas of 'straight line,' 'circle,' 'square' were derived from experience, in the sense that they were caused by my seeing and moving among material things that appeared straight, round, and square. But the proposition seems to me one of merely antiquarian interest; since all competent persons are agreed that, in the degree of refinement in which these notions are now used in mathematical reasonings, it is impossible to produce any objects of experience which perfectly exemplify them. In physical sciences, however, this change of meaning is often more marked. Take the notion 'Force.' This seems indubitably derived from experience of muscular exercise, and hence its original significance must have

INCOHERENCE OF EMPIRICAL PHILOSOPHY 379

included, at least, some vague representation of the movements of muscles, or of the limbs moved by muscles, and also some of the specific feeling of muscular effort. But by 'Force,' as used in physical reasonings, we mean merely a cause which we conceive obscurely through its relation to its effect, motion; which motion, again, may be merely possible, not actual. Hence, whatever be the conditions within which our knowledge of forces is confined, it does not appear that the origin or original content of the notion can have much to do with these conditions. Similarly in chemistry, the ideas of 'acid' and 'salt' must have originally represented merely the flavours experienced by tasting the things so called: but now we regard such flavours as mere accidents of the relation of the things we call 'acids' and 'salts' to our palate, and not even universally inseparable accidents. In psychology, again, the difference between the original character of the ideas by means of which we think about mental processes, and the character they ultimately acquire when our reasoning has become scientifically precise, is still more striking. For almost all our terms originally represented physical, not psychical, facts; and the physical significance often clings to the idea in such a way as to confuse our psychological reasonings, unless we take pains to get rid of it; while, at the same time, thinkers of all schools would agree that we *have* to get rid of it. Thus, 'impression' meant the physical fact of stamping or pressing, 'apprehension' meant 'grasping with the hand,' 'intention' and 'emotion' suggested physical 'straining' and 'stirring up.' But we all put these physical meanings out of our view, when we are trying to think clearly and precisely about psychical phenomena, however interesting it may be to note them when we are studying the history of thought. Hence I conclude that the settlement of the time-honoured question of the "origin of our ideas"—so far as it admits of being settled by received scientific methods—will not really determine anything of fundamental importance, either as regards the *materials* of our actual knowledge, or as regards the mode of constructing knowledge out of them.

After this preliminary clearing of the ground, I pass to consider how the cardinal doctrine of Empiricism as above defined—that all trustworthy cognitions are either mediately or immediately empirical—is philosophically established. We may begin by laying down that this general criterion of truth must itself be based on experience—*i.e.* upon particular cognitions of the truth of this, that, and the other empirical cognition: since it would be palpably inconsistent for Empirical Philosophy to start with the general assumption, *not* based on experience, that no general propositions are trustworthy, *except* those based on experience. If, again, we ask how these particular cognitions are to be obtained, it is obvious that they must either be proved or assumed; and that if we say that they are proved, this proof can only be given by assuming similar particulars, since it would be inconsistent with the criterion to be established if we allowed any part of its proof to rest on universal propositions as an ultimate basis; so that ultimately we must be led back to particular cognitions assumed without proof.

What, then, are these particular knowledges of which Empirical Philosophy must assume the validity at the outset of its procedure? Popular Empiricism seems to me to give at different times two different answers to this question; and by shifting about from the one to the other, and sometimes mixing the two, its argument, I think, gains in plausibility what it loses in clearness.

(1) Sometimes the answer is—whether explicitly or, as is more often the case, implicitly—that we start with what is generally admitted to be solid knowledge; that is, not the disputed and controverted matter which is found to some extent in all departments of study, and of which Metaphysics and Theology entirely consist; but the undoubted facts of history, natural and civil, and the generalisations of positive science of which, as they are commonly supposed to be based upon experience, the examination leads us *prima facie* to the empirical criterion. Let us grant for the present that being founded on experience alone is a characteristic which we find, on examination, to belong to the majority of beliefs that are commonly admitted as constituting solid knowledge. It must still be clear that, if we make a complete survey of the classes of beliefs that are supported by the common sense of mankind, we come upon important aggregates of beliefs which, in the

382 INCOHERENCE OF EMPIRICAL PHILOSOPHY

absolute universality with which they are commonly accepted, are certainly not based upon experience. I do not now dispute the empirical arguments used to prove that these beliefs, when duly restricted, have really a solid empirical basis—as, for instance, if we believe not (as common sense holds) that a straight line is always the shortest line between its extremities, but merely that it is so in the space with which we are familiar. But such modifications of current beliefs implicitly accuse common sense of error too extensive to leave its guarantee philosophically trustworthy: so that it becomes impossible in strict philosophical reasoning for an Empiricist to start with assuming the validity of what is commonly taken as knowledge. We may allow him to accept for practical purposes whatever is believed by "every sensible man" or "every one with the least knowledge of physical science"; but he must not introduce in philosophising propositions guaranteed by this kind of warrant alone.

This seems so plain that I need not enter into further difficulties involved in the acceptance of the criterion of General Consent,—as that the consent of the majority to science and history is ignorantly given, or not really given at all; that the consent of one age and country differs from that of another, and that in past ages the criterion would have certified many doctrines that we now reject as erroneous and superstitious, etc.,—especially since these considerations have been forcibly urged by more than one empirical philosopher. In fact, empirical philosophers do not, for the most part, appeal expressly to the criterion of General Consent, so far as their philosophical procedure is concerned. If formally asked what the cognitions are which they assume to be true in the reasoning by which they establish the empirical criterion, they would usually answer (2) that they assume, first, what is immediately known, or what we are immediately conscious of, and, secondly, whatever may be cogently inferred from this.

The second part of this answer has been frequently attacked; and it certainly appears to me that no perfectly cogent inference is possible on strictly empirical principles; because no cogent inference is possible without assuming some general truth, the validity of which cannot itself be guaranteed by any canon of cogent inference. But the assumption of the validity of immediate cognitions seems to me equally open to attack; and it is to this that I now wish specially to direct attention. I must begin by removing an ambiguity in the term 'immediate.' When an Empiricist speaks of a cognition as 'immediate' he must not be understood to mean that it has not among its causes some antecedent psychical or physical phenomena—some feelings, or some movements of the matter of the organism of the cognising individual; for no empiricists maintain that *any* cognitions or any other mental phenomena are *un*caused; and if they are caused at all, they must stand in the relation of effect either to psychical or physical phenomena, or to both combined. The 'mediation' that is excluded by terming any cognition 'immediate' must therefore be logical mediation or inference.

If then it be asked, why should we make the general assumption that error is absent from non-inferred cognitions and from these alone, the answer would seem to be, first, that immediate knowledge carries with it its own warrant; that when we immediately know we also, by a secondary inseparable act of the mind,—generally latent but becoming explicit if any doubt is raised,—know that we know certainly; and, secondly, that we have no experience of error in non-inferred cognitions; error being always found to come in through inference.

But it is practically of no avail to say that immediate cognition is infallible, unless we have a no less infallible criterion for ascertaining what cognitions are immediate: and the difficulties of ascertaining this are profound and complicated. Are we to accept each man's own view of what he immediately knows? This certainly seems in accordance with empirical principles, as all experience must be primarily the experience of individual minds. But if we take, unsifted and uncriticised, what any human being is satisfied that he or she immediately knows, we open the door to all sorts of mal-observation in material matters, and to all sorts of superstition in spiritual matters,—as superstitious beliefs commonly rest, in a great measure, upon what certain persons believe themselves to have seen, heard, or otherwise personally experienced. And, in fact, no empiricist adopts this alternative; there is no point upon which empirical philosophers are more agreed than on the incapacity of ordinary persons to distinguish their immediate from their mediate knowledge. Shall we, then, say that we take each man's experience so far as it commends itself to other men? But if we mean 'other men generally,' this is only our old criterion of General Consent, in a negative instead of a positive aspect, and the acceptance of it would therefore bring us round again to the difficulties already discussed; with this further difficulty, that it is hard to see why, on empirical principles, any one man's experience stands in need of being confirmed by that of others. I do not see what right an empiricist has to assume that one man's immediate cognitions *ought* to coincide with the immediate cognitions of others; still less, that they ought to coincide with their inferences. And if empiricists do not trust common men's judgment as to their own immediate knowledge, they can hardly put them forward as trustworthy judges of the immediate knowledge of others.

It may, however, be said that to distinguish accurately immediate from mediate cognitions requires a skill beyond that of ordinary men, only attainable by training and practice: that, in short, it requires the intervention of psychological experts. This seems to be the doctrine of James and John Mill, and, in the main, of the school of which they, with Mr. Bain, are the founders; but, in my opinion, it is open to several fatal objections. In the first place, I do not see how even an expert can claim to know another man's immediate knowledge without assuming that all human minds are similarly constituted, in respect of immediate cognition; and I do not see how this assumption is legitimate on empirical principles. And this difficulty is increased when we consider that the psychological expert, if he is an Empiricist, has to throw aside as untrustworthy the affirmations, as to their own immediate knowledge, of thoughtful persons who have given much attention to the subject—I mean the Intuitional Metaphysicians, who say that they immediately know universal truths. If we admit these to be experts, I do not see how we can hope to establish the cardinal doctrine of Empiricism. Yet how can we exclude them, except by assuming the empirical philosophers to be the only real experts?—and this seems hardly a legitimate assumption in an argument that aims at proving the empirical philosophy to be true. Nor is it any answer to this objection to show that Intuitional Metaphysicians have in certain cases affirmed as immediately known propositions that are not true; since the question is not whether error is incident to non-empirical cognitions, but whether we may legitimately assume that it is not incident to empirical cognitions.

But further, even supposing that we only recognise, as experts in discriminating immediate knowledge, persons who will not allow anything to be immediately known, except particular facts, serious difficulties still remain; because we find that these experts disagree profoundly among themselves. We find—

not to speak of minor divergences—that there is a fundamental disagreement between two lines of empirical thought which—if I may coin a word for clearness' sake—I will call respectively *materialistic* and *mentalistic*. When a Materialistic Empiricist affirms that physical science is based upon experience he means that it is based on immediate knowledge of particular portions of something solid and extended, definitely shaped and sized, moving about in space of three dimensions. Whether he regards this matter as also coloured, resonant, and odorous, is a more doubtful question; but probably he would say that colour, sound, and odour are effects on the mind—or perhaps on the brain?—of the molecular movements of material particles. I can hardly profess to give a consistent account of his views on this point, if he is a thorough-going materialist, but it is enough for my present purpose that he at any rate believes himself to know immediately—through touch, if in no other way—matter with the qualities first mentioned.

The Mentalistic Empiricist, on the other hand, maintains that nothing can be immediately known except mental facts, consciousness or feeling of some kind; and that if we are right in assuming a non-mental cause of these mental facts—which he is generally inclined to doubt—we must at any rate regard this cause as unknown in every respect except its mere existence, and this last as only known by inference.

How, then, is Empiricism to deal with this disagreement? It cannot be denied to be rather serious;

since, though materialism has plenty of support among philosophising men of science, the tendency of the main line of English empirical philosophy, from Locke downwards, is definitely towards Mentalism. I may observe that the more thoughtful Materialists, like Dr. Maudsley, do not exactly say that there are no mental facts which we may contemplate introspectively. But they hold that no scientific results have ever been reached by such contemplation; and they say very truly that physical science has always progressed by taking the materialistic point of view, and that there is no admitted progressive science of psychology, proceeding by the introspective method, which can be set beside the physical sciences. Hence they boldly infer that there never will be such a science; and in fact, they are inclined to lump the Mentalists along with Transcendentalists and others, under the common notion of "Metaphysicians" (used as a term of abuse), and to charge them all together with using the Subjective Method, condemned as fruitless by experience. The Mentalists do not quite reply in the same strain; indeed, they have rather a tenderness for the Materialists, whose aid, as against Transcendentalism and Superstition, is not to be despised. But they say that the Materialists are inexpert in psychological analysis, and that what they call "matter" is really, when analysed, a complex mental fact, of which some elements are immediately known and others added by inference. In so saying, the Mentalists appear to me to use the term "inference" loosely, and also to fall into the confusion before pointed out between the *antecedents* (or concomitants) and the *elements* of a cognition. Certainly I find myself unable to analyse my notion or perception of matter into feelings or ideas of feelings, tactual, visual, or muscular; though I do find that such sensation-elements present themselves as inseparable accompaniments of my notion or perception of matter, when attention is directed to it introspectively. But my object now is not so much to enter into this controversy between two sets of Empiricists, as to point out the serious obstacle it opposes to a satisfactory determination of the question what is immediate cognition.

Let us suppose, however, that this controversy has been settled to the satisfaction of both parties, in the manner in which some empiricists have tried to settle it. Let us suppose that both Materialists and Mentalists agree to affirm (1) that we immediately know the external world, so far as it is necessary to know it for the purpose of constructing physical science; (2) that we immediately know nothing but our own consciousness; and (3) that these two statements are perfectly consistent. It still remains to ask who are the "we" who have this knowledge. Each one of us can only have experience of a very small portion of this world; and if we abstract what is known through memory, and therefore mediately, the portion becomes small indeed. In order to get to what "we" conceive "ourselves" to know as "matter of fact" respecting the world, as extended in space and time—to such merely historical knowledge as we commonly regard not as "resting" on experience, but as constituting the experience on which science rests—we must assume the general trustworthiness of memory, and the general trustworthiness of testimony under proper limitations and conditions. I do not for a moment say that we have no right to make these assumptions; I only do not see how we can prove that we have such a right, from what we immediately know.

At this point of the argument Empiricists sometimes reply that these and similar assumptions are continually "verified" by experience. But what does "verified" exactly mean? If it means "proved true," I challenge any one to construct the proof, or even to advance a step in it, without assuming one or more of the propositions that are to be verified. What Empiricists really mean, I conceive, by "verification" in this case is that these assumptions are accompanied by anticipations of feelings or perceptions which are continually found to resemble or agree with—though not identical with—the more vivid feelings of perceptions which constitute the main stream of consciousness. Now, granting that such resemblance or agreement may be immediately known, I yet cannot see that anything is gained towards the establishment of the cardinal doctrine of Empiricism. For there is a similar agreement between actual experience and the anticipations accompanying all the general propositions—mathematical, logical, or physical—which philosophers of a different school affirm themselves to know immediately; so that this "verification" can hardly justify one set of assumptions, as against the other.

If, finally, the reader who has got through this paper should say that my cavils cannot shake his confidence in experience, or in the aggregate of modern knowledge that has progressed and still progresses by accumulating, sifting, and systematising experience—I can only answer that my own confidence is equally unshaken. The question that I wish to raise is not as to the validity of received scientific methods, but as to the general epistemological inferences that may legitimately be drawn from the assumption of their validity. It is possible to combine a practically complete trust in the procedure and results of empirical science with a profound distrust in the procedure and conclusions—especially the negative conclusions—of Empirical Philosophy.

A DIALOGUE ON TIME AND COMMON SENSE

(Reprinted from *Mind*, vol. iii. N.S., October 1894.)

I WAS interested in a conversation that I had, a short time ago, with a Russian Professor of Philosophy—who, I ought to say, spoke English with a fluency rarely attained out of Russia. What interested me in our talk, when I came to think it over, was the peculiarity that while it ranged rather widely it was almost entirely occupied with the effort to explain our views each to the other, with hardly any aim at either confuting or convincing, and no sense of a cause that had to be defended or a school that might be attacked. He had never read my books and I had never read his: he was on his travels, curious to know what we thought in England: I was also curious—though perhaps not equally—to know what was thought in Russia: time was short, and as I have never myself been convinced of anything important in half an hour, I never expect to convince any one else in that limited space. But when I tried to write down the talk I found I had forgotten too much of it: if I aimed at exactness, the result would be meagre and uninteresting; so in what follows I have allowed imagination to supplement the defects of memory, merely trying to preserve the general attitude of our minds towards each other, and the general impression that my visitor had given of his philosophical position.

The talk began with an account of his recent visit to America, where he had been for some months : he had been much impressed with the activity with which philosophical and psychological studies were being developed there, and the wide range and diversity of their development. One set of minds were working with transatlantic energy at the minutest problems of psychophysics, in the psychological laboratories that have sprung up like mushrooms during the last ten years or so: another set were agitating the largest questions of speculative philosophy: and my visitor's admiration seemed to be equally divided between metaphysicians and experimental psychologists.

While we were thus chatting about academic institutions and persons in America, he suddenly said, "Excuse me, but there is a question I always ask of a philosopher, which perhaps you will not mind answering. What do you think really exists?"

My first impulse was to borrow Hegel's famous answer to Cousin, when the Frenchman asked him for a succinct account of Hegelianism. But I remembered that earlier in our talk my guest had permitted himself a mild complaint of the reserve of Englishmen, as contrasted with the communicativeness of his American friends. So, feeling that our reputation for international cordiality was at stake, my second impulse was to gain time.

"No doubt," I said, "you put this question to your American friends."

"Oh yes," said he.

"And what did they answer?"

"Well," he said, "it is difficult to remember all their answers. But I think that a majority of those whom I persuaded to take an interest in the question were of opinion that God is the one ultimate reality."

"But did they all mean the same thing," said I, "or may we not rather invert the oft-quoted Greek phrase—

$$\pi o \lambda \lambda \hat{\omega} \nu \ \dot{o} \nu o \mu \dot{\alpha} \tau \omega \nu \ \mu o \rho \phi \dot{\eta} \ \mu \dot{\iota} \alpha —$$

and say that, in current thought, 'God' is one name for many and diverse ideas?"

I thought this might be a successful diversion, as the topic seemed both wide and attractive. But I had overshot my mark; it was too obvious an invitation to go off into infinite space; and declining this, he returned to the charge and reminded me that I had not answered his question.

Well, there was no help for it, but I thought I saw still a way of gaining time.

"Do you mean," I said, "what really exists *now*? or do you include what has existed and what will exist?"

"Ah," said he, "but that is a part of the question I am asking you. Do you think that the past really exists?"

"Well," I said, "one has to distinguish different modes of real existence. It would be absurd to say that the great study of History is not conversant with reality. So far as the historian attains truth—as doubtless he does in some degree—the past exists for him as an object of thought and investigation: but so far as it is past it has ceased to exist in the sense in which the present exists."

"Ah," said he, brightening, "then in spite of Kant you think Time really exists as a condition of things, and not merely as a form of perception. Why, I thought that even your empiricists and your scientists all held now that science only deals with phenomena, and that Time is only a sum of relations among phenomena."

"I think," I said, "that you must not take our men of science too much *au pied de lettre* when they talk of a 'phenomenon.' For instance, I was referring to a text-book on physics the other day, and I found 'a phenomenon' defined as 'any change that takes place in the condition of a body.' I think scientific men commonly mean by 'phenomenon' a real event that occurs in real time: they call it a phenomenon, only because the real event as conceived by their science is something other and more than the event as first perceived through the senses."

"Then," he said, "you think Time really exists, and you can conceive Time pure and simple, apart from the changes that make up experience."

"I have not said that," I replied, "but I certainly distinguish it in thought from the changes:—for I can conceive any particular series of changes going quicker or slower, and occupying more or less time: and that conception would be impossible if I did not distinguish the course of time from the course of change."

"Well," he said, "I have no wish to prove Time unreal: for the most real thing to me is my own existence: and though as a thinking, knowing being I can think myself out of Time, I admit that I can form no idea of myself as a living, feeling being except under the condition of Time. And perhaps my life is, on the whole, more interesting to me than my knowledge. But still—there are the antinomies. How do you get over the antinomies? Can you help me to conceive either a beginning of Time or an infinite past—a 'finished infinite' as Kant says,—or any tertium quid?"

"No," I said, "I am afraid I cannot help you over that stile. I admit that these alternatives are at present both inevitable and inconceivable to me, and I infer from this that I do not comprehend past time as a whole. But to conclude, therefore, that Time is unreal seems to me—what is the German phrase?—to be 'throwing out the child in emptying the bath.' If Time is unreal, succession is unreal: and if succession is unreal, the interest of the study of the past is destroyed."

"Are you not forgetting," he said, "that Kant's solution of the antinomies is critical and not sceptical, and leaves ample room for the scientific study of past experience, in order to discover the general laws of the empirical world? Surely the particular succession of past events is of no interest except as a basis for scientific generalisation: the study of them is only of practical value, so far as it enables us to grasp the present and foresee the future by the ascertainment of general laws. And surely, so far as we get hold of these general laws, we have a grasp of reality which remains unimpaired, even if we grant that the element of Time in our conception of these laws is due to the necessary form of our apprehension and does not belong to the reality of things."

"I admit the force of what you say," I replied, "so far as the empirical laws with which physics and chemistry deal are concerned; though by the way I do not think the Kantian theory will explain why we succeed—so far as we do succeed—in discovering these laws. Kant explains ingeniously why we inevitably *seek* for the causes of phenomenal change, but not why we *find* them. However, putting this aside, and granting all you say, I do not think the interest of human history is saved by it. For the interest of human history lies not merely in the general laws of change that we can discover in it, but in the general fact of progress through stages each different from the one before. If Time is unreal progress is unreal, and if progress is unreal the interest goes."

"Still surely," he said, "the important point for *practice* is that we should discover the general laws of social change and be able to foresee what is coming."

"Well," I said, "I will follow you into the region of practice. Surely all our notions of practice become unmeaning if you suppose Time to be unreal —a mere form of our apprehension. I always feel this in reading Kant. So long as he is engaged with his destructive work I can get on with his 'things in themselves': but when he tries to become constructive on the basis of moral experience I feel that all the fundamental conceptions he uses—the conceptions of rational action, springs of action, means and ends and so forth—become altogether unmeaning if his view of Time be accepted. The real man, in Kant's practical philosophy, seems to me a being who, in an unintelligible position out of Time, makes an absolutely incomprehensible and unaccountable choice of partial irrationality. A more unexplanatory explanation of the mystery of our fallen nature it is impossible to conceive."

"I agree," said he, "that Time is indispensable to my notion of human action—and human life generally. But the case seems to me quite otherwise with knowledge. The knowing subject, that combines experiences in Time and Space and so makes a world —surely we necessarily conceive that out of Time. Time belongs to the object of knowledge, and therefore not to the knowing subject as such."

"Let me see," I said: "Time is an object of my thought, therefore the subject of thought is not in Time. Is that the argument?"

"Something like it," he said; "an object or condition of the object."

"Suppose," I said, "that we consult your American friends who say that the ultimate reality is God. God then is an object of thought — *the* object of thought—to each of these philosophers; yet surely no one would say that he was therefore out of God. You, on the other hand, say that self is to you the most real existence; in thinking this you make yourself an object of thought, but you are not, therefore, out of yourself. Why are you any more out of Time?"

"I don't think the cases are analogous," said he: "at any rate, I do not find that your argument convinces me. For my own part, I am not a Pantheist, because—as I said—what is most certain to me is my own existence as an individual; and though I know I am not the whole of things, I cannot feel sure that all the rest is God. But still less am I an atheist: for when I consider my relation as a thinking being to Truth, I find myself irresistibly led through Finite Thought to the conception of Infinite Thought, and so to an Infinite Thinker of Infinite Truth, of which the truth apprehended by me is only an infinitesimal part. Now truth is essentially unchangeable, otherwise it would not be truth—though it may relate to things subject to change,—hence as Time is essentially changing, in laying hold of truth I carry myself out of Time, and accordingly I have to conceive God, the Infinite Thinker, as essentially out of Time."

While he was speaking, I took out my watch. "You say," I answered, "that you are more certain of your own existence than of anything else. Well, I am as certain as I am of my own existence that my ideas about Truth, Infinite Thought, Infinite Thinker, as avowed by your words, have occurred in succession between five and six minutes past three on the 20th of April 1894—or at some other definite point of time, for my watch is not infallible,—and, further, that these ideas would not have been what they actually were, had they not had as essential antecedents other ideas which have occurred before at definite points of time. Granting that Truth is not subject to change, my intellectual life is as much subject to it as any other element of my life."

"Well, but," said he, "what do you say of God's existence?"

"I say as little as I can," I replied, "under this head; since the relation of God to Time is one of the things that I do not understand."

"In short," he said, "you do not believe in a Divine Being out of Time."

"I have not said that," I rejoined; "I am led by the same consideration of Truth that you gave just now—but especially by a consideration of ethical Truth—to regard a belief in a Divine Being as indispensable to a normal human mind; and though I may not always keep this in mind in philosophical speculation, I was a man before I became a philosopher, and I do not forget it for long——"

"Well," he said, interrupting, "I have no wish to dispute the correctness of your attitude as a man and a citizen. But we are talking philosophy now, we are not talking about beliefs practically necessary for the plain man or the good citizen; and in any case you can hardly say that it is normal to humanity to believe in a God out of Time. The good people who go to church believe in an everlasting deity, enduring through Time, not out of Time."

"Yes," I replied, "but I understand that the better opinion—as lawyers say—among students of theology is that the efflux and succession of Time takes place only for finite beings and is not a condition of Divine existence; and I respect this preponderant opinion,—although I am unable to share it, because what it affirms is to me inconceivable. I follow these theologians in conceiving the past and the future as simultaneously present in knowledge to the Divine Mind; but I am forced to conceive this presence of all the known to the Infinite Knower as perpetual, if I would avoid conceiving it at a point of time."

"You will pardon me," he said, "the question I am about to ask; I know some of you English philosophers are anxious to keep in touch with orthodoxy—I found this also in America—and I do not wish to be indiscreet. But, between ourselves, do you think the theologians really know anything about the matter?"

"You need not be afraid of indiscretion," I said, laughing. "For if I were more concerned about my reputation for orthodoxy than is in fact the case, I could still answer your question in the negative and yet claim the support of many highly orthodox persons, who would emphatically and piously declare that the human mind was not intended to find an answer to such questions as these, and that to ask them was a sign of idle—and perhaps worse than idle—curiosity. Indeed, I think the prevailing opinion of theologians at the present time would be in favour of giving these transcendental inquiries a wide berth."

"I thought," he replied, "you said that the preponderant opinion was inclined to regard the Divine existence as independent of Time."

"I meant," said I, "the preponderant opinion of persons who had thought seriously about the matter; I never attach importance to a man's judgment on questions he does not care to consider."

"Well, but," he said, "you seem to attach importance to the movement of what you call the normal mind in these matters; and if the normal mind of religious persons is moving away from certain questions —it would not affect me in the least, but ought it not to influence you?"

"I think it would affect me more," I answered, "if I had not observed that the normal mind seems to move about these questions in a spiral way; so that the philosopher may avoid too wide a divergence from it, and save himself unnecessary motion, by keeping nearer the axis of the spiral."

"That depends," said he, "on the goal he wants to reach."

"I think we are agreed," I said, "on his goal, which can be nothing less than to understand the whole of things. To do this I think he must try to get the whole of our normal thought free from confusion and contradiction; and therefore not ignore the answers given by Theology to any questions he is led to ask, any more than he ignores the answers given by physicists to questions about the material world. For Theology is the result of the efforts of generations to understand the universe as manifested in the religious consciousness, just as sciences are the results of the similar effort to understand it as apprehended through sense-perception."

"But surely if one finds the answers of Theology confused and contradictory, it is a sign that the method is altogether wrong. You would not surely maintain that there is similar confusion and contradiction in the fundamental conceptions and methods of physical science?"

"Your former question," I said, smiling, "was not indiscreet, but this one, I am afraid, is; or is it with deliberate malice that you are tempting me to provoke more formidable antagonists—at the present time—than theologians? But I think I see a pacific way of answering. I think we shall agree that two centuries ago—or perhaps even a century ago—the fundamental notions and methods of natural science had not been brought to the condition of clearness and consistency that they have now reached; yet surely it would have been unphilosophical then to throw their methods and conclusions aside, and not rather to endeavour to aid in clearing them from confusion and contradiction. And that is how I would deal with Theology now, and with other subjects besides Theology—for instance, Ethics and Politics."

"I am not sure," said he, "that I understand your view of philosophy. You think it the business of philosophy to put together a number of different sciences and arts—or whatever you call them. But will they not be an aggregate rather than a whole, and the student a polymath—as we call it—rather than a philosopher?"

"I should not exactly say 'put together,'" I replied, "as that would imply that they were not already in intimate and essential relation—and if that were so, the task of the philosopher would doubtless be impossible. I should rather say 'exhibit the essential coherence which is now somewhat latent and obscured in their relations.' The philosopher may not succeed in this, but the polymath—as you call him—does not try."

"Well," he said, "I rather fear that your philosopher will get bewildered and lost in the multiplicity of the bits of his puzzle. I had rather aim directly at the whole: find out and make clear the fundamental conditions of its being a whole for *me*—my whole, my universe—since I must begin from myself; and having made this out, then descend to particulars and connect them while distinguishing them by their varying relation to these fundamental conditions."

"Well," I said, "the world is wide both for living and for philosophising. I am glad you feel energy enough for this adventure, which grows more daring as the world grows older. *Ex Oriente Lux!*"

He looked dreamy but hopeful. Then a thought struck him, and he said, "But I do not see that you have, after all, told me what you think really exists."

"Do you not think," I replied, "that it is now time for you to go and ask this question of some other Cambridge philosopher?"

He looked at his watch and assented; we rose and went downstairs: and as we bent our steps westward through the grounds of the college, I occupied his mind with a series of questions about the academic institutions of Russia.

THE PHILOSOPHY OF COMMON SENSE

AN ADDRESS DELIVERED TO THE GLASGOW
PHILOSOPHICAL SOCIETY ON JANUARY 10, 1895

(Reprinted from *Mind*, vol. iv. N.S., April 1895.)

WHEN I received, some months ago, the invitation to address your society, my mind was carried irresistibly back to a period in the last century, in which, through my study of three eminent teachers whose works have had a permanent influence on my thought, I seem to feel more at home in the intellectual life of your famous University than in that even of my own. It is a period of about fifty years; beginning in 1730, when Francis Hutcheson was summoned from Dublin to fill in Glasgow the chair now worthily occupied by my friend Professor Jones; and ending in 1781, when Thomas Reid retired from the same chair to put into final literary form the teaching that he had given here for seventeen years. Between the two, as the immediate predecessor of Reid, though not the immediate successor of Hutcheson, stands the greater name of Adam Smith. I felt "in private duty bound" to select the work of one of the three as the theme of my address: the difficulty was to choose. I should have much liked to try to explain the attraction which the refinement, balance, and comprehensiveness of Hutcheson's ethical views have always had for me; but on such an occasion it seemed prudent to defer to the sometimes capricious judgment of history: and in face of that judgment, I felt diffident of my power of persuading you to regard Hutcheson's system with more than antiquarian interest. With Adam Smith, as I need hardly say, the case was altogether different. His doctrine has gone out into all lands, and his words unto the ends of the world: and hardly a year passes without some attempt being made somewhere to extract fresh instruction from his epoch-making work, or to throw fresh light on its method or its relations. But for this very reason I doubted whether I should not seem superfluous in adding my pebble to the imposing cairn of literary products that has thus been raised to his memory. The intermediate position of Reid, unquestionably a more important leader of thought than Hutcheson, unquestionably less familiar to current thought than Adam Smith, seemed on the whole to fit the opportunity best: I propose therefore this evening to present to you—not with the fulness and exactness of a critical historian, but in the lighter and more selective style allowed to an occasional utterance—such features of Reid's philosophical work as appear to me of most enduring interest.

I will begin by endeavouring to remove a prejudice, which perhaps my very title may have produced.

"The Philosophy of Common Sense," you may say, "is not this, after all, an intellectual monstrosity?

Philosophy is a good thing, and Common Sense in its place is a good thing too : but they are both better kept apart. If we mix them, shall we not find ourselves cutting blocks with a scalpel, and using a garden-knife for the finer processes of scientific dissection ? "

And I am the more afraid of this prejudgment, because in the only passage of Kant's works in which he speaks of Reid's philosophical labours, it is this antithesis that he applies in condemnation of them: and, speaking as I do in a University where the leading expositor of Kant, to Englishmen as well as Scotsmen of our age, has taught for so many years, I cannot but feel this condemnation a formidable obstacle to my efforts to claim your sympathy for Reid.

The passage I refer to is that in Kant's *Prolegomena to any Future Metaphysic* (1783) in which he "considers with a sense of pain" how completely Hume's opponents, "Reid, Oswald, Beattie, and even Priestley," missed the point of Hume's problem. Instead of answering Hume's sceptical reasoning by "probing more deeply into the nature of reason," as Kant believed himself to have done, "they discovered a more convenient means of putting on a bold face without any proper insight into the question, by appealing to the common sense of mankind . . . a subtle discovery for enabling the most vapid babbler" without a "particle of insight" to hold his own against the most penetrating thinker.

The censure, you see, is strong : but is it thoroughly

intelligent? Reid, says the critic, has not caught Hume's point. Has Kant caught Reid's? I venture to doubt whether he ever gave himself a chance of catching it.

This for two reasons. First, look at the names he puts together, "Reid, Oswald, Beattie";—the first a thinker of indubitable originality; the third a man of real, but chiefly literary, ability, a poet by choice and a philosopher from a sense of duty; the second a theological pamphleteer. Is it likely that Kant would have thus bracketed the three, if he had really read them? How came he then to put them on a par? That is easily explained. He had doubtless read Priestley's examination which treats the three together, and which, written as it was primarily from a theological point of view, gives even a larger space to Oswald. This explains Kant's odd conjunction of names, "Reid, Oswald, Beattie, and even Priestley,"— even, that is, their critic Priestley. I imagine Kant was on general grounds more likely to be attracted by Priestley's book than by Reid's, since he had a keen interest in the progress of contemporary physical science, and Priestley had here a well-deserved reputation: and certainly the Reid who appears in Priestley's pages, misquoted, misrepresented, and misunderstood, was likely enough to be regarded as another Oswald.

My second reason is that if Kant had ever studied Reid's *Inquiry into the Human Mind* he could hardly have failed to extend his studies to the Hume to whom Reid was replying. This may startle you.

"What," you may say, "Kant not read Hume: why, any shilling handbook of the history of philosophy will tell you that Hume's scepticism woke up Kant from his dogmatic slumbers." Certainly, but it was not the same scepticism as that which woke up Reid to construct the Philosophy of Common Sense: it was the veiled, limited, and guarded scepticism of the *Inquiry into the Human Understanding*, not the frank, comprehensive, and uncompromising scepticism of the *Treatise on Human Nature*. Kant's Hume is a sceptic who ventures modestly to point out the absence of a rational ground for his expectation that the future will resemble the past, while in the same breath hastening to assure the reader that his expectation remains unshaken by his arguments. Reid's Hume is a sceptic who boldly denies the infinite divisibility of space, who professes to have in his intellectual laboratory a solvent powerful enough to destroy the force of the most cogent demonstration, and who ventures to tell his fellowmen plainly that they are each and all "nothing but bundles of different perceptions, succeeding each other with inconceivable rapidity." I think that if Kant had even looked into Reid's *Inquiry*, the difference between the earlier and the later Hume must have struck him, and he must have been led on to read the *Treatise on Human Nature*; whereas it is evident and admitted that he never did read it.

Do you still want proof that Kant did not catch Reid's point? I have a witness to bring forward whom Kant himself would have allowed to be a good witness—Mr. David Hume: who was persuaded by a common friend to peruse parts of Reid's work before it appeared, and to write his view of them to the author. Hume did not much like the task in prospect. "I wish," he grumbles to the common friend, "that the parsons would confine themselves to their old occupation of worrying one another, and leave philosophers to argue with moderation, temper, and good manners." In fact, he expects another Warburton: but when he has read the MS. his tone changes. "It is certainly very rare," he writes to Reid, "that a piece so deeply philosophical is wrote with so much spirit, and affords so much entertainment to the reader. . . . There are some objections," he goes on, "that I would propose, but I will forbear till the whole can be brought before me. I will only say that if you have been able to clear up these abstruse and important topics, instead of being mortified, I shall be so vain as to pretend to a share of the praise: and shall think that my errors, by having at least some coherence, had led you to make a strict review of my principles, which were the common ones, and to perceive their futility."

Well, I think you will agree with me that this is a charmingly urbane letter, from a freethinker of established literary reputation to a parson turned professor, as yet hardly known in the world of letters, who had hit him some smart blows and ventured to laugh at him a little as well as argue with him. But Hume recognises that the parson unexpectedly writes like a philosopher: and Hume, as we saw, has a high ideal of the manner in which philosophers should conduct their debates; and it is a pleasure to find him acting up to his ideal, a pleasure all the greater from the rarity with which it is afforded to the student of philosophical controversy.

But it was not on Hume's urbanity that I wished now to dwell: I wished to point out that it never occurs to Hume that Reid has appealed from the expert to the vulgar, and endeavoured to avoid his conclusions without answering his arguments. What rather strikes Hume is the philosophic depth that his antagonist has shown in attacking his fundamental assumptions;—which were, as he says, the common ones, and which Reid accordingly had traced back through Berkeley and Locke to the start of modern philosophy in Descartes. It is difficult, I think, for us to appreciate equally the penetration shown in this historical *aperçu*, because the connexion of ideas that Reid makes apparent now seems to us so obvious and patent. But this is the case with many important steps in the development of philosophical thought: when once the step has been taken, it appears so simple and inevitable that we can hardly feel that it required intellectual force and originality to take it. You remember, perhaps, the depreciatory remark made on Christopher Columbus by a schoolboy who "didn't see why so much fuss should be made about his discovery of America, since, if he went that way at all, he could not well miss it." Similarly it now seems to us that if Reid "went that way at all" he

THE PHILOSOPHY OF COMMON SENSE 413

could not fail to find the source of the Idealism of Berkeley and the pulverising scepticism of Hume in Locke's assumption that the immediate object of the mind in external perception is its own ideas: and that finding this view equally in Malebranche, he could not fail to trace it to Descartes. His merit lay in the independence of thought required to free himself from this assumption, question it, and hunt it home : and this merit Hume evidently recognised.

And now, perhaps, I may have persuaded some of my hearers that Kant entirely failed to see what Reid and his followers were driving at. But if so, I have gone too far, and persuaded them of more than I intended. The appeal to vulgar common sense *has* an important place in Reid's doctrine: he does rely on it: nor can I defend him from the charge that he relies on it too much. He does hold that the mere ridiculousness of Hume's conclusions is a good reason for disbelieving them: and even in his later and maturer treatise he speaks of the sense of the ridiculous as a guide to philosophic truth, in language that lacks his usual circumspection. For our sense of the ridiculous is manifestly stirred by the mere incongruity of an opinion with our intellectual habits: a strange truth is no less apt to excite it than a strange error. When the Copernican theory was slowly winning its way to acceptance, even the grave Milton allowed himself a jest on "the new carmen who drive the earth about": and I can remember how, when the Darwinian theory was new, persons of the highest culture cracked their jokes on the zoologist's supposed private reasons for the absurd conclusion that his ancestor was a monkey. And this is doubtless all for the best: laughter is a natural and valuable relief in many perplexities and disturbances of life, and I do not see why it should not relieve the disturbance caused by the collision of new opinions with old: only let us remember that it is evidence of nothing except the mere fact of collision. But, though Reid does rely more than he ought on the *argumentum ad risum*, he is not so stupid as to think that a volume is required to exhibit this argument. He does say to the plain man, " If philosophy befools her votaries, and leads them into these quagmires of absurdity, beware of her as an *ignis fatuus*": but he immediately adds, "Is it, however, certain that this fair lady is of the party? Is it not possible that she may have been misrepresented?" and that she has been misrepresented is the thesis which he aims at proving.

In the course of the proof, no doubt, he leads us again to Common Sense, as the source and warrant of certain primary data of knowledge at once unreasoned and indubitable: but the Common Sense to which we are thus led is not that of the vulgar as contrasted with the philosopher: Reid's point is that the philosopher inevitably shares it with the vulgar. Whether a philosopher has been developed out of a monkey may possibly be still an open question; but there can be no doubt that he is developed out of a man; and if we consider his intellectual life as a whole, we may surmise that the larger part of it is occupied with the beliefs that he still shares with the unphilosophical majority of his contemporaries. It is on this fact that Reid's appeal to him is based. He refers to Hume's account of the manner in which, after solitary reflection has environed him with the clouds and darkness of doubt, the genial influence of "dinner, backgammon, and social talk" dispels these doubts and restores his belief in the world without and the self within: and Reid takes his stand with those who are "so weak as to imagine that they ought to have the same belief in solitude and in company." His *essential* demand, therefore, on the philosopher, is not primarily that he should make his beliefs consistent with those of the vulgar, but that he should make them consistent with his own; and the legitimacy of the demand becomes, I think, more apparent, when we regard it as made in the name of Philosophy rather than in the name of Common Sense. For when we reflect on plain Common Sense,—on the body of unreasoned principles of judgment which we and other men are in the habit of applying in ordinary thought and discourse,—we find it certainly to some extent confused and inconsistent: but it is not clear that it is the business of Common Sense to get rid of these confusions and inconsistencies, so long as they do not give trouble in the ordinary conduct of life: at any rate it is not its most pressing business, since system-making is not its affair. But system-making is pre-eminently the affair of Philosophy, and it cannot willingly tolerate inconsistencies: at least if it has to tolerate them, as I sadly fear that it has, it can only tolerate them as a physician tolerates a chronic imperfection of health, which he can only hope to mitigate and not completely to cure.

Accordingly, in Reid's view it is the duty of a philosopher—his duty *as* a philosopher—to aim steadily and persistently at bringing the common human element of his intellectual life into clear consistency with the special philosophic element. And Reid is on the whole perfectly aware—though his language occasionally ignores it—that for every part of this task the special training and intellectual habits of the philosopher are required. For the fundamental beliefs which the philosopher shares with the plain man can only be defined with clearness and precision by one who has reflected systematically, as an ordinary man does not reflect, on the operations of his own mind; even the elementary distinction between sensation and perception is, Reid admits, only apprehended by the plain man in a confused form. To bring the distinction into clear consciousness, to attend to "sensation and perception each by itself, and to attribute nothing to one which belongs to the other," requires, he tells us, "a degree of attention to what passes in our own minds, and a talent for distinguishing things that differ, which is not to be expected in the vulgar." The philosopher alone can do it: but in order to do it, he must partially divest himself of his philosophic peculiarities; that is, he must temporarily put out of his mind the conclusions of any system he may have learnt or adopted, and merely bring his trained faculty of reflective attention to the observation and analysis of the common human element of his thought.

But if it be admitted that the philosopher alone is capable of the steady and clear attention required to ascertain the fundamental beliefs of Common Sense, what valid evidence is there of the general assent to these beliefs on which Reid lays stress, and which, indeed, the term implies? He seems to be in a dilemma; either the many must be held capable of reflective analysis, or the decision on questions of fundamental belief must after all be limited to the expert few. The difficulty is partly met by pointing out that the philosophical faculty required to distinguish and state such beliefs with precision much exceeds that required to judge of such a statement when made; just as few of us could have found out the axioms required in the study of geometry, but we could easily see the truth of Euclid's at a very early age. Still, granting this, I think that Reid presses too far the competence of plain men even to *judge* of philosophical first principles. It is true, as he urges, that this judgment requires no more than a "sound mind free from prejudice and a distinct conception of the questions": but it does not follow, as Reid seems to think, that "every man is a competent judge, the learned and unlearned, the philosopher and day-labourer alike": because a good deal of the painful process we call 'learning' is normally needed to realise these apparently simple requirements, freedom from prejudice and distinctness of conception. I will not affirm that no day-labourer could attain a distinct conception of the positions that Reid is defending against Berkeley and Hume: but I venture to think that a day-labourer who could convince us that he had attained it would be at once recognised as a born philosopher, incontrovertibly qualified by native genius for membership of the society that I have the honour to address.

At the same time, I cannot think Reid wrong in holding that the propositions he is most concerned to maintain as first principles are implicitly assented to by men in general. That for ordinary men sense-perception involves a belief in the existence of a thing perceived, independent of the perception: that similarly consciousness involves a belief in the existence of a permanent identical subject of changing conscious states: that ordinary moral judgment involves the belief in a real right and wrong in human action, capable of being known by a moral agent and distinct in idea from what conduces to his interest: that in ordinary thought about experience we find implicit the unreasoned assumption that every change must have a cause, and a cause adequate to the effect,—all this, I think, will hardly be denied by any one who approaches the question with a fair mind. He may, of course, still regard it as unphilosophical to rest the validity of these beliefs on the fact of their general acceptance. But here again it must be said that Reid's own deference to general assent is of a strictly limited and subordinate kind. He is far from wishing truth to be determined by votes: he only urges that "authority, though tyrannical as a mistress, is useful as a handmaid to private judgment." He points out that even in the exactest sciences authority actually has this place: even a mathematician who has demonstrated a novel conclusion is strengthened in his belief in it by the assent of other mathematical experts who have examined his demonstration, and is "reduced to a kind of suspense" by their dissent.

This is, I think, undeniable: and perhaps we may separate Reid's just and moderate statement of the claims of Authority from his exaggerated view of the competence of untrained intellects to deal with philosophical first principles; and simply take it as a cardinal point in the philosophy of Common Sense that a difference in judgment from another whom he has no reason to regard as less competent to judge than himself, naturally and properly reduces a thinker to a "kind of suspense." When the conflict relates to a demonstrated conclusion, it leads him to search for a flaw in the opponent's demonstration; but when it relates to a first principle, primary datum, or fundamental assumption, this resource appears to be excluded: and then, perhaps, when he has done all that he can to remove any misunderstanding of the question at issue, the Common Sense philosopher may be allowed to derive some support from the thought that his own conviction is shared by the great majority of those whose judgments have built up and continually sustain the living fabric of our common thought and knowledge. And this, I think, is all that Reid really means to claim.

I have now, I hope, succeeded in making clear the general relation which Reid's epistemology bears to his psychology. I have not used these modern terms, because Reid himself blends the two subjects under the single notion of "Philosophy of the Human Mind": but it is necessary, in any careful estimate of his work, to distinguish the process of psychological distinction and analysis through which the fundamental beliefs of Common Sense are ascertained, from the arguments by which their validity is justified. I do not propose to enter into the details of Reid's psychological view, which has largely become antiquated through the progress of mental science. But if Locke is the first founder of the distinctively British study, Empirical Psychology, of which the primary method is introspective observation and analysis, I think Reid has a fair claim to be regarded as a second founder: and even now his psychological work may be studied with interest, from the patient fidelity of his self-observation, the acumen of his reflective analysis, and, especially, his entire freedom from the vague materialism that, in spite of Descartes, still hung about the current philosophical conception of Mind and its operations. It is, indeed, in the task of exposing the unwarrantable assumptions generated by this vague materialism that the force and penetration of Reid's intellect is most conspicuously shown.

Let me briefly note this in the case of the beliefs

involved in ordinary sense-perception, since this problem occupies a leading place in his discussion. Not, I ought to say, that he is specially interested in this problem on its own account: he makes it quite clear that it is on far greater issues that his thought is really set. God, Freedom, Duty, the spirituality of human nature,—these are, for Reid as for Kant, the grave matters really at stake in the epistemological controversy. But these greater matters, for the very reason of their supreme importance, are apt to stir our deepest emotions so strongly as to render difficult the passionless precision of analysis and reasoning which Reid rightly held to be needful for the attainment of philosophical truth: while at the same time it is clear to him that all the questions hang together, and that the decision of one in the sense that he claims will carry with it the similar determination of the rest.

Accepting this view then, and remembering that in a trivial case we are trying no trivial issue, let us examine his treatment of the cognition by Mind of particular material things. Here Reid's task, as he ultimately saw, was merely carrying further the work of Descartes. By clearly distinguishing the motions of material particles antecedent to perception from perception itself as a psychical fact, Descartes had got rid of the old psychophysical muddle, by which forms or semblances of things perceived by the senses were supposed somehow to get into the brain through the 'animal spirits' and so into the mind. But he had not equally got rid of the view that perception was the getting of an idea in the mind, from which the existence of a thing outside the mind *like* the idea had to be somehow inferred. This view is definitely held, not only by his disciple Malebranche but by his independent successor Locke. They do not see what Reid came to see, that the normal perception of an external object presents itself to introspection as an immediate cognition: that is, as a cognition which has no psychical mediation, no inference in it. What prevented them and others from seeing this was, mainly, a naïve assumption that the mind can only know immediately what is 'present' to it, and that things outside the body cannot be thus present; as the mind cannot go out to them and they cannot get into the mind, only the ideas of them can get in. It was reserved to Reid to point out the illegitimacy of this assumption, and to derive it from a confused, half-unconscious transfer to Mind and its function of cognition, of the conditions under which body acts on body in ordinary physical experience. When the assumption is made explicit and traced to its source, it loses, I think, all appearance of validity.

It is to be observed, that in affirming external perception to be an immediate cognition, Reid does not of course mean that it is physically uncaused. He only means that the perceiving mind has not a double object, its own percept and a non-mental thing like its percept: and accordingly that our normal conviction of the present existence of the non-mental thing perceived is not a judgment attained by reasoning, but a primary datum of knowledge. He recognises like his predecessors that it has physical antecedents, movements of material particles both without and within the organism. And he recognises, more distinctly than his predecessors, that it has psychical antecedents and concomitants, *i.e.* sensations which he carefully distinguishes from the perception that they suggest and accompany. A consideration of these antecedents may possibly affect our reflective confidence in the cognition that follows them,—that question I will deal with presently,—but at any rate it cannot properly modify our view of the content of this cognition as ascertained by introspective observation. This, I think, remains true after duly taking account of the valuable work that has been done since Reid's time, in ascertaining more accurately the antecedents and concomitants of our common perceptions of extended matter. Whatever view we may take on the interesting but still disputed questions as to the precise manner in which visual, tactual, and muscular feelings have historically been combined in the genesis of our particular perceptions and general notions of matter and space,—there can still be no doubt of the fundamental difference in our present consciousness between these perceptions or notions and any combinations of muscular, tactual, and visual feelings.

It has indeed been held, by an influential school of British psychologists, that this manifest difference is merely apparent and illusory: it has been held that by a process of "mental chemistry" sensations and images of sensation have been "compounded" into what we now distinguish as perceptions and conceptions of matter in space, and that the latter really consist of sensations and images of sensation, just as water really consists of oxygen and hydrogen. But this view involves a second illegitimate transfer of physical conditions to psychical facts; and Reid would certainly have rejected 'mental chemistry' in this application as unhesitatingly as he does reject it when applied to support the conclusion that a "cluster of the ideas of sense, properly combined, may make up the idea of a mind." He would have rejected it for the simple reason that we have no ground for holding any fact of consciousness to be other than careful introspection declares it to be. In the case of material chemistry, the inference that a compound consists of certain elements depends on experimental proof that we can not only make the compound out of the elements, but can also make the elements again out of the compound. But even if we grant that our cognitions of Matter and Space, of Self and Duty, are derived from more elementary feelings, it is certain that no psychical experiment will enable us to turn them into such feelings again: the later phenomena, if products, are biological not chemical products, resulting from evolution, not from mere composition.

Still, it may be said, granting the existence of cognitions and beliefs that cannot now be resolved into more elementary feelings, and that present themselves in ordinary thought with the character of unreasoned certitude, systematic reflection on these beliefs and their antecedents must render it impossible to accept them as trustworthy premises for philosophical reasoning. It is a commonplace that the senses deceive, and the more we learn of the psychophysical process of sense-perception, the more clear it becomes why and how they must deceive. Even apart from cases of admitted illusion, philosophical reflection on normal perception continually shows us, as Hume urges, a manifest difference between the actual percept and what we commonly regard as the real thing perceived. Thus, Hume says, "the table which we see seems to diminish as we remove farther from it: but the real table which exists independent of us suffers no alteration. It was, therefore, nothing but its image which was present to the mind. These are the obvious dictates of reason." In answering this line of objection Reid partly relies on a weak distinction between original and acquired perception, which the progress of science has rendered clearly untenable and irrelevant. Apart from this his really effective reply is twofold. First he points out that the very evidence relied upon to show the unreality of sense-percepts really affords striking testimony to the general validity of the belief in an independent reality known through sense-perception. It is by trusting, not by distrusting, this fundamental belief that Common Sense organised into Science continually at once corrects and confirms crude Common Sense. Take Hume's case of the table. If nothing but images were present to the mind, how could we ever know that there exists a real table which does not alter while the visible magnitude changes with its distance from us? The plain man knows this through an acquired perception, by which he habitually judges of real magnitude from visible appearances : but science carries the knowledge further, enabling us to predict exactly what appearance a given portion of extended matter will exhibit at any given distance from the spectators. Now all this coherent, precise, and unerring prediction rests upon innumerable sense-perceptions; and the scientific processes which have made it possible have been carried on throughout on the basis of the vulgar belief in the independent existence of the matter perceived. "Is it not absurd," Reid asks, "to suppose that a false supposition of the rude vulgar has been so lucky in solving an infinite number of phenomena of nature?"

Suppose, however, that the opponent resists this argument : suppose he maintains that, though physical science may find the independent existence of matter a convenient fiction,—as mathematicians find it convenient to feign that they can extract the square root of negative quantities,—still in truth Mind can only know mental facts—feelings and thoughts. Suppose he further urges that the common belief in the independent existence of the object of perception is found on reflection to have no claim to philosophic acceptance, because while admittedly unreasoned it cannot be said to be strictly intuitive :— granted that I may directly perceive the table before me, I cannot directly perceive that it exists independently of my perception. To this line of argument Reid has another line of reply. He points out to the

Idealist that he does not escape from this kind of unreasoned belief by refusing to recognise a reality beyond consciousness. He has still to rely on data of knowledge which are open to the same objections as the belief in the independent existence of matter. For instance, he has to rely on memory. If sense-perception is fallible, memory is surely more fallible; if we do not know intuitively and cannot prove that what we perceive really exists independently of our perception, still less can we either know intuitively or prove that what we recollect really happened: if on reflection we find it difficult to conceive how the Non-ego can be known by the Ego, there is surely an equal difficulty in understanding how the Present Ego can know the Past. And yet once cease to rely on memory, and intellectual life becomes impossible: even in reasoning beyond the very simplest we have to rely on our recollection of previous steps of reasoning. A pure system of truths reasoned throughout from rational intuitions may be the philosophic ideal: but it is as true of the intellectual as of the physical life that living somehow is prior to living ideally well: and if we are to live at all, we must accept some beliefs that cannot claim Reason for their source. Is it not then, Reid urges, arbitrary and unphilosophical to acquiesce tranquilly in some of these beliefs of Common Sense, and yet obstinately to fight against others that have an equal warrant of spontaneous certitude? May we not rather say that it is the duty of a philosopher to give impartially a provisional acceptance to all such beliefs, and then set himself to clarify them by reflection, remove inadvertencies, confusions, and contradictions, and as far as possible build together the purged results into an ordered and harmonious system of thought?

If, finally, the opposing philosopher answers that he cannot be satisfied by any system that is not perfectly transparent to reason, Reid does not altogether refuse him his sympathy, though he cannot encourage him to hope. "I confess," he says, "after all that the evidence of reasoning, and of necessary and self-evident truths, seems to be the least mysterious and the most perfectly comprehended . . . the light of truth so fills my mind in these cases that I can neither conceive nor desire anything more satisfying. On the other hand, when I remember distinctly a past event, or see an object before my eyes," though "this commands my belief no less than an axiom . . . I seem to want that evidence which I can best comprehend and which gives perfect satisfaction to an inquisitive mind." And "to a philosopher who has been accustomed to think that the treasure of his knowledge is the acquisition of his reason, it is no doubt humiliating to find" that "his knowledge of what really exists or did exist comes by another channel," and that "he is led to it" as it were "in the dark." "It is no wonder" then "that some philosophers should invent vain theories to account for this knowledge": while others "spurn at a knowledge they cannot account for and vainly attempt to throw it off." But all such "attempts," he holds, are as impracticable as "an attempt to fly."

The passage from which I have quoted was published in 1785, when Reid was seventy-five years of age. Even before it was published attempts at aerial navigation had suddenly come to seem less chimerical in the physical world; and before the end of the century, in the world of thought, attempts to transcend and rationally account for the beliefs of Common Sense—more remarkable than any dreamt of by Reid—had begun to excite some interest even in our insular mind. The nineteenth century is now drawing to its close; and these attempts to fly are still going on, both in the physical and in the intellectual world; but in neither region, according to my information, have they yet attained a triumphant success. At the same time our age, which has seen so many things achieved that were once thought impossible, may without presumption contemplate such attempts in a somewhat more hopeful spirit than was possible to Reid: and I should be sorry to say anything here to damp the noble ardour or to depress the high aspirations that ought to animate a society like yours. But if there should be any one among you who, desirous to philosophise and yet fearing the fate of Icarus, may prefer to walk in the dimness and twilight of the lower region in which my discourse has moved,—then I venture to think that he may even now find profit in communing with the earnest, patient, lucid, and discerning intellect of the thinker who, in the history of modern speculation, has connected the name of Scotland with the Philosophy of Common Sense.

CRITERIA OF TRUTH AND ERROR

(Reprinted from *Mind*, vol. ix. N.S., January 1900.)

THE present essay is a partial discussion of what I regard as the central problem of Epistemology. In order that its drift may be clearly seen from the outset, I will begin by explaining briefly—without argument—my view of Philosophy, Epistemology, and their relation. I take it to be the business of Philosophy—in Mr. Spencer's words—to 'unify' or systematise as completely as possible our common thought, which it finds partially systematised in a number of different sciences and studies. Now before attempting this unification, we must wish to be somehow assured that the thoughts or beliefs which we seek to systematise completely are true and valid. This is obvious; no rational being with his eyes open would try to work up a mixture of truth and error into a coherent system without some attempt to eliminate the error.

It is *prima facie* necessary, therefore, as a preliminary to the task of bringing into—or exhibiting in—coherent relation the different bodies of systematic thought which furnish the matter for Philo-

CRITERIA OF TRUTH AND ERROR   431

sophy, to have some criteria for distinguishing truth from error. It may, however, be thought that this need—though undeniably urgent in the case of such studies as, *e.g.*, Politics and Theology—will not be practically presented, so long as the philosopher's work is confined to the positive sciences. The prevalence of error in Politics is kept prominently before our minds by the system of party government; and the effective working of this system almost requires the conviction on either side that the political programme of the other party—unhappily often in a majority—is a tissue of errors. So again in Theology, it is the established belief of average members of any religious denomination that the whole world outside the pale of the denomination lies in the darkness of error on some fundamental points; and even within the pale, the wide-spread existence of right-hand backslidings and left-hand defections from the standard of orthodoxy is continually attracting the attention of the newspapers. But no doubt, in elementary study of the positive sciences, error is commonly only brought before our minds in the strictly limited form of slight discrepancy in the results of observation, as something reducible to a minimum by an application of the theory of probabilities.

Still the danger of error is only thus kept in the background, so long as we confine our attention to the more settled parts of the established sciences in their present condition. Around and beneath these more settled portions, in the region where knowledge is growing in range or depth, and the human intellect endeavouring to solve new questions, or penetrate to a more solid basis of principles, we find continually conflict and controversy as to the truth of new conclusions—which appear established and demonstrated to the adventurous minds that have worked them out—as to the legitimacy of new hypotheses, and the validity of new methods; and wherever we find such conflict and controversy, there must be error on one side or the other, or possibly on both.

And the fact of error is still more prominently brought before our minds when we turn from the present to the past, and retrace the history of the now established sciences: since we find that in almost all cases human knowledge has progressed not merely by adding newly ascertained facts to facts previously ascertained, but also, to an important extent, by questioning and correcting or discarding beliefs—often whole systems of connected beliefs—previously held on insufficient grounds. In this way, convinced by Copernicus, the human mind dropped the Ptolemaic astronomy and reconstructed its view of the planetary and celestial motions on the heliocentric hypothesis; convinced by Galileo, it discarded the fundamental errors of Aristotle's view of matter; convinced by Lavoisier, it rectified its conception of chemical elements, and relegated the remarkable substance 'phlogiston'—that had enjoyed an imaginary existence for something like a century—to the limbo of recognised non-entities; convinced by Darwin, it abandoned its fundamental notion of the fixity of organic species, and accepted a revolution in morphological method.

Now the student of science is ordinarily not much disturbed by this evidence that his class forms no exception to Pope's oft-quoted characterisation of man as "sole judge of truth, in endless error hurled." When, in the progress of thought, any prevalent scientific belief is recognised as erroneous, he simply discards this—with more or less endeavour to ascertain the particular causes of error and guard against their recurrence,—and, on the whole, continues his natural processes of acquiring, evolving, systematising beliefs with undiminished confidence. But to the philosophical mind the ascertained erroneousness of some beliefs is apt to suggest the possible erroneousness of all. If a belief that I once held to be certainly true has turned out to be false, what guarantees me against a similar discovery in respect of any other belief which I am now holding to be true? The mind is thus overspread with a general and sweeping distrust of the processes of ordinary thinking, which is not exactly to be called philosophical scepticism—since this usually presents itself as systematically deduced from premises accepted by philosophers,—but is rather to be conceived as the naïve, untechnical scepticism of a philosophic mind, which may turn out to be (as in the classical case of Descartes) a mere stage in its progress toward a dogmatic system. At any rate, it is the removal of this philosophic uncertainty—in respect of beliefs that, in ordinary thought, are commonly assumed to be true—that I regard as the primary aim of Epistemology.

I have said that this task lies in the way of philosophy; but I ought to add that it does not appear to lie in the way of all philosophers. Some of those who have devoted their minds to the solution of philosophical problems seem hardly to have contemplated error except as a kind of misconduct into which the rest of the human race —and especially other philosophers—are inexcusably prone to fall. It is, indeed, a common experience of mankind in all departments of theory and practice that the liability to error is more equally distributed among human beings than the consciousness of such liability. But the variations of self-confidence that we find among persons who have devoted themselves to the business of philosophy are perhaps less than elsewhere to be attributed to differences of individual temperament: it would rather seem that in the social movement of philosophic thought there are general ebbs and flows; an age of confidence followed by an age of diffidence. It is partly the fact that the philosophic mind of the modern world is now rather at the ebb, with its constructive impulses comparatively feeble, which explains the development and the prominence that the epistemological aspect or function of philosophy is now receiving; and has accordingly led to the composition of the present paper.

I will begin by somewhat limiting my subject for clearness of discussion. I have contrasted ordinary

CRITERIA OF TRUTH AND ERROR 435

certitude with philosophic doubt; but even the plain man is not always cocksure. Sometimes he even doubts and suspends his judgment; but even when he believes and positively affirms, many of his beliefs and affirmations—most of those relating to the future —are intended to be taken as not certain but probable. By a 'probable' belief I do not now mean a belief relating to probabilities; for this may be as certain as any other—as for instance the belief that the chances are even that a penny I toss will come down tails. The theory of chances has been described as a method of extracting knowledge out of ignorance; it is undoubtedly a method of converting probable judgments into certain ones—though the certainty is of a peculiar kind, and its verification presents a special epistemological problem of some interest. But the probable beliefs that I now wish to distinguish from certain ones are beliefs which involve no attempt at a quantitative estimate of 'amount of probability'; and they are often in form of expression indistinguishable from beliefs held with certitude:—thus when a man affirms in conversation that the new plan of international arbitration will have no practical effect, or that the Liberal Party must return to power after the next general election, it will be generally understood that though the speaker may appear to express certitude on these points, he only means that the events are extremely probable. I draw attention to this ambiguity of expression, because it facilitates an indeterminateness of thought, of which we have to take note in applying the distinction that I now draw between 'certain' and 'probable' beliefs. Often in ordinary thought we do not know whether we are *sure* of what we affirm unless we are led to reflect on the point; sometimes we do not know after reflection; sometimes we are conscious of elements of uncertainty which we decide to disregard, and then we say that we are 'morally certain'—meaning that we should unhesitatingly act as if we were certain. This last state of mind I shall consider hereafter; at present I wish to confine attention to beliefs which present themselves in ordinary thought as certain without qualification. Of these I may roughly distinguish three chief classes: (1) particular beliefs about the present and recent past of the changing world of which we are part; (2) general beliefs more or less systematised in the sciences, especially the exact sciences, which we may happen to know; (3) beliefs that *prima facie* relate not to mere matters of fact but to moral or æsthetic valuation—to what we ought to do as individuals, or what government ought to do, or what is good and bad in manners, literature, and art. Of course in these latter regions of belief any educated person is aware that there is much doubt and controversy; still there are plenty of propositions in each of the regions indicated, which it would seem in ordinary thought as absurd to dispute or qualify as propositions with regard to the most familiar matters of fact. When Charles Lamb took a candle to examine the cerebral bumps of the soap-boiler who affirmed that Shakespeare was a first-rate dramatic writer, it was, I suppose, because the irrefragable certainty of the proposition seemed to render its express statement absurdly superfluous.

Concentrating attention, then, on beliefs that in ordinary thought are certain in the sense explained, let us—with a view to a necessary limitation of our inquiry—take a second distinction. Reflecting upon the beliefs of the truth of which I have no doubt, I perceive that some of them (*e.g.* the propositions of Euclid) have only derivative or dependent certainty —my belief in them rests on my belief in some other proposition or propositions; while in other cases (*e.g.* most of the axioms of Euclid) my certitude may be distinguished as primary or independent. In the instance given—as I have personally followed the reasonings of Euclid and satisfied myself as to their cogency—I might employ a clearer antithesis, and say that some of my geometrical beliefs have 'intuitive' and others demonstrative certainty. But this antithesis is too narrow for my present purpose. For, firstly, I do not profess to have intuitive certainty with regard to all beliefs for which proof does not seem to be required. I am certain that I read through the three first pages of this essay before I sat down to write the fourth half an hour ago; but it would be contrary to usage to call this certainty 'intuitive,' though the belief does not present itself to me as requiring proof. Secondly, I wish to include among beliefs with derivative certainty that comparatively large body of scientific conclusions which I believe to have been scientifically proved, though not to me, and which I accordingly accept on the authority of one or more other persons. Of course, in a wide sense of the word, a statement of my grounds for trusting any conclusion arrived at by some other mind might be called my 'proof' of the proposition; but at any rate it would not be scientific demonstration, and it would be odd to call the certainty of any such belief to me 'demonstrative certainty.' For simplicity, let us here provisionally disregard any doubts of the authority of others as others: then the distinction will be between beliefs which requiring proof seem to have obtained it, and beliefs which do not seem to require it.

Now the errors due to taking invalid proof for valid are the special subject of investigation in the science of Logic; and it is widely held that the labours of logicians have provided adequate criteria for excluding them: that they have discovered by analysis certain forms of reasoning into one or other of which any cogent inference may be thrown, and by the application of which the validity or invalidity of any process of inference may be made manifest. Suppose we grant this: then our epistemological problem is solved in respect of dependent or inferential beliefs—so far as the process of inference by which they are reached is capable of being thrown into a logically cogent form. That is, I can in this way obtain assurance that all my apparently proved beliefs are true if the premises from which they are inferred are true: and if these premises are themselves arrived at by inference I can similarly apply the test to the proof of them—and so on till we come to the ultimate premises. I propose to assume for the purpose of this paper that Logic has done satisfactorily what it commonly professes to have done; and that our task, accordingly, may be limited to the verification of ultimate premises, or beliefs that are in ordinary thought accepted as not requiring proof.

The importance of the task thus limited has been fully recognised by some philosophers. J. S. Mill, indeed, seems disposed to bestow on this inquiry the venerable name of "Metaphysics." "The grand question," he says, " of what is called Metaphysics is 'what are the propositions that may reasonably be received without proof?'" And it is, I suppose, to propositions of this kind that Descartes' famous criterion—expressed in the formula "that all the things which we very clearly and distinctly conceive are true"—was primarily designed to apply.

On the other hand, it seems to be also primarily to this class of propositions that Kant's unqualified rejection of "a general criterion of truth" applies[1] —since Kant regards Logic as having adequately furnished criteria of formal truth, and therefore of all kinds of inference. In fact, Kant's condemnation of the task on which I am engaged is so strong and sweeping that I think it well to examine his arguments before proceeding further. I give it somewhat abbreviated.

[1] See § 3 of the *Introduction to Transcendental Logic* (*Kritik der reinen Vernunft*. Hart. p. 86).

"If truth consists—as is admitted—in the agreement of a cognition with its object, that object must, by the true cognition, be distinguished from some other object or objects. Now it is implied in the idea of a general criterion of truth that it is valid with regard to every kind of cognition, whatever the objects cognised may be. But then, as such a criterion must abstract from the particular contents of particular cognitions, whereas, as we have seen, truth concerns those very contents, it is impossible and absurd to suppose that such a general criterion can give us a sign of the truth of cognition in respect of its content or matter. Therefore a sufficient and at the same time general criterion of truth cannot possibly be found."

In examining this passage I may begin by pointing out that Kant's view of truth as 'consisting in the agreement of cognition with its object'—which he takes as universally accepted—cannot be applied to all propositions without a difficult extension of the notion of 'object' (*Gegenstand*). This will appear, if we try to apply it to strictly hypothetical propositions, or to categorical propositions of ethical import.

To this consideration I shall hereafter return; meanwhile, in discussing Kant's definition, I shall assume for clearness, that we are dealing with judgments that are intended to represent some fact, past, present, or future, particular or general. Thus restricted, Kant's argument is simple and at first sight plausible; but I think it contains a *petitio principii.* For it proceeds on the assumption that true cognitions cannot as such have any *common* characteristic, except that of agreeing with their objects; but that is surely to assume the very point in question. To illustrate this, let us take Descartes' criterion before referred to, as the first that comes to hand in the history of modern philosophy. How can the diversity of the objects of cognition be a logical ground for denying that "what is clearly and distinctly conceived" is necessarily true?—since the distinction between clear and obscure, and between distinct and confused conception, does not become less applicable when we pass from one kind of object to another.

It may be answered on Kant's behalf that "clearness and distinctness of conception" belong to the form of thought, not to its matter; that clearness and distinctness of conception may prevent us from attributing to any subject an incompatible predicate, but not from attributing a predicate that though compatible does not actually belong to the subject. But it is just this dogmatic separation of form from matter that I regard as an unproved assumption. It is surely conceivable that the relation of the knowing mind to knowable things—to the whole realm of possible objects of knowledge—is such that, whenever any matter of thought is clearly and distinctly conceived, the immediate judgments which the mind unhesitatingly affirms with regard to it are always true. As will presently appear, I do not hold a brief for the Cartesian criterion; on the contrary, I have no doubt whatever that the Cartesian criterion taken by itself is inadequate. All I urge is that its inadequacy is not established by Kant's summary argument.

Let us turn to consider Kant's sweeping negation in relation to a different criterion, laid down by Empiricists.

I take the principle of Empiricism, as an epistemological doctrine, to be that the ultimately valid premises of all scientific reasonings are cognitions of particular facts; all the generalisations of science being held to be obtained from these particular cognitions by induction, and to depend upon these for their validity. I do not accept this principle; I think it impossible to establish the general truths of the accepted sciences by processes of cogent inference on the basis of merely particular premises; and I think the chief service that J. S. Mill rendered to philosophy, by his elaborate attempt to perform this task, was to make this impossibility as clear as day. But I wish now to avoid this controversy; and, in order to avoid it, I shall take the Empirical criterion as relating only to particular cognitions; leaving open the question how far we also require universal premises in the construction of science.

The criterion is briefly discussed by Mill (*Logic*, Book IV. chap. i. §§ 1, 2). It being understood that the validity of the general truths of the sciences depends on the correctness of induction from correct observation of particular facts, the question is what guarantee there is of the correctness of the observa-

CRITERIA OF TRUTH AND ERROR   443

tions?—in Mill's words "we have to consider what is needful in order that the fact supposed to be observed may safely be received as true." The answer is, "in its first aspect," very simple. "The sole condition is that what is supposed to have been observed shall really have been observed; that it be an observation—not an inference." The fulfilment, indeed, of this sole and simple condition is not—as Mill goes on to explain—so easy as it may appear; "for in almost every act of our perceiving faculties, observation and inference are intimately blended; what we are said to observe is usually a compound result of which one-tenth may be observation and nine-tenths inference." *E.g.* I affirm that I saw my brother at a certain hour this morning; this would commonly be said to be a fact known through the direct testimony of my senses. But the truth, Mill explains, is far otherwise; for I might have had visual sensations so similar as to be indistinguishable from those I actually had without my brother being there; I might have seen some one very like him, or it might have been a dream, or a waking hallucination; and if I had the ordinary evidence that my brother was dead, or in India, I should probably adopt one or other of these suppositions without hesitation. Now, obviously, "if any of these suppositions had been true, the affirmation that I saw my brother would have been erroneous"; but this does not, in Mill's view, invalidate the Empirical criterion, for "whatever was matter of direct perception, namely, the visual sensations, would have been real"; my apparent cognition of this reality (he tacitly assumes) would have been a true and valid cognition. In short, only separate observation from inference, and observation—or apparent knowledge obtained through observation —is absolutely valid and trustworthy; the idea that these are 'errors of sense' is itself a vulgar error, or at least a loose thought or phrase; there are no errors in direct sense-perception, but only erroneous inferences from sense.

Now I shall presently consider how far this criterion, taken in any sense in which it would be available for its purpose, is completely trustworthy. But, however that may be, it seems to me that Kant's sweeping negative argument—which we are now examining—has really no force against its validity. No doubt, according to Kant's general view of the form and matter of thought, this criterion, like the other, relates primarily to the form; for it rests on the distinction between two different functions of the knowing mind—Observation or Perception and Inference. But I see no reason to infer that it is *therefore* incapable of guaranteeing the material truth of Empirical cognition; or that the relation of the knowable world to the knowing mind cannot possibly be what Empiricism affirms it to be.

If now we contemplate together the two criteria that have been examined—the Cartesian and the Empirical—it is evident that, at least in its primary intention, neither alone covers the whole ground of

CRITERIA OF TRUTH AND ERROR 445

the premises for which verification is *prima facie* required. The Empirical criterion only verifies particular premises, and the Cartesian appears to be applied by its author primarily to universals—to what is "clearly and distinctly conceived by the pure understanding."

This leads me to suggest that Kant has perhaps taken too strictly the demand for a 'universal' (*allgemein*) criterion of truth. He has understood it to be a demand for some ascertainable characteristic —other than truth—always found to belong to valid cognitions, and never found in invalid ones. And no doubt a criterion of this scope is what any philosopher would like to get; but any one who has realised the slow, prolonged, tortuous process by which the human intellect has attained such truth as it has now got, will thankfully accept something less complete. If (*e.g.*) any epistemological doctrine offers, among the commonly accepted premises of scientific reasoning, to mark out a substantial portion to which the stamp of philosophic certainty may be affixed; or if, again, it offers to cut out a class of invalid and untrustworthy affirmations, to warn us off a region in which our natural impulse to affirm or believe must, if indulged, produce mere illusion and semblance of knowledge—then, if either offer is made good, we shall gratefully accept it as a philosophic gain.

Now it is remarkable that in both these ways, but especially in the latter way, Kant undoubtedly does offer general criteria of truth which, if valid, are of immense importance. Indeed, it is the very aim and purpose of his *Critical Philosophy*—as its name indicates—to establish such criteria: it is its aim, by a critical examination of our faculties of knowledge, to cut off and stamp as manifest illusion the whole mass of beliefs and affirmations with regard to 'things in themselves' which common sense naïvely makes, and which—or some of which—previous dogmatic philosophers had accepted as valid. At the same time, by the same critical analysis, Kant seeks to stamp with philosophic precision and certitude the fundamental principles of physical knowledge—as that every event has a cause, and the quantum of substance in the physical world is unchangeable—while restricting the application of these principles to phenomena.

And here I would remark that the main importance for philosophy of the epistemological question brought into prominence by Kantian Criticism—the question as to the Limits of human knowledge—seems to depend upon its connexion with the question with which we are now concerned—the inquiry after criteria. For our interest in Kant's inquiry into the limits of knowledge certainly depends on the fact that the limits which the critical thinker aims at establishing have been actually transgressed by other thinkers. It therefore implies an actual claim to validity on behalf of assertions transgressing the limits which the criticist denies: so that he may be viewed as propounding in respect of these assertions a criterion for distinguishing truth from error, which stamps them as error. It is true that as regards a part of the assertions he discusses—*e.g.* as to the infinity or finiteness of Space and Time, or the infinite or finite divisibility of matter—the criticist finds a controversy going on which implies error on one side or the other: but by his criterion he decides that there is error on both sides, the 'antinomy' which leads to controversy in each case arising from a fundamental misconception common to both sides.

It is no part of my plan to criticise Kant's epistemology: what I am rather concerned to point out is that his system is embarrassed in a quite special manner by the difficulty that besets every constructive epistemology—the difficulty of finding a satisfactory answer to the question, 'Quis custodiet custodem?' For the claim of Criticism is to establish the limits of human knowledge by an examination of man's faculties of knowledge: but the proposition that we have faculties of cognition so and so constituted can only be an inference from the proposition that we have such and such valid cognitions. It would thus seem that the Critical procedure must presuppose that truth adequately distinguished from error has already been certainly obtained in some departments. And in fact this presupposition is frankly made by Kant so far as Mathematics and Physical Science are concerned. He expressly takes their validity as a *datum*. Mathematics, he tells us (*Proleg.* § 40), "rests on its own evidence," and Physical Science "on experience and its thoroughgoing confirmation": neither study stands in need of Criticism "for its own safety and certainty." And he similarly assumes the validity and completeness of Formal Logic as the starting-point for his *Transcendental Analytic*.

If, therefore, we ask for a criterion of truth and error in Mathematical and Logical Judgments—and error undeniably occurs in both—or in the Empirical cognitions which confirm the general propositions of physical science, we cannot obtain this from Kantian criticism without involving the latter in a *circulus in probando*. We are therefore *prima facie* thrown back in the former case on the Cartesian or some similar criterion for guaranteeing 'truths of reason,' in the latter case on some Empirical criterion for guaranteeing 'truths of fact.'

I turn, therefore, to examine more closely these two criteria. With regard to the former, however, it may be thought that such examination is now superfluous, since the historic failure of Descartes' attempt to extend the evidence of mathematics to his physical and metaphysical principles has sufficiently shown its invalidity. "*Securus judicat orbis terrarum*"; and the inadequacy of the Cartesian criterion may be thought to be now '*res judicata.*' On the other hand, Mr. Spencer has in recent times put forward a criterion which, so far as it relates to universal cognitions, has at least a close affinity to the Cartesian. I propose, therefore, to begin by some consideration of the earlier proposition.

I may begin by saying that Descartes' statement

of his criterion hardly satisfies his own requirements, *i.e.* it is not quite clear what he means by the 'clearness' of a notion. I think that it will render Descartes' meaning with sufficient precision to drop the word 'clear,' keeping 'distinct' (which, he says, involves 'clear'), and explain a distinct notion of any object to be one that is not liable to be confounded with that of any different object—'object' being taken to denote any distinguishable element or aspect of Being, in the sense in which Descartes uses 'Being' as a wider term than Existence, and includes under it the objects of mathematical thought.

One further modification of Descartes' statement seems expedient: Descartes applies the term 'clear' (or 'distinct') 'conception' to the cognition of the connexion of subject and predicate in a true judgment, as well as to the notions taken separately. But it seems desirable to make more explicit the distinction between the two; since the indistinctness that causes error may be held to lie not in the latter but in the former.

We may state our question, then, as follows: "Is error in universal judgments certainly excluded by a distinct conception of the subject and predicate of the judgment and of their connexion?" But this at once suggests a second question: "Why does Descartes hold it to be excluded?" And here it is noteworthy that he nowhere affirms the infallibility of his criterion to be intuitively known. He seems to have three ways of establishing it: (1) He presents it as implied in the certainty of his conscious existence (*Meth.* iv.

and *Med.* iii.); (2) he presents it as a deduction from the veracity of God (*Princ.* xxix., xxx.); (3) he rests it on an appeal to the experience of his readers (*Réponses aux II^{des} Objections*, Demande vii.). The first two procedures appear to me obviously unsatisfactory;[1] I therefore propose only to consider the Empirical basis of the criterion.

Let us ask, then, whether, when error occurs and we are convinced of it, in mathematical or logical assertions, experience shows it to have occurred through want of distinctness in our conceptions? Now — excluding the case of reasoning in which symbols are used more or less mechanically, so that error when it occurs is usually due to a casual lapse of memory—I find that Descartes' view is confirmed by my experience in a certain sense; but not in a sense which tends to establish the adequacy of his criterion. That is, the discovery of any such error seems always to involve the discovery of a past confusion of thought; but, in some cases at least, *before* the discovery of the error the thought *appeared* to be quite free from confusion, so that the most conscientious application of the criterion would not have saved me from error. I suppose the experience of others to be similar. Let me take as an illustration a mathematical error of an eminent thinker which I transiently shared.

[1] The certainty of the proposition 'sum cogitans' surely does not carry with it the certainty of the only discoverable general reason for accepting it as certain; and—as the veracity of God has to be demonstrated—the second procedure involves Descartes in a logical circle, as has often been observed.

In an attack on Metageometry (*Metaph.* Book II. chap. ii.) Lotze, discussing Helmholtz's fiction of an intelligent being whose life and experience are confined to the surface of a sphere, remarks that such a being, if it moved in a small circle of the sphere, would find that "the meridians known to it from other experiences make smaller angles with its path on the side" towards the pole of the circle, "and greater on the opposite side." On first reading this sentence I thought I could see clearly the fact as stated; then, on further consideration, I saw that the meridians must cut the small circle at right angles; then—reflecting on my momentary error in order to see how I had been misled—I perceived that the object I had been contemplating in idea was not a true spherical surface, but a confused mixture or *tertium quid* between such a surface and its projection on a plane. When discovered, the confusion seemed very palpable; but the opposite view had seemed clear and distinct when I agreed with Lotze's assertion, and I could not doubt that it had seemed so to Lotze himself.

I do not therefore think the Cartesian criterion useless; on the contrary, I believe that I have actually saved myself from error by applying it. But the experience to which Descartes appeals seems to me to show that judgments, universal and particular, often present themselves with an illusory semblance of distinct conception or perception which cannot be stripped from them by direct reflection; though it often vanishes at once when the judgment is otherwise demonstrated to be erroneous. In the case of perception Descartes expressly recognises this; he speaks (*Med.* iii.) of the existence of things outside him exactly like his ideas as something which "I thought I perceived very clearly, though in reality I did not perceive it all." In this case, however, the Empirical criterion offers a guarantee against error by the rigorous separation of observation from inference. This guarantee I will now proceed to examine.

I may begin by remarking a curious interchange of *rôles* between Rationalism and Empiricism as regards the evidence claimed for their respective criteria. While the Rationalist's criterion is partly supported, as we have seen, on an appeal to experience, the validity of the Empirical criterion appears to be treated as self-evident. At least this seems to be implied in Mill's language before referred to; where, after pointing out various possible sources of error in the affirmation that "I saw my brother this morning," he says that if any of these possibilities had been realised, "the affirmation that I saw my brother would have been erroneous: but *whatever was matter of direct perception, namely, the visual sensations, would have been real.*" For his argument requires us to understand the last sentence as meaning not merely that there would have been sensations for me to perceive, but that my perception of them would certainly have been free from error: and as no empirical proof is offered of this last proposition, it seems to have been regarded as not requiring proof.

But—even if we assume, to limit the discussion, that a man cannot, strictly speaking, observe anything except his own states of consciousness—it still seems paradoxical to affirm that the elimination of all inference from such observation would leave a residuum of certainly true cognition : considering the numerous philosophical disputes that have arisen from the conflicting views taken by different thinkers of psychical experiences supposed to be similar. Take (*e.g.*) the controversy since Hume about the impossibility of finding a self in the stream of psychical experience, or that as to the consciousness of free-will, or the disinterestedness of moral choice, or the feeling-tone of desire; surely in view of these and other controversies it would be extraordinarily rash to claim freedom from error for our cognitions of psychical fact, let them be never so rigorously purged of inference.

The truth seems to be that the indubitable certainty of the judgment 'I am conscious' has been rather hastily extended by Empiricists to judgments affirming that my present consciousness is such and such. But these latter judgments necessarily involve an *implicit* comparison and classification of the present consciousness with elements of past conscious experience recalled in memory: and the implied classification may obviously be erroneous either through inaccuracy of memory or a mistake in the comparative judgment. And the risk of error cannot well be avoided by eliminating along with inference this implicit classification : for the psychical fact observed cannot be distinctly thought at all without it: if we rigorously purge it away, there will be nothing left save the cognition of self and of we cannot say what psychical fact. Nay, it is doubtful whether even this much will be left for the Empiricist's observation: since he may share Hume's inability to find a self in the stream of psychical experience, or to maintain a clear distinction between psychical and material fact. Thus the Empiricist criterion, if extended to purge away comparison as well as inference, may leave us nothing free from error but the bare affirmation of Fact not further definable.

Here again I am far from denying the value of the Empirical criterion. I have no doubt of the importance of distinguishing the inferential element in our apparently immediate judgments as far as we can, with a view to the elimination of error. Only the assertion that we can by this procedure obtain a residuum of certainly true cognition seems to me neither self-evident nor confirmed by experience.

I pass to examine the criterion propounded by Mr. Herbert Spencer in his *Principles of Psychology* (part vii. chaps. ix.-xii.): which, in his view, is applicable equally to particular and universal cognitions. It is there laid down that "the inconceivableness of its negation is that which shows a cognition to possess the highest rank—is the criterion by which its unsurpassable validity is known." . . . "If the negation of a proposition is inconceivable"—*i.e.* "if its terms cannot by any effort be brought before consciousness in that relation which the proposition asserts between them"—we "have the highest possible logical justification for holding it to be unquestionable." This is, in Mr. Spencer's view, the Universal Postulate, on the validity of which the validity of all reasoning depends.

Before we examine the validity of the criterion, the meaning of the term 'inconceivable' requires some discussion. In replying to a criticism by J. S. Mill, Mr. Spencer—while recognising that 'inconceivable' is sometimes loosely used in the sense of 'incredible'—repudiates this meaning for his own use. But I agree with Mill in regarding this repudiation as hasty, so far as the criterion is applied to propositions that represent particular facts—e.g. "I feel cold." For in most cases in which such a statement is made it would not be true to say "I cannot conceive myself not feeling cold," since only very intense sensation excludes the imagination or conception of a feeling opposite in quality. We might, no doubt, say, "I cannot conceive that I am not feeling cold": but the form of this sentence shows that I have passed from conception, strictly taken, to belief. Spencer's contention that in this case the connexion of the predicate-notion "feeling cold" with the subject-notion "self" is for the time "absolute," though only "temporarily," seems to me to ignore the complexity of consciousness. According to my experience, disagreeable sensations, when not too violent, even tend to excite the opposite imagination, e.g. great thirst is apt to be attended by a recurrent imagination of cool spring water gurgling down my throat. I cannot therefore agree that the utmost certainty in a proposition representing a transient empirical fact involves the 'inconceivability' of its negation—except in a peculiar sense of the term in which it is equivalent to 'intuitive incredibility.'

It is, no doubt, otherwise in the case of universal propositions intuitively known—or, in Mr. Spencer's phrase, "cognitions in which the union of subject and predicate is permanently absolute." I cannot imagine or conceive two straight lines enclosing a space : here 'intuitive incredibility' coincides with 'inconceivability' in the strict sense; only either attribute must be taken with the qualification that I can suppose my inability to conceive or believe to be due to a defect of my intellect.

With this explanation, I shall allow myself to use Mr. Spencer's term in a stricter or looser sense, according as the cognition in question is universal or particular. I have no doubt that 'inconceivability of negation,' so understood, is normally an attribute of propositions that appear self-evident truths; I think that, in trying to comprehend distinctly the degree of certainty attaching to any such proposition, we commonly do apply—more or less consciously—Mr. Spencer's test, and that a systematic application of it is a useful protection against error. But I think that the objection before urged against the infallibility of the Cartesian criterion applies equally to Mr. Spencer's. Indeed he admits "that some propositions have been wrongly accepted as true, because their negations were supposed inconceivable when they were not." But he argues that this "does not disprove the validity of the test"; chiefly because (1) "they were complex propositions, not to be established by a test applicable only to propositions no further decomposable"; and (2) this test, like any other, is liable to yield untrue results, "either from incapacity or from carelessness in those who use it." The force of the second admission depends on the extension given to 'incapacity.' Casual and transient incapacity—similar to the occasional logical fallacies that occur in ordinary reasoning—would not seriously impair the value of the criterion; but how if the historical divergences of thought indicate obstinate and wide-spread incapacity? Mr. Spencer seems to hold that this is not the case if we limit the application of the criterion to simple propositions; thus he contrasts the complexity of the erroneous proposition maintained by those who regarded the existence of antipodes as inconceivable with the simplicity of the propositions that "embody the ultimate relations of space." But the proposition that "heavy things must fall downward" is apparently as simple as the proposition that "two straight lines cannot enclose a space"; and if analysis reveals complexity in the notions connected in the former proposition, this is equally the case with the latter, according to Spencer's own account of spatial perception: since, in his view, any perception of space involves "an aggregate of simultaneous states of consciousness symbolising a series of states to which it is found equivalent."

The difficulty of applying this criterion is forcibly presented when we examine the philosophical doctrine to support which it is especially propounded. For Mr. Spencer's primary aim in establishing it is to defend Realism against Idealism: this he regards as vital to his system, since "if Idealism is true, the doctrine of Evolution is a dream." Now, he nowhere, I think, expressly defines Realism: but his argument throughout implies that what is defended is the proposition that the Non-ego exists independently of the Ego. It is this proposition of which he seems to hold the negation inconceivable in any particular case of external perception: as (*e.g.*) where he speaks (*Princ. of Psych.* § 441) of the "primary deliverances of consciousness which yield subject and object as independent existences": and it is in this sense, as I understand, that in his *First Principles* (§§ 44, 45) he speaks of the "division of self from not-self" as "the primordial datum of Philosophy." If now we ask what 'self' and 'not-self' exactly mean, it is explained that we apply the term *Self, Ego*, to an aggregate or series of faint states of consciousness, and the terms *Not-self, Non-ego*, to an aggregate or series of vivid states: "or rather more truly—each order of manifestations carries with it the irresistible implication of some power that manifests itself, and by the words *Ego* and *Non-ego* respectively we mean the power that manifests itself in the faint forms, and the power that manifests itself in the vivid forms" (*First Principles*, § 44).

Now the proposition that an aggregate of vivid

states of consciousness *plus* a power that manifests itself in them is independent of an aggregate of faint states *plus* a power that manifests itself in these is certainly not simple; while, if we try to decompose it into more elementary propositions, it seems impossible to obtain any which we can even suppose Mr. Spencer to regard as guaranteed by his criterion. For, since states of consciousness *prima facie* imply a conscious self to which they are attributed, we cannot suppose Mr. Spencer to regard as inconceivable the negation of the independent existence of an external object so far as this is taken to be an aggregate of vivid states of consciousness; especially as he sometimes uses the term 'existence beyond consciousness' as an equivalent for the independent *non-ego*. Are we to take, then, as the fundamental doctrine of Realism, established by the criterion, the proposition that the power manifested in the vivid states exists independently of the power manifested in the faint states? But again it seems impossible to suppose that Mr. Spencer regards the negation of this proposition as inconceivable, because, first, he holds that "it is one and the same ultimate reality that is manifested to us subjectively and objectively" (*Princ. of Psych.* § 273); and secondly, he holds that this ultimate reality or Power "is totally and for ever inconceivable" and "unknowable" (*First Principles*, part i. chap. v.).

I cannot indeed reconcile these two statements—I should have thought that we could not reasonably attribute either unity or duality to a totally unknowable entity: but if either of the two is maintained, it surely cannot at the same time be maintained that the negation of two independent Powers is inconceivable.

I conclude, therefore, that Mr. Spencer's Universal Postulate is inadequate to guarantee even the primordial datum of his own philosophy; and, on the whole, that—however useful it may be in certain cases—it will not, any more than the criteria before examined, provide the bulwark against scepticism of which we are in search. With this negative conclusion I must here end. In a later article I hope[1] to treat the problem with which I have been dealing in a somewhat more positive manner.

[1] [Owing to the illness and death of the author some months later this hope was never realised; but appended is the concluding portion of the second of two lectures entitled *Verification of Beliefs*, which probably furnishes in rough outline some part of what the later article would have contained. The lectures belong to a course on Metaphysics.]

APPENDIX TO THE PRECEDING ESSAY

ON the whole, then, I have to reject the claims of Empiricism no less than of Rationalism to put forward a simple infallible criterion for the kind of knowledge which is to be taken as the ultimately valid basis of all else that is commonly taken for knowledge. I regard both criteria as *useful*, as a means of guarding against error, but neither as infallible. I propose, then, to turn from infallible criteria to what I call methods of verification: from the search after an absolute test of truth to the humbler task of excluding error.

One of these methods I call the Intuitive Verification. It includes as two species the Rationalist and the Empiricist criteria somewhat modified. They may be regarded as two applications of a wider rule : Assure yourself of the self-evidence of what appears self-evident, by careful examination. As regards universals, especially scrutinise both the clearness and distinctness of the notions connected in a judgment, and the intuitive certainty of their connexion. As regards particular judgments, especially purge observation of inference so far as reflection enables you to do this.

These, I think, are valuable rules; but even after they have been observed as carefully as they can be observed, we may be convinced of error through *conflict* of the judgment thus apparently guaranteed with some other judgment relating to the same matter which is equally strongly affirmed by us.

This indeed is the most common way in which error is discovered. Such conflict does occur, even as regards the universal intuitions of reason or the conclusions demonstrated from them : indeed in this region it is sometimes obstinate and is then called an 'antinomy.' It is more familiar in the case of particular judgments—whether relating to matter or to mind. But perhaps the most important case of the kind is a conflict between a universal judgment accepted as self-evident, and the particular judgments of perception, or inference from these. The fate of the belief that "a thing cannot act where it is not" may illustrate this. It was found to conflict apparently with the hypothesis of universal gravitation, which rested on a multitude of particular observations of the position of the heavenly bodies; and this has, I think, destroyed any appearance of intuitive certainty in it for most of us. And I may illustrate it further by the method by which in my work on Ethics Common Sense is led to Utilitarianism.[1] This was, indeed, suggested by the method of Socrates, whose ethical discussion brought to light latent conflicts of this kind. It was evident (*e.g.*) to Polemarchus that 'it was just to give every man his own'; but being convinced that it is not just to restore to a mad friend his own sword, his faith in his universal maxim was shaken.[2]

Now it is possible that what I have called the Intuitive Verification might exclude error in some of these cases, one of the conflicting intuitions being due to inadvertence. If we had examined more carefully the supposed universal truth, or the supposed particular fact of observation, we might have detected the inadvertence, or at any rate have seen that we had mistaken for an intuition what was merely inference or belief accepted on authority. But the history of thought shows that I cannot completely rely upon the Intuitive Verification alone.

It seems, then, that the Intuitive or Cartesian Verification needs to be supplemented by a second, which I will call the Discursive Verification, the object of which is to exclude the danger of the kind of conflict I have indicated. It consists in contemplating the belief that appears intuitively certain along with other beliefs which may possibly be found to conflict with it. Of course we are always liable to obtain new beliefs which will conflict with old ones; therefore this verification is necessarily fallible. Still we may reduce the danger of failure by carefully grouping the intuitions that we see to be related, and

[1] Cf. *Methods of Ethics*, Bk. III. chaps. iii.-xi.
[2] Cf. Plato's *Republic*, Bk. I. p. 331.

surveying them together in the most systematic order possible. It would, I think, be a gain if ethical and metaphysical writers would take more pains to state implicitly in the best attainable order the propositions they ask the reader to accept without proof. I may observe that among the chief of our particular beliefs which we commonly regard as intuitively certain —those relating to the External World—there is a natural concatenation which enables us to dispense with an artificial one; we may trust our ordinary physical beliefs with regard to the [roughly measured] size, shape, and relative position of familiar objects, because if we made a mistake we should find it out.

The most noteworthy application of the Discursive Verification is to the relations between universal propositions which appear self-evident, and the particular beliefs which they implicitly include. We continually have this verification in the case of Mathematics, though in the case of Geometry only indirectly and approximately. We see universally and necessarily that two straight lines cannot enclose a space; the lines we meet with in experience as boundaries are not exactly straight, but the more nearly straight they are the less space is it possible for two such lines to include, if they meet in two points. We might call this case of the Discursive Verification, Inductive Verification: it may be applied either to intuitive beliefs directly, or to beliefs demonstratively inferred from them.

Comparing the Intuitive and Discursive Verifications, we see that while the former lays stress on the need of clearness, distinctness, precision, in our thought, the latter—the Discursive —brings into prominence the value of *system*. The gain of system in any part of our thought is not merely (1) that it enables us to *grasp* a large and complicated mass of cognitions, or even (2) that it prevents our overlooking any hiatus, or lapse through forgetfulness, which may be either important in itself or in its bearing on other cognition, but (3) that it provides against the kind of error which the conflict of beliefs reveals. And this, I may say, is the kind of service which Philosophy may be expected to render to the sciences.

I have spoken of the history of thought as revealing discrepancy between the intuitions of one age and those of a subsequent generation. But where the conflicting beliefs are not contemporaneous, it is usually not clear that the earlier thinker would have maintained his conviction if confronted by the arguments of the later. The history of thought, however, I need hardly say, affords abundant instances of similar conflict among contemporaries; and as conversions are extremely rare in philosophical controversy, I suppose the conflict in most cases affects intuitions—what is self-evident to one mind is not so to another. It is obvious that in any such conflict there must be error on one side or the other, or on both. The natural man will often decide unhesitatingly that the error is on the other side. But it is manifest that a philosophic mind cannot do this, unless it can prove independently that the conflicting intuitor has an inferior faculty of envisaging truth in general or this kind of truth; one who cannot do this must reasonably submit to a loss of confidence in any intuition of his own that thus is found to conflict with another's.[1]

We are thus led to see the need of a third Verification, to supplement the two former; we might call it the Social or Oecumenical Verification. It completes the process of philosophical criteria of error which I have been briefly expounding. This last, as we are all aware, with many persons, probably the majority of mankind, is the Criterion or Verification practically most prominent; if they have such verification in the case of any belief, neither lack of self-evidence in the belief itself, nor lack of consistency when it is compared with other beliefs, is sufficient to disturb their confidence in it. And its practical importance, even for more reflective and more logical minds, grows with the growth of knowledge, and the division of intellectual labour which attends it; for as this grows, the proportion of the truths that enter into our systematisation, which for any individual have to depend on the *consensus of experts*, continually increases. In fact, in provisionally taking Common Sense as the point of departure for philosophical construction, it was this criterion that we implicitly applied. The Philosopher, I conceive, at the present day, starts with the

[1] Cf. *Methods of Ethics*, pp. 341-342. Chap. xi. contains a discussion of these criteria in special application to Ethics.

particular sciences; they give the matter which it is his business—I do not say his whole business, but a part of his business—to systematise. But how is he to know what matter to take? He cannot, in this age, be an expert in all sciences; he must, then, *provisionally* accept the judgment of Common Sense. Provisionally, I say, not finally; in working out his Epistemological principles in application to the sciences, he may correct or define more precisely some fundamental conception, point out a want of cogency in certain methods, limit the scope of certain premises and certain conclusions. Especially will he be moved to do this when he finds confusion and conflict in comparing and trying to reduce to system the fundamental conceptions, premises, and methods of different sciences.

Let me now sum up briefly the triple exclusion of error which I have been expounding. I disclaim the pretension of establishing absolute truth or absolute exclusion of error. But if we find that an intuitive belief appears clear and certain to ourselves contemplating it, that it is in harmony with our other beliefs relating to the same subject, and does not conflict with the beliefs of other persons competent to judge, we have reduced the risk of error with regard to it as low as it is possible to reduce it.

At a later period I shall try to co-ordinate and compare the different kinds and degrees of imperfect certitude or provisional acceptance in which we have to acquiesce in cases where this triple verification cannot be obtained. Practically, the most important points are raised when one of the three verifications is wanting, while the other two are obtained entirely, or to a great extent.

Thus there are chiefly three questions :—

1. How to regard fundamental assumptions which lack self-evidence, but are confirmed or not contradicted by other beliefs relating to the same matter and accepted by Common Sense.

2. How to deal with 'antinomies,' or obstinate conflicts of beliefs not peculiar to the individual thinker but shared by others.

3. How to deal with points of unsettled controversy, where,

after clearing away all misunderstandings, we come upon what seems to be an ultimate difference of intuitive judgment.[1]

By way of summary, I may point out that modern Epistemology began with an inquiry for a universal criterion for distinguishing truth and error. Rationalism in Descartes propounded a simple infallible criterion [for 'truths of reason']; Empiricism the like for the particular judgments of experience which it regards as the only ultimate valid premises. But I have not proposed any such infallible criterion. After discarding the dogmatism as to the limits of knowledge, of the *soi-disant* Critical Philosophy, I turned from criteria to Verifications: *i.e.* I converted the original 'search after an absolute test of truth to the humbler task of devising modes of excluding error.'

These verifications are based on experience of the ways in which the human mind has actually been convinced of error, and been led to discard it: *i.e.* three modes of conflict, conflict between a judgment first formed and the view of this judgment taken by the same mind on subsequent reconsideration; conflict between two different judgments, or the implications of two partially different judgments formed by the same mind under different conditions; and finally, conflict between the judgments of different minds.

Each of these experiences reveals a danger of error, and on each we may base a process for partially excluding error.

The first danger we meet by a serious effort to obtain clearness, distinctness, precision in our concepts, and definite subjective self-evidence in our judgment. The second we meet by a similar effort to attain system and coherence. The third we meet by endeavouring to attain Consensus of Experts, and so from individual variations and temporary conflicts of opinion educe the judgments of the general mind that, as Browning says, "receives life in parts to live in a whole." But I do not put these on a par. Indeed, it will be evident from the very words used that the second is of special and pre-eminent

---

[1] Another interesting question which chiefly comes into view practically in dealing with inferior grades of certainty is the relation of volition to belief, what constitutes practical or moral certainty, and whether certitudes can—and, if so, ought to be—attained by volition.

importance. For the ideal aim of philosophy is systematisation —the exhibition of system and coherence in a mass of beliefs which, as presented by Common Sense, are wanting therein. But the special characteristic of *my* philosophy is to keep the importance of the others in view.

INDEX

Absolute: for Hamilton, 196 f.; can it be known, and how far? Kant's answer to these questions, 204, 205; different uses of the term, 203 ff.; Fichte's view of (cf. Unconditioned), 205 f.; for Kant, is God, 204, 205; Subject, 140, this not to be confused with Simple Substance, 141, 142, 145, 146, 148
Agnosticism, 178, 268-270; and Relativism, 267, 274; (Kantian or Spencerian) and Common Sense and Science, 210 f.
Analogies of Experience: 98-116; principle of, 99 (cf. Substance, Causality, Community)
'Antecedents' and 'Elements,' confusion between, 376, 389 (cf. 'Mental Chemistry')
Anticipations of Perception (or Observation), principle of, 93 f.
Antinomies, 137; questions raised by, 139; mathematical, 152-161, 162 f., 396; critical solution of, 156; first of the, 152 ff., 162-168; Leibnizo-Wolffian solution of the second, 157 f.; the second, 153 ff.
Antinomies, dynamical, 162 ff., especially 168-178, *passim*; both negative and affirmative answers to, may be true, 170; positive and negative, relation between, 174; and theology, 178; first and third, 163 ff.; Kant's different answers to mathematical and dynamical antinomies, 166
'Appearance' (or Phenomenon), meaning of, 283 f.
Aristippus, 343
Aristophanes, 358
Aristotle, 41, 329, 339, 343, 346, 352, 358, 432; his *Ethics*, 362, 365 f.; his *Logic*, 78, 78 n., 79, 80, 81, 82
Association, psychology of, 376
Axioms of Intuition (or Perception), principle of, 90 f.

Bain, 385
Beattie, 408, 409
Beliefs, certain: may be known primarily or derivatively, 437 f.; three chief classes of, 436 f.; and probable, 435 f.
Berkeley, 217, 286, 412, 413, 418; Kant's estimation of, 11; on Idealism, 74

Caird, Dr. E., 74, 105, 196; his *Philosophy of Kant*, 74 n.
Campbell, Prof., 323 f., 337 n.
Categories, Kant's: 62 f.; of Quantity and Quality, 82, 85 f.; of Relation, 98 f.; of Modality, 116 f.; schematism of, 88 f.
Causality: Free, Unconditioned, and Natural, 164, 168-177, *passim*; principle of, 109, 110, 136, 137; transcendental proof of principle of, 106-113, *passim*; this proof criticised, 110-113
'Cause,' 106
Certainty (or Knowledge): rational and empirical, apodeictic and assertoric, 22, 119, 128; *a priori* and *a posteriori*, 124, etc.
Chrysippus, 345 n.
Clarke, Samuel, 164
Cognitive Faculties, threefold division of, 21, 22
Coleridge: and Schelling, 267; his *Biographia Literaria*, 267 n.
Common Sense, 291; and Philosophy, reconciliation between, attempted by Berkeley and Brown, by Reid and Hamilton, 310; Philosophy of, 406-429; this title defended, 407 f.; plain, 415; Scottish, philosophy of, and Kantism, 272; the starting-point for philosophical construction, 464
'Constitutive' and 'Regulative' principles, 99
Contingency and Mutability, 175

469

Convention' and 'Nature' (νόμος and φύσις), 365; distinction between, incident to dawn of ethical reflection, 363 f.
Cope, 324, 365
Cousin, 393
Criteria: of Truth, 4, 5, 8, 430-467; summary of, 466; the central problem of Epistemology, 430; of General Consent, difficulties involved in, 381 f., 385; of Immediacy, 383, and appeal to experts on behalf of, 385, and objections to, 383 f., 390; Cartesian (Rationalist) and Empiricist, evidence for, 452; different scope of the Empiricist and Cartesian, 444, 445; Empiricist, as given by J. S. Mill, 442 f.; of inferred beliefs, provided by Logic, 438 f.; Intuitive, 318-319
Critical standpoint, 1 ff.
Crude Realism, 293, 320
Curtius, 323, 357
Cynics, 337

Darwin, 432
Darwinian Theory, 413
Descartes, 11, 12, 178, 184 f., 198, 373, 412, 413, 420, 421, 433, 448, 449 f., 452; his Criterion of Truth, 319, 439, 441; this not disposed of by Kant's argument, 441, 442; his *Discourse on Method*, 7, 449; his *Meditations*, 450, 452; his *Principles of Philosophy*, 450; his *Answers to Objections*, 450
Diogenes Laertius, 339 f., 341 n.
Dionysodorus, 336, 342
Divine Mind (or Spirit): for Green, 242, 244 f., 258-266, *passim* (cf. God, Spiritual Principle, Eternal Consciousness, etc.); (or Divine, or Primal, Being) and its relation to finite minds and material world, 282
Dogmatism, 181, 182, 183; and Empiricism, compared by Kant to Platonism and Epicureanism, 9 n.

Empedocles, 330
Empirical or Experiential, meaning of terms, 372-373
Empirical Philosophy, an *Epistemological* doctrine, 372; its incoherence, 372-391 (cf. Empiricism)
Empiricism (cf. Empirical Philosophy), 196 f.; according to Kant, 180 f.; and Mathematics, as types of definite knowledge, 373-374; and Natural Science, 373; English, its antagonism to German post-Kantian Philosophy, 197 ff.; Epistemological principle of, 442; fundamental doctrine of, 374 f., 380; how this can be philosophically established, 380 f.; Materialistic and Mentalistic, 387 f.; two accounts of its preliminary assumptions, 381 f. Empiricist criterion examined, 452 f.
Ens Realissimum, 188, 191 f., 199
Epicurus, 276
Epistemology, its primary aim, 431-434; term not used by H. Spencer, 275
Erdmann, J. E., 357
Eristic, 336 f., 339, 347, 348; only one kind in Plato's view, 338; Plato's changing views of, 346; and Dialectic, 336 f., 346 f.; and Sophistic, 349, and Plato's use of these two terms, 346, 347
Euclid, 437
Euripides, 344
Euthydemus, 342
'Experience': not explicable by 'Natural' history, 214 f.; ways in which knowledge may be 'founded on,' 374 ff.; world of, How does it come to be for human minds? Common Sense and Kantian answers, 61 f.
Externality and *a priority*, ambiguity of these notions, 38, 39, 40, 158

Fichte, his 'Absolute Ego,' 204, 206, 207
Finite minds and their relation to the material world, 282 f.
First Cause, 279 f.
'Force,' change in meaning of, 378 f.
Freedom, 169, 180 f.; and moral consciousness, 169, 170; Divine, 173, 178; human, 170; practical and transcendental, 170, 172

Geometrical knowledge, Kant's view of its relation to intuition, examined, 49-54
God: metaphysical idea of, 184 f.; Existence of: ontological proof of, 184, 186; Kant's argument against ontological proof of, stated, 192, and examined, 193-195; cosmological proof of, 188 f.; physico-theological proof of, 189; speculative and practical proofs for, 180 f.; Freedom and Immortality, 180, 182, and their relation to speculative and practical reason, 17-20, 23 (cf. 36, 37, Freedom)
Gorgias, 325 f., 332 f., 347, 348, 351, 353, 367, 370

INDEX

Grant, Sir A., 324, 365; his *Ethics of Aristotle*, 365 n.
Green, T. H., 1, 196, 209-266, *passim*; and Locke and Common Sense, 217, 238, 265; controversy of, with Sensationalism and Phenomenalism, 238, 239, 243, 265; his treatment of Error, 225, 253 f.; his relation to Kant, 227-230; his Spiritual (or Non-natural, or Eternal) Principle (or One Subject), 230 f.; his Spiritual Principle (or Conscious Intelligence) criticised, 231 f., 250, etc., 264; this Conscious Intelligence the unifying principle in the world of reality, as well as in the Cosmos of Experience, 220, 222 f., 230 f., 240, 242, 243 f., 255, 258-266, *passim*; his Metaphysical System is Idealistic and Spiritualistic Mentalism, 257 ff.; polemical aspect of his Metaphysical System, 265; in his view, Man a Free Cause, 248 f., 251 f., and self-conscious, 245, 251, 253, 264 f., and a composite or dual being, 258 f.; his view of the relation of God (the Spiritual Principle) to man, 222 f., 243 f., 258, and to the world, 262 f.; his Metaphysics and his Ethics cannot be reconciled, 263; can we really accept his account of Spirit, and does Green himself succeed in *thinking* it? 260 f.
Grote, G., 323-371, *passim*; his *Plato*, 354

Hamilton, Sir W., 1, 196 f., 203, 268 and n., 276; and Mansel, 268, 279; his acceptance of Free-Will, 270; his Agnosticism, 268 f., 270 f.; his metaphysical compromise, 270; his Natural Realism, 270, 271; his philosophical inconsistency, 272; his 'Philosophy of the Conditioned,' 268 and n., 279; his Primary, Secundo-primary, and Secondary qualities, 271; his edition of Reid's *Works*, 268 n.; his *Discussions on Philosophy*, 272 n.; his *Dissertations* in his edition of Reid's *Works*, 271 and n., 274 and n.; his *Lectures on Metaphysics*, 270 n., 272 n.
Hegel, 197, 198, 199, 393
Human consciousness and Eternal consciousness, relation between, in Green's view, 244 f., 245 n., 250; this view criticised, 245 f.
Human sensibility, fundamental forms of, 62
Hume, D., 32, 217, 223, 408, 409, 410 f., 418, 425, 453, 454; and Spencer, 309 n.; his treatment of Cause, 11, 79; Kant's estimation of, 11; his *Inquiry into the Human Understanding*, 410; his *Treatise on Human Nature*, 309 n., 410, 415
Hutcheson, Francis, 406, 407

Idealism: repudiated by Kant, 203, 206; problematical and dogmatic, 30
Imagination, function of, 63 f.
'Immediate,' ambiguity of, 383
'Inconceivable,' meaning of, 317, 455 f.
Inconsistency commonest sign of error, 461 (cf. Antinomy)
Independent, 280
Infinite, 269 f.; and Absolute (or Unconditioned), 196-207, *passim*, 279 f.
Intuitional Metaphysicians, 386
Isocrates, 334, 345 f., 353, 358; his *Encomium of Helen*, κατὰ τῶν Σοφιστῶν and περὶ Ἀντιδόσεως, 328 f.

Jones, Prof. H., 406
Jowett, Dr., 324
Just, The, 363 f., 369 f.

Kant, 1-207, *passim*, 220, 239, 261, 276, 395 ff., 408 f., 413; his problem in the *Critique of Pure Reason*, 15 f.; and Coleridge, 267-268; and Falckenberg, 1 n., 2; his relation to Spencer's Agnosticism and Green's Spiritualism, 1; his general relation to Descartes, Leibniz, and Wolff, 184; and Leibniz, 11, 12; and Locke, 10; his metaphysical criterion, 9 f.; his view on general criterion of truth stated and examined, 439 f., 445 f.; constructive and destructive sides of his doctrine, 267, 268 f.; his Epistemology specially embarrassed, 447, 448; his inconsistency, 30, 31; his limitation of human knowledge and inquiry after Criteria, 446 f.; his Cosmological Antinomies and Hamilton's Philosophy of the Conditioned, 269 f.; his philosophical aim, 3, 17, 18; his distinction between Metaphysics and other knowledge, 4; his Metaphysical system rather Phenomenalism than Spiritualism or Mentalism, 27; his view of the reality underlying phenomena, inconsistent, 28, 29 (cf. 36, *re* Time); his influence in England, 267-274; his *Critique of Judgment*: its relation to the *Critique of Pure Reason*, and *Critique* of *Practical Reason*, 205, 206 ; his *Critique of Practical Reason*, 18, 19, 28, 36 ; his *Introduction to Transcendental Logic* (*Critique of Pure Reason*), 439 and n., 440 ; his *Prolegomena to any Future Metaphysic*, 2, 2 n., 13, 17, 26, 27, 28, 29, 30, 31, 32, 39, 43, 291, 408 ; his *Critique of Pure Reason*, 2, 12, 13, 18, 21, 27, 30

Külpe, 287 n.

Leibniz, 144, 157, 160, 162, 163, 164, 183, 184 f., 198
Leibnizo-Wolffian Metaphysics, 148
Locke, 27, 271, 342, 420, 422 ; and Common Sense, 310 ; his Empiricism mentalistic, 388 ; his Epistemological position, 377-378
Logical priority, 41, 42
Lotze, error in his attack on Metageometry, 451 ; his *Metaphysics*, 451

Malebranche, 413, 422
Mansel, 1
Maudsley, Dr., 388
'May be,' 'must be,' and 'is,' different uses of, 116 ff.
Megarians, 337 ; their Eristic, 337
'Mental Chemistry,' 423, 424
Mentalism, 238 ; its fundamental assumption (that 'Nature' implies a non-natural principle), 227
Metaphysical propositions regarded as *a priori* and synthetical, universal, and necessary, 14, 15
'Metaphysical system,' meaning of, 275
Metaphysics : for Kant, 13, 14, 16, 21 ff. ; and Criticism, 6 ; Dogmatic, 22 ; chief question of, 282 ; compared with mathematical and physical science, 4, 5, 6, 7, 8, 9, 22, 24, 25, 49 ; compared with Pure Mathematics, 54 f. ; criterion of, for Kant, 9, 10, 11 ; limitation of, for Kant, 9, 10, 11
Methods of Verification : as opposed to infallible criteria, 461 f. ; questions in connexion with, 465 f. ; summed up, 465
Mill, James, 385
Mill, John Stuart, 196, 198, 385 ; his *Examination of Sir W. Hamilton's Philosophy*, 198 n. ; his *System of Logic*, 317, 442
Milton, 413
Mind and Matter, relation of, 32, 33

Modality, 116-127, *passim* ; categories of (Possibility, Actual Existence, and Necessity), 116-127
Moral Theology, 202
'Morally certain,' 426

Nature, 'a process of change,' 225-226 ; (for Green), an ordered system of objects, 224, 'a single unalterable all-inclusive system of relations,' 226, and implies a 'non-natural' principle, 226 f. ; Common Sense assumption concerning knowledge of, 107 ; Materialist (and Common Sense) view of, 222 ; Mentalist and Sensationalist view of, 223
'Necessary,' 280, 281 ; Being (Unconditional Substance), and Contingent Being, 174 f.

'Object,' 'objective,' Kantian use of, discussed, 69-77, 94, 95
Ontology, Wolff's view of, 145
Origin and validity, 375 ff.
Origin of ideas, an antiquarian inquiry, 378 f.
Oswald, 408 f.

Paralogisms of Pure Reason, 138 ff., 142 ; the author's view of, 143 ff.
Persistence of Force, 295, 297 f.
Phenomenalism, 239
'Philosopher,' contrasted with 'Polymath,' 404
Philosophic mind, naïve scepticism of, 433
Philosophy : aim of, 467 ; and Common Sense, relation between, 408, 412, 413 f. ; and Epistemology, and their relation, 430 f. ; as taught to Kant, 133 ff. ; of H. Spencer, 267, 321 ; of Common Sense (or Natural Dualism), 224—this contrasted with that of Green (Idealistic-Spiritualist) and of the Sensationalists, 224 ; Critical or Transcendental, 17, and the three divisions of this, 21 f.
Physical Science, Kant's view of its relation to the true Metaphysics, 167
Plato, 9 n., 325-371, *passim*, 373 ; his twofold use of the term *Sophist* (cf. Isocrates, 328 f.) corresponding to a twofold grouping of his dialogues, 332 f., 338 f., 359 f. ; his *Dialogues*, suggested chronological order of, 346 f., 359
Pope, 433
'Possibility,' ambiguity of, 123, 124
Postulates of Empirical thought, 116 ;

INDEX 473

examined and criticised, 120 ff.; Kant's schematism of, 121 ff.
Postulates of Practical Reason, 201, 202; Kant's view of, contrasted with English empiricism and post-Kantian philosophy in Germany, 202 f.
Priestley, 408, 409
Proof, transcendental method of, distinguished and described, 100; application of this proof to principle of Permanence of Substance, 100-105
Protagoras: 325 f., 329, 332 f., 339, 348, 351, 354, 358 f.
Psychical antecedents and concomitants of a cognition, their effect on its validity, 424 f.
Psychical experience, controversy as to the nature of, 452
Psychology, Rational: 143 ff.; and Empirical, 148, 149
Pure Mathematics, Kant's view of its relation to Intuition examined, 54-57
Pure Reason, Categorical Idea of (Psychological Idea), 140, 141
Pure Science of Nature: Does it exist? 58-60; How is it possible? 58 f.; principles of, 60
Pure Thought: its contribution to our knowledge of empirical objects, 77 f.; its relation to general (or formal) logic, 77 ff., and Kant's view of this relation criticised, 80 ff.

Quality, Kant's schematism of, criticised, 93-97
Quality, judgments and categories of, 82; schematism of categories of, 93 f.
Quantity, judgments of, 82 f.; categories of, 85; schematism of categories of, 88 f.
Quantity and Quality, their origin and explanatory efficacy discussed, and Kant's view criticised, 82 ff.; Kant's schematism of, criticised, 88-93
Quintilian, 345

Rational: and Empirical method, 132; Psychology, Cosmology, and Theology, 132, and Kantian criticism of, 133 ff.; Theology, 179 ff., and its importance, in Kant's view, 183-184
Real and Phenomenal, 158 f., 166
Realism and Mentalism, issue between, 313
Reality and Appearance, 171, 172, 173, 174
Reason, function of, 135 ff.; narrower and wider use of, 21
Reciprocal action (Community), transcendental proof of principle of, examined and described, 113-116
Refutation of Idealism, Kant's, 28
Reid, Thomas: 406-429, *passim*; and Locke, their relation to Empirical Psychology, 420; and the philosophy of Common Sense (Natural Dualism), 217, 238; his account of external perception, 421 ff.; his appeal to vulgar Common Sense, 413, and exaggerated estimate of it, 417 ff.; his dependence on the *argumentum ad risum*, 413, 414; his attitude to God, Freedom, Duty, and man's spirituality, 421; his dilemma as between Common Sense and expert opinion, 417; his *essential demand* is for *consistency* of philosophic beliefs, 415 f.; his estimation of Authority (general assent), 418, 419; his Psychology distinguished from his Epistemology, 420; his Psychology free from Materialism, 420; his view of the duty of the philosopher as philosopher, 416; his view that the Common Sense of the vulgar is shared by the philosopher, 414; his view of relation between philosopher and plain man, 416 f.; his *Inquiry into the Human Mind*, 409 f.
Reinhold, 197
Relation, categories of, 98-116, *passim*
Relativism, 268; and Natural Dualism, 268
Relativity: of Knowledge, 198 f., 270 f.; meanings of, 272-274

Schelling, 197, 199
Schematism, Kant's, 86 f., 121
Schwegler, 357
Science, 403 f.
Self, as Subject and as Object of knowledge, in Kant's view, 147 f., 149; emptiness of Kant's notion of, 150; Kant's notion of, criticised, 150, 151
Sensationalism, 312
Sensibility: forms of (Space and Time), 22 f., 26 f.; passivity of, 67
Sidgwick, H., his *Methods of Ethics*, 462, 464; his *Outlines of the History of Ethics*, 267
Simple: subject, and simple substances, 162, 163; substance, 141 (cf. Absolute)
Simplicity of the Soul, and simplicity of substance underlying empirical matter, 183
Smith, Adam, 406, 407

Socrates, 325-371, *passim*
Space: (for Kant), 91, 269 f.; (real), 158; and Time, 31 f.; 'Metaphysical exposition' of, 26 f., 38 f.; 'Transcendental exposition' of, 44 f.; examination of doctrine that universal synthetic judgments of, depend on Space being a form of intuition, 44-48
Speculative Reason, results of, modified by those of Practical Reason, 202
Speculative Thought and practical interests, 180 f., 183
Spencer, Herbert: 1, 196 f., 430, 455 f.; and Common Sense, 303; and English Empiricism, 277; and Hume, 309 n., 310; and Kant, 268, 277; and Monism, 287 and n., 307; and Realism, 310 f., 313, 320 f.; and Sir W. Hamilton, 268 f., 277; his Agnosticism, 277 ff.; and Mentalism, 285, 287, 298; and Natural Dualism, 285 f., 302; his Criterion (Universal Postulate), 296, 314, 316 f., 448 f.; its inadequacy, 458-460; his Dualism, 283 ff.; his doctrine of First Cause, 279 f., and of 'the Unknowable,' 276, 282 f., 286, 288; his Epistemological doctrines, 308-321; his Metaphysical doctrines, 275-308; his Philosophical *datum*, 286, 289, 458; his Philosophy, its scope and relations, 283 n.; his 'Supreme or Ultimate Verity,' 207, 281, 282, 287, 297-298; his use of Self, Ego, Not-self, and Non-ego, 458 f., and of the *term* 'Metaphysician,' 275; his view of Force, 295 f., of Matter (Non-ego), 282 f., and Mind (Ego), 302 f., and of Logic, 289 f.; his 'Transfigured Realism,' 292 f., 299 f.; his view of 'Religious Ideas,' etc., 276 f., 281 f.; on Space and Time, 32, 33; his 'vivid' and 'faint' manifestations or states, and their equation to 'Object' and 'Subject,' Non-ego and Ego, 284 f., 285-286, 292 f., 296 f., 299 f., 303 f.; Philosophy in his view concerned with phenomena, 283; why his system is called *Phenomenalism* and *Agnosticism* by the author, 283 and n.; his *First Principles*, 275 ff.; his *Principles of Psychology*, 303 ff.
Spinoza, 11
Stallbaum, 355
Subject and Object in cognition, 232 f.; Green's view of, criticised, 233 f.
Subjective Method, 388

Substance, 64, 98 f.; and Cause, schematism of, 64 f., 86 f.; principle of the permanence of, 99-105
Succession, objective and subjective, 108, 109
Successive apprehension of phenomena, 102, 107 f.

Thales, 276
Theology, 403 f.; and practical interests, 179 f.; and the thesis of the Antinomies, 182
Thing-in-itself, 73, 201, 203 f.
Thompson, Dr., 323 f., 345; his *Gorgias*, 367 n.
Thought: and Feeling, Green's view of the relation between, criticised, 265, 266; and Reality, relation of, 185 f.
Time, 101, 269 f.; (real), 158; and Change, 109; and Common Sense, 392-405; and Number, 56, 57; and Space, Are they entities of relational quality, or merely forms of sensibility? 33, 34, 35; consequence of regarding it as a form of human sensibility, 35, 36
Transcendental Æsthetic, 21 f.; the two main points of, 31
Transcendental Analytic, 24, 25, 26, 28, 58 f.; subject and scope of, 57 f., 61; problem of, 58, 61
Transcendental Dialectic, 26, 128-142; its aim, 23
Transcendental Ideal, the, 187 f.
Transcendental Ideas of Reason, the, 134 ff., 153
Transcendental Illusion, the, 134
Transcendental Reality, 62
Transcendental schematism of the Categories, 60 f., 68, 85, 86
Transcendentalism, 196

Ultimate beliefs, verification of, 439 f.
Ulysses, 359
Unconditioned (or Absolute), notion of: not applied to God in pre-Kantian philosophy, 198-199; in Kantian thinkers, 199; in Kant's philosophy, 199 f.; its speculative use only regulative, 200, 201
Understanding, function of, 63 f., 66 f., 78, 135; Kant's forms of, 26, 63 f.
Unity of Apperception, Transcendental: its function, 67, 68; its importance, in Kant's view, 146, 147
Universe, origin of, 277 f.

Verification, methods of, 461 ff.; In-

tuitive or Cartesian, 461 f. ; Discursive (including Inductive), 462 f. ; Social or Oecumenical, 464 f.
Volitionism, 265
Vorstellung, 73

Warburton, 411
Watson, Prof.: his *Philosophy of Kant as contained in Extracts from his own Writings* (=*Selections from Kant*), 22, etc.
Welcker, 323, 346
Wolff, 141, 142, 144, 148, 152, 157, 158, 163, 183, 184 ; and Kant, 11, 12 ; his Philosophic system, 132 f.

Xenophon, 328, 329, 358, 363, 364

Zeller, 356, 370

THE END

www.ingramcontent.com/pod-product-compliance
Lightning Source LLC
Chambersburg PA
CBHW071136300426
44113CB00009B/990